Antitrust in Emerging and Developing Countries: *Featuring Africa, Brazil, China, India, Mexico…*

2nd Edition

Editors
Eleanor M. Fox
Harry First
Nicolas Charbit
Elisa Ramundo

Assistant Editor
Duy D. Pham

Concurrences Review, 2016

60 Broad Street, Suite 3502, NY 10004
www.concurrences.com
contact@concurrences.com

Printed in the United States of America
First Printing, 2016

Publisher's Cataloging-in-Publication
(Provided by Quality Books, Inc.)

Antitrust in Emerging and Developing Countries (Conference)
(2015 : New York University School of Law)
Antitrust in emerging and developing countries :
featuring Africa, Brazil, China, India, Mexico :
conference papers / editors, Eleanor M. Fox, Harry
First, Nicolas Charbit, Elisa Ramundo. -- 2nd edition.
pages cm
Includes bibliographical references.
LCCN 2016939156
ISBN 9781939007520
ISBN 9781939007537

1. Antitrust law—Developing countries—Congresses.
2. Competition—Developing countries—Congresses.
3. Conference papers and proceedings. I. Fox, Eleanor, M., editor.
II. First, Harry, 1945- editor. III. Charbit, Nicolas, editor.
IV. Ramundo, Elisa, editor. V. New York University. School of Law, sponsoring body. VI. Institute of Competition Law (New York, N.Y.), sponsoring body. VII. Title.

K3850.A6A68 2015 *343.07'21*
QBI16-600068

Cover and book design: Yves Buliard, www.yvesbuliard.fr
Layout implementation: Darlene Swanson, www.van-garde.com

Editors' Note

Eleanor M. Fox
Harry First
Nicolas Charbit
Elisa Ramundo

On October 23, 2015, Concurrences Journal in partnership with New York University School of Law presented for the second time the conference, "Antitrust in Emerging and Developing Countries." Five panels of 24 prominent speakers representing 10 jurisdictions, two eminent keynote speakers and a closing conversation with an influential South African jurist explored the economic context and addressed the challenges and developments in competition law and policy in emerging and developing jurisdictions. Recognizing the coming of age of developing countries' competition law systems, the panelists (academics, enforcers and practicing lawyers) engaged in passionate debates about what this means in law, policy, and on-the ground reality for business, consumers, and the world.

The conference underscores the reality that, in this globalized business landscape, firms must have regard to the competition laws of emerging economies, including in particular China, India, Mexico, Brazil and South Africa, whether they are merging, collaborating with competitors, or designing distribution systems. Businesses are facing dedicated enforcers who are trying to make their markets work in the face of challenges posed by public and private power. The conference revealed that the challenges and therefore the responses are not always the same in the developed and developing world.

In this book, 20 prominent authors offer 13 contributions that tackle some of the most stimulating topics debated during this one-day event: **Susan Ning** discusses the enforcement of the Chinese Anti-Monopoly Law against state administrative monopolies; **Jonathan Orszag** lays out principles to guide governments from developing countries when intervening in the market and in network industries; **Kirti Gupta** provides an overview of the Indian experience in dealing with issues relating to FRAND patents; **Aditya Bhattacharjea** and **Fiyanshu Sindhwani** analyze the antitrust cases concerning pharmaceuticals in India; **Thomas K. Cheng** discusses the history of the pharmaceutical industry in China and suggests there may be future antitrust issues that the Chinese authorities will have to address; **Carlos Mena-Labarthe** uses the Mexican experience in enforcing competition law in the pharmaceutical sector to provide guidance to developing countries on how to implement effective competition policy in that sector; **George S. Cary**, **Elaine Ewing** and **Tara Tavernia** relay the concerns of the business community by arguing that the global proliferation of merger control regimes is imposing substantial and often unnecessary costs on businesses; **D.M. Davis** provides an illuminating discussion of South Africa's controversial public interest approach to merger review; **Samir Gandhi** lays out the history of merger control in India and interestingly suggests that it may be have been influenced by India's industrial policy; **J. Mark Gidley** and **Maxwell J. Hyman** intriguingly use insights from institutional economics to argue that one of the indirect benefits from the proliferation of antitrust based on international best practices is the distillation of due process norms in the legal institutions of developing countries, which ultimately leads to a stronger economy; **Francis Wang'ombe Kariuki** and **Simon Roberts** discuss the historical growth of the Competition Authority of Kenya and how it has contributed to Kenya's development goals; **Mariana Tavares de Araujo** analyzes how Brazil has incorporated international best practices to improve its competition law; and lastly, **Timothy T. Hughes**, **Russell W. Damtoft** and **Randolph W. Tritell** provide an historical overview of the US Federal Trade Commission's technical assistance program and highlight how it has contributed to the economic development of developing countries.

This volume guides readers through some of the most important and cutting-edge issues faced by developing countries in their application of antitrust.

The editors would like to give their sincere thanks to the 20 authors for their hours of labor dedicated to this unique collection of articles.

Table of Contents

PART III: Public Interest, Industrial Policy, and Mergers

PART IV: International Antitrust Enforcement and Economic Development

Contributors

Aditya Bhattacharjea
Delhi School of Economics

George S. Cary
Cleary Gottlieb Steen & Hamilton

Thomas K. Cheng
University of Hong Kong

Russell W. Damtoft
US Federal Trade Commission

Dennis M. Davis
South African Competition Appeal Court

Elaine Ewing
Cleary Gottlieb Steen & Hamilton

Samir Gandhi
AZB Partners

J. Mark Gidley
White & Case

Kirti Gupta
Qualcomm

Timothy T. Hughes
US Federal Trade Commission

Maxwell J. Hyman
White & Case

Francis Wang'ombe Kariuki
Competition Authority of Kenya

Carlos Mena-Labarthe
Mexican Competition Authority

Susan Ning
King & Wood Mallesons

Jonathan Orszag
Compass Lexecon

Simon Roberts
University of Johannesburg

Fiyanshu Sindhwani
Delhi School of Economics

Mariana Tavares de Araujo
Levy & Salomão Advogados

Tara Tavernia
Cleary Gottlieb Steen & Hamilton

Randolph Tritell
US Federal Trade Commission

China's Anti-Monopoly Law and Its Enforcement against State Monopolies: Achievements and Limitations

Susan Ning*

susan.ning@cn.kwm.com

Partner, King & Wood Mallesons

Abstract

This paper tries to briefly introduce China's attempt to control state restraints with the Anti-monopoly Law of the People's Republic of China ("AML") against the two most common forms of China's state restraints, the administrative monopolies and the monopolies carried out by state-owned enterprises. The article starts by presenting the problems of state restraints in the economic context of China, and then it sets forth the relevant legal framework against the state restraints under the AML, which includes both the administrative-oriented enforcement conducted by the anti-monopoly enforcement authorities, and the judicial-oriented enforcement. The analysis of the relevant high profile cases will also be included in this section. The article moves on to evaluate the effectiveness of such enforcement and to provide the observations on the achievements and limitations of the AML enforcement against state monopolies. Lastly, the article suggests an outlook of the reforms where China could implement to deal with illegal state involvements in the economy.

* I am grateful to Cheng Liu, Ting Gong, and Yumeng Li for their contributions to this paper.

I. Introduction

On August 1, 2008, China's AML,[1] the first comprehensive anti-monopoly legislation in China, came into effect. The AML is expected to serve as the legal foundation for the sustained development of China's thriving market economy. Over the past decades, China has made extraordinary economic progress in a relatively short period of time. Notwithstanding this development, China's transition to a modern market system is still on-going and the legacy of a centrally planned and highly administered and regulated system still remains in some areas of the economy.

This paper tries to briefly introduce China's attempt to control state restraints with the Anti-monopoly Law of the People's Republic of China ("AML") against the two most common forms of China's state restraints, the administrative monopolies and the monopolies carried out by state-owned enterprises ("SOEs"). The article starts by presenting the problems of state restraints in the economic context of China, and then it sets forth the relevant legal framework against the state restraints under the AML, which includes both the administrative-oriented enforcement conducted by the anti-monopoly enforcement authorities ("AMEAs")[2], and the judicial-oriented enforcement. The analysis of the relevant high profile cases will also be included in this section. The article moves on to evaluate the effectiveness of such enforcement and to provide the observations on the achievements and limitations of the AML enforcement against state monopolies. Lastly, the article suggests an outlook of the reforms where China could implement to deal with illegal state involvements in the economy.

II. Administrative Monopolies

1. The Problem of Administrative Monopolies in China

Possibly without exception, every country with a functioning government has administrative monopolies to some extent.[3] Economic theory generally holds that administrative monopolies, like other monopolies, hamper overall social welfare because they lead to increased prices, reduced output, and restricted competition. In China, as in other countries, an administrative monopoly is fundamentally an issue of economic governance, i.e., the relationship between the state and the market. It is a well-recognized problem in China and a basic aspect of the economy that China is seeking to reform.

As some scholars suggest,[4] one of the most intriguing sections of the AML is its Chapter V on *Abuse of Administrative Power to Eliminate or Restrict Competition*, which aims to prevent government agencies from using their power to interfere in competition, especially the government agencies at the local level.

---

1 The AML was promulgated by the Standing Committee of the National People's Conference on August 30, 2007, and went into effect on August 1, 2008.

2 China's AML enforcement is shared by three government authorities: the Ministry of Commerce ("MOFCOM") has exclusive competence for merger control; the State Administration of Industry and Commerce ("SAIC") shares responsibility with the National Development and Reform Commission ("NDRC") for the enforcement of the AML's non-merger provisions. Further, the SAIC is assigned oversight of non-price related conduct, and the NDRC handles price-related offenses.

3 Jacob S. Schneider, *Administrative Monopoly and China's New Anti-Monopoly Law: Lessons from Europe's State Aid Doctrine*, 87 Wash. U. L. Rev. 869, pp 1-2 (2010).

4 *See, e.g.*, Salil K. Mehra & Meng Yanbei, *Against Antitrust Functionalism: Reconsidering China's Antimonopoly Law*, 49 Va. J. Int'l L, p 379, p 383 (2008).

2. Legal Framework to Deal with Administrative Monopolies

The AML prohibits the abuse of administrative powers that eliminates or restricts competition or favors enterprises at the expense of other market players. Specific forms of abuse and their consequences include:

» Protecting local companies at the expense of other companies by way of discriminatory treatment, which often leads to the creation of regional monopolies;

» Creating barriers to the trade among provinces, which often leads to market fragmentation at the national level, preventing the free movement of goods, services, capital, and technology; and

» Providing regulated industries and SOEs with preferential treatment or protection (at both the local and regional level), which often leads to the enactment or maintenance of rules and measures contrary to AML provisions, especially Articles 13, 14, and 17. Other common consequences of all these abuses are corruption and rent-seeking.

As for the legal requirements to qualify as an abuse of administrative monopoly, although there is no explicit test in the AML, some scholars consider that abuse of administrative power is composed of three elements: the subject, the behavior, and the consequence. The subjects are the administrative authorities or other organizations authorized by laws and regulations; the behavior is the misuse of administrative power with no legal basis or in violation of the relevant laws; and the consequence is the elimination or restriction of competition in a relevant market.[5]

Article 51 of the AML serves as the primary enforcement provision for Chapter V, instead of directly granting the AMEAs the power to punish government agencies for violating the AML, establishes that the AMEAs can only identify such violations and propose corrective actions to the relevant superior authorities of the agencies in question. According to the AML, the government officials who are directly in charge and/or other directly responsible public servants can be individually held liable and disciplined. In addition, under provisions promulgated by the SAIC,[6] undertakings that benefit from an AML violation by participating in cartel arrangements or engaging in abuses of dominance—even though under the order or arrangements of government agencies—are subject to the fine ranging from 1 to 10% of their previous year's sales revenue.

The enforcement power granted in Chapter V is shared between the NDRC, which is responsible for price-related anti-competitive conducts, and the SAIC, which is responsible for non-price related conducts. The NDRC and the SAIC can also delegate their powers to their provincial counterparts. To provide more clarity and details regarding the procedures, the NDRC[7] and SAIC[8] each promulgated their respective provisions on the enforcement regarding abuses of administrative monopolies.

---

5 Zheng Peng Cheng, The Legal Studies related to Administrative Monopoly, p 43 (2002).

6 Provisions for Administrative Authorities for Industry and Commerce on Prohibiting Abuses of Dominant Market Positions were promulgated on Dec. 31, 2010, and came into effect on Feb. 1, 2011.

7 The NDRC promulgated Provisions on Anti-Price Monopoly, which came into effect on Feb. 1, 2011, and Regulations on Procedures for Enforcement of Administrative Law on Anti-Price Monopoly, which came into effect on Feb. 1, 2011.

8 The SAIC promulgated Provisions for Administrative Authorities for Industry and Commerce on Prohibiting Abuses of Dominant Market Positions on Dec. 31, 2010, which came into effect on Feb. 1, 2011, and Provisions for Administrative Authorities for Industry and Commerce to Prevent Abuses of Administrative Powers to Exclude or Restrain Competition on Dec. 31, 2010, which came to effect on Feb. 1, 2011.

3. Enforcement against Administrative Monopolies

As of this writing, we have not seen any decisions published by the SAIC on AML enforcement against administrative monopolies.[9] In contrast, the NDRC (including its provincial counterparts) have published three decisions relating to administrative monopolies.

a. Case 1: The Yunnan Communication Administration's Abuse of Administrative Power by Forcing Companies to Engage in Monopolistic Activities

In 2014, the Yunnan provincial branch of the NDRC discovered that the Yunnan Provincial Communication Administration ("YPCA") had organized a cartel arrangement involving restrictions on the refunding of benefits to customers. The cartel was carried out by the Yunnan branches of China Mobile, China Telecom, China Unicom, and China Railcom.

The NDRC concluded that the cartel arrangement facilitated by the YPCA and entered into by four major competitors was in violation of Articles 8 and 36 of the AML. The NDRC reported this suspected violation to the National Communication Administration ("NCA"), the sector's supervisory authority and the superior authority that according to Article 51 of the AML holds the power to rectify such a violation.

In the end, the NCA ordered the YPCA to immediately cease the illegal practice.

Moreover, China Mobile, China Telecom, and China Unicom each received a fine equaling two percent of their previous year's sales revenue for being part of the cartel. China Railcom did not comply with the cartel, and therefore was given a reduced penalty of RMB 500,000.

b. Case 2: The Shandong Provincial Department of Transport's Abuse of Administrative Power in the Market for Road Navigation Satellite Systems

On March 27, 2014, the NDRC deemed that the Shandong Department of Transport ("Shandong DOT") was in violation of Articles 8, 32, and 37 of the AML for abusing its administrative power to exclude and restrict competition in the vehicle monitoring platform services and vehicle mount terminal markets.

The NDRC found that, since 2011, Shandong DOT had initiated several policies to require information on three types of vehicle (tourist group-use vehicles, certain types of passenger vehicles, and vehicles used for transporting hazardous chemicals, fireworks, firecrackers, and civil explosives) to be connected to a provincial technological service platform, and information related to heavy-duty trucks and semi-trailer towing vehicles would be connected to another system called the "Bei Dou dynamic information platform." The Shandong DOT further specified that the technological support services for the two technology platforms would be exclusively provided by a company named 9TONG. It also required that the vehicle

9 According to Professor Wang Xiaoye, the SAIC (including its local counterparts) have assisted in the investigation of 519 cases involving state monopolies (including administrative monopolies as well as anticompetitive conduct carried out by SOEs) between 1995 and 2005. However, there have been no formal decisions involving administrative monopolies published by the SAIC (including its local counterparts) so far. *See* Wang Xiaoye, *Reconsideration into State Monopoly Problems*, p 4, L. & Soc'y (July 2009). *See also* SAIC, Antitrust Classic Decisions and AML Investigations (2007).

satellite positioning terminals would have to pass testing organized by 9TONG in order to enter the Shandong market.

The NDRC found that such conduct excluded and restricted competition in the vehicle monitoring and control platform service and the vehicle mount terminal markets, deprived road transportation companies of the freedom to choose products, and unreasonably pushed up platform service fees and the sale prices of vehicle mount terminal products.

Consequently, the NDRC put forward suggestions that the Shandong provincial government should order Shandong DOT to rectify its behavior in the following ways:

» Fully open up the vehicle monitoring and control market for two-passenger, hazardous, heavy-duty truck, and semi-trailer towing vehicles, and allow road freight carriers to freely choose the platforms to be connected to the Ministry of Transportation's ("MOT") national monitoring and service platform;

» Remove restrictions on market entry for terminal product providers in Shandong Province, allow road transportation companies to freely choose terminals that gained MOT approval, and allow qualified terminals to be connected to the relevant monitoring and control platforms; and

» Scrap the earlier policy of capping the prices of vehicle satellite positioning terminals at the bid-winning price in the MOT's BeiDou demo projects.

c. Case 3: The Hebei Provincial Government's Abuse of Administrative Power by Enforcing a Discriminatory Toll Policy

In September 2014, the NDRC found that the Hebei provincial government was in violation of Articles 8 and 33 of the AML for enforcing a discriminatory toll policy and abusing its administrative power.

In its investigation, the NDRC found that the Transportation Department, the Finance Department, and the Price Bureau in Hebei province had jointly issued a policy in October 2013 under which local passenger transport companies in Hebei enjoyed a 50% discount on toll roads. Non-Hebei companies did not receive any discounts. The discriminatory toll charge was a form of subsidy for local operators, giving them an unfair competitive edge by allowing them to run at a far lower cost than non-local competitors.

According to the report published on the NDRC's website, the NDRC sent an enforcement letter to the Hebei provincial government asking the three departments to rectify the discriminatory policy.

d. Conclusion: the AMEAs' Enforcement Approach Toward Administrative Monopolies

In view of the decisions published by the NDRC, the agency's enforcement approach towards administrative monopolies could be summarized as follows:

(a) In contrast with other AML provisions, Chapter V on administrative monopolies targets the conduct of government agencies, rather than the conduct of private undertakings. The factors to be taken into account when assessing whether there is abusive government behavior are therefore different from those relating to abuse of dominance by private undertakings.

(b) In order to identify whether certain actions are illegal under Chapter V, an investigation to uncover the facts, such as whether the government agencies carried out the proscribed acts or not, is sufficient.[10] Chapter V, in this regard, largely resembles the *per se* approach to illegality to the extent it does not require a detailed analysis of the trade-off between the costs and benefits of certain actions before reaching a decision. Chapter V thus does not necessarily require a market definition, which is normally a pre-requisite to establish that a private undertaking has a dominant position.

(c) It is important to note there are no justification defenses provided under Chapter V. When a private company undertakes certain acts that are in violation of the AML based on government legislative measures,[11] the company cannot use the compliance with such measures as a defense for its AML violation. It therefore seems that the AML opts for a severe approach when dealing with the abuses of administrative monopolies.

(d) Article 51 only grants the AMEAs the power to make suggestions. As such, the AMEAs cannot impose direct punishment. All they can do is report the violation to the superior authority of the government agency that is violating the AML and make recommendations.

III. The Anti-Competition Conduct of SOEs

1. SOEs in China

With the establishment of the People's Republic of China in 1949, the Chinese government opted for a centrally planned economy, where neither private enterprises nor significant foreign investments were allowed. As a consequence, SOEs were the main actors in almost all economic sectors in China.

After Deng Xiaoping's adoption of his policy to open up the economy in 1972, and especially during the early 1990s, China implemented several measures to introduce more competition into stagnant sectors controlled by the state. As the owner of the SOEs, the government restructured some of these enterprises in order to stimulate competition in specific sectors (also known as "the liberalization process"). While China was able to reduce the role of SOEs in some economic sectors, SOEs still have a significant, or even increased, control in certain sectors that are deemed of strategic importance to the economy. In fact, on December 18, 2006, the State Assets Supervision and Management Commission announced that seven strategic industries, including petrochemicals, telecommunications, coal, civil aviation, and waterway transportation, would be controlled by SOEs.[12] In addition, for other important industries, including automobiles, steel, and technology, the government will seek to maintain a "strong influence" through government held capital in the leading companies.[13]

---

10 The main categories of prohibited conduct contained in Chapter V are the following: local protectionism and unequal treatment of local and non-local goods; protectionist bidding procedures; forcing businesses to engage in monopolistic activities; and other forms of unequal treatment of non-local businesses.

11 The government legislative measures refer to the ones issued by the relevant government agencies, rather than legislation issued by the People's Congress at the various levels.

12 *See* State Assets Supervision & Mgmt. Comm'n, Guidance on the Restructuring of State Capital and State Owned Enterprises (2006). *See also SOEs to Maintain Overwhelming Control in Seven Sectors*, XINHUA Net, Dec. 19, 2006.

13 *Id.*

2. The Legal Framework Dealing with SOEs' Anti-Competitive Conduct

The AML aims to achieve a balance between maintaining the dominant status of SOEs in important sectors and subjecting them to antitrust enforcement. Article 7 of the AML states that:

> The SOE-controlled sectors concerning the health of national economy and national security and in sectors where state trading is authorized by law, the legal operations of the enterprises are protected by law, yet the government will supervise and regulate the price of the goods and services provided by those enterprises to protect the interests of consumers and promote technology advancement.
>
> The enterprises referenced in the foregoing clause shall conduct businesses in accordance with law, be honest, exercise strict self-discipline, and be subject to the supervision of the public. Those enterprises shall not hurt the interests of consumers by virtue of their dominant status or state trading status.

An important achievement of the AML was the inclusion, in Article 7, of the provision that SOEs are subject to the law and its enforcement, which has already been witnessed in practice.

3. AML's Enforcement against SOEs

According to its official statement, the SAIC has investigated seven cases relating to antitrust violations by SOEs.[14] Among them, six of the decisions are related to abuses of dominant position by the SOEs for an arrangement that imposed unreasonable conditions on equally qualified trading firms. The other case concerns a cartel arrangement that was organized by an SOE to facilitate market division.

From the NDRC's decisions, it also appears that the NDRC does not necessarily grant privileges to SOEs. For instance, in 2013, the NDRC investigated two top state-owned liquor companies, Kweichow Moutai and Wuliangye, for their resale price maintenance arrangements. The two companies were imposed fines of RMB 247 million and RMB 202 million, respectively. In early 2011, the NDRC investigated China Telecom and China Unicom on broadband pricing issues (including differentiated pricing and overpricing). The investigation was closed without any formal decision but with both China Telecom and China Unicom subsequently announcing a price decrease for broadband access.

From the publicly available decisions, I notice that, in practice, Article 7 of the AML does not necessarily give an "exemption" to the SOEs in strategically important sectors. On the other hand, I also notice that SOEs have received lighter punishments when compared with the fines imposed on private entities. In view of the available published statistics, the average fine for private undertakings was around 4 to 6% of sales revenue in the previous financial year. Some undertakings even incurred fines of 8 to 10% given the seriousness and duration of their anticompetitive conduct. However, based on the decisions announced by the AMEAs so far, the fines imposed on SOEs range from 1 to 2% of their total revenue.

---

14 See the attached Annex for a brief summary of the decisions by the SAIC (including its provincial counterparts) regarding anticompetitive conduct by SOEs. The summaries are for all cases up to September 12, 2015.

IV. Judicial Actions against State Restraints

1. Private Litigation against Administrative Monopolies

An individual may rely on Article 53 of the AML to bring legal actions against administrative monopolies. However, for MOFCOM's merger decisions, administrative review is a pre-condition to initiate administrative litigation. For the NDRC or SAIC's decisions, an individual can either apply for administrative review or directly bring an administrative lawsuit without the need to first proceed with an administrative review.

In 2015, the first private litigation against an administrative monopoly was initiated, *Shenzhen Sware Technology vs. Guangdong Provincial Department of Education*. On February 2, 2015, the Guangzhou Intermediate People's Court ruled that the Guangdong Provincial Department of Education ("GDOE") had violated Article 32 of the AML by selecting a company, Glodon Software, as the sole software supplier for a professional skill exam. As a result of the decision to source from a single supplier, other software suppliers, including the plaintiff, were excluded from the possibility of competing to provide software.

This case, however, is currently under appeal[15] by the GDOE. In the appeal, the GDOE argues that selecting a software vendor for a professional skill exam was not an administrative decision. The GDOE further argues that the decision to select Glodon Software as the sole designated software provider at the annual provincial professional skill exam was not directly issued by it, but by the exam's organizing committee. Therefore, the decision cannot be deemed a department's administrative order and should not be treated as an abuse of an administrative monopoly.

2. Private Litigation against SOEs

Article 50 of the AML serves as a general provision that allows a plaintiff to obtain judgment against undertakings that are pursing anticompetitive practices. The provision provides that, if in committing anticompetitive acts, an undertaking causes a third party to incur losses, the former shall bear civil liability in accordance with the law. A private action against an SOE for a cartel arrangement or an abuse of dominance is covered under this clause and, as such, the action would fall under the scope of civil litigation.

a. Yunnan Yinding Bio-energy's Accusation of Sinopec for Its Refusal to Deal

On December 8, 2014, the Kunming Intermediate People's Court decided that Sinopec had abused its dominant market position by refusing to deal with a private company, Yunnan Yingding Bio-energy, which produced biodiesel. Sinopec had refused without any justifiable reasons to incorporate biodiesel that the plaintiff made from waste cooking oil into its distribution system. The diesel distribution system in China is dominated by SOEs (including Sinopec) in accordance with the law.

15 At the time of writing on September 30, 2015, the case is still in process of being appealed.

The decision, however, was remanded on appeal by the Yunnan High People's Court in September 2015 on the basis that the market definition and the determination of Sinopec's dominant position were not properly established in the first instance at trial. The final result of this case still remains to be seen.

V. Achievements, Limitations, and Outlook

1. Achievements and Limitations

There is no doubt that significant achievements were made by the AML against state restraints. Recent decisions underline the point that the AMEAs have targeted abuses by administrative monopolies as their enforcement priority.[16] In doing that, it appears that there is no privilege given to SOEs compared to other undertakings, including foreign companies.

As for private litigations, although there are few successful cases against administrative monopolies so far, there is an increasing trend that suggests Chinese courts are willing to accept such cases.

There are, however, certain limitations such as the lack of direct power to enforce Chapter V against state restraints. Article 51 merely provides the AMEAs with the power to refer matters so they can be considered by the superior authority of the infringing body. This inherent weakness of the AML makes the AMEAs comparable to a toothless tiger.

Another limitation is that there is a legal barrier that prevents private individuals and enterprises from initiating administrative litigation in China. The previous Administrative Litigation Law[17] makes a distinction between "abstract administrative act" and "concrete (individualized) administrative act." A private individual or entity can only bring to court cases against concrete administrative acts or administrative acts specifically issued against an individual or company. This approach is similar to the EU's direct effect principle, which enables a private individual or entity to bring a competition law case before a national court. In contrast, administrative litigation against "abstract administrative activity" (i.e., a legislative measure issued by a government agency) was explicitly excluded by the previous Administrative Litigation Law. The abuses of administrative monopolies, in practice, are usually carried out in the form of legislative or other similar measures. If these measures are not concrete or addressed to individuals, under the previous Administrative Litigation Law, no administrative litigation could be successfully initiated. The revised Administrative Litigation Law,[18] however, has removed such limitations. Notwithstanding, whether the revised Administrative Litigation Law will in practice expand the scope of administrative jurisdiction still remains to be seen.

---

16 The following link contains news reports of such decisions: http://news.xinhuanet.com/legal/2014-10/23/c_1112939052.htm.

17 The Administrative Litigation Law was promulgated by the National People's Conference on Apr. 4, 1989, and became effective on Oct. 1, 1990. Pursuant to Article 11, only certain kinds of concrete administrative activity could be litigated. The previous practice under the 1989 Administrative Litigation Law was that the People's Court would not accept litigation related to "abstract administrative activity."

18 The Administrative Litigation Law was revised by the National People's Conference on Nov. 11, 2014, and the revised version took effect on Jan. 1, 2015. In the revised Administrative Litigation Law, the distinction between "abstract administrative activities" and "concrete administrative actives" is no longer referred to. Some scholars comment that the removal of this distinction is intended to remove the previous limitations on administrative litigation. See e.g., Chen Liping, *Interpretation of the Revised Administrative Litigation Law*, which can be retrieved from http://www.cssn.cn/fx/fx_fxxf/201411/t20141105_1390919.shtml.

2. Outlook

Administrative monopolies, sectors with SOEs, and certain features of China's industrial policy continue to obstruct competition in several areas of the economy. The monopolistic and anticompetitive practices arising from these systemic factors limit the effectiveness of the competition policy regime and, in a number of instances, the practices lie outside the jurisdiction of the AML. Reforms to strengthen competition and to take steps to ease the tensions between competition policy and other features of China's economic system are therefore needed.

To address the issue, during the Third Plenary Session of the 18th Central Committee of the Communist Party of China, decisions were made to proceed with reforms in order to make the market play the decisive role in resource allocation, to establish a "a unified, open, competitive and orderly market system," to reduce market entry barriers, including the replacement of a positive list of industries where investment is allowed with a negative list of industries where investments are restricted.[19] Moreover, China is currently in the process of liberalizing certain sectors (for example the sectors characterized as natural monopolies, such as electricity, telecommunications,[20] and oil and gas[21]). This is part of the initiatives contained in the Opinions on Accelerating Implementation of Innovation-Driven Development Strategy through Strengthening Institutional Reforms (the "Opinions") released by the Communist Party of China's Central Committee and the State Council in March 2015. To implement the Opinions, the NDRC was entrusted with the task of establishing and enforcing a review mechanism to ensure fair competition across all sectors in the Chinese economy. This review mechanism mainly targets state restraints that must be amended or eliminated. It seems that this proposed mechanism largely resembles the EU's state aid rules,[22] which provide both *ex ante* and *ex post* control over state involvement in economic activity.

These reforms, conceived by the highest level of the Chinese government, represent a significant change in the government's thinking about the role of the state and its relationship with the economy. The gradual reduction of state interference in economic activity across most sectors of the economy is most welcomed and in need of further development. Another recommended reform is the establishment of an independent competition agency that is authorized to look into state restraints, and that has the power to directly enforce any necessary correction measures.

19 Communiqué of the Third Plenary Session of the 18th Central Committee of the Communist Party of China, adopted on Nov. 12, 2013, *available at* http://www.china.org.cn/china/third_plenary_session/2014-01/15/content_31203056.htm.

20 China National Radio recently reported that orders were issued to telecommunications operators to stop them from restricting competition in schools and universities following reports that the major carriers were engaging in agreements to geographically divide the market among themselves.

21 It was reported that a proposal to spin off of the national oil and gas pipeline assets in order to set up independent pipeline companies is being discussed by relevant governmental authorities, including the NDRC. The report is available at http://money.163.com/15/1217/09/BB1BTQN900253B0H.html.

22 *See* Dep't for Bus., Innovation & Skills, *What state aid is and how public authorities can make sure they comply with the rules*, Dec. 12, 2012, https://www.gov.uk/guidance/state-aid ("State aid is any advantage granted by public authorities through state resources on a selective basis to any organisations that could potentially distort competition and trade in the European Union. The definition of state aid is very broad because 'an advantage' can take many forms. It is anything which an undertaking (an organisation engaged in economic activity) could not get on the open market.").

Annex 1

Brief Summary of SAIC Decisions regarding Anti-Competitive Conduct by SOEs

Date	Infringing Entity	SOE Business	Anticompetitive Conduct	Amount of Penalty (RMB)
August 2015	Liaoning Fushun Tobacco Company	The tobacco monopoly in Fushun City	Abuse of dominant position by selling goods through tying arrangements and by imposing other unreasonable trade conditions	1% of sales revenue from the tied products in the preceding year, which amounted to 43,344,980,000
May 2015 (investigation terminated)[1]	China Railcom, China Unicom, and China Telecom	Major state-owned telecommunication service providers	Abuse of dominant position by selling goods through tying arrangements	Required to stop tying
November 2014	Chongqing Gas Group	One of the two state-owned gas service providers in the relevant geographic market	Abuse of dominant position by imposing unreasonable trade conditions	1% of sales revenue from the affected products in the preceding year, which amounted to 1,793,588.55
October 2014	Jiangsu Xuzhou Tobacco Company Pizhou Branch	The tobacco monopoly in Pizhou	Abuse of dominant position by discriminating between companies	1% of sales of revenue from the affected products in the preceding year, which amounted to 1,723,745.04

1 During the investigation, China Railcom, China Unicom, and China Telecom made full confessions regarding their anticompetitive conduct and promised to implement corrective measures. As a result, Ning Xia Administration of Industry and Commerce terminated the investigation in accordance with the Provisions of the Industry and Commerce Administration Organs on the Procedures for the Prevention of Administrative Powers Abuse to Exclude or Restrain Competition.

Date	Infringing Entity	SOE Business	Anticompetitive Conduct	Amount of Penalty (RMB)
July 2014	Inner Mongolia Chifeng Tobacco Company	The tobacco monopoly in Chifeng	Abuse of dominant position by selling goods through tying arrangements and by imposing other unreasonable trade conditions	1% of sales revenue from tied products in preceding year, which amounted to 5957,000
January 2014	Guangdong Huizhou Dayawan Yiyuan Water-supply Company	One of the two state-owned service providers of water in the relevant geographic market	Abuse of dominant position by selling goods through tying arrangements	2% of sales revenue from tied goods in preceding year, which amounted to 2,363,597.45
July 2013	Jiangxi Taihe LPG Stored and Delivered Station	Gas monopoly in Taihe	Anticompetitive agreement to divide the market	Confiscated illegal gains of 205,537 and fined 130,230

The summaries are for all cases up to September 12, 2015.

State Involvement in a Market Economy: Principles to Guide Interventions and a Discussion about Network Industries

JONATHAN ORSZAG*
jorszag@compasslexecon.com
Senior Managing Director, Compass Lexecon

Abstract

This paper explores two important issues regarding the role of government in a market economy. First, it examines the key principles that should guide government interventions to enhance economic efficiency. The principles are then combined into a "decision tree" for policymakers to evaluate proposed governmental actions; the decision tree provides a useful framework for government policymakers to decide whether to provide directly a good or service. Second, it examines government intervention in antitrust matters where network effects are present. The key economic problem is that in markets characterized by network effects, the termination of an anticompetitive practice may not restore effective competition. In such cases, an effective remedy must go beyond simply prohibiting a specified practice. The remedy must seek to recreate a level playing field and then to permit "undistorted competition" on the merits on a going-forward basis.

* The views and opinions expressed in this paper are solely those of the author and do not necessarily reflect the views and opinions of any of the organizations with which the author is or has previously been affiliated.

This short paper covers two topics relevant to the issue of "State Involvement in a Market Economy." First, I discuss the broad-based economic principles that should govern when and how governments intervene in private markets. These principles are based on a paper that I wrote in the early 2000s with my brother, Peter, and Joseph Stiglitz.[1] Second, I briefly discuss issues related to government intervention in antitrust matters where network effects are present.

I. Principles for Government Intervention

It is well understood among economists that there is a role for government involvement in a market economy. In other words, a market economy with no regulation and no government intervention will produce an inefficient allocation of economic resources. However, over regulation or too much market intervention can similarly harm economic efficiency. In this section, I focus on the broad-based economic principles that should guide government intervention.

The government has a proper role to intervene in a market economy in three key areas: (1) providing public data and information; (2) improving the efficiency with which governmental services are provided; and (3) the support of basic research.

I briefly explain the logic behind each of these principles:

First, it has long been recognized that providing basic public information and data is a public function. As Thomas Jefferson is reported to have said, "Information is the currency of democracy."

Second, improving the efficiency with which inherently governmental services are provided is socially beneficial. Such improvements in efficiency should be undertaken despite any potential displacement or reduction in revenue of private firms. For example, the displacement of private-sector "facilitators," who help to speed up passport applications for a fee, should not impede the government from improving the efficiency of the passport system. The granting of passports is an inherently governmental function, and it should be undertaken as efficiently as possible.

Lastly, basic research is a public good. It is often difficult to exclude others from sharing in the gains from research advances, and providing the information regarding those advances to others entails no additional cost. Because it is difficult to exclude others from enjoying the benefits of innovation, despite intellectual property protections, some estimates suggest that the social gains from innovation exceed private returns by between 35 and 60 percent. Given this differential, private markets will under-provide basic research.[2] Government support, but not necessarily provision, of basic research is therefore appropriate.

The most prominent example of a government-sponsored research project that later produced large social benefits is the Internet itself. The precursor of the Internet was a Department of Defense project in 1969, which was created to link together government computers at different sites to share information and data. Interestingly, the Department of Defense contracted with a private firm to develop the military communications network that was the precursor of the Internet. A private technology firm, Bolt, Beranek and Newman,

---

1 Joseph Stiglitz, Peter Orszag & Jonathan Orszag, The Role of Government in a Digital Age (2000).

2 Council of Econ. Advisers, Economic Report of the President 1993 at 190 (1993).

won that contract. The initial development of the Internet thus involved public financing, but private production.[3]

The government continued to sponsor innovations critical to the development of the Internet; the National Science Foundation, for example, funded the research that led to Mosaic, the first user-friendly web browser. The original Defense Department network began with four nodes; today, billions of people worldwide have access to the Internet.

The line between basic research and applied research is often blurry, and the government should exercise increasing caution as the substance of the research moves more toward commercial applications.

The government needs to be more cautious when it intervenes in private markets by adding specialized value to public data and information or provides private goods, even if private-sector firms are not providing them.

The more specialized the benefit of a government information service (i.e., that adds value to the underlying data or information), the more cautious the government should be in providing it. For example, the government should produce statistics on macroeconomic activity (e.g., Gross Domestic Product), but should be cautious in producing market studies of specific industries (e.g., analyses of the coal industry in West Virginia and the Powder Basin).

One example of this principle is the estimation of online retail sales. For years, private-sector firms have estimated the value of retail sales conducted online. Until early 2000, these firms were filling a gap in official statistics: There were no official statistics on online retail sales. Yet the extent of such online retail sales—and their projected growth—had important implications, for issues ranging from market forecasts to sales tax revenue projections. The private-sector estimates were highly variable and often were based on different concepts.

Fundamentally, providing estimates of aggregate economic statistics—such as online sales—is justified under the principle that the proper role of government is to provide public data and information.[4]

But at what point does the government go beyond providing a public good such as basic information and data? For example, providing detailed projections of online sales in specific markets (e.g., forecasts of online book sales) would seem to go too far. Such projections fundamentally represent market research, which does not serve a direct public purpose and can be (and is) provided by the private sector. The government should exercise increasing caution as it adds more and more value to raw data or information, or as it provides a more and more specialized service.

Similarly, the government should provide tools to assemble data, but more specialized tasks—such as "cleaning" databases or linking official information to related academic articles—should generally be left to non-governmental entities (including academic institutions, non-profit organizations, and private-sector firms). Such case- or individual-specific tasks have less of a public good nature than the provision of the underlying data.

---

3 Elinor Harris Solomon, Virtual Money 4 (1997).

4 The entry of private-sector firms in this case reflects the government's sluggishness in estimating online activity; such sluggishness, however, does not provide a justification for further delay. Indeed, the government should always pursue an aggressive policy of updating national statistics for new developments in the economy.

One indication of a specialized service is a high marginal cost. The higher the marginal cost of providing the service or information to a specific user, the more specialized the benefit of the service would appear to be.

In general, therefore, the presence of a large governmental user fee for user-specific activity should raise questions about whether the activity should instead be undertaken by the private sector. (It is worth emphasizing that if the government *does* undertake activities with substantial marginal costs, user fees should be imposed. But the government should generally not be undertaking such tasks.)

The government may occasionally be able to "jump start" new markets or provide universal access to a private good that is deemed important enough that all citizens should have access to it.

The government's decision to provide electricity in markets that were not adequately served by the private sector is an example of this principle. One of the original motivations for federal production of electricity was to ensure that every household had access to it. At the beginning of the 20th century, less than 10 percent of all households had access to electricity. By the 1950s, nearly every household had electricity.[5] This example, however, also illustrates a danger: temporary government activities can often become permanent. Indeed, federal agencies—including the Tennessee Valley Authority and the five Power Marketing Administrations—still account for roughly eight percent of the Nation's electricity production.[6] According to the Congressional Budget Office, "Compared with other major industries, the federal presence in what is primarily a private and local function is in many ways an anomaly, having changed little since the New Deal era of the 1930s."[7]

But the government should be cautious in entering such markets. The experience with electricity production also suggests that, when the government decides to enter a private market, it should intervene modestly, and—whenever possible—work in conjunction with private-sector actors. Cooperative ventures with private-sector entities are a means of spurring the new activities and ensuring at least a minimal level of private-sector interest, without which the long-run prospects for private-sector provision would appear dim.

Even if a public good or other market imperfection is present, the government should not provide the good directly if private provision coupled with appropriate regulation (including contracting with a private provider) or taxation would be more effective. In many situations, the government may be able to achieve its social objectives more efficiently by harnessing private firms rather than by providing the good or service directly. Indeed, given the weaker incentives often faced by government employees to innovate and reduce costs, the principal motivation for direct government provision involves imperfect information and uncertainty—in particular, when the government has difficulty in anticipating all possible contingencies or in monitoring the performance of a private provider.

The benefit of direct provision relative to private provision with regulation/taxation depends on many factors, including the internal efficiency of the government relative to the private sector in providing the good, principal-agent and other information problems in regulating a private-sector entity, and the potential for innovation and dynamic benefits from private provision. Andrei Shleifer of Harvard University, for example, argues that public provision is preferable only when innovation is relatively unimportant,

5 Council of Econ. Advisers, Economic Report of the President 2000 at 100 (2000). It is also worth noting that, at least prior to a national electricity grid, electricity (especially hydro-electricity) likely represented a local monopoly requiring significant regulation—and therefore it is not clear that private production was more desirable than public production.

6 Cong. Budget Office, Should the Federal Government Sell Electricity? at xi (1997).

7 *Id.* at xii.

competition is weak, information problems are substantial, or private sector concerns regarding reputation are inconsequential.[8]

Continuing to develop the appropriate standards for protecting privacy, security, and consumer protection is one of the most difficult tasks facing both policymakers and businesses. Before the government mandates standards in these areas, it should first encourage the private sector to develop its own voluntary standards that would be monitored by the government. Should voluntary approaches ultimately prove ineffective, the government would have to stand ready to set the standards itself (after consultation with stakeholders).

Promoting network externalities—either through direct government provision of a specific type of good or service, or through a government technology standard with which private providers must conform—is fraught with potential dangers for policymakers. In particular, policymakers face two types of risks: They can fail to promote a network that the private sector is incapable of promoting (and thereby forgo the benefits from the network that would have resulted), or they can promote an inefficient technology (and thereby lock into a network with lower benefits than an alternative network that might have developed in the absence of government action).

History highlights the relevance of both types of risks. The government and the private sector have each had both successes and failures in promulgating technology standards. For example, the government's adoption of common standards for map-making through the Federal Geographic Data Committee seems to have been successful. In addition, one of the most prominent examples of a flawed government-set standard involves color television. In the 1940s, RCA and CBS were competing to develop a color television system. RCA was working on an electronic approach, whereas CBS was developing a mechanical system. The CBS system progressed more quickly, and, in 1950, the Federal Communications Commission ("FCC") adopted the CBS system. Despite its superior performance during the FCC tests held in 1950, however, the CBS system had significant drawbacks: For example, it was incompatible with extant black-and-white broadcast signals without special equipment. In 1953, the FCC therefore switched and adopted the RCA technology, which had by then been sufficiently developed. The Europeans, by contrast, waited another decade to adopt color television standards—and wound up with a better system (PAL and SECAM). Arguably, the US government's intervention in the standard-setting process produced an inferior result.

The government is not alone, however, in settling on standards that appear inefficient: Private markets can also produce standards that are not efficient. Many analysts, for example, believe that Sony's Betamax format for video cassette recorders was technically superior to JVC's VHS format, which ultimately became the industry standard.[9]

Put simply, the presence of potential network externalities raises difficult policy choices, with no easy answers and no simple rules of thumb. As economists Carl Shapiro and Hal Varian argue, "[W]idespread availability is desirable for many kinds of networked goods. However, it is a large leap from there to say that such access should occur only through government provision or subsidies. After all, many goods with network externalities are provided by the private sector."[10] Nobel Prize-winning economist Paul Krugman

8 Andrei Shleifer, *State versus Private Ownership*, 12(4) J. Econ. Persp. 130-40 (1998).

9 *See* Peter Passell, *Why the Best Doesn't Always Win*, The N.Y. Times Mag., May 5, 1996, at 60. It should be noted, however, that some analysts do not concur that VHS was technologically inferior.

10 Carl Shapiro & Hal Varian, Information Rules: A Strategic Guide to the Network Economy 315 (1999).

adds, "[W]hile an acknowledgement of the importance of QWERTY refutes the near-religious faith of conservatives in free markets, it is not at all easy to decide which direction the government should pursue."[11]

The fundamental purpose of patents and copyright protection is to provide a financial incentive to private innovators: Without such protection for intellectual property, the incentives for investing in research and development would be substantially attenuated. It is therefore necessary to trade off the costs of the temporary monopoly granted to inventors against the benefits of the innovation and effort that the promise of such a temporary monopoly induces.

Public entities, however, are not governed by the same profit incentives that apply in the private sector. In particular, a patent or copyright should not generally be necessary in order to induce research or creative work within public-sector entities.[12] Since such an incentive effect is the primary motivation for protecting intellectual property, the government should be allowed to exercise a patent or copyright only in limited situations.

It should be noted that the *exercise* of a patent or copyright is distinct from the *holding* of such intellectual property. Public entities should be entitled to hold the patent on products or ideas, if only to avoid allowing the patent to be reserved by someone else. But the public sector should generally not exercise such rights—in other words, it should not restrict the use of the technology or product, or charge for its use, despite holding the patent.

More broadly, a governmental entity should generally not be allowed to withhold information from the public solely because it believes such withholding increases its net revenue. As discussed below, maximizing net revenue is generally not an appropriate objective for public-sector entities.

The presence of significant private-sector activity generally raises a *prima facie* case against the existence of a public good. Therefore, the presence of such firms suggests that one of the primary motivations for direct government provision of a good or service—that it is a public good—is likely to be absent.

Furthermore, the government should generally *not* enter markets to provide more competition to existing firms. If the government is concerned about the lack of competition in a market, it should use antitrust and other tools to address the underlying barriers to such competition. To the extent that the government is concerned that extant private-sector activity is either insufficient or excessive relative to some social optimum, it should generally encourage or discourage such activity through other incentives (e.g., taxes and subsidies) rather than direct provision itself.

In general, maximization of net revenue (or "profits") is not an appropriate objective for public-sector entities. Commercial activities in which the government's goal is net revenue maximization should therefore raise concern, either because the activity should be undertaken in the private sector (if no governmental role is warranted) or because the public-sector entity is not appropriately fulfilling its mission (if a governmental role is warranted).[13]

A vivid example of the dangers associated with net revenue maximization by governmental agencies or corporations is offered by the US Enrichment Corporation ("USEC"), a government corporation created

---

11 Paul Krugman, Peddling Prosperity: Economic Sense and Nonsense in the Age of Diminished Expectations 243 (1994).

12 To some degree, the government is already limited in its ability to enjoy copyright protection. According to Title 17, Section 105 of the United States Code, "Copyright protection . . . is not available for any work of the United States Government, but the United States Government is not precluded from receiving and holding copyrights transferred to it by assignment, bequest, or otherwise."

13 Limited circumstances may exist in which profit maximization is the best objective for a public enterprise. *See, e.g.*, G. De Fraja & F. Delbono, *Alternative Strategies of a Public Enterprise in Oligopoly*, Paper Presented at the 1st Congress of the European Economic Association (1986). I suspect, however, that the necessary conditions for this result are relatively rare in practice.

in 1992 that was subsequently privatized in 1998.[14] USEC inherited the Department of Energy's role in enriching uranium for use in nuclear power reactors. As a government corporation (and subsequently as a private corporation), USEC's net revenue maximization was inconsistent with a crucial non-proliferation program of the US government: the highly enriched uranium ("HEU") deal with Russia, under which 500 metric tons of Russian weapons-grade uranium is blended into reactor fuel and sold to US utilities. USEC serves as the US government's executive agent with the Russians. But USEC's marginal cost of producing enriched uranium from domestic sources is significantly lower than the cost of the Russian material, so that the more it imports, the higher its costs. Net revenue maximization in this case is therefore inconsistent with national security objectives (since net revenue maximization would imply importing none of the Russian material, whereas national security would be best served by importing as much of the Russian material as possible).

Governmental agencies or corporations should also not undertake actions that reduce competition—such as imposing higher costs on existing rivals, erecting entry barriers, or circumventing restrictions on below-cost pricing. Interestingly, entities that seek to maximize revenue rather than profits may have a *stronger* incentive to engage in such anticompetitive behavior than profit-maximizing entities. Indeed, one paper identified "a variety of plausible settings in which public enterprises have stronger incentives than profit-maximizing firms to pursue activities that disadvantage competitors. Quite often, the less concerned is the public enterprise with profit, the stronger are its incentives to undertake activities that disadvantage competitors."[15] Intuitively, a concern over revenue maximization could more easily lead public-sector enterprises to engage in costly activities (e.g., pricing below marginal cost) that reduce profits but raise revenue.

A related issue is that predatory pricing and other antitrust laws do not generally apply to governmental agencies. The same paper therefore argued that "the optimal design of antitrust law as applied to public enterprises also merits extensive study."[16] The application of predatory pricing laws to public entities could help to minimize the opportunities for such entities to behave in a socially counterproductive manner.

The difficulty is thus that neither profit maximization nor revenue maximization is generally an appropriate objective for public enterprises. Much more attention must be given to defining appropriate objectives for such enterprises; an objective of profit maximization or even revenue maximization should serve as a warning sign that further scrutiny is necessary.[17]

---

14 For a discussion of USEC and the problems inherent in its privatization, *see* Peter R. Orszag, *Privatization of the U.S. Enrichment Corporation: An Economic Analysis*, Presented at the Brookings Institution (Feb. 2000), *available at* http://citeseerx.ist.psu.edu/viewdoc/download?doi=10.1.1.25.2071&rep=rep1&type=pdf.

15 David E.M. Sappington & J. Gregory Sidak, *Incentives for Anticompetitive Behavior by Public Enterprises* 1 (AEI-Brookings Joint Ctr. Reg. Stud., Working Paper 99-11, Nov. 1999). *See also* John R. Lott, *Predation by Public Enterprises*, 43 J. Pub. Econ. 237 (1990).

16 Sappington & Sidak, *supra* note 16, at 24.

17 One argument sometimes proposed for profit-maximizing behavior by some governmental agencies is the cross-subsidization possibilities that the resultant profits can offer. But even if the activities that are being cross-subsidized are important policy objectives, it is not clear that the best source of revenue for them is profit-maximizing behavior. To be sure, it is possible in some situations that the distortions imposed by the profit-maximizing behavior are lower than the distortions that would be imposed by any other source of government revenue. But such situations would seem to be relatively rare, and therefore one arm of the government should generally not engage in profit-maximizing behavior merely to cross-subsidize another arm. To the extent that budgetary accounting rules encourage such cross-subsidization, modifications to the rules should be explored.

II. A Decision Tree for Policymakers

The preceding principles can be combined into a "decision tree" for policymakers to evaluate proposed governmental actions.

In evaluating whether a good or service should be provided by the government, the first question policymakers should ask is whether the good or service is a public good or whether any externalities (or other market failures) are present. If the answer to that question is "no," the government should *not* provide the good or service. If the answer is "yes," policymakers must proceed to the next question, which is whether the good or service can be provided more efficiently through appropriate regulation or subsidization, relative to direct public provisions. If the answer to that question is "yes," the government should proceed with appropriate regulation or subsidization if private-sector entities are already active, and not attempt to enter the market as a direct or indirect service provider itself. If either public-sector provision would be more efficient or if no private-sector entities exist, policymakers should proceed with direct provision only if privacy and pricing issues have been appropriately addressed.

In practice, implementing this decision tree is difficult. For example, determining whether a good or service can be provided more efficiently through appropriate regulation or a subsidy is a complicated empirical issue. Nonetheless, the decision tree should serve as a useful framework for government policymakers to decide whether to directly provide a good or service.

III. Principles for Intervention in Antitrust Matters

1. Where Network Effects Are Present

One issue that antitrust authorities in countries with emerging markets will almost certainly confront at some point are markets characterized by network effects. Here I briefly discuss a particular form of market intervention in such markets: antitrust remedies.

The key problem is that in markets characterized by network effects, the termination of an anticompetitive practice may not restore effective competition. Consider a highly stylized example. There are two firms in a network industry—let us say, operating systems. As soon as one firm has less than 40 percent share, some software companies will cease to write applications for that operating system, which will result in the operating system losing even more share, which, in turn, creates a vicious cycle. Now further assume that one firm engages in an anticompetitive act (e.g., predatory pricing, tying, etc.) and pushes the second firm below that "magical" 40 percent threshold. The antitrust authority steps in and orders Firm 1 to stop engaging in the anticompetitive act. Without any other remedy, Firm 1 will see the market "tip" to it since Firm 2 will start a downward spiral with network effects operating against it.

In such cases, an effective remedy must go beyond simply prohibiting a specified practice. The remedy must seek to recreate a level playing field and then to permit "undistorted competition" on the merits on a going-forward basis. In particular, it must attempt to reverse the ill-gotten network benefits enjoyed by the firm due to its anticompetitive actions.

In such an environment, an effective remedy of eliminating the network effect and thus restoring conditions of competition may impose short-term costs on economic efficiency. But, in the long run, the imposition of an effective remedy allows for competition on the merits and innovation incentives in other related sectors. As a result, in the long run, imposing a truly effective remedy in such a case can increase consumer welfare. The reason is that, with the remedy, the best product in the eyes of consumers can "win" while, without the remedy, consumers may be stuck with a lower-quality product since the market realities (i.e., the network externalities garnered through anticompetitive practices) make it difficult to undo the dominant firm's position (even if the dominant firm's product is of lower-quality). It would thus appear that the costs to economic efficiency from price regulation (or another form of market intervention, perhaps a very large fine with the "excess" proceeds going to Firm 2) may be worth the potential long-run benefits, especially if it is found that the costs to economic efficiency are present due to acts by a particular company (e.g., Firm 1).

Imposing such an effective remedy in network industries may be particularly important because of a "deterrent effect." An ineffective remedy conveys a message that a firm may have to pay a substantial fine, but there is nevertheless a benefit to engaging in foreclosure. While such a remedy will prevent the continuation of the abuse, it would not undo the network effects *and, in such a case, the firm which engaged in anticompetitive conduct would be able to continue to enjoy the benefits of past anticompetitive actions even after being enjoined from continuing such actions*. So long as the firm is allowed to retain the substantial benefits derived from its anticompetitive acts, the deterrent effect will be insufficient. An ineffective remedy will, therefore, not only undermine the potential for undistorted competition, it will likely distort incentives for innovation in related and future product markets, with potentially substantial adverse consequences for the pace of innovation generally.

Given the substantial consumer benefits that result from innovation, there is a sound economic argument for sending a strong signal to firms that acquire a dominant position in a network industry through anti-competitive conduct that they will not be allowed to retain the advantage gained from anticompetitive actions. One goal of antitrust law is deterrence by imposing meaningful penalties on firms convicted of anticompetitive acts. The primary economic benefit from antitrust penalties is thus not their *ex post* effect in providing compensation to those injured, but rather their *ex ante* effect in deterring the anticompetitive acts in the first place.

FRAND in India: Emerging Developments

Kirti Gupta*

kgupta@qualcomm.com

Director of Economic Strategy, Qualcomm

Abstract

There is an ongoing debate about the Intellectual Property Rights ("IPR") policies of major Standard Setting Organizations ("SSOs") and how the licensing disputes related to the valuation of IPR related to standards, or the Standard Essential Patents ("SEPs") should be resolved. The licensing commitments, often based on Fair Reasonable and Non-Discriminatory ("FRAND") terms, have been the focal point of various discussions and questions abound about their purpose, interpretation and whether or not they need further clarification. At this time of intense global debate, IPR policies related to the newly formed Indian telecommunications standards SSO are in formation, as is the jurisprudence on the FRAND licensing practices – both in the Indian courts and the Indian antitrust authority—the Competition Commission of India ("CCI"). This article connects the underlying issues of the global dialogue on SSO IPR policies and disputers related to licensing of SEPs to the Indian jurisprudence in formation. What policies India implements and how the jurisprudence evolves is of key importance towards the long term prospects of the wireless and telecommunications technologies that heavily rely on the creation and use of common technology standards.

---

* All the views reflected in this paper are my own and do not reflect that of any affiliation.

I. Introduction

Standard setting organizations ("SSOs") are industry groups that set common industry standards in a variety of important technological areas. In the Information and Communications Technology ("ICT") industry specifically, technology standards have enabled mobile phones to communicate with each other, to operate on the internet, etc. India itself has a long history in the development of various types of standards via the Bureau of Indian Standards ("BIS") established in 1947, and has a growing interest in ICT standards, with the recent formation of the Telecommunications Standards Development Society, India ("TSDSI") in 2013, for developing and contributing to global telecommunications standards while addressing India-specific requirements.

In many ways, today's digital economy is based upon standards. Without standards, we would not have had hundreds of firms coming together to create the mobile wireless revolution, and bind decades of engineering inventions into the 2G, 3G, and 4G wireless cellular standards that power most of our smartphones and tablets today. Nor would the ubiquitous Wifi (802.11) standards and products exist. Printers, cameras, and medical devices all operate due to standards that enable different firms in the industry to cooperate in creating common solutions to technological problems. Therefore, it is imperative for the economy that standards-based innovation continues, and all firms continue to have incentives to voluntarily participate in these standards, an issue that the SSOs have dealt with successfully over the last several decades.

Although the importance and benefits of standards are well recognized for businesses and consumers, they have recently attracted some concern by policy makers, regulators, and certain business groups.[1] A debate based on theory, and more recently based on empirical data, on these issues is raging in several jurisdictions such as the United States and EU, and is now reaching India. Recently, patents deemed as potentially essential to developing standards, referred to as standard-essential-patents ("SEPs"), have gained a lot of attention in India. Three proceedings on the licensing of SEPs in the Delhi High Court (*Ericsson v. Micromax*, *Ericsson v. Intex*, and *Ericsson v. Xiaomei*) and pending investigations of Ericsson's licensing practices of its SEPs by the Competition Commission of India ("CCI") have attracted intense international attention. The newly formed TSDSI has been working towards the formation of its intellectual property rights ("IPR") policies related to the standards it develops, and has attracted heavy corporate participation from various firms involved in international standards.

This debate over standards and SEPs is a part of a larger debate related to IPR and patents. Yet, it has some unique features. This paper provides an outline of some of the major issues of the debate related to SEPs and FRAND disputes in the literature by balancing various view points and puts them in the context of the recent SSO IPR policy discussions as well as the court decisions and antitrust investigations in India. The rest of the paper is organized as follows: Part II of the paper provides a background of the IPR policies in SSOs relevant to recent discussions in the TSDSI. Part III discusses the concerns of "hold-up" related to standards, and proposes some measures that may be used for a first-order empirical analysis for assessing any effect on competition. Part IV discusses how aggregate royalties may be viewed with regard to standards-compliant products and how any effect on competition may be measured. Part V analyses the recent cases involving SEPs in India. Part VI concludes.

---

1 *See, e.g.*, Anne Layne-Farrar, A. Jorge Padilla & Richard Schmalensee, *Pricing Patents for Licensing in Standard-Setting Organizations: Making Sense of FRAND Commitments*, 74(3) Antitrust L.J. 671 (2007). *See also* Kirti Gupta, *The Patent Policy Debate in the High-Tech World*, 9(4) J. Competition L. & Econ. 827 (2013).

II. IPR Policies and FRAND

As India's TSDSI frames its IPR policies, this Part summarizes some guidelines that have been followed by various SSOs around the globe over the last few decades, and an analysis of the reasons behind those guidelines.

By way of background, this section starts by examining why SSOs need IPR policies. Standards have a significant role to play, especially in the ICT industry, where multiple devices need to connect and communicate with each other using compatible and interoperable technology solutions. Before there were wireless cellular standards, for example, consumers could not roam between countries and still connect on their mobile devices. Different systems were used by different countries and industry groups, each requiring heavy investments to build a complex system that works regionally. The telecommunications industry therefore organized itself with the formation of standards bodies that dictate new technological standards and create them such that they are scalable and interoperable so that everyone can use and leverage them. Today's devices are enabled with mobile connections due to 3G and 4G wireless cellular standards, and are enabled with WiFi due to the 802.11 standards, with each standard bringing together hundreds of companies and organizations who come together to play their role. Some specialized in developing core and fundamental communications technologies over decades (the "inventors"), others specialized in creating products utilizing these technologies, such as smartphones and tablets (the "manufacturers"), and yet others specialized in deploying large networks and providing wireless services to consumers (the "operators" or "service providers").

SSOs carry an important responsibility to create transparent procedures, and to balance the incentives of multiple stakeholders so that they voluntarily choose to participate in the process of standard setting. To this end, one of the functions of primary importance performed by SSOs is to develop IPR policies that create an incentive for firms that invest in R&D to produce standards (inventors), as well as firms that only implement (manufacturers) to participate in the adoption of standards, to develop standards-compliant products, and to make the standardized technology successful. Typically, as an incentive for firms to participate in and contribute to the standard setting process, the participants are allowed to seek IPRs for their technical contributions and investments during the standardization process. And because all manufacturers of a standard need a license from patent owners holding patents essential to the implementation of a standard, the IPR policies of several SSOs require their members to publicly declare any IPRs that may become essential to the implementation of the standard, i.e., the SEPs, and to license them to any interested parties on "fair, reasonable, and non-discriminatory terms" ("FRAND").[2]

Some have argued that SEPs confer market power to their owners because there is necessarily no design-around for patents that are essential to implement a standard, therefore allowing patent owners to potentially hold-up implementers (or product manufacturers).[3] However, others have pointed out that a FRAND commitment is a contract enforceable in court and designed to bring licensors and licensees together to negotiate appropriate terms such that the interests of both the parties are balanced.[4] It follows that a breach

---

2 Although the IP policies of SSOs vary widely, FRAND terms are a common practice in the most commonly used ICT standards for wireless technologies. For a recent survey of IPR policies across SSOs, *see* Rudi Bekkers & Andrew Updegrove, A Study of IPR Policies and Practices of a Representative Group of Standards Setting Organizations Worldwide (2012).

3 *See, e.g.*, Mark A. Lemley & Carl Shapiro, *Patent Holdup and Royalty Stacking*, 85(7) Tex. L. Rev. 199 (2007).

4 Roger G. Brooks & Damien Geradin, *Interpreting and Enforcing the Voluntary FRAND Commitment*, 9(1) Int'l J. IT Standards & Standardization Res. 1, 2011, page 2, "[This paper…] reviews the basic fact that a FRAND commitment is the result of a voluntary contract between essential patent holders and a standards-setting organization, with the important corollary that the meaning of that commitment must be determined through the legal methods of contractual interpretation.

of that contract by failure of a SEP owner to provide a license on FRAND terms to a qualified potential licensee – that is, the alleged exercise of market power that commentators argue can result in hold-up – can be thwarted by the potential licensee by bringing a breach of contract claim against the SEP owner.[5] Therefore, although a license to SEPs is required by implementers of standards-compliant products, the SEP owners do not enjoy unilateral power over setting any price they desire to impose on the implementers due to the binding FRAND commitment.

It is also important to recognize the underlying motivation behind the FRAND contract. Some scholars have asserted that the *raison d'être* of a FRAND contract is to prevent "patent hold-up."[6] However, most SSOs' IPR policies clearly state that one of the main purposes of the FRAND commitment is to ensure access to the standardized technology as well as to fairly compensate the contributors to the standardized technology. For example, the International Telecommunication Union's ("ITU") IPR policy states that "securing access to the SEPs . . . is the sole objective of the code of practice."[7] Similarly, the European Telecommunications Standards Institute ("ETSI") states that the purpose of its policy is to "reduce the risk that the investment in the preparation . . . of [standards] could be wasted as a result of an [essential] IPR . . . being unavailable"[8] and that, "IPR holders . . . should be adequately and fairly rewarded for the use of their IPRs."[9] Thus, by implementing the FRAND contract, SSOs seek to prevent an SEP holder from refusing to license its SEPs on reasonable terms and denying implementers access to the technology, and, at the same time, aim to ensure that SEP holders will be fairly compensated for their contributions to the standard.

Even though FRAND may be enforceable as a contract between the patent holder and the SSO, some commentators have raised concerns about the meaning and completeness of FRAND as a contract, and what that has meant to SSO members.[10] It has been argued that the risk of patent hold-up arises because of the ambiguity inherent in the term, i.e., its failure to define a specific rate. To that end, Tsai and Wright, who have dug deep into the changes in the contractual provisions of SSOs, including the IPR policies that deal with the FRAND commitment and its meaning, find that contract incompleteness has been a persistent and historical feature across SSOs, even after taking several antitrust considerations into account. They conclude that incompleteness may be an intended and efficient feature of a competitive contracting process, rationally chosen by the SSOs, as it allows for flexible bilateral negotiations between firms.[11]

---

5 A "qualified" potential licensee is a potential licensee (infringer) that is capable of being a third party beneficiary of the relevant FRAND commitment. In most courts, such licensees can also raise a defense to an injunction sought in patent litigation to enforce an SEP on the basis that the SEP owner has not complied with its FRAND commitment. By contrast, a SEP owner cannot typically seek enforcement of its unilateral FRAND commitment, and is limited to bringing suit for patent infringement if a licensing dispute arises.

6 *See, e.g.*, Joseph Farrell, John Hayes, Carl Shapiro & Theresa Sullivan, *Standard Setting, Patents, and Hold-Up*, 74 Antitrust L.J. 603 (2007); Jorge L. Contreras, *Fixing FRAND: A Pseudo-Pool Approach to Standards-Based Patent Licensing*, 79 Antitrust L.J. 47 (2013).

7 Int'l Telecomm. Union, Common Patent Policy for ITU-T/ITU-R/ISO/IEC, *available at* http://www.itu.int/en/ITU-T/ipr/Pages/policy.aspx.

8 Eur. Telecomm. Standards Inst., ETSI Rules of Procedure at ann. 6 § 3.1 (2014), *available at* www.etsi.org/images/etsi_ipr-policy.pdf.

9 *Id.* §3.3.

10 *See* Mariniello, Mario. "Fair, Reasonable and Non-Discriminatory (FRAND) terms: a challenge for competition authorities." *Journal of Competition Law and Economics* 7.3 (2011): 523-541.

11 *See* Joanna Tsai & Joshua D. Wright, *Standard Setting, Intellectual Property Rights, and the Role of Antitrust in Regulating Incomplete Contracts*, 80(1) Antitrust L.J. 157 (2015).

III. Hold-up: A Two-Way Street?

Since the patents essential to implementing standards-compliant products must be made available to implementing firms for the technology to prosper, most of the key SSOs had addressed this issue early-on by the 1990s by putting in place policies for patent owning firms to disclose their patents, and for FRAND commitments to make licenses fairly and widely available. The definitions of these commitments have stood the test of time under the wake of several antitrust concerns.[12]

In the early 2000s, the law and economics literature began to raise the concern that the FRAND commitment was intended to but was not enough to prevent patent hold-up. The concern is that after a technology standard is set, the implementers of these given technologies must obtain licenses of this technology from the patent owners and they have no other alternative, which allows patent owners to abuse this opportunity by holding-up the implementers.[13] Indeed, the literature has acknowledged that such a model of patent hold-up assumes that all the bargaining power is available to the patent holder at the outset, and none to the implementer (who may be potentially infringing a patent right),[14] which may not be valid when either party can bargain and bring a dispute to court if and when negotiations fail. Another issue has been the lack of empirical evidence of patent hold-up after over a decade of this theory in the context of standard setting.[15]

To understand why the theory and the availability of any empirical evidence are at such odds with each other, let us briefly summarize the theory and review its implications. As a general economic theory, hold-up[16] is a well-known idea introduced by Nobel Laureate and economist Oliver Williamson that applied to traditional physical products and contracting.[17] Hold-up has a precise definition in economics: It arises when part of the return on an agent's relationship-specific investment is appropriable *ex post* by its trading partner. A textbook example of hold-up arises in the banana industry between a planter and a shipper. Once a planter picks the fruit, it rapidly begins to decay. The shipper can take advantage of the planter by changing terms of their contract on the dock (*ex post*) after the fruit has been picked. However, once the shipper's boat is half full of the perishable fruit, the planter can now take advantage of the shipper by changing the terms of the contract (*ex post*). Since each side can hold-up the other, in a negative equilibrium, no one has an incentive to plant trees or ship bananas, and the industry shrinks.[18] To get around this, an efficient contract is established between the two parties.

---

12 *See* Anne Layne-Farrar, *Proactive or reactive? An empirical assessment of IPR policy revisions in the wake of antitrust actions*, (59) Antitrust Bull. 373 (2014).

13 *See supra* text accompanying note 2.

14 *See* Gregory J. Sidak, *Holdup, Royalty Stacking, and the Presumption of Injunctive Relief for Patent Infringement: A Reply to Lemley and Shapiro*, 92(3) Minn. L. Rev. 714 (2008).

15 During the *Microsoft v. Motorola* trial before Judge Robart in the Western District of Washington (United States) in 2012, Microsoft's economic experts were unable, under cross-examination, to identify any SEP license or empirical evidence that they believed reflected patent hold-up driven terms. *See, e.g.*, Hearing Transcript at 180, Microsoft Corp v. Motorola Inc., No. 10-cv-1823 (W.D. Wash. Nov. 13, 2012) (testimony of economist Kevin Murphy stating that the existence of hold-up is an "open question"); *id.* at 201-02 (stating that "hold-up has not necessarily been a problem"); *id.* (testimony of economist Timothy Simcoe stating that he "can't nail down any particular license from any company as an example of hold-up"); *id.* at 135-36 (testimony of economist Matthew Lynde acknowledging that "I have no basis from economic evidence to conclude whether or not patent hold-up is a real problem").

16 Notably, the original idea of hold-up is distinct and different from the newly formed definition of "patent hold-up."

17 *See* Oliver E. Williamson, *Credible Commitments: Using Hostages to Support Exchange*, 73(4) Am. Econ. Rev. 519 (1983).

18 Alexander Gelatovic, Stephen Haber & Ross Levine, *Patent Holdup: Do Patent Holders Holdup Innovation?* 9 (Hoover IP[2] Working Paper Series No. 14011, 2014), *available at* http://www.hoover.org/sites/default/files/ip2-wp14011-paper.pdf.

In the context of standard setting, hold-up can occur between an inventor of standardized technology (patent owner), and a manufacturer of standards compliant products (implementer). The patent owner can opportunistically increase the price of the licensed technology after the standard is set and other potential solutions are ruled out (*ex post*). Similarly, the implementer can refuse to pay the licensing fee after the standard is set and the patent owner has incurred significant sunk costs in R&D investment (*ex post*).[19] In equilibrium, inventors would not invest in upfront risky R&D towards creating technology standards in light of the potential of not being paid *ex post* and implementers would not manufacture standards-compliant products under the risk of having to pay excessive royalty rates to patent owners *ex post*. The FRAND commitment should enable the parties involved to have an efficient contract while their incentives to participate in the standards are balanced. Even if FRAND, or the agreement to license patents can be exploited, it can be done by either party—for example, by patent owners offering licensing terms that may not be deemed "fair or reasonable" and forcing the implementers to pay excessive royalties to get on with manufacturing standards-compliant products, or by the implementers not behaving as willing licensees and negotiating in good faith, forcing the patent owners to give up by allowing the implementer to infringe and freeride on their sunk R&D investments. In this case, the courts must balance the rights of both the parties by offering them full legal remedies and tools.

Although the theory of hold-up is symmetric, the idea of one-sided patent hold-up has become a concern based on concerns heard by regulatory agencies.[20] The fact that the concern of patent holders potentially holding up implementers ex-post (and not vice-versa) is heard more often may explained by the very nature of technology standards: among all the industry participants in the technology ecosystem, only a minority are inventors that invest in upfront R&D towards creating new standards-compliant technologies for the future, while a majority are implementers of the standards compliant products.[21] This may be because investment in R&D years in advance of any commercialization is a risky proposition—some standards technologies fail, others only enjoy weak market adoption—after decades of investment in developing complex technological solutions.[22] Only a few studies have tried to study the issue of hold-up with empirical rigor. One such study compared SEP intensive with non-SEP intensive and non-patent intensive industries, and found that the former are associated with rapidly falling consumer prices, at a faster pace than other comparison industries—this reveals a trend that is at odds with what the hold-up theory would suggest.[23]

---

19 The literature refers to the potential hold-up of the implementer by the patent owner as "patent hold-up," and the potential hold-up of the patent owner by the implementer as "hold-out" or "reverse hold-up." But the idea expressed is the same: hold-up is a symmetric problem with each party on the two sides of the bargaining table able to behave opportunistically *ex post*.

20 *See, e.g.*, Fed. Trade Comm'n, The Evolving IP Marketplace: Aligning Patent Notice and Remedies with Competition (2011), *available at* http://www.ftc.gov/sites/default/files/documents/reports/evolving-ip-marketplace-aligning-patent-notice-and-remedies-competition-report-federal-trade/110307patentreport.pdf. The report is not based on empirical analysis, and cites several companies such as Intel, Cisco, and others to find evidence of a one-sided patent hold-up concern.

21 Kirti Gupta, *The process and data behind standard setting in wireless communications*, (Northwestern Searle Center Working Paper, 2013), *available at* http://www.law.northwestern.edu/research-faculty/searlecenter/events/innovation/documents/Gupta_standard-setting-process-3gpp.pdf. *See* page 22, "Only 34% of the attendees ever submitted one or more change requests to any one of the [3GPP] RAN working groups".

22 There are some well-known examples of inter-standard competition and failed ICT standards because the market take-up did not occur. For example, VHS and its failed rival BetaMax in the video standard wars, 4G wireless cellular LTE and its failed rival WiMAX (IEEE 802.16e), as well as the failure of Minidisc, Global Videophone, Digital Video Broadcasting for handheld devices ("DVB-H"), MediaFlo, Wireless Home Digital Interface, WiMedia standards.

23 *Supra* note 19.

IV. Valuation of Patents and Determination of Royalties

Courts and regulators in India and around the world have been faced with a number of issues when considering how to apply IPR and competition laws to the licensing of SEPs.

At the outset, one issue under discussion is whether the cases involving FRAND commitments are a matter of antitrust law at all, since they have traditionally been addressed as a contract law (or tort law) matter.[24] The issue of jurisdiction is now playing out in India, with cases involving the same parties involved in FRAND licensing disputes being heard both in the Delhi High Court and pending investigation at the CCI. While the specifics of the cases are discussed in Part IV, this Part addresses the complex and difficult issues a competition authority must deal with in light of the efforts to invoke competition law to set or limit royalties in complex commercial license agreements.

With antitrust agencies setting royalty rates, the price of a technology is not determined by market forces, but rather, based on fact-specific merits on a case-by-case basis as they address the question of whether a particular royalty rate fairly and adequately compensates innovators for their investment and risk. However, if this question is not determined appropriately, it may seriously harm the incentives for innovators to invest in risky R&D or the incentives for manufacturers to implement standards compliant products. Although the concerns of potential patent hold-up and exorbitant royalties have been raised by certain groups, competition authorities must seek concrete evidence that establishes anticompetitive effects on an industry for a commercial dispute to be an antitrust concern. It is, of course, also an exceedingly difficult proposition for a central authority to try and determine royalty rates and to set one-size-fits-all regulations, rather than letting the markets determine the rates based on good faith negotiations between parties under the threat of litigation, which can be initiated by either party. To provide a flavor of these difficulties and the inaccuracies that may result, some proposed measures to calculate royalty rates are reviewed in this Part.

First, some have raised a concern that the choice of a specific royalty base to be used in calculating royalties may have an anticompetitive effect and constitute abuse of dominance, for e.g., the use of the price of an entire licensed device rather than of particular components within the device as the royalty base for patent portfolios that enable specific wireless communications functionalities in the device.[25] This is likely to raise complex and fact-specific questions. First of all, in this example, the wireless communications industry has had the historical and wide-spread industry practice of using the end-user device prices as the royalty base for a variety of practical reasons.[26] For example, for large patent portfolios that include patents on several components of the device, licensing on the whole device rather than individual components significantly reduces the industry's transaction costs. Device volumes and prices are more readily ascertainable. Second, the inventions incorporated in the cellular standards have a

24 Bruce H. Kobayashi & Joshua D. Wright, *Federalism, Substantive Preemption, and Limits on Antitrust: An Application to Patent Holdup*, 5(3) J. Competition L. & Econ. 469, (2009) See, example, page 6, "[The] contract law offers a promising alternative to antitrust enforcement in the case of patent hold-up involving breach of FRAND commitments made in good faith as contract doctrine provides tools designed to identify and distinguish hold up from good faith negotiations of long term contracts." Part V deals exclusively with this analysis.

25 *See, e.g.*, Joseph Kattan, *The Next FRAND Battle: Why the Royalty Base Matters*, 1 CPI Antitrust Chronicle (Mar. 2015).

26 *See* Russell L. Parr & Gordon V. Smith, Intellectual Property: Valuation, Exploitation, and Infringement Damages (11th ed. 2013). *See also* Eric Stasik, *Royalty Rates And Licensing Strategies For Essential Patents On LTE (4G) Telecommunication Standards*, 3 Les Nouvelles 114 (2010).

system-wide effect, i.e., they help towards the improvement of the entire system. For such inventions, the value of the invention may or may not be directly related to where it happens to be implemented, in this example, in a chip or any other component in a specific part of the overall system. Thus, if faced with this issue, regulators will need to consider carefully all perspectives around charging higher royalties on devices that have advanced features to take greater advantage of underlying technologies.

Another proposal by antitrust economists is the use of an "incremental value test" for determining the royalty rates, i.e., only the incremental value of the patented invention over the next-best alternative should be used as a benchmark for a reasonable royalty calculation.[27] Traditionally, the theory of incremental value has been discussed in terms of inventions that lead to cost savings for manufacturing. It suggests that a patent holder should receive the value of the incremental improvement that their patented technology offers compared to the closest rival. For example, if a plate already exists and someone patented a design on a plate, only the value of the plate design is considered a part of that patent. Building on an early theory that extends this to licensing that suggests the price of a patent in the standard setting context should be commensurate with the price it could have obtained if there had been an auction among competing technologies prior to the standard being set (ex-ante)[28], Farrell, Hayes, Shapiro and Sullivan suggest the incremental value test for the calculation of reasonable royalties.[29] Considering a simple interpretation with two entities competing in an R&D race, for example, one firm produces an invention valued at level X and another produces an invention valued at level Y, where $X - Y = \Delta > 0$. X is chosen to be included in the standard. Under this interpretation of the incremental value test, only the first firm receives a royalty payment of $\Delta < X$, that is, strictly lower than the full value of the technology X it contributes and more importantly, may be strictly lower than the R&D cost of creating the technology X. In other words, this interpretation of incremental value may only relates to a comparison of alternatives in a patent race, not to the starting point of an innovation. For a competitive process or a race to begin, inventors must have an incentive to innovate new technologies. If they are systematically compensated lower than the R&D cost of participating in the innovation process, their incentive may be reduced. Therefore, any proposal for the incremental value will have to take into account for the ex-ante timeline not only prior to when a technology is chosen for being incorporated in the standard, but when firms are making decisions on whether or not to invest in R&D that may be contributed into a standard.

Yet another proposal has been the use of numeric proportionality to value SEPs. This proposal suggests that all patents essential to the standard should be regarded as equally valuable and treated symmetrically since they all afford the same market power, or *ex post* hold-up power.[30] This premise leads to proposed royalties calculated to be proportional to the number of essential patents contributed to the standard. For example, a firm owning 100 SEPs out of a total of 1000 patents in that standard can claim 10% of the total royalty that the standard can command. First, this simple rule defies the well-established empirical result in the patent literature that patents differ greatly in their inventive and economic significance, and

---

27 Fed. Trade Comm'n, *supra* note 19, at pages 28-29, 174, e.g. "Courts should cap the royalty at the incremental value of the patented technology over alternatives available at the time the standard was set."

28 *See* Daniel G. Swanson & William J. Baumol, *Reasonable and Nondiscriminatory (RAND) Royalties, Standards Selection, and Control of Market Power*, 73(1) Antitrust L.J. 1 (2005).

29 Farrell, Hayes, Shapiro & Sullivan, *supra* note 8, e.g., at page 41, "the proportionality default could be modified, either ex ante or ex post based on information about the ex ante incremental values of the essential patent."

30 Philippe Chappatte, *FRAND Commitments—The Case for Antitrust Intervention*, 5(2) Eur. Competition J. 319, 340-43 (2009).

that the distribution of patent values is known to be highly skewed.[31] Second, not all patents declared essential to the standard are truly technically or commercially essential.[32]

Any proposal that suggests a central planner type approach in determining royalties would have to take these and various other factors into account on a case-by-case basis for reaching appropriate incentives for all the parties involved.

V. ICT Standards and FRAND Proceedings in India

Although India is one of the world's largest wireless cellular markets, the Indian jurisprudence on FRAND licensing practices for SEPs has begun to take shape only recently.

It all started with Ericsson, a well-known and leading inventor of wireless cellular technologies, bringing a lawsuit against Indian suppliers Micromax and Intex in 2013 and 2014, respectively, in the Delhi High Court for the infringement of its SEPs related to 2G and 3G technologies after years of failed licensing agreement negotiations with both parties. In turn, both Micromax and Intex filed a complaint with the CCI alleging that Ericsson abused its allegedly dominant position by imposing exorbitant royalties for its SEPs, thus violating the Indian Competition Act. In January 2014, the CCI made a prima facie determination of abuse of dominant position and ordered the Director General ("DG") to investigate the allegations against Ericsson. However, following a writ petition filed by Ericsson challenging the CCI's jurisdiction in cases related to the licensing of patents, the court directed the DG of CCI to refrain from passing any final order/report pending adjudication of this matter in court. Additionally, in December 2014, Ericsson filed a lawsuit against the Chinese manufacturer Xiaomei Technology Company in the Delhi High Court for infringement of its 2G and 3G SEPs. And in May 2015, iBall, an Indian supplier of smartphones, filed a complaint against Ericsson with the CCI.

As of September 2015, the Delhi High Court has issued interim orders and calculated appropriate royalties for the two FRAND-related patent infringement cases while the investigations before the CCI remain pending. In this Part, I briefly discuss the six FRAND proceedings to date and follow with a brief analysis of some of the key issues involved in these proceedings and the potential impact of the proceedings on the formation of Indian jurisprudence on these issues.

1. Ericsson v. Micromax in the Delhi High Court

In March 2013, Ericsson brought a suit against Micromax, an Indian supplier of mobile devices, for infringement of its eight patents related to 2G and 3G SEPs registered in India seeking damages and a permanent injunction against Micromax.[33] According to the court documents, Ericsson initiated licensing

---

31 *See, e.g.*, Mark Schankerman & Ariel Pakes, *Estimates of the Value of Patent Rights in European Countries During the Post-1950 Period*, 96(384) Econ. J. 1052 (1987).

32 *See* David J. Goodman & Robert A. Myers, *3G Cellular Standards and Patents*, Paper Presented at IEEE WirelessCom 2005 (Jun. 13, 2005), http://eeweb.poly.edu/dgoodman/wirelesscom2005.pdf.

33 Order, Telefonaktiebolaget LM Ericsson v. Mercury Elecs. & Another, Interim Application No. 3825 of 2013 in Civil Suit (Original Side) No. 442 of 2013, High Ct. of Delhi (Mar. 6, 2013), *available at* http://delhihighcourt.nic.in/dhcqrydisp_o.asp?pn=46519&yr=2013.

negotiations with Micromax in 2009 after sending an initial notice of infringement. After repeated notices, Ericsson and Micromax finally did agree to negotiate a FRAND license, and pending negotiations Micromax agreed to pay the rates Ericsson had initially proposed in November 2012.[34] However, Micromax never entered into any agreement to license Ericsson's SEPs, thus leading Ericsson to file a lawsuit.

After the hearing in December 2014, the Delhi High Court granted an injunction to Ericsson against Micromax based on the infringed 2G and 3G technology, and directed Micromax to pay royalties to Ericsson ranging from 0.8-1.3% of the net selling price of the devices containing the infringed technology. In order to compute the royalty rates, the Court asked Ericsson to produce comparable licenses and based its calculation on 26 licenses that Ericsson had signed with other Indian parties.[35] The interim agreement also stated that Micromax and the Customs department would have to notify Ericsson when a consignment of Micromax devices arrives in India. Following an inspection by Ericsson's representative the consignment will be cleared for release and immediately handed over to Micromax. Upon sale, Micromax will transfer royalties to Ericsson based on the Court's established rate.

2. Ericsson v. Intex in the Delhi High Court

In April 2014, Ericsson sued Intex for the infringement of eight SEPs related to 2G and 3G standards and sought a permanent injunction and damages.[36] In March 2015, the Delhi High Court issued an interim decision granting an injunction against Intex and directed Intex to transfer the determined royalties to Ericsson. The facts of the case are colorful and are considered carefully in the interim decision by the presiding judge, Justice Manmohan Singh.[37]

Ericsson argued that because its asserted patents are 2G and 3G SEPs, any entity that makes, uses, or sells devices complying with these standards by definition infringes on these patents. Ericsson produced a record of having initiated a licensing negotiation with Intex in December 2008, with repeated interactions until 2013, but no agreement was reached.[38] Ericsson argued that Intex had taken two contradictory stands on the issue of validity and infringement of Ericsson's SEPs. Ericsson produced a record that its licensing negotiations continued with Intex in 2013, during which time, on the one hand, Intex continued to correspond with Ericsson about a potential licensing agreement but, on the other hand, initiated proceedings against Ericsson with the Intellectual Property Appellate Board ("IPAB") for the revocation of Ericsson's patents, as well as initiated a complaint against Ericsson with the CCI alleging abuse of dominance by Ericsson due to its prominent position in ownership of SEPs for a standard for which there is no other alternative.[39] Intex argued that the Court should not grant an injunction against it because there was no clear evidence of validity of Ericsson's patents and damages were adequate to compensate Ericsson for its claim.

---

34 Order, Telefonaktiebolaget LM Ericsson v. Mercury Elecs. & Another, Interim Application No. 4694 of 2013 in Civil Suit (Original Side) No. 442 of 2013, High Ct. of Delhi (Mar. 19, 2013), *available at* http://delhihighcourt.nic.in/dhcqrydisp_o.asp?pn=57850&yr=2013.

35 Judgment, Telefonaktiebolaget LM Ericsson v. Mercury Elecs. & Another, Interim Application No. 3825 of 2013 and Interim Application No. 4694 of 2013 in Civil Suit (Original Side) No. 442 of 2013, }} 1 – 4, High Ct. of Delhi (Nov. 12, 2014), *available at* http://lobis.nic.in/ddir/dhc/GSS/judgement/17-11-2014/GSS12112014S4422013.pdf.

36 Judgment, Telefonaktiebolaget LM Ericsson v Intex Techs. (India) Limited, Interim Application No. 6735 of 2014 in Civil Suit (Original Side) No. 1045 of 2014, }} 1, 8, High Ct of Delhi (Mar. 13, 2015), *available at* http://lobis.nic.in/ddir/dhc/MAN/judgement/16-03-2015/MAN13032015S10452014.pdf.

37 *Id.*at 2-34.

38 *Id.* at 26-28.

39 *Id.* at 28-30.

The Delhi High Court determined that the asserted patents prima facie appear to be valid. The Court referred to Intex's statements in its complaint to the CCI that Ericsson's patents are essential to 2G and 3G, leaving companies complying with these standards no choice other than implementing these SEPs.[40] The Court observed that Intex's complaint to the CCI is admission of its infringement of Ericsson's SEPs. The Court also brought to attention Intex's statement before the IPAB, where it admitted that the patents in suit were directly related to its business, a further admission of infringement. Based on these facts and the contradictory positions taken by Intex, the Court found Intex an unwilling licensee.[41]

In addition, the Delhi High Court did an analysis of Ericsson's practice of charging royalties based on the price of the device and considered them consistent with its FRAND commitments, citing the US decision in *CSIRO v Cisco*, where the District Court for the Eastern District of Texas had rejected that the royalty base should be based on the chipset price, and the Chinese decision by the National Development and Reform Commission ("NDRC") for Qualcomm's 3G and 4G SEPs, where it calculated royalty rates as a percentage of the net selling price of devices incorporating those technologies.[42] The Court upheld the royalty rates calculated for the *Ericsson v Micromax* interim decision as the facts in both the cases were similar.

Notably, the Delhi High Court's decision of granting an interim injunction to an unwilling licensee predates a recent hallmark decision by the European Court of Justice on the *Huawei Technologies v ZTE Corporation*, which provides useful guidance that a SEP owner does not abuse its dominant position when seeking injunctive relief against an unwilling licensee.[43]

3. Ericsson v. Xiaomei in the Delhi High Court

In December 2014, Ericsson sued Xiaomei in the Delhi High Court for the same set of its 2G and 3G SEPs that it asserted against Micromax and Intex.[44] Ericsson had allegedly asked Xiaomei to take a license for its SEPs, but Xiaomei launched infringing products in India, and created an Indian subsidiary for marketing the infringing products without obtaining a license. The Court issued an interim injunction against Xiaomei to restrain it from importing or selling any infringing devices in India. Xiaomei appealed and argued that since it had obtained the chipset implementing Ericsson's asserted patented technology from Qualcomm Inc., which had a license from Ericsson, its products did not infringe Ericsson's patents. As a temporary arrangement, Xiaomei is allowed to import and sell only devices containing Qualcomm's chipsets in India. Unlike the Micromax and Intex cases, no royalty rate has been determined by the court.

---

40 *Id.*

41 *Id.*

42 *Id.* at 249-50.

43 Case C170/13, Huawei Technologies v. ZTE Corporation [not yet reported], *available at* http://curia.europa.eu/juris/document/document.jsf;jsessionid=9ea7d2dc30dda3db711f97bb4c0d8dfeefb36e3beda0.e34KaxiLc3qMb40Rch0SaxuSahr0?text=&docid=165911&pageIndex=0&doclang=EN&mode=lst&dir=&occ=first&part=1&cid=2106054.

44 Judgment, Telefonaktiebolaget LM Ericsson v. Xiaomi Technology and Others, Interim Application No. 24580 of 2014 in Civil Suit (Original Side) No. 3775 of 2014, 1 – 2, High Ct of Delhi (Dec. 8, 2014), *available at* http://delhihighcourt.nic.in/dhcqrydisp_o.asp?pn=250092&yr=2014.

4. Micromax's Complaint against Ericsson with the CCI

In 2013, after Ericsson filed a lawsuit against Micromax in the Delhi High Court, Micromax filed a complaint with the CCI alleging that Ericsson had abused its dominant position by asking for exorbitant royalties for its SEPs.[45] Micromax argued that the royalty rates being charged by Ericsson were on the basis of the value of the device and not the value of the chipset in which the patented technology was implemented, thus constituting a "misuse of SEPs" that would ultimately harm consumers.[46] Micromax also submitted that Ericsson had subjected all its present and prospective licensees to signing a non-disclosure agreement ("NDA"), which prevented the disclosure of commercial terms between similarly placed patent seekers, allegedly demonstrating that "the royalty charged from Micromax may be many times more than the royalty being charged from others."[47]

The opinion by the CCI determined Ericsson to be a dominant player due to being the largest holder of SEPs for 2G, 3G, and 4G technologies, for which there is no alternate technology available in the market. The CCI suggested that "FRAND licenses are primarily intended to prevent patent hold-up and royalty stacking," noting some alleged harms of patent hold-up, but not citing any evidence of harm to competition.[48] The CCI also stated that the practices adopted by Ericsson were excessive and discriminatory, and contrary to FRAND terms, as the royalty rates being charged had "no linkage to the patented product"—in other words, the CCI took issue with the royalties being charged as a percentage of the net selling price of the device rather than the chip implementing the 2G or 3G technology. The CCI argued that for the use of the GSM chip in a phone costing Rs 100, the royalty of 1.25% would be Rs 1.25, but for the use of the same chip in a phone of Rs 1000, the royalty would be Rs 12.5, and that this "increase in the royalty for the patent holder is without any contribution to the product of the licensee." The CCI argued that the charging of two different license fees per unit phone for the use of the same technology prima facie is discriminatory and reflects excessive pricing.[49]

The CCI concluded that Micromax had established a prima facie case of Ericsson's abuse of its dominant position and directed the DG to further investigate without being swayed in any manner by the strong observations already made by the CCI in its opinion.

5. Intex's Complaint against Ericsson with the CCI

In 2013, Intex Technologies (India) Limited filed a complaint against Ericsson with the CCI. Intex, like Micromax, alleged that Ericsson's licensing rates were "exorbitant" and thus constituted an abuse of its allegedly dominant position in India's telecommunications market. In addition, Intex argued that Ericsson's demand that potential licensees sign an NDA was restrictive and violated Ericsson's FRAND commitment.[50] Intex argued that the NDA was "strongly suggestive" that different royalty rates/commercial terms were being offered to potential licensees of the same category, and alleged that Ericsson had abused its position

45 Micromax Informatics Ltd v. Telefonaktiebolaget LM Ericsson, Case No. 50/2013, Competition Commission of India (Nov. 12, 2013), *available at* http://infojustice.org/wp-content/uploads/2013/12/CCI-Case-no-50-2013.pdf.

46 *Id.* at 4 ("Due to this, royalty for use of same chipset in a smart phone is more than 10 times the royalty for ordinary phone, while the chipset gives no additional value to a smart phone, then it gives to an ordinary phone. *Such misuse of SEPs would ultimately harm consumers*" (emphasis added)).

47 *Id.*

48 *Id.* at 6 ("Patent Hold-up is one of the serious problems faced by the information and communications industry worldwide.").

49 Part III of this paper refers to practical considerations that need to be taken into account for such licensing practices.

50 Intex Techs. (India) Ltd v. Telefonaktiebolaget LM Ericsson, Case No. 76 of 2013,} 6, Competition Commission of India (Jan. 16, 2014).

to force Intex to sign the NDA, which unreasonably restricted Intex from discussing the infringement of Ericsson's patents with its vendors whom Intex needed to rely on for making representations regarding non-infringement.

On the basis of this complaint, the CCI's prima facie opinion expressed the same conclusions as its response to Micromax's complaint. On many of the conclusions, however, the CCI opinion is directly at odds with the Delhi High Court's interim decision.

6. iBall's Complaint against Ericsson with the CCI

In May 2015, Best IT World (India) Private Limited (known as iBall) filed a complaint against Ericsson with the CCI.[51] Unlike Micromax and Intex's complaints, iBall focused more on Ericsson's "strict and onerous terms" through the NDA that Ericsson required iBall to sign for conducting the licensing negotiations. These terms included settling all disputes through arbitration in Stockholm, requiring confidentiality for 10 years, and covering past as well as future sales within the ambit of the license agreement. iBall alleged that this conduct—including the threat of patent infringement proceedings, the demand of "unreasonably high royalties" calculated as a percentage of the price of the standard-compliant products, and the bundling of "patents irrelevant to iBall's products" in the license agreement—violated the Competition Act.

The CCI, similar to its opinions for the Micromax and Intex complaints, observed that, because there is no alternate technology available for Ericsson's patents in the 2G, 3G, and 4G standards, Ericsson enjoys dominance over its present and prospective licensees. The CCI opined that Ericsson's practice of "forcing a party to execute NDA and imposing excessive and unfair royalty rates, prima facie, amount to abuse of dominance in violation of section 4 of the Act." The CCI directed the DG to investigate further Ericsson's licensing practices and highlighted that iBall's allegations were similar to the allegations made by Micromax and Intex.

7. Key Observations

There are some noteworthy developments from the Delhi High Court's interim decisions on the *Micromax* and *Intex* cases, as well as from the opinions expressed by the CCI.

The Delhi High Court viewed these cases to be commercial IP disputes and adjudicated them as such, and directed the DG of the CCI to refrain from passing any final order/report pending adjudication of this matter before the Court.

On the substantive issue of whether the royalty rate should be based on the net selling price of the device, the Court agreed that "Ericsson's practice of charging royalty on the device price is non-discriminatory," and cited decisions involving similar issues from the United States and China. This analysis takes into account both the common industry practice of licensing these technologies at the device level, as well as recent judicial trends. The economic reasoning, as discussed in Part III, also supports the Court's analysis, as the technologies embodied in the 2G, 3G, and 4G standards are system level inventions that improve the performance of the entire network and often provide the foundation for the user experience by enabling fast connectivity, high quality communication, and high speed data rates. Thus, the complementarity and

51 Best IT World (India) Private Ltd. v. Telefonaktiebolaget LM Ericsson, Case No. 4 of 2015, Competition Commission of India (May 12, 2015), *available at* http://www.cci.gov.in/sites/default/files/042015_0.pdf.

network effects generated by these technologies cannot be valued appropriately based on the value of a component where they may happen to be implemented. The CCI's position on this issue is contrary to the Court's since the CCI found Ericsson's practice of basing the royalty on the price of the end-product an abuse of dominance.

The Court also relied upon comparable licenses to derive FRAND rates, and therefore relied upon real-world market valuations of the asserted SEPs. From an economic perspective, comparable licenses reveal what a willing licensor and a willing licensee consider fair compensation for the use of a patented technology, and thus represent a mutually beneficial agreement. From a judicial perspective, the value of comparable licenses for the calculation of patent damages has been recognized by US courts as well. For example, the US Court of Appeals for the Federal Circuit has emphasized that "actual licenses to the patented technology are highly probative as to what constitutes a reasonably royalty for those patent rights because such actual licenses most clearly reflect the economic value of the patented technology in the marketplace."[52] The reliance on real-world comparable licenses reduces the risk of errors in coming up with the valuation of a technology, an extremely difficult exercise for third-party observers of a commercial dispute. Again, the CCI took a contradictory view in its opinion, and found Ericsson's royalty rates to be "exorbitant" and "in violation of its FRAND commitments," despite not examining any potential evidence based on pre-existing and long-standing comparable licenses in the industry.

The CCI opinion's mention of patent hold-up and royalty stacking as concerns that may lead to consumer harm. Aside from the active discussion and debate around these theories noted in Part II, evidence of harm to competition is currently not included. In the recent *Ericsson v. D-Link* case, the Court of Appeals of the Federal Circuit upheld the District Court's analysis that such concerns would not be admissible unless there was evidence of *actual* hold-up or royalty stacking, which the defendants in the case had failed to provide, and noted "something more than a general argument that these phenomena are possibilities is necessary."[53]

Therefore, jurisprudence in India on the issues related to FRAND is in formation and it would be interesting for the international community to watch how it evolves. The issues in all the cases are directly related to the broader issues that are currently being debated on a global scale, as have been discussed in Sections II and III of this Article.

52 LaserDynamics, Inc. v. Quanta Comp., Inc., 694 F.3d 51, 79 (Fed. Cir. 2012).

53 Ericsson, Inc. v. D-Link Systems, Inc., Nos. 13-1625, -1631, -1632, -1633, at 54 (Fed. Cir. Dec. 4, 2014).

VI Conclusion

With the world's second largest mobile market, India is an important and attractive market for the key global firms in the wireless communications industry, both to supply and sell products, as well as to set-up local manufacturing plants and design centers. Currently, policies and jurisprudence in India on the issues related to SSO IPR policies and FRAND licensing disputes are in formation, and the issues involved at the core of all these matters are currently being debated on a global scale. How India chooses to shape its policies related to IP enforcement and FRAND licensing issues will be interesting for the international dialogue, but more importantly, it would be instrumental in determining India's future in the global wireless value chain. The key issues for the ICT industry are rooted in standard setting and related IPR policies, thus the policies implemented by the local SSOs, including the newly formed TSDSI, as well as the evolving jurisprudence on SEP-related issues both in the courts and the CCI, will be critical toward shaping the future of the ICT industry in India. With the government's initiatives on "Make in India" and "Design in India," it is imperative that the adopted IPR policies are attractive both to implementers and inventors of new technologies, so that local investment in R&D and manufacturing is lucrative, as well as for activities in India to climb further in the value chain towards long-term innovation.

The Indian Pharmaceutical Sector: Antitrust Issues and Cases*

Aditya Bhattacharjea

aditya@econdse.org

Professor, Delhi School of Economics, University of Delhi

Fiyanshu Sindhwani

fiyanshu@econdse.org

Research Scholar, Delhi School of Economics, University of Delhi

Abstract

Most Indians suffer from a lack of access to essential drugs, although the country is home to a large and internationally competitive pharmaceutical sector. In seeking to explain this paradox, we begin with an exploration of the market structure and marketing practices of the industry, which allow high prices and anticompetitive behaviour to be sustained despite the existence of a large number of competitors. We then critically review all the decisions of the Competition Commission of India ("CCI") concerning this sector since the Competition Act was brought into force in 2009. A nationwide agreement between associations of the major manufacturers and distributors, in operation since 1982, was found to have restricted the number of distributors in each region and also imposed distribution margins. Although heavy fines were imposed on the distributors, the manufacturers were let off without examining whether they benefited from these restrictions. All mergers in the sector were approved, with behavioural or structural remedies in a few cases. However, many mergers may have escaped scrutiny because of the high notification thresholds in the Act, and the CCI failed to look into possible coordinated effects or to recognize that export capacity could be a source of potential competition.

---

* This chapter draws upon and substantially updates a project report submitted to CUTS International in 2013. The authors are grateful to CUTS International for sponsoring the project.

I. Introduction

From a competition perspective, India's pharmaceuticals sector presents two paradoxes that are both puzzling and troubling. First, "the country now ranks 3rd world wide by volume of production and 14th by value."[1] It has more than 10,000 drug manufacturing units.[2] Indian- and foreign-based suppliers between them supply over 20,000 different brands in the Indian market,[3] distributed by over 700,000 wholesalers and retail "chemists" (the Indian term for pharmacies or drug stores),[4] most of them small single-proprietorship or partnership operations. Concentration ratios and price-cost margins, measured at the aggregate industry level, have been falling in recent years.[5] The combination of a large market and a highly fragmented market structure at both the production and distribution levels should not create significant competition concerns, except for patented medicines. But in fact the sector has witnessed pervasive and long-lasting cartelization involving players at both levels. Recent mega-mergers, whose value exceeded the fairly high notification thresholds in India's Competition Act, have also required antitrust scrutiny.

The second paradox resides in the twin facts that although India's pharmaceuticals sector has come to be regarded as "the world's pharmacy," exporting about half its $30 billion turnover to over 200 countries,[6] the majority of India's own population is deprived of access to many essential drugs, and bears a heavy burden of paying for those drugs that are accessible. According to the latest available data, in 2013 "out of pocket" ("OOP") expenditure accounted for 86% of private expenditure on health, which in turn constituted 68% of total expenditure on health. Both figures are high by even the standards of developing countries. The first figure reflects the low coverage of private health insurance (which funded only about 5% of private health expenditure) and employer-provided medical benefits; the second reflects the low public financing of healthcare (with healthcare accounting for about 4.5% of total government expenditures, or about 1.2% of GDP).[7] These figures are deplorable even by the standards of poor countries. OOP expenditure on healthcare is a major cause of families falling into poverty and/or indebtedness. To the extent they cannot access adequate healthcare, they suffer low productivity at work or lost workdays due to high morbidity and diversion of family members to caregiving, further contributing to chronic poverty. Healthcare costs are therefore directly implicated in issues of poverty, quality of life, and productivity.

Drugs, of course, are only one component of healthcare spending, the others being hospitalization expenses, outpatient consultations, and diagnostic tests. According to the official 2009-10 Consumer Expenditure

---

1 Dep't of Pharmaceuticals, *Indian Pharmaceutical Industry – a Global Industry*, *available at* http://pharmaceuticals.gov.in/pharma-industry-promotion.

2 In 2011, there were 10,563 pharma manufacturing units in India. *See* Dep't of Pharmaceuticals, Annual Report of the Department of Pharmaceuticals 2010-11, at 66 (2011) [hereinafter 2010-11 Report].

3 Estimates of this figure vary widely, but this is the number cited by the Chairman of India's National Pharmaceutical Pricing Authority. *See* Injeti Srinivas, *The Myth of Branded Generics*, 49(38) Econ. & Pol. Wkly. 12, 14 (2014) (mentions that if one accounts for different strengths and dosages, there are 90,000 actively sold varieties).

4 Strictly speaking, they are called "chemists and druggists." Only those retailers who prepare a medicine on-site are called pharmacies or dispensing chemists.

5 *See* Aditya Bhattacharjea & Fiyanshu Sindhwani, Competition Issues in the Indian Pharmaceutical Sector ch. 3 (2014), *available at* http://www.cuts-ccier.org/Compeg/PDF/Report-Pharmaceutical_Sector_Study.pdf.

6 *Indian Pharmaceutical Industry*, as n 2 above. The same website also states that "India is the only country with [the] largest number of US-FDA compliant plants (more than 262 including APIs) outside of USA. We have nearly 1400 WHO-GMP approved Pharma Plants, [and] 253 European Directorate of Quality Medicines (EDQM) approved plants with modern state of the art Technology. No other country can boast of such an infrastructure."

7 Health expenditure ratios, by country, 1995-2013 India, http://apps.who.int/gho/data/view.main.HEALTHEXPRATIOIND (last visited Dec. 27, 2015).

Survey, expenditure on drugs accounted for over two-thirds of households' OOP expenditure on healthcare, rising to three-fourths for the poorest 20% of households.[8] In addition, according to internationally comparable and validated surveys undertaken in six Indian states in 2004-05, India had almost the highest availability for a standardized basket of drugs (counting only the lowest-price generics) in the private sector, and their median prices were almost the lowest of all developing countries. However, these were still more than 50% above international reference prices, while the median availability of these drugs in the public sector (where they are supposed to be provided free) was less than 20% in all but one of the states that were surveyed.[9] A more recent 2011 survey using the same methodology showed that public-sector availability is only slightly better in the National Capital Territory of Delhi, which is much better endowed with public healthcare facilities than the rest of the country. Several essential medicines were not available at all except in selected tertiary-care hospitals. Patients had to rely on the private sector, where availability was very high, but at prices much higher than international reference prices. For many of the medicines only one high-priced generic version was available at most outlets.[10]

The twin paradoxes can be partially resolved if we examine certain features of the market structure of the pharmaceuticals industry. First, the 10,563 pharma manufacturing units in India are not competing in the same market. For one thing, they produce at different vertical levels: 2,389 were producing bulk drugs (intermediates) and 8,174 were producing formulations (the final products).[11] Among producers of formulations, many small firms undertake contract manufacturing for larger firms which market the drugs under their own brand names, so the actual number of competitors is less than reported. Drugs are further divided into non-competing therapeutic segments like cardio-vascular, oncology, anti-infectives, etc. Even within a therapeutic segment, competition takes place at the level of a narrower range of drugs for particular conditions.

This takes us to the second remarkable feature of the industry: it consists of what can be succinctly described as a small number of very large firms co-existing with a large number of very small firms. One indication of this is that although the pharmaceuticals census enumerated over 10,000 manufacturing units in 2010-11, the official Annual Survey of Industries for the same year listed only 3,957 operating factories under the corresponding industry code 21 ("Basic Pharmaceutical Products and Pharmaceutical Preparations").[12] The ASI covers only units in the "organized" sector (those employing ten or more workers and using electric power), so this lower figure could mean that a large number of the units covered by the Pharmaceutical Manufacturing Census were either in the unorganized sector (employing less than ten workers) or were not operational. Moreover, both figures would overstate the degree of competition, as a firm (ownership unit) may own or control (horizontally or vertically) several manufacturing units. In the same year, some 600 companies accounted for over 80% of the sector's sales, with considerable dispersion in the size of these companies.[13]

---

8 Sakthivel Selvaraj & Anup Karan, *Why Publicly-Financed Health Insurance Schemes Are Ineffective in Providing Financial Risk Protection*, 47(11) Econ. & Pol. Wkly. 60 (2012).

9 *See* Alexandra Cameron et al., The World Medicines Situation 2011: Medicines Prices, Availability and Affordability ann. 2 (2011), *available at* http://apps.who.int/medicinedocs/documents/s18065en/s18065en.pdf.

10 *See* Anita Kotwani, *Where are we now: Assessing the price, availability and affordability of essential medicines in Delhi as India plans free medicines for all*, 13 BMC Health Services Res. 285 (2013)

11 2010-11 Report, *supra* note 2, at 66.

12 Ministry of Statistics & Programme Implementation, Annual Survey of Industries 2010-11: Summary Results for Factory Sector, Statement 5A, at 27.

13 We have computed this figure by taking the ratio of sales of the companies reported in the widely-used CMIE Prowess database to the aggregate industry production reported in the Indian Drugs Manufacturers' Association's annual publication for 2012.

The final feature to which we wish to draw attention is that in India, even generic drugs are branded. According to the Chairman of India's National Pharmaceuticals Pricing Authority, generic drugs sold under brand names comprise 98% of the domestic market, with the rest equally divided between patented drugs and unbranded generics (which are mainly sold to the public healthcare system).[14] Branding of generics allows manufacturers to differentiate varieties that are otherwise chemically identical (in the sense of having the same active pharmaceutical ingredient, or API). These brands are marketed through incentives provided to doctors and pharmacists:[15] the latter are often the first-line prescribers for poor patients unable to afford doctors' fees. As in other countries, including highly developed ones, many medicines are classic "credence goods" characterized by extreme information asymmetry: consumers lack the knowledge to exercise their free choice, and passively accept the recommendations of the supposedly better informed prescribers. This results in what is sometimes called "supplier-induced demand."

No doubt, the regulatory body for the medical profession exhorts its members that, "Every physician should, as far as possible, prescribe drugs with generic names and he/she shall ensure that there is a rational prescription and use of drugs,"[16] but this exhortation is almost universally ignored. India has no law requiring pharmacies to substitute cheaper generics; in fact, they are prohibited from substituting any medicine listed in Schedules H and X of the Drugs and Cosmetics Act (which list drugs that can be sold only on prescription).[17] However, many pharmacies routinely do so, claiming that the prescribed medicine is not in stock, and they may actually substitute a more expensive brand.

The result of all these complications is that despite an apparently fragmented market, there is considerable market concentration and market power at the level of individual drugs, manifested in high concentration ratios and a wide range of prices and retail margins for different brands of the same drug, sometimes even those produced by the same firm. In many cases, the highest-priced brands perversely command the highest market shares, and/or exhibit prices that are large multiples of prices of the same drug procured competitively by state procurement agencies for distribution through public clinics and hospitals.[18] In a country with a large number of very poor people, extremely limited health insurance coverage (which usually does not pay for outpatient treatment), and an overburdened public healthcare system, competition issues in the pharmaceutical sector contribute significantly to the social and economic problems discussed above.

Against this background, we now look at specific antitrust issues in so far as they pertain to the pharmaceuticals sector, under the rubrics of anticompetitive agreements and mergers. In each section, we briefly describe the relevant provisions of the Indian Competition Act and then review all the cases in which final orders have been issued by the Competition Commission of India ("CCI") up to the end of October 2015.[19]

---

14 Srinivas, *supra* note 3, at 13.

15 *Id.*; Kotwani, *supra* note 10, at 12. For the personal account of an Indian doctor, *see* Sanjay Nagral, *The Cost of Drugs: Beyond the Supreme Court Order*, 48(17) Econ. & Pol. Wkly. 13 (2013).

16 The Indian Medical Council (Professional Conduct, Etiquette and Ethics) Regulations, 2002 § 1.5.

17 "No person dispensing a prescription containing substances specified in Schedule H or X, may supply any other preparation, whether containing the same substance or not, in lieu thereof." *See* Drugs and Cosmetics Rules, No. 52 of 1945 (as corrected up to Nov. 30, 2004), r. 65(11-A).

18 *See* Bhattacharjea & Sindhwani, *supra* note 5, at 50-54; and generally, Selvaraj & Karan, *supra* note 8; Srinivas, *supra* note 3; Kotwani, *supra* note 10; Anita Kotwani, *Tracking Medicine Prices in the Supply Chain: Who Benefits from the Free Market in India?*, 48(52) Econ. & Pol. Wkly. 104 (2013).

19 The official text of all CCI orders is accessible from www.cci.gov.in, and will be cited below only by reference number and date of decision. It should be kept in mind that many of these orders are under appeal at the Competition Appellate Tribunal, and may be appealed beyond that to the Indian Supreme Court.

II. Anticompetitive Agreements

Under Section 3 of India's Competition Act, agreements between persons, enterprises, or associations of enterprises or persons are prohibited and void if they cause or are likely to cause an appreciable adverse effect on competition ("AAEC"). Like the competition laws of most countries, Section 3(3) of India's Act singles out so-called "hard core" horizontal agreements for special treatment. These are agreements between competitors to fix prices, restrict quantities, rig bids, or allocate markets. Such agreements (subject to a specific exemption for joint ventures) are *presumed* to have an AAEC. This does not quite amount to *per se* prohibition, because this presumption can be rebutted with reference to certain potential benefits enumerated in Section 19(3). So far no rebuttal has been successful. Other agreements, including vertical agreements listed explicitly in Section 3(4), are prohibited only if they cause an AAEC, which subjects them to the rule of reason. Finally, Section 3(5) carves out an exemption for agreements that impose "reasonable conditions, as may be necessary for protecting any . . . rights" granted under six specific laws governing intellectual property. No such case has been decided so far in respect of pharmaceuticals, so we do not discuss the intellectual property-antitrust interface in this paper.[20]

Since the 1990s, antitrust agencies in the developed world have detected and punished several international cartels involving pharmaceutical manufacturers, the so-called vitamins conspiracy being especially notorious. India was undoubtedly a victim of such cartels, but lacked an effective competition law with jurisdiction based on the effects doctrine that could counter them.[21] Section 32 of the Competition Act does explicitly assert jurisdiction over "[a]cts taking place outside India but having an effect on competition in India," but no such case has been decided so far in regard to pharmaceuticals. We briefly discuss a recent case of bid-rigging which did involve two multinational drug companies, one of them with manufacturing facilities in India.[22]

Once a year since 2002, a department of India's Ministry of Health and Family Welfare procures a large quantity of meningitis vaccine for vaccinating pilgrims going on the Hajj pilgrimage to Mecca. Until 2007 GlaxoSmithKline ("GSK"), which imported the vaccine from its parent, was the sole bidder. In 2008 Sanofi, which produced it from a facility in India, also made a bid. In 2009 and 2010, the sole Indian manufacturer, Bio-Med Products Pvt Ltd, successfully outbid the two multinationals. However, in 2011 the procurement agency increased the minimum turnover requirement for qualified bidders, with the result that Bio-Med became ineligible to bid. In that year, the two multinationals quoted a much higher price than in earlier years, and also offered to supply only a limited number of doses that would have effectively divided the required quantity almost equally between themselves. Bio-Med alleged that the government agency had abused its dominant position and that the two rival firms had cartelized the order.[23] The CCI did not pursue

20 Several cases regarding patent validity, "evergreening," and one of compulsory licensing, have been decided under the Patents Act by the regular courts and the office of the Patent Controller. For a survey of these cases, *see* Bhattacharjea & Sindhwani, *supra* note 5, at 75-78.

21 For an assessment of the Monopolies and Restrictive Trade Practices Act which was in force during this period, *see* Aditya Bhattacharjea, *India's New Competition Law: A Comparative Assessment*, 4 J. Competition L. & Econ. 609 (2008), *reprinted in* Economic Development: The Critical Role Of Competition Law And Politics (Eleanor Fox & Abel Mateus eds., 2011).

22 The next two paragraphs summarize the salient aspects of the case from the CCI order *In Re: M/s Bio-Med Pvt Ltd and Union of India and Others*, Case No.26 of 2013, decided June 4, 2015. A note on legal terminology: under the Indian Competition Act, the person bringing the complaint is termed the "informant." Unlike a plaintiff or complainant in other jurisdictions, the informant does not have to pursue the case once it is admitted by the CCI. In fact, Bio-Med did not appear in the hearings. The parties named in the complaint are designated as "other parties" rather than respondents or defendants. Hence the title of the cases are in the form *In Re: X and Y* rather than the adversarial *X vs Y*.

23 Many of the torturous details of the case need not be summarized here, but it bears mentioning that Bio-Med also approached the Delhi High Court, which upheld the increase in the turnover threshold. After the bids for the 2011 tender were received, the procurement agency had second thoughts and called for a limited tender from the three parties, including Bio-Med. Sanofi then went to the High Court, which allowed it to supply half the order if it matched the lowest bid price, which turned out to be from Bio-Med.

the case against the procurement agency as it was not an "enterprise" and therefore not subject to the Act, but it did inquire into the allegation against the firms. After a detailed investigation by its Director General ("DG"), the CCI found that GSK and Sanofi had engaged in bid-rigging. It imposed a penalty on each of them at the rate of 3% of their average annual turnover over the three years preceding the violation.

As in many other cartel cases decided by the CCI, the investigation could not uncover any direct evidence of an agreement, and the decision was based on circumstantial evidence. This included the sharp increase in bid prices in 2011, disproportionate to any increase in the firms' costs, inflation, or exchange rate changes. GSK did not bid in 2012, and Sanofi, despite being the sole bidder, quoted a lower price than it had bid in 2011. The CCI also noted the homogeneity of the product, the predictability of the order, the fact that the same firms were repeat bidders, and the fact that GSK had successfully catered to the entire tender at short notice in earlier years without pleading supply constraints. There was also evidence that representatives of the two firms had entered the office of the procurement agency almost simultaneously on two occasions, including the date of submission of their bids, and that Sanofi routinely prepared two bids and submitted one of them only after finding out whether other bidders had participated. In addition to the very similar bid prices, these findings are fairly persuasive as "plus factors," but the CCI order would have been on much stronger ground if it had found hard evidence of collusion.[24] The role of the procurement agency in disqualifying the erstwhile lowest bidder by raising the eligibility threshold, although not directly a matter of competition law, should also be considered.[25]

Direct evidence was plentiful in a series of cases in which brazen collusion was found at the level of drug distribution. These cases forcefully illustrate the first paradox described above. Textbook cartel theory predicts that highly fragmented industries should not be able to form and sustain cartels. Two major factors are supposedly at play: the practical problems of coordinating and monitoring the behavior of a large number of participants, and the incentive problems inherent in the large immediate gain that a small firm can expect from defection relative to the loss of its small share of future collusive profits if the cartel breaks down. It is surprising, therefore, that the majority of cartel cases in the Indian pharmaceutical sector have involved regional associations of hundreds, if not thousands, of small chemists (pharmacies). In India, most such outlets operate out of small premises with two or three employees. Along with wholesalers, they are organized into regional associations at the level of towns, districts, and states in a pyramidal formation with the national body, the All India Organization of Chemists and Druggists ("AIOCD"), at the apex. These eight cases reveal a truly Lilliputian situation in which thousands of small distributors had for decades collectively tied down and dictated terms to the giants of the pharmaceutical industry, enforcing several blatantly anticompetitive practices all over the country. Here too, government policy played a facilitating role, but in a very different way.

The first two cases were originally filed before India's erstwhile competition agency, the Monopolies and Restrictive Practices ("MRTP") Commission, in 2009. Shortly thereafter, the Commission was wound up and the MRTP Act was repealed to make way for enforcement of the Competition Act. Under Section 66(6) of the Competition Act, investigations initiated by the MRTP Commission were transferred to the CCI, to be disposed of as the CCI thought fit. The CCI ordered reinvestigation in the two cases and assessed them

24 For a review of other cartel cases decided by the CCI based on circumstantial evidence, *see* Aditya Bhattacharjea & Oindrila De, *Cartels and the Competition Commission*, 47(35) Econ. & Pol. Wkly. 14 (2012). That paper also urged the CCI to undertake the equivalent of "dawn raids," for which it has to approach a magistrate's court, and to lay down guidelines on penalties so as to avoid the impression of arbitrariness. In different cases, it has imposed penalties ranging from 2% to the maximum legally permissible 10% of turnover, sometimes listing aggravating and mitigating factors without quantifying how much each of them affected the penalty calculation.

25 Abuse of dominance by the procuring agency, in setting discriminatory product specifications or eligibility conditions for bidders, has been alleged in several other cases as well. *See* Aditya Bhattacharjea, *India's New Antitrust Regime: The First Two Years of Enforcement*, 57 Antitrust Bull. 449, 471 (Fall 2012) [hereinafter Bhattacharjea, *India's New Antitrust Regime*].

under the relevant provisions of the Competition Act.[26] The remaining six cases were filed directly before the CCI under the Competition Act.[27] The "informants"[28] were usually dissident members of the regional associations, or potential distributors who had been denied entry into the local market by the associations' policies. Apart from naming the concerned regional associations as "opposite parties," some of the cases also named the AIOCD, particular drug manufacturers, and/or the two major national manufacturers' associations, the Organization of Pharmaceutical Producers of India ("OPPI") and the Indian Drugs Manufacturers' Association ("IDMA"). The range of anticompetitive practices alleged was fairly similar in each case, as the regional associations had been implementing the guidelines of their national body, the AIOCD, set out in Memoranda of Understanding ("MoUs") signed with the OPPI and IDMA as far back as 1982 and revised periodically thereafter. The informants' evidence in each case was broadly confirmed, with more practices being brought to light, by further investigations that the CCI ordered its DG to undertake. In particular:

» Following the AIOCD guidelines, the regional affiliates had imposed limits on the number of stockists (wholesalers) in each territory, and had prevented pharmaceutical companies from appointing stockists without a no-objection certificate ("NOC") from the local association. The pharmaceutical companies could appoint stockists and retailers only from among the members of the associations.

» The associations also made distribution of any drug (whether a new launch or any change in product brand, dosage, form, strength, etc.) contingent on the manufacturers paying them a token amount under the Product Information System ("PIS"), ostensibly to disseminate information about drugs. No drugs could be distributed without PIS approval, which was often withheld or delayed to extract better terms from the manufacturers.

» In a few cases, the AIOCD and the regional associations had fixed trade margins of wholesalers and retailers at 10% and 20% respectively, and, in some cases, the regional associations had prohibited retailers from giving discounts to consumers and restricted wholesalers from giving discounts of more than 2% to retailers.

» Finally, the regional associations had in some cases imposed fines on distributors and ordered boycotts of the drugs supplied by pharmaceutical companies who violated these conditions. In one case, the association went much further and formed local vigilance committees to monitor compliance with its decision on prohibiting discounts. It repeatedly called for an "organizational movement" against members who continued to offer discounts, as well as against non-members (especially new chain stores which were offering substantial discounts and free home delivery, while remaining open 24 hours, 7 days a week, thereby cutting into the sales of member pharmacies). Minutes of the meetings of the association's executive committee referred only to meetings with the deviators to "persuade" them, but statements taken in evidence during the investigation revealed incidents of picketing, intimidation, and forced closures of non-complying outlets.[29]

---

26 In Re: C-127/2009/DGIR/(4/28), *Varca Chemist and Druggist and others vs Chemists and Druggists Association, Goa* (CDAG), decided June 11, 2012;In Re: C-87/2009/DGIR, *Vedant Bio Sciences vs Chemists & Druggists Association of Baroda*, decided Sept. 5, 2012. For the idiosyncratic way in which competition cases are titled in India, *see supra* text accompanying note 22. In a follow-up to the first case, the association was found to have continued some of its practices despite the original orders against it, and a further fine was imposed. *See* Suo-Moto Case No. 05 of 2013, *In re: Collective boycott/refusal to deal by the Chemists & Druggists Association, Goa (CDAG), M/s Glenmark Company and, M/s Wockhardt Ltd.*, decided Oct. 27, 2014.

27 Case 20/2011, *In re: M/s Santuka Associates Pvt. Ltd. and All India Organization of Chemists and Druggists and Ors.*, decided Feb. 19, 2013; Case 41/2011, *In Re: Sandhya Drug Agency and Assam Drug Dealers Association and Ors.*, decided Dec. 9, 2013; Case 30/2011, *In Re: Peeveear Medical Agencies and AIOCD and Ors.* decided Dec. 9, 2013; Case 60/2012, *In Re: Arora Medical Hall and Chemists and Druggists Association, Ferozepur and Ors.*, decided Feb. 5, 2014; Suo-Moto Case 02 of 2012, *In Re: Bengal Chemist and Druggist Association*, and Reference Case No. 01 of 2013, decided Mar. 11, 2014; Case 78/2012, *In Re: Rohit Medical Store and Macleod's Pharmaceuticals and Ors.*, decided Jan. 29, 2015. The Commission's order in the Bengal Chemist case also covered a submission (technically known as a "reference") from the Director of Drugs Control of the Government of West Bengal regarding the same practices.

28 For an explanation of this terminology, *see supra* note 22.

29 *See* Suo-Moto Case 02 of 2012, *In Re: Bengal Chemist and Druggist Association*.

Unusually for a cartel, in which firms usually collude without leaving any documentary evidence, in these cases there was ample evidence in the form of MoUs with the manufacturers' associations, annual reports, guidelines, letters, e-mails, minutes of meetings of the associations, as well as depositions by their members and some of the pharmaceutical companies. (Many others, including some of the biggest names in the pharmaceutical industry, had been so intimidated that they gave evasive answers or flatly denied knowledge of some of the industry practices that the others had attested to.)

The CCI found these activities to be violations of Sections 3(3)(a) and 3(3)(b) of the Competition Act, which deal respectively with horizontal agreements that fix prices and restrict quantities.[30] Such agreements are presumed to be anticompetitive. The CCI directed that these activities should cease, and the distributors' associations should inform the manufacturers and their own members accordingly. It also imposed fines of 10% of the average annual turnover—the maximum penalty permissible under the Act—of the respective distributors' associations. As their turnover consisted mainly of their membership fees, this was a negligible amount compared to the members' profits from their cartel. Fines ranging from 7% to 10% of income or turnover (as reported in tax returns) were imposed on individual members of the associations' executive committees, and deferred for those who did not submit their tax returns. These amounts were much larger than the fines on the associations themselves.

While a crackdown on the blatantly anticompetitive practices prevailing in the sector was long overdue, some aspects of these decisions are troubling. Although the drug manufacturers and their associations (the OPPI and IDMA) had been party to the MoUs that had established some of the practices, they were exonerated by the CCI on debatable grounds, despite its own DG finding them in violation of the Act. The associations had stated that they had terminated or not renewed their MoUs with the AIOCD. But the DG investigation had found that they had not publicized this fact or informed their members, and the practices were continuing.[31] The CCI, however, opined that the OPPI and IDMA (the manufacturers' associations) and the AIOCD (the distributors' association) were not operating at the same level of trade, so Section 3(3), which concerns horizontal agreements, could not be applied to the MoU between them. This argument was trite and unexceptionable. Nevertheless, one would have expected the MoU to be caught by Section 3(4), which covers vertical agreements. But the CCI argued that the associations were not "enterprises" as defined in the Competition Act, so the MoUs "cannot be said to be part of a vertical chain as envisaged under Section 3(4) of the Act and, consequently agreement in form of MoU does not fall under the ambit of Section 3(4) of the Act."[32] Section 3(3) of the Act covers both enterprises and associations of enterprises, which made it possible to fix liability on the distributors' associations for their horizontal practices. But Section 3(4) omits associations, a loophole that enabled the manufacturers' associations to escape.[33]

---

30 In the first few cases, a few of the seven members of the Commission gave partially dissenting orders, disagreeing with the majority on whether some of the practices could be considered anticompetitive, but concurring that the other practices were indeed anticompetitive and merited a penalty. For details, *see* Aditya Bhattacharjea, *The Competition Commission of India fines an association of pharmaceutical distributors for price-fixing and limiting competition on the basis of the Competition Act*, e-Competitions, Feb. 2013-II. Subsequently, the dissenting members were among those who were replaced in the normal course at the end of their five-year terms, and the Commission's orders in the later cases were all unanimous.

31 Case 20/2011, *Santuka Associates*, ¶¶ 29.1-29.6. Similar findings were recorded in other cases as well.

32 *Id.* ¶¶ 29.10- 29.12.

33 In the most recent case, the CCI has changed its stance somewhat. Referring to its decision in an earlier case (not related to pharmaceuticals), it held that "an agreement, even if it is not falling under section 3(3) or 3(4) of the Act, is amenable to the jurisdiction of the Commission under section 3(1) if the same has an appreciable adverse effect on competition (AAEC)." But it nonetheless held that there was insufficient evidence of an agreement between the individual manufacturers and the regional association, or of an AAEC, so no contravention of the Act could be established against the manufacturers. *See* Case 78/2012, *Rohit Medical Store*, ¶¶ 6.16-6.20.

The CCI in fact went further and wondered why the manufacturers would want to limit their own supply or fix their distributors' margins, and opined that they were "victims of the exploitative tactics of AIOCD."[34] This may well have been true, but some analysis of how the manufacturers were actually affected by the limitation of downstream competition was called for. As is well known, limiting the number of distributors, fixing their margins, and prohibiting discounts prevents freeriding on retail services by rival distributors and thereby encourages retailers to invest in such services, benefiting manufacturers as well as consumers. However, unlike electronics or cars, medicines do not need to be explained or demonstrated at the point of sale. The minimal requirement that each outlet should have a qualified pharmacist can be enforced by law. And in any case, the NOC requirement limited the number of wholesalers, not retailers. The usual arguments in favor of restrictions on downstream competition are therefore inapplicable to drug distribution. On the other hand, reducing intrabrand competition by limiting the number of distributors in a territory can soften interbrand competition and increase both upstream and downstream profits at the cost of consumers and social welfare.[35] And maintaining downstream prices can facilitate upstream collusion: transparency and stability of retail margins ensures that changes in retail costs are not automatically transmitted into prices, which could otherwise be misinterpreted by other upstream firms as a deviation from a collusive arrangement, thereby triggering a price war. The CCI did not go into any of these issues.

The issue of pricing transparency takes us to the second area of concern, which speaks to the role of government policies in restricting competition. The distributors' associations had pointed out that the government's own National Pharmaceutical Pricing Authority ("NPPA") had fixed the margins for "scheduled" drugs (those under price control), at 8% for wholesalers and 16% for retailers. The associations had argued that the margins of 10% and 20% respectively that they had fixed for non-scheduled drugs (those which are not under price control) were therefore "reasonable." (A minority of Commission members had agreed with them in the earlier cases.) But this points to a more serious issue that goes far beyond drugs or price controls. These margins were fixed as a percentage of the Maximum Retail Price ("MRP"), which is set by the manufacturers, not the distributors. For decades, the government has required manufacturers of all packaged products to print the MRP on the package itself. The latest such regulation is the Legal Metrology (Packaged Commodities) Rules, 2011. Although this is a well-intentioned measure to prevent consumers from being overcharged by retailers, it also mandates price transparency that can facilitate collusion amongst manufacturers, retailers, or both.

34 Case 20/2011, *Santuka Associates*, ¶¶ 29.13-29.14.

35 Patrick Rey & Joseph Stiglitz, *The Role of Exclusive Territories in Producers' Competition*, 26 RAND J ECON 431 (1995).

III. Mergers and Acquisitions

The merger-related provisions of the Competition Act were extremely controversial, and their enforcement was delayed until June 2011, more than two years after the other sections of the Act had been brought into force.[36] These provisions are supplemented by extremely detailed implementing regulations, which have been revised frequently to clarify the nature of transactions that need to be notified to the CCI.[37] Briefly, "combinations" (broadly defined to include mergers, acquisitions, and acquiring of control) are to be notified in advance to the CCI if they exceed any of several thresholds in terms of assets or turnover. These thresholds are specified separately for the combined assets or turnover of the parties, and for the group to which the target firm would belong after the merger. Each such threshold is specified separately for assets or turnover within India and globally. At the same time that the merger provisions were brought into force, the government notified a separate, lower, threshold for the assets and turnover of the target firm alone. No combination can be consummated unless it is approved by the CCI, or before 210 days, whichever is earlier.

Over 250 combination decisions have been handed down by the CCI up to October 2015. In every case, the proposed combination has been allowed to go ahead, in a few cases with conditions attached. Such behavioral or structural remedies were most frequently observed in the pharmaceuticals sector, in four out of the 14 cases decided so far. We briefly summarize the reasons given by the CCI for approval and the remedies that it imposed.

In three cases (Reckit/Paras/Halite, Orchid Research/Orchid Chemicals, and PHL Holding/Piramal Enterprises), the combination involved restructuring of the affiliates of the same owning group with no change in control, and therefore no AAEC. In seven other cases, no AAEC was expected because there was little or no horizontal overlap or vertical relationship, the combined entity would command a small market share, and many other significant competitors were present. Importantly, as most of the firms had diversified product portfolios, the analysis was undertaken at the level of therapeutic categories or even individual molecules. For combinations with a vertical dimension, the CCI looked into whether acquisition of an upstream producer of APIs could foreclose rival downstream manufacturers of formulations using the same API. The CCI also considered the possibility that the combined entity might stop development of products in the pipeline of one of the parties in case they competed with those of the other party. Although the CCI did not lay down a market share threshold that it would regard as triggering competition concerns, in some cases it did point out that the combined market shares would be less than 10%. In some cases, it also took comfort in the fact that the drugs that both parties were producing were under price control.

In the remaining four cases, the CCI imposed behavioral or structural remedies to ameliorate a possible AAEC. In three cases (Orchid/Hospira, Mylan/Strides, and Torrent/Elder) it required modification of the scope and duration of non-compete agreements whereby the target firms and their promoters[38] had committed not to develop, manufacture, or sell a broad range of products for periods of up to eight years

---

36 *See* Bhattacharjea, *India's New Antitrust Regime*, *supra* note 25, at 461.

37 For more details, and a review of India's experience with merger control in general, based on a review of the first 125 decisions up to August 2013, *see* Aditya Bhattacharjea, *Recent Trends in Mega-mergers in India and Lessons for Competition Policy: Insights from Merger Cases under the Competition Act*, *in* Trade and Industrial Development in India: Emerging Trends, Patterns and Issues (C. Veeramani & R. Nagaraj eds., forthcoming).

38 These transactions were asset acquisitions of only some of the plants or products of the target firms, which therefore remained in business as potential competitors. Many Indian firms are closely held or controlled by their "promoters," who can launch new ventures, so similar strictures were placed on them.

after the transaction. These agreements covered drugs that the targets did not produce, and also restrained them from conducting research on new molecules. The CCI approved the deals after the agreements were modified so as to shorten their duration to four years, and to confine the non-compete clauses to drugs currently being manufactured by the targets or in their development pipeline. It also insisted that the targets and their promoters could conduct research into currently non-existing molecules.

The only structural remedy was applied in the Sun/Ranbaxy merger, which gave rise to the world's fifth largest drug producer. This was the first case which went into a second-stage inquiry, in which the parties are required to publish details of the combination so that persons who might be adversely affected can file objections to be considered by the CCI. After conducting a market share analysis at the molecule level, the CCI ordered Sun and Ranbaxy to divest one and six products respectively. A monitoring and compliance mechanism was set up to ensure that the buyers were and remained independent of the parties to the combination.

It is possible that these 14 cases under-report the extent of merger activity because the notification thresholds are rather high by international standards. In 2011, a high-level committee was appointed by the government to look into the issue of foreign acquisitions of Indian companies, which was generating much political concern in the wake of several large cross-border acquisitions that had taken place before the merger regulations came into force. The committee pointed out (without giving any specific examples) that many acquisitions by multinationals are made by subsidiaries or special purpose vehicles created for that purpose. As these entities would have negligible assets and turnover, the global assets or turnover of their parent companies would have to be taken into account—but these would come under the much higher thresholds for "groups." The committee tabulated the size of the world's pharmaceutical giants and pointed out that only the top 18 would exceed the turnover threshold. Moreover, only the top 10 to 12 Indian companies would exceed the turnover threshold for target firms.[39] The committee recommended that the notification thresholds be reduced for the pharmaceuticals sector, but this suggestion was not implemented. Consequently, many mergers may have remained below the radar of the CCI. However, inflation would have raised some smaller transactions above the thresholds, which have not been revised since 2011.

On the other hand, some potential large mergers may have been stopped before they could reach the stage of notification to the CCI. Soon after the committee submitted its report, the government reacted in a different way to the concerns about foreign acquisitions in the sector. It imposed a requirement that all "brownfield" foreign direct investment (i.e., foreign acquisition of an Indian company) in the pharmaceutical sector would first need to be approved by the oddly-named Foreign Investment Promotion Board ("FIPB"); only then would the question of notification to the CCI arise. The FIPB imposes conditions regarding non-compete clauses, continued post-merger production of designated essential medicines, and maintenance of R&D expenditure levels. Although the FIPB decisions are in the public domain, extending the analysis to cover them is beyond the scope of this paper. What cannot be determined is whether these restrictions discouraged some acquirers from even applying. Be that as it may, four out of the 14 cases that came to the CCI (Mitsui/Arch, Orchid/Hospira, Mylan/Unichem, and Mylan/Strides) did involve foreign firms acquiring Indian companies. Two other cases (GSK/Novartis and Pfizer/Hospira/Perkins) involved local affiliates of foreign companies. All these cases were approved by the CCI after regular competition analysis.

---

39 Arun Maira Comm., High Level Committee Report on FDI in Existing Indian Pharma Companies 20 (2011), *available at* http://pharmaceuticals.gov.in/sites/default/files/ArunMiaraCommitteeReport.pdf.

On the whole, the CCI has done a commendable job of reviewing mergers expeditiously, identifying AAECs, and prescribing remedies where needed. We have reservations on only two aspects of its track record in respect of decisions in the pharmaceutical sector. First, although it did well to examine potential competition from the parties' pipeline products, and to insist that future drug development be kept out of non-compete agreements, it ignored another source of potential competition. In two cases (Mylan/Unichem and Mylan/Strides) it noted that one or both parties exported most of their output, and used this as an argument *against* the likelihood of the merger causing an AAEC in the domestic market. But capacity currently being used for producing for export can be quickly redirected to serve the domestic market, and thus constitutes a source of potential competition which might be thwarted by the combination. Second, the CCI seems to have confined itself to examining only the unilateral effects of the combinations; there seems to have been no recognition of the possibility that a market with fewer players of more equal size might facilitate collusion via coordinated effects. It is, of course, possible that these combinations would still have gone through even after examining these dimensions.

IV. Conclusions

Hamstrung by a small and inexperienced staff, the CCI has done a fairly good job of addressing competition concerns in the pharmaceuticals sector. Its crackdown on blatantly collusive behavior in the distribution chain should have a salutary effect on downstream competition and ultimately on prices paid by consumers. But the anticompetitive implications of asymmetric information, compulsory price labelling and "branded generics" still remain outside the purview of antitrust remedies. In the last 40 years, three official committees have recommended a phased program of mandatory debranding of generics. But the industry has proved too powerful to reform on this count, arguing that branding safeguards consumers against substandard and spurious drugs in the context of unreliable regulation by state agencies.[40] Other remedies are required: mandatory prescription by generic names, greater publicity to the "incentives" provided by drug companies to doctors and pharmacies, more sensible drug price control, and greatly expanded public procurement and distribution of drugs,[41] with the CCI intervening to penalize collusion in the procurement process.

40 To the contrary, Srinivas, *supra* note 3, at 12, cites tests of random drug samples by official and non-official investigators who found only a minuscule fraction to be substandard.

41 For discussion of these measures, *see* Bhattacharjea & Sindhwani, *supra* note 5, at 81-85.

Antitrust Issues in the Pharmaceutical Sector in China

Thomas K. Cheng*

thomas.cheng@hku.hk

Associate Professor, Faculty of Law, University of Hong Kong

Abstract

Although China adopted the Anti-Monopoly Law in 2007, the Chinese pharmaceutical industry has traditionally not received much attention in antitrust law. This article aims to fill this gap in the literature by tracing the development of the regulatory structure of pharmaceuticals in China, scrutinizing the impact of the recent NDRC reform implemented in 2015, reviewing the current industry regulation and enforcement under the AML and projecting possible issues which may arise in the future, particularly in the area of patent protection and innovation.

* The author would like to express his gratitude for the research assistance provided by Tiffany Wu, who made particularly substantial contributions to Sections II and III of this chapter.

I. Introduction

Since the adoption of the Anti-Monopoly Law ("AML") in 2007, a number of industries have received particular attention from the enforcement authorities from the People's Republic of China ("PRC"). The most notable is probably the automotive industry, which has been subject to multiple enforcement actions. The PRC's enforcement authorities are in the process of drafting specific guidelines for this sector. Other sectors which have been subject to the scrutiny of the enforcement authorities have included baby formula, contact lens, Chinese spirits, and telecommunications. One industry that has been noticeably absent from the news is pharmaceuticals. With the exception of one exclusive dealing/price fixing case and three abuse of administrative monopoly cases, the pharmaceutical industry has largely escaped the attention of the enforcement authorities. This is doubly surprising as the pharmaceutical industry has borne the brunt of much enforcement activity in other jurisdictions, such as the United States and the EU, in recent years. One reason that competition issues have not arisen in the industry thus far may be because drugs have been subject to direct price control by the Chinese authorities over the years. Therefore, the scope for using anticompetitive or exclusionary practices to raise prices was reduced. All this is about to change as the Chinese government recently lifted price control over a majority of drugs. The liberalization of drug prices may present pharmaceutical companies with the opportunity to raise their profits by way of anticompetitive practices. Moreover, the Chinese pharmaceutical market is set to grow in the future, as the Chinese population undergoes rapid aging and the middle class continues to grow. The ever-expanding middle class will be able to afford more expensive treatment, which will render the Chinese pharmaceutical market more lucrative. All this means that the hitherto lack of attention to the industry under the AML is set to change. Now would be a good time to take stock of the development of the industry, to examine how recent regulatory reforms will change the landscape, and to look ahead to possible future enforcement in the industry.

II. An Overview of the Pharmaceutical Industry in China

1. An Evolving Regulatory Structure

China's drug regulatory system has undergone several significant changes over the decades. With the "Open Door" policy adopted in the late-1970s, the Chinese government set about opening the economy to foreign trade and investment. One of the sectors that received attention from the central government was the pharmaceutical industry. The main policy goal at that time was to promote and accelerate economic development. The central government promoted the pharmaceutical industry mainly to create jobs and further industrial development.[1] One of the major problems at the time was the lack of coordination among government departments, which the central government deemed problematic for the development of the industry. It therefore established the Pharmaceutical Administration ("PA") to organize the industry.

---

1 Qiang Sun et al., *Pharmaceutical Policy in China*, 27(4) Health Aff. 1042, 1043 (2008), *available at* http://content.healthaffairs.org/content/27/4/1042.

However, this was largely unsuccessful as the PA received funding directly from the pharmaceutical enterprises that it was supposed to regulate.[2] Despite some growth in drug production, there was no effective quality control system and thus the quality of drugs remained poor. Counterfeit drugs were also prevalent. Substandard drugs plagued the Chinese pharmaceutical industry for years to come.

In the 1980s, the central government set up the State Drug Administration, an independent regulatory body that was prohibited from undertaking any profit-making activities. In 1998, the body started to receive direct government funding. It was replaced by the State Food and Drug Administration ("SFDA") in 2003, which was renamed in 2013 as the China Food and Drug Administration ("CFDA"). The CFDA is under the auspices of the State Council and regulates all drugs, medical devices, food, and cosmetics. Provincial administrative authorities also supervise drug production within their respective administrative regions. Meanwhile, the National Development and Reform Commission ("NDRC") is responsible for the overall economic development and administration of the healthcare industry.

In recent decades, the government's main policy is to achieve the twin goals of promoting innovation and research and development ("R&D") in the pharmaceutical industry while keeping drug prices low. On the one hand, it aims to expand the domestic pharmaceutical industry and encourage drug manufacturers to invest in drug innovation. On the other hand, it has to ensure that the poor and uninsured patients have access to essential drugs, especially when public healthcare has largely fallen by the wayside with the dismantling of the state-owned enterprises and the enterprise-based healthcare system.

2. Price Control Mechanisms

To ensure that drug prices are affordable to the general population, the Chinese government has long imposed price control over drugs. This is achieved through two principal means: direct price control and the Centralized Tendering System.

a. Price Ceilings and the National Essential Drugs List ("EDL")

The Chinese government exercised direct price control mainly in the form of fixed prices or price ceilings. Pursuant to the Drug Administration Law as well as the *Circular of the National Development and Reform Commission on Adjustment of Price-Controlled Pharmaceutical Products*,[3] certain drugs are subject to a fixed price or price ceiling set by the government. Drug manufacturers are not allowed to set prices above the price ceiling or deviate from the fixed prices imposed by the government.[4] From time to time, the NDRC publishes and updates the list of medicines subject to price controls. The quantum of the fixed prices and price ceilings is fixed by the government according to the pricing principles stipulated in the Pricing Law.[5] Other factors include the type and quality of the medicine, average production costs, and the prices of substitute medicines.

---

2 Haona Li, He Sun & Frances J. Richmond, The Historical Evolution of China's Drug Regulatory System 9 (n.d.), https://regulatory.usc.edu/files/2014/08/Evolution_China_Reg_system_2014.pdf.

3 国家发展改革委关于调整《国家发展改革委定价药品目录》等有关问题的通知 [Circular of the National Development and Reform Commission on Adjustment of Price-Controlled Pharmaceutical Products] (promulgated by the Nat'l Dev. & Reform Comm'n, Mar. 5, 2010, effective Mar. 5, 2010), *available at* http://jgs.ndrc.gov.cn/zcfg/201003/t20100323_748523.html.

4 Yaopin guanli fa [Drug Administration Law] (promulgated by the Standing Comm. Nat'l People's Cong., Feb. 28. 2001, effective Dec. 1, 2001), *available at* http://eng.sfda.gov.cn/WS03/CL0766/61638.html.

5 *Id.*

The existence of price controls does not mean that all drugs, regardless of whether they are imported branded drugs or locally produced generics, are priced the same. The price control regime did provide for different prices for imported drugs and local drugs, and for branded drugs and generics. Generally, an imported drug that has just entered the Chinese market will be priced at a level approximate to its free market price, unless there is already an original developer or patent holder selling the same substance in China.[6] In China, many patients still consider imported drugs to be of higher quality. That has allowed them to be priced well above locally produced generics, sometimes even higher than the same drugs in other parts of the world. It has been revealed that certain drugs are priced 40% higher in China than in other countries.[7] Meanwhile, between imported generics and branded products, an imported generic drug is usually given a price lower than that of the imported patented product but higher than the price of locally made generics. Even though imported drugs are much more expensive than domestic generic drugs, their quality is more reliable, and therefore many doctors are inclined to use them.

However, pursuant to the *Opinion on the Promotion of Drug Price Reform*, the price caps on all pharmaceutical products, except for certain classes of drugs, have been removed. In case of any inconsistency between the *Opinion on the Promotion of Drug Pricing Reform* and the previous drug pricing policy, the former shall prevail. This reform will be discussed in greater detail in the next section.

In order to ensure that there is equal access to drugs that are essential for the population's well-being, the Ministry of Health together with eight other ministries and commissions issued the *National Essential Drugs List*[8] and the *Guidelines on the Implementation of the National List of Essential Drugs System*.[9] This list contains both Western and Chinese medications and treatment that cover at least 60% of the most common illnesses in China.[10] The government requires certain small public clinics and healthcare centers as well as hospitals to stock these essential drugs. It is expected that by 2020, all state-owned facilities will be fully equipped with the medicines on this list.[11] The list is updated every three to five years by the Ministry of Health.

b. Centralized Tendering System

Another method of price control implemented by the Chinese government is the Centralized Tendering System. The Centralized Tendering System, which was promulgated in 1999, operates at the provincial level and is aimed at "overcoming the problem of 'high drug prices and problems of corruption'."[12] The system requires all state-run, non-profit healthcare institutions to procure their drugs through a centralized bidding process at the provincial level and to purchase their drugs from the official list approved by the

---

6 *Market Access in China: Drug Listing, Bidding, Pricing and Reimbursement*, Pac. Bridge Med., July 1, 2014, http://www.pacificbridgemedical.com/news-brief/market-access-in-china-drug-listing-bidding-pricing-and-reimbursement/.

7 *Foreign Drugmakers Face Pressure to Lower Prices in China*, Bloomberg News, May 26, 2015, http://www.bloomberg.com/news/articles/2015-05-25/foreign-drugmakers-face-more-pressure-to-lower-prices-in-china.

8 国家基本药物目录(2012年版)[National Essential Drug List (2012 edition)] (promulgated by the Ministry of Health, Sept. 21, 2012, effective May 1, 2013), *available at* http://www.sfda.gov.cn/WS01/CL0053/79110.html.

9 关于建立国家基本药物制度的实施意见 [Guidelines on the Implementation of the National List of Essential Drugs System] (promulgated by the Ministry of Human Res. & Soc. Security, Aug. 18, 2009), *available at* http://www.mohrss.gov.cn/SYrlzyhshbzb/ldbk/shehuibaozhang/yiliao/200908/t20090818_86845.htm.

10 Pac. Bridge Med., China Regulatory and Market Access Pharmaceutical Report 59 (2014), *available at* http://www.pacificbridgemedical.com/wp-content/uploads/2015/04/China-Regulatory-and-Market-Access-Pharmaceutical-Report-2014.pdf.

11 *Id*.

12 Mariko Watanabe & Luwen Shi, *Sufficient but expensive drugs: a double-track system that facilitated supply capability in China*, *in* Intellectual Property, Pharmaceuticals and Public Health: Access to Drugs in Developing Countries 253, 271 (Kenneth C. Shadlen et al. eds., 2011).

provincial government agencies, except for certain narcotic, psychotropic, and radioactive drugs, as well as certain types of traditional Chinese medicines.[13]

The typical procedure would involve a tenderer, a bidder, and a procurement agent. The tenderer is the healthcare institution and the bidder the drug manufacturer. A third-party would typically take up the role of the procurement agent and run the bidding process. The procurement agents are forbidden to have any ties with the industry regulators. By 2009, most public hospitals at the county level or higher have implemented a public tendering system. It was hoped that the Centralized Tendering System would enhance the transparency of the procurement process and allow the government to harness the purchasing power of hospitals to lower drug prices. The reality, however, has fallen short of expectations. Although sometimes bid prices resulting from the tendering process are low, the quality of the drugs procured is also low. The Anhui tender system is one example, where both patients and physicians have found the quality of the cheaper EDL drugs so unacceptable that they turned to branded drugs instead, even though they are more expensive.[14] Therefore, although the government has made concerted efforts to ensure equal access to medical service and drugs for all, the price control mechanisms have frequently resulted in a compromise in the quality of the drugs.

3. Branded Drugs vs. Generics in China

The pharmaceutical market in China can be described as being segmented between the local generics and the branded drugs. There are now around 5000 drug manufacturers in China, many of which are small producers of generic drugs.[15] Domestically produced generics are widely distributed due to their low prices, despite their poor quality. Moreover, a single drug can be manufactured by multiple drug manufacturers because a manufacturer can apply for a new drug status simply by slightly changing the packaging or dosage or adding an irrelevant component.[16] For instance, in 2004 the SFDA approved more than 10,009 new drug applications, compared to only 148 by the US Food and Drug Administration.[17]

---

13 Chen Yang & Lei Li, *Drug Procurement Bidding*, China Bus. Rev., Jan. 1, 2010, http://www.chinabusinessreview.com/drug-procurement-bidding/.

14 Benjamin A. Shobert, *Anhui medicine wrong for China*, AsiaTimes, Feb. 14, 2012, http://www.atimes.com/atimes/China_Business/NB14Cb02.html.

15 This is as of 2006. *See* China Data Online, http://chinadataonline.org (last visited Nov. 8, 2015).

16 Xue-feng Liang, De-quan Zheng & Li-juan Yang, *The Dilemma of Drug Price Regulation and Countermeasures in China*, Paper Presented at the Conference on Asian Social Protection in Comparative Perspective 3 (Jan. 7-9, 2009), *available at* http://www.umdcipe.org/conferences/policy_exchanges/conf_papers/Papers/1401.PDF; Sun et al., *supra* note 1, at 1045.

17 Liang, Zheng & Yang, *supra* note 17, at 4.

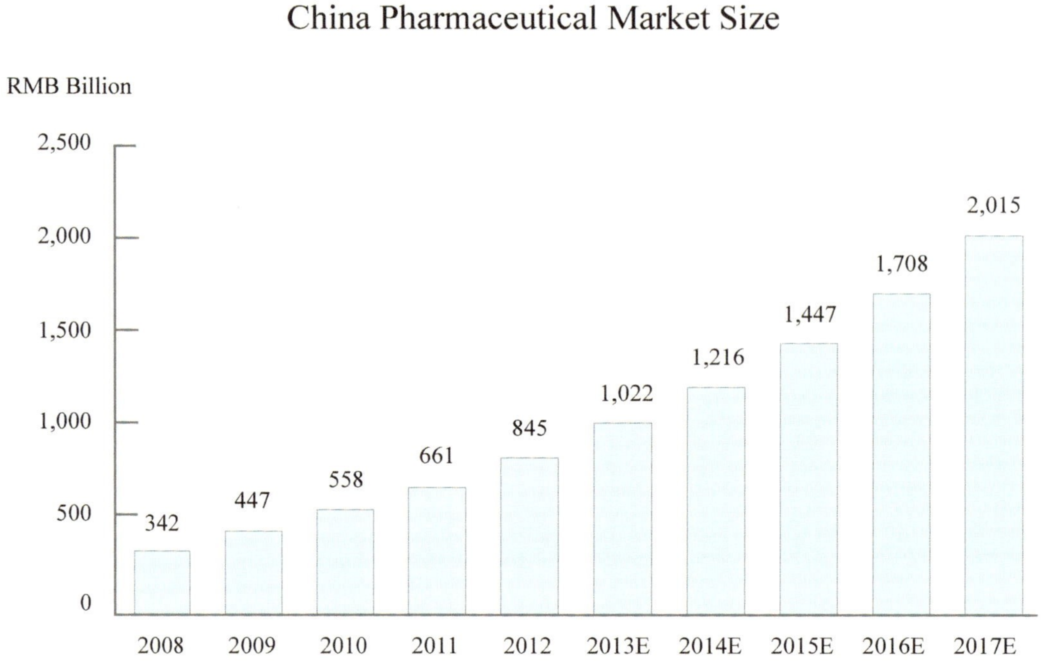

Source: Chinese Pharmaecutical Association. Chinese Association of Pharmaceutical Commerce, Frost & Sullivan analysis.

Locally produced generics compete based on price rather than quality and innovation. R&D only accounts for 2% of the average sales revenue of local drug manufacturers, compared to 14-18% for leading global pharmaceutical companies.[18] Locally produced generics are generally deemed to be of poorer quality than those produced by the foreign drug manufacturers. In fact, the quality of domestically produced drugs was so poor that counterfeit drugs were responsible for the death of approximately 192,000 people in China in 2001.[19] Thus it can be argued that generics and imported branded drugs are not substitutes for each other and appeal to different consumers. Local patients are said generally to favor imported products because of their perceived superior quality, despite their higher prices.[20] Major hospitals still dispense highly priced, imported branded drugs.[21]

Global drug manufacturers have held a strong position in the Chinese pharmaceutical market. However, many of these global manufacturers' patents are about to expire in the coming years. It has been estimated that within the next 4 years, over 441 foreign drug patents will expire.[22] This presents a huge business opportunity for local Chinese drug manufacturers to supply the market with generic versions of the patented

18 Sun et al., *supra* note 1, at 1043.

19 Martin Fackler, *China's Fake Drugs Kill Thousands*, San Francisco Examiner, Jul. 29, 2002, http://en.minghui.org/html/articles/2002/7/31/24700p.html.

20 Chee-Ruey Hsieh, *Pharmaceuticals, Health Policy and Intellectual Property Rights in China*, *in* The New Political Economy of Pharmaceuticals: Production, Innovation and TRIPS in the Global South 48, 55 (Hans Löfgren & Owain David Williams eds., 2013).

21 Hepeng Jia, *China clampdown on GSK linked to drug costs*, 31 Nature Biotechnology 861, 861 (2013), *available at* http://www.nature.com/nbt/journal/v31/n10/full/nbt1013-861.html.

22 *Big pharma looks to enter China's generics market*, Want China Times, Dec. 11, 2014, http://www.wantchinatimes.com/news-subclass-cnt.aspx?id=20141211000174&cid=1202.

drugs.[23] Faced with a potentially significant loss of revenue from the expiration of patents, as well as the government's price cuts, the global drug manufacturers have pursued mainly two strategies: conducting research in highly specialized drugs and cooperating with local companies to take advantage of their low costs and wide distribution channels.[24] As such, many global drug manufacturers have entered into joint ventures with local pharmaceutical companies ahead of the expiration of their patents in order to maintain and gradually expand their market shares. For instance, Pfizer set up a joint venture company with Zhejiang Hisun Pharmaceutical Co. in Hangzhou in order to tap into the generic drugs market, as many of its patents, including the cholesterol-lowering drug Lipitor, have expired (which contributed to a 24% decline in Lipitor sales and 50% annual decline in net profits).[25] Local drug makers are keen to enter into such joint ventures as these allow them to enhance their technological and management expertise.

4. The Pharmaceutical Industry and Corruption

Seventy-eight percent of prescription drugs in China are sold through hospital pharmacies, with only 22% sold via retail pharmacies.[26] The majority of hospitals in China receive government funding to operate their general medical services and to buy medical supplies. However, due to insufficient funding, the public hospitals often look for alternative means to generate revenue, one of which is to prescribe more drugs.[27] At the end of 2009, 15% of Chinese hospitals were profit-oriented.[28]

Two factors aggravate the reliance of hospitals on profits generated from drug sales. First, since the mid-1950s, the Chinese government has officially permitted a 15% mark-up for prescription drugs and diagnostic testing at hospitals. The government's policy, therefore, has increased hospitals' reliance on drug sales to finance their operating costs, with hospitals earning up to 50% of their revenue and 90% of their profits from prescribing drugs and tests.[29] Hospitals thus have strong financial incentives to prescribe and dispense high-priced drugs. Second, salaries for physicians are low. It is estimated that doctors in China only earn a national average salary of RMB 6,000 (roughly USD$1,000) per month.[30] They are also paid bonuses based on the hospital's overall revenue or the quantity of services the physician prescribes, which again incentivizes them to over-prescribe medication and treatment. For instance, 75% of patients suffering from common colds and 79% of all hospitalized patients are prescribed antibiotics, which far exceeds the global average.[31]

Responding to this incentive of hospitals and doctors to profiteer, foreign drug makers have been accused of offering bribes to doctors through various methods such as sponsoring doctors' academic meetings in

---

23 *Id.*

24 KPMG, Healthcare & life sciences in China – Towards growing collaboration 9-10 (2013), *available at* https://www.kpmg.com/CN/en/IssuesAndInsights/ArticlesPublications/Documents/China-healthcare-life-sciences-201303.pdf.

25 *Pfizer and Merck set up Chinese joint ventures for generic drugs*, Want China Times, Sept. 19, 2012, http://www.wantchinatimes.com/news-subclass-cnt.aspx?id=20120919000112&cid=1206.

26 *The generics market in China*, Generics & Biosimilars Initiatives J., Nov. 21, 2014, http://gabi-journal.net/news/the-generics-market-in-china.

27 Pac. Bridge Med., *supra* note 10, at 14.

28 *Id.* at 15.

29 *See* Arthur Daemmrich, *The political economy of healthcare reform in China: negotiating public and private*, 2 SpringerPlus 448 (2013), available at http://www.ncbi.nlm.nih.gov/pmc/articles/PMC3776089/.

30 *China's Bitter Medicine for Foreign Drug Companies*, Knowledge@Wharton, Sept. 27, 2013, http://knowledge.wharton.upenn.edu/article/chinas-bitter-medicine-foreign-drug-companies/.

31 Daemmrich, *supra* note 30.

order to get hospitals to buy and prescribe their drugs. In recent years, there has been a series of clampdowns on multinational pharmaceutical companies in China, the most notable one being the GlaxoSmithKline ("GSK") case.[32] In July 2013, the Chinese government arrested four senior Chinese GSK executives on corruption charges. It is sometimes speculated that these bribery investigations targeted at international pharmaceutical companies in China are motivated by a desire to lower drug prices.[33]

III. Recent Reforms

The NDRC, which is in charge of the regulation of the economic aspects of the pharmaceutical market, announced a far-reaching reform on May 4, 2015. The reform signified a move from the previous regime of price control to one that entrusts market forces with the determination of drug prices. There are three main pillars in the reform agenda: (1) abolition of direct price control for a vast majority of drugs; (2) a relaxation of the rules governing drug price re-negotiations between hospitals and drug suppliers; and (3) a six-month intensive monitoring campaign of drug price-setting in order to forestall any anticompetitive activity.

1. Elimination of Price Control

The reform was set in motion by the repeal of Article 55 of the Drug Administration Law by the Standing Committee of the National People's Congress on April 24, 2015.[34] Article 55 had previously empowered administrative authorities to fix prices or set maximum retail prices for a large number of drugs.[35] Following the legislative amendment, the NDRC, together with six other authorities, issued the *Opinion on the Promotion of Drug Price Reform* ("*Opinion*") on May 4, 2015.[36] The *Opinion* provides that the prices for all drugs are to be determined by business operators based on their costs of production and supply and demand, apart from the following four exceptions: (1) anesthetics and first class psychotropic drugs remain subject to maximum retail price control; (2) drugs purchased by health insurance funds will be determined by a reasonable price setting mechanism under procedures formulated by the insurance fund authorities and other authorities; (3) the prices for patented and exclusively-produced drugs are to be determined by a transparent multilateral negotiation mechanism; and (4) blood products that are outside of the health insurance catalog, and AIDS/HIV drugs and contraceptives that are provided by the state for free will be determined by tender or negotiation.[37]

While removing price control for most drugs, the NDRC and other authorities are mindful of the possibility that drug prices will rise rapidly because of the removal of price control and that pharmaceutical manufacturers may resort to anticompetitive measures to acquire or exercise market power. Therefore, the *Opinion* also announced a number of regulatory measures to ensure that drug prices remain reasonably

32 Jia, *supra* note 22.

33 *Id.*

34 Jianwen Huang, *Analysis of the revisions in the Drug Administration Law*, China L. Insights, Apr. 30, 2015, http://www.chinalawinsight.com/2015/04/articles/healthcare/analysis-of-the-revisions-in-the-drug-administration-law/.

35 Drug Administration Law, art. 55.

36 推进药品价格改革的意见 [Opinion on the Promotion of Drug Price Reform] (promulgated by State Council, May 4, 2015, effective June 1, 2015), *available at* http://www.nhfpc.gov.cn/ewebeditor/uploadfile/2015/05/20150505142837875.pdf.

37 *Id.* at 1-2.

affordable. These measures include: (1) strengthening the drug procurement mechanism; (2) relying on health insurance funds to help control medical costs; (3) imposing closer monitoring over the prescription of drugs and the ordering of treatment by doctors to minimize over-prescription and over-treatment; and (4) strengthening the regulation of drug price-setting behavior.[38] The last measure will be further pursued through a number of means. Price regulatory authorities are to instruct business operators to set prices according to principles of reasonableness, legality, and good faith through regulations on drug price setting.[39] Efforts are to be made to establish an integrated platform for multiple authorities to monitor the real transaction prices for drugs, especially focusing on drugs that do not face sufficient competition.[40] Particular attention is to be paid to drugs that are subject to frequent or substantial price changes, or whose domestic price varies significantly from its international prices, or whose prices manifest substantial regional variations.[41]

This reform serves two main objectives. First, the reform aims to create a transparent, market-driven pricing environment to encourage development and innovation in drugs, especially from foreign firms, which often experienced unexpected price cuts and a loss in revenue due to government policy changes. Due to government price cuts, foreign pharmaceutical companies have experienced a substantial loss of revenue in the past few years.[42] In response to the loss of revenue, the US pharmaceutical giant Merck called a halt to its joint venture with its Chinese partner, Simcere Pharmaceutical Group, resulting in possible job losses for more than 300 employees.[43] It is hoped that by opening up the market and lifting price controls, both domestic and foreign manufacturers would be able to promote innovative drugs, ensure stable supplies, and maintain low prices. Second, the reform aims to solve the problem of shortages and the poor quality of drugs. The central government's tight rein on prices often resulted in prices dropping below the manufacturing costs, leading to several drug shortages, even for essential drugs. For instance, in April 2014, the government removed price caps on a limited number of drugs after a severe shortage of critical medications used to treat hyperthyroidism and other ailments.[44] As a result of the low prices, the quality of drugs has also often been compromised. In 2012, it was revealed that several commonly used drugs were made of capsules containing an excessive amount of chromium.[45]

---

38 *Id.* at 2-4.

39 *Id.* at 3.

40 *Id.* at 4.

41 *Id.*

42 Both foreign and domestic pharmaceutical companies have seen slower growth because of the government's price control. However, the decline in growth has proven especially acute for the foreign pharmaceutical companies because they usually charge a higher price and have been required to offer greater discounts. For instance, the tender system whereby provincial governments determine the wholesale prices have created a downward pressure on price, forcing these foreign pharmaceutical companies to lower their prices by 30-80%, to the extent that some firms have been forced to walk away from the tender. Jean-François Tremblay, *China's Weakening Health*, Chemical and Engineering News, Aug 31, 2015, http://cen.acs.org/articles/93/i34/Chinas-Weakening-Health.html. Drugs prices were cut almost 30 times between 1997 and 2011. In particular, prices for imported drugs were cut by as many as 35 times in 2011. Susie Lunt, *China: a dangerous game that pharma must play*, Pharmafile, Sept. 1, 2014, http://www.pharmafile.com/news/193561/china-dangerous-game-pharma-must-play.

43 Li Yan, *China Market Causes Headache for Big Foreign Drug Companies*, Caixin Online, Mar. 7, 2015, http://english.caixin.com/2015-07-03/100825046.html.

44 Li Jing, *China scraps price caps for most drugs*, S. China Morning Post, May 5, 2015, *available at* http://www.scmp.com/news/china/policies-politics/article/1786573/china-stop-setting-prices-most-medicines-june-1.

45 *Id.*; Laurie Burkitt, *China Halts Sale of Some Drugs*, Wall St. J., Apr. 17, 2012, *available at* http://www.wsj.com/articles/SB1000142405 2702304299304577347563418936068.

2. Strengthening of Regulation of Price-Setting Conduct

On the same day that the NDRC and other authorities issued the *Opinion*, the NDRC also issued the *Notice Regarding the Strengthening of Regulation of Drug Price-Setting Conduct* ("*Notice*").[46] In the *Notice*, the NDRC announced a six-month intensive inspection of drug prices by the various levels of price regulators.[47] The targets of the inspection include drug manufacturers, hospitals, disease prevention and control centers, blood centers, and medication procurement platforms.[48] The focus of the inspection is on drugs that do not face sufficient competition and drugs that are used by patients with special or rare diseases. The *Notice* enumerates 10 specific kinds of conduct that will form the target of the inspection, some of which fall within the ambit of competition law, while some of which do not. Conduct that falls within competition law include manipulation of market prices through collusion and abuse of dominance through charging of unfairly high prices.[49] Other proscribed conduct includes fabrication and dissemination of information about price increases, and the violation of mark-up control by state-owned hospitals and medical facilities.[50] As mentioned earlier, some state-owned hospitals and medical facilities are subject to a maximum mark-up of 15%. Some are subject to what is known as the zero mark-up policy.

3. Reform of Negotiation between Hospitals and Manufacturers

The reform also enables hospitals and manufacturers to enter into direct price negotiations at the provincial level without direct government intervention.[51] This reform is expected to change the provincial drug tender and bidding process by removing government involvement, thus allowing hospitals and drug makers to enter into direct price negotiations. It is an attempt to put an end to the notorious practice of second-round price negotiations in the province whereby hospitals often bargain for an even better price from the drug manufacturers after the official price had been agreed upon.[52] This has led to a "race to the bottom" with drug manufacturers quoting prices that almost fall below their own production costs in order to get hospitals to prescribe their drugs.[53] The intense price-cutting has caused certain drug makers to withdraw from the bidding process, hence depriving hospitals access to their drugs and treatment.[54] While the guidance provided by the government does not expressly remove restrictions on price re-negotiations by public hospitals, some flexibility has been introduced in this regard. In particular, public hospitals in

---

46 国家发展改革委关于加强药品市场价格行为监管的通知 [Notice Regarding the Strengthening of Regulation of Drug Price-Setting Conduct] (promulgated by Nat'l Dev. Reform Comm'n, May 4, 2015, effective May 4, 2015), *available at* http://www.sdpc.gov.cn/gzdt/201505/t20150505_690683.html.

47 *Id.*

48 *Id.*

49 *Id.*

50 *Id.*

51 国务院办公厅关于完善公立医院药品集中采购工作的指导意见 [State Council Legislative Affairs Office Guiding Opinion Concerning Improvement of Group Procurement by Public Hospitals] (promulgated by State Council, Feb. 28, 2015, effective Feb. 28, 2015), *available at* http://www.gov.cn/zhengce/content/2015-02/28/content_9502.htm.

52 *China removes price controls as part of amendments to Drug Administration Law*, IHS Life Sci. Blog, Jan. 5, 2015, https://www.ihs.com/country-industry-forecasting.html?ID=1065998980.

53 *Id.*

54 *Id.*

pilot cities are no longer bound by provincially negotiated prices, but rather can directly negotiate drug prices with pharmaceutical companies or distributors. It remains to be seen how these reforms will be implemented into local practice.

4. An Evaluation of the Reform

This reform signals a shift in the Chinese government's role in the pharmaceutical industry from controlling prices to supervising the price-setting process and penalizing illegal pricing behavior. Given the short history of the reform, it is too early to assess its long-term impact. While the reform represents a significant step in the liberalization of the pharmaceutical market in China, it is important to note that the prices for patented and exclusively-produced drugs are not fully liberalized. These prices will need to be determined through multilateral negotiation. Therefore, multinational pharmaceutical manufacturers will not have a free hand in determining the prices for their drugs. Moreover, the NDRC has made it clear that it is concerned about substantial price increases following the reform by specifying that the charging of unfairly high prices will be pursued under the AML as an abuse of dominance. While the pursuit of excessive pricing under competition law is highly controversial in other jurisdictions, the NDRC has made it quite clear through its enforcement record and the *Notice* that it will not shy away from it. Given the repeated emphasis on the price-cost relationship and supply and demand in the *Opinion* and the *Notice*, one can surmise that the NDRC will be making a determination of the excessiveness of a price with reference to the production cost of the drug. This is where the situation becomes complicated. If the NDRC determines the excessiveness of a price only with reference to the production cost of the drug, and ignores the R&D cost of the drug, the NDRC will arrive at prices that are so low that they do not allow the pharmaceutical companies to recoup their R&D costs. However, if the NDRC eventually accepts that the R&D costs of the drug should be taken into account in determining its costs, which it should, pharmaceutical companies will likely claim that the R&D costs for failed drug development should be taken into account as well. Obviously not every drug development turns out to be successful so pharmaceutical companies must absorb the costs of these failed projects. Therefore, there is a good argument that the costs of the failed development projects should be spread across the successful drugs. Once that is accepted, the determination of the excessiveness of a price will become fraught with difficulty.

One of the purported objectives of the reform is to reduce price uncertainty for multinational pharmaceutical manufacturers whose profits had been cut in recent years due to the constant price cuts under the price control regime. Whether this objective will be achieved will depend on how the multilateral negotiation mechanism for patented and exclusively produced drugs is implemented, given that most products of the multinational manufacturers are patented. If the negotiated drug prices are subject to constant revision, the new regime will bring no greater certainty to the multinational manufacturers than did the old regime. However, if the mechanism is genuinely based on negotiation, the manufacturers will presumably have greater say over the setting of the price for their drugs than under the old regime, where prices were set by the administrative authorities with little input from the manufacturers. This will hopefully help to reduce the uncertainty faced by the multinational manufacturers.

Another purported objective of the reform is to increase the quality of domestically produced generics, which were criticized for being of substandard quality due to the artificially low prices imposed by the government. It is important to note that it is not an inherent flaw of a price control mechanism that it would lead to substandard quality drugs. This problem presumably would not have arisen if the price regulators had set more appropriate prices (although one may argue that price regulators will generally set excessively low prices and that experiences with price control tend to confirm this). One can also argue that price uncertainty need not be an inherent feature of price control if the price regulators had committed themselves to setting prices that would apply for a longer period of time. Perhaps an explanation for the failure of the price control system is that when trying to determine the appropriate prices for drugs, regulators face the conflicting demands of ensuring affordability for patients while guaranteeing sufficient profits for the manufacturers. And the Chinese regulators, for one reason or another, perhaps due to a relative lack of regulatory capture, generally err in the interest of consumers and have a tendency to set excessively low prices.

By eliminating price control, the PRC's authorities have removed a pro-consumer bias in the setting of drug prices. But they have not eliminated the conflict between ensuring affordability for patients and generating sufficient profit for pharmaceutical companies. If overseas experiences are any indication, once drug prices are open to full market forces, consumers tend to lose out and drug prices tend to rise progressively higher. Therefore, at some point, the PRC's authorities may be forced to intervene in the market to prevent excessive price increases. Perhaps the threat to pursue excessive pricing claims under the AML is an implicit message to pharmaceutical manufacturers that price increases will only be tolerated so long as they are within reason and that the authorities will not hesitate to intervene if they are deemed to be excessive. The important question that remains is how much of a price increase will be deemed to be excessive.

In a way, this new regime introduces even greater uncertainty to pharmaceutical companies. Under the old regime, the main source of uncertainty was that the authorities would lower the official prices frequently. But at least if the manufacturers followed the official prices, they would know that they were in compliance with the law. Under the new regime, the manufacturers in theory have full liberty to set prices, as long as they are not too high. However, there is no clear indication of how high would be deemed too high. And if prices are deemed to be too high, not only would the manufacturers be forced to lower prices, they would also be subject to potentially hefty fines for violating the AML. The operational risks are thus arguably greater under the new regime. How real these risks are will depend on how vigorously the authorities pursue excessive pricing claims.

IV. Regulation of the Pharmaceutical Industry under the AML

1. Relevant Provisions and Guidelines under the AML

Aside from the sector-specific regulations of the pharmaceutical industry that have been described above, the pharmaceutical industry is also subject to the AML. The most relevant provisions within the AML are Articles 13 to 15 and Articles 17 to 19.[55] Articles 13 to 15 are concerned with what are referred to as monopolistic agreements (which essentially amount to restrictive agreements) under the AML. Article 13 focuses on horizontal agreements, and specifically prohibits agreements that fix prices, limit output, allocate markets, restrict access to new technology or the development of new products, or further a group

55 Fan longduan fa [Anti-Monopoly Law] (promulgated by the Standing Comm. Nat'l People's Cong., Aug. 30. 2007, effective Aug. 1, 2008) 2007 Standing Comm. Nat'l People's Cong. Gaz. 517.

boycott.[56] Article 14 tackles vertical agreements and expressly prohibits resale price maintenance.[57] Article 15 provides a list of procompetitive benefits that serve as possible defenses for agreements that have been deemed monopolistic under Articles 13 and 14. The procompetitive benefits include: (1) improvement of technology and research, and development of new products; (2) improvement of product quality, reduction of costs, enhancement of efficiency, and standardization of products; (3) improvement of operational efficiency and enhancement of competitiveness of small- and medium-sized enterprises; (4) advancement of public interest, including energy efficiency, environmental protection, and disaster relief; (5) alleviation of oversupply due to economic depression; and (6) protection of legitimate interests in foreign trade and foreign economic cooperation.[58]

Articles 17 to 19 are concerned with abuse of dominance. Article 17 prohibits abuses of a dominant position in a relevant market, specifically enumerating the following conduct: (1) excessive pricing; (2) predatory pricing; (3) refusal to deal; (4) exclusive dealing; (5) tying; and (6) discriminatory pricing or treatment.[59] Article 18 lists out the factors that will be considered when determining the existence of a dominant position. These include market share, ability to control the final product market or the raw material procurement market, the firm's financial resources and technical capabilities, degree of dependence of contractual counterparties, and entry barriers.[60] Article 19 provides a number of market share-based presumptions of dominance. Dominance is presumed if: (1) one firm accounts for 50% of the market; (2) two firms together account for two-thirds of the market; or (3) three firms together account for three quarters of the market, unless the firm at issue possesses a less than 10% market share.[61]

Even though the AML enforcement authorities have issued a slew of regulations and guidelines to provide greater clarity in their enforcement approaches, none of them so far are particularly relevant to the pharmaceutical sector. The most relevant one is arguably the *Provisions on Prohibiting the Abuse of Intellectual Property Rights to Exclude and Restrain Competition* ("*Provisions*") issued by the State Administration of Industry and Commerce ("SAIC") in April 2015.[62] These *Provisions* only govern enforcement by the SAIC. The three enforcement authorities are drafting a new set of intellectual property-competition guidelines under the auspices of the Anti-Monopoly Commission. It is fair to say that the *Provisions* were probably drafted more with the ICT industries in mind. For example, Article 10 of the *Provisions* prohibits a number of licensing restrictions that are relatively more common in the ICT industry.[63] Articles 12 and 13 are concerned with patent pools and standardization, which again are more common in the ICT industry.[64]

Conspicuously absent from the *Provisions* is any discussion about reverse payments, product hopping, or evergreening, which are antitrust issues that have featured prominently in the pharmaceutical industry in other jurisdictions, especially the United States. This may be a reflection of the fact that the general

---

56 *Id*. at art. 13.

57 *Id*. at art. 14.

58 *Id*. at art. 15.

59 *Id*. at art. 17.

60 *Id*. at art. 18.

61 *Id*. at art. 19.

62 关于禁止滥用知识产权排除、限制竞争行为的规定 [Provisions on Prohibiting the Abuse of Intellectual Property Rights to Exclude and Restrain Competition] (promulgated by State Admin. Trade & Commerce, Apr. 7, 2015, effective Aug. 1, 2015), *available at* http://www.saic.gov.cn/zcfg/xzgzjgfxwj/xxb/201504/t20150413_155104.html.

63 *Id*. at art. 10.

64 *Id*. at arts. 12-13.

perception of the significantly different standards of quality between imported branded drugs and domestically produced generics means that the two do not really compete in the same market. Consumers who can afford the branded drugs do not see generics as substitutes for the branded drugs regardless of the difference in prices. Therefore, imported branded drugs are subject to minimal competitive pressure from domestically produced generics, obviating the need to forestall generic competition by way of the above mentioned anticompetitive practices.

Perhaps the most relevant to the pharmaceutical industry is the Article on the essential facilities doctrine contained in the *Provisions*. Article 7 states that a dominant business operator shall not, for the purpose of restricting or excluding competition, refuse to license other business operators on reasonable terms intellectual property rights that constitute an essential facility.[65] Article 7 enumerates three factors for consideration when applying the doctrine to intellectual property rights. First, whether there are no reasonable alternatives to the intellectual property right concerned in the relevant market and whether the intellectual property is required by other business operators to compete in the relevant market.[66] Second, whether the refusal to license would adversely affect competition or innovation in the relevant market, and prejudice consumer or public interests.[67] Third, whether the compulsory license will cause unreasonable damage to the owner of the intellectual property right.[68] Particularly noteworthy is that Article 7 authorizes compulsory licensing when the refusal to license prejudices the public interest. What constitutes public interest is not defined in the *Provisions*. Presumably, access to an essential drug at affordable prices could constitute such an interest. Therefore, Article 7 could conceivably be invoked by a generic manufacturer against a branded manufacturer when the branded drug is sold at a sufficiently high price that places the drug beyond the reach of most consumers. As it turns out, this is not the only provision that can be invoked to impose compulsory licensing on a pharmaceutical manufacturer. The PRC's Patent Law also provides for compulsory licensing on public health grounds. Further explanation is provided below in another section of the paper.

2. Enforcement under the AML

The pharmaceutical sector has received a fair amount of enforcement activity by the PRC's enforcement authorities. Given that the PRC's enforcement cases are often not reported to the public, information about them is often not readily accessible. This Author is only aware of five enforcement cases by the PRC's enforcement authorities in the sector. One of them concerns market allocation and exclusive dealing in the Shandong Province. One of them concerns a refusal to supply case in Sichuan Province. The other three concern abuse of administrative monopoly in Anhui, Zhejiang, and Sichuan Provinces. The case in Anhui poses particularly interesting analytical issues.

The *Shandong Pharmaceutical* case was an enforcement decision by the NDRC.[69] In that case, two distributors of pharmaceutical ingredients had signed an exclusive distribution agreement with the only two domestic manufacturers of a key ingredient of an important hypertension drug. The drug was listed

65 *Id.* at art. 7.

66 *Id.*

67 *Id.*

68 *Id.*

69 两医药公司垄断复方利血平原料药受到严厉处罚 [Two Pharmaceutical Companies Severely Punished for Monopolizing Market for Ingredients for Compound Reserpine Tablets] (announced by Nat'l Dev. Reform Comm'n, Nov. 15, 2011), *available at* http://jjs.ndrc.gov.cn/gzdt/201111/t20111115_444599.html.

on the National Essential Drug List. Upon entry of the agreements, the two distributors raised the price of the ingredient from RMB 200 per kilogram to RMB 300 to 1350 per kilogram. Unable to bear the inflated price, a number of the manufacturers ceased production of the hypertension drug, resulting in a shortage in the market. The NDRC found an infringement of the AML without elaborating whether the exclusive distribution agreements, absent what was obviously a cartel arrangement between the two distributors, would be deemed illegal. However, it is noteworthy that in addition to imposing fines, the NDRC also required the two distributors to terminate their exclusive distribution agreements. Two exclusive distribution agreements that account for the entire market supply of a product would probably be highly problematic. The fact that the NDRC required the termination of the distribution agreements suggests that it held a similar view.

The Sichuan case concerned a suppler of an ingredient for a drug called allopurinol API, which is used to produce allopurinol. This drug is primarily used to treat excessive uric acid in the blood and its complications, including gout. The local AIC of Chongqing issued a decision on December 22, 2015 to sanction Qingyang Yaoye for refusal to supply. The facts of the case are very similar to the facts in the EU Commercial Solvents case.[70] Qingyang is a dominant producer of the ingredient for the drug. The decision highlighted that there are no credible competitors in that market and high barriers to entry due to extensive licensing restrictions and high R&D costs. Qingyang also sells the end product drug of allopurinol. Qingyang entered into two sets of exclusive distribution agreements with a Hunan drug distributor under which the distributor would become the sole distributor for allopurinol API and national distributor for allopurinol tablets produced by Qingyang. Qingyang allegedly terminated supply of the ingredient to rival drug manufacturers. After that, four out of seven rivals ceased production and exited the market. Qingyang's market share in the final drug market increased by 47% to 57% within one year.

The Anhui abuse of administrative monopoly case is somewhat peculiar.[71] The case originated from a complaint by the China Pharmaceutical Innovation and Research Development Association, which is a trade association of Chinese pharmaceutical companies, against the Health and Family Planning Commission of Bengbu, Anhui. The Health and Family Planning Commission was accused of demanding a more than 25% discount from pharmaceutical companies that wanted to participate in local tenders. Companies that refused to offer the discount were banned from future local tenders. The NDRC found against the local authority, holding that the latter had abused its administrative monopoly by restricting local and non-local pharmaceuticals firms from fair procurement by imposing discriminatory qualification requirements and assessment standards. It also found that the local authority had arbitrarily selected pharmaceutical firms as suppliers for procurements. The local authority reportedly was not receptive of the NDRC decision, arguing that its procurement policy had been implemented in accordance with the law.[72] It seems that the local authority had the backing of the Anhui provincial government. The first charge of discriminatory qualification requirements in procurement clearly violated the AML. Article 34 of the AML states that administrative authorities shall not abuse their administrative powers to exclude or restrict the participation

70 重庆市工商行政管理局行政处罚决定书 [Chongqing Administration of Industry and Commerce Administrative Penalty Decision], *available at* http://www.saic.gov.cn/zwgk/gggs/jzzf/cfjd/201512/t20151221_165120.html.

71 国家发展改革委办公厅关于建议纠正蚌埠市卫生计生委滥用行政权力排除限制竞争有关行为的函 [National Development and Reform Commission Recommendation for the Rectification of Abuse of Administrative Monopoly by Bengbu Municipal Health and Planning Commission] (adopted by Nat'l Dev. Reform Comm'n, Aug. 17, 2015, effective Aug. 17, 2015), *available at* http://jjs.ndrc.gov.cn/fjgld/201508/t20150826_748682.html.

72 *Bengbu health authority considers NDRC conclusions one-sided*, PaRR, Sept. 2, 2015, http://app.parr-global.com//intelligence/view/1297927.

of undertakings from other regions in local bidding activities by means such as prescribing discriminatory qualification requirements or standards or by not publishing information according to law.[73]

From the reports of the case, it is not entirely clear what provisions of the AML the Bengbu authority violated by stipulating a minimum discount. Article 34 of the AML states that administrative authorities shall not abuse their administrative powers to exclude or restrict the participation of undertakings from other regions in local bidding activities by means such as prescribing discriminatory qualification requirements or standards or by not publishing information according to law.[74] In this case, there is no suggestion that the compulsory discount requirement was imposed to exclude non-local firms. And there is no suggestion that local firms were better able to meet the compulsory discount requirement. In fact, it is not even clear that there were local pharmaceutical manufacturers. Nor is the compulsory discount requirement discriminatory. There is no suggestion that the requirement is applied selectively. From the reports of the case, it seems that the requirement was applied across the board. So there is no issue of discriminatory qualification requirements.

The local authority was further accused of arbitrarily selecting pharmaceuticals firms as suppliers for procurements. The NDRC seemingly objected to the fact that the local Health and Family Planning Commission appointed suppliers of certain drugs without going through a competitive tender. It was not explained in the NDRC decision the motivation behind the Bengbu authority's action. The NDRC's reasoning can be interpreted as imposing a compulsory tender requirement for public procurement, which the AML does not explicitly entertain. The NDRC based its decisions on two provisions of the AML, Article 32, which prohibits administrative bodies from requiring business operators to purchase or use products from a designated business operator, and Article 37, which broadly prohibits administrative bodies from adopting measures that restrict or eliminate competition.[75] Article 32 arguably does not apply to the current situation. From its wording, it seems to only apply to situations where administrative bodies require unrelated business entities to procure products from a designated business operator. It should not apply to a situation in which an administrative body organizes a public procurement on behalf of its subsidiary entities and requires them to abide by the procurement result. Pushed to its logical extreme, the NDRC's interpretation of Article 32 could result in a prohibition of government entities from organizing procurement tenders on behalf of their subsidiaries. Presumably under the NDRC's interpretation, if one of the hospitals within the Bengbu Health and Family Planning Commission's jurisdiction wants to procure medical supplies on its own, it could invoke Article 32 to prevent the Commission from requiring the hospital to take part in the Commission's procurement process. That cannot be the intention behind Article 32. Meanwhile, the conduct of the Bengbu authority arguably does fall within the broad language of Article 37. However, one can distinguish between situations in which a market already exists and an administrative body uses measures to stifle competition and situations in which no market exists and an administrative body is compelled to create competition. Requiring a competitive tender in public procurement would fall under the latter interpretation, which would be an expansive reading of Article 37. While adopting this interpretation may serve a laudable purpose in this instance, it may give rise to unintended consequences in future cases. The NDRC should carefully consider whether it would be wise to adopt such an expansive reading.

---

73 Anti-Monopoly Law, art. 34.

74 Anti-Monopoly Law, *supra* note 53, at art. 34.

75 *Id.* at arts. 32, 37.

The only possible characterization of the discount requirement as an anticompetitive practice is perhaps as an instance of the exercise of monopsonistic power. The Bengbu authority is likely to account for a large proportion of the purchase of drugs in the local market. However, the mere exercise of buyer power to demand lower prices should not be considered an abuse of dominance, especially when the low prices are demanded in order to reduce healthcare costs for patients. In any case, the abuse of dominance provisions of the AML only apply to business operators[76] and the Bengbu authority would not qualify as one. Therefore, the exercise of buyer power by a local authority would not fall within the ambit of the AML.

This case is particularly troubling because the conduct at issue seems to be nothing more than a price cap imposed by a local authority in its public tender for drugs. There is nothing discriminatory or anticompetitive about the requirement. One would think that it is the job of a local authority to try to obtain low drug prices for local patients. And the local authority would be well positioned to do so given its buyer power. The NDRC's decision does not directly address the discount requirement imposed by the Bengbu authority, which renders the decision less damaging. If the NDRC had prohibited the discount requirement, the NDRC would be effectively prohibiting local authorities from exercising their buyer power to obtain lower drug prices for local patients. This would be particularly problematic given the recent removal of direct price control of drug prices, which means that local procurement authorities now bear a greater burden to help control healthcare costs. Without direct price control, the most effective mechanism for keeping drug prices down is the negotiation between the local authorities and the manufacturers. The NDRC's decision could inadvertently open the door for rampant drug price inflation.

In contrast the Anhui case, the two abuse of administrative monopoly cases in Zhejiang and Sichuan were decided on sounder grounds. In November 2015, the NDRC announced that it had taken action against the Health and Family Planning Commissions of Zhejiang and Sichuan Provinces for alleged abuse of administrative monopoly.[77] The Sichuan Health and Family Planning Commission enacted a number of policy measures to favor local pharmaceutical producers, including stipulating minimum procurement requirements from local producers by local medical institutions, barring certain non-local drugs from online procurement, and adopting preferential economic and technical assessment policies in favor of local producers. The NDRC concluded that these measures violated Articles 33 and 34 of the AML. The Zhejiang Health and Family Planning Commission allegedly issued policies that favored local producers as well, such as including locally produced drugs in the provincial emergency medicine reserves to the exclusion of non-local drugs and barring producers that did not have a transactional history in the provincial centralized procurement platform from taking part in public tender. The latter policy apparently resulted in the exclusion of non-local producers. The two provincial authorities undertook remedial measures to rectify their policies.

All of the measures adopted by the Sichuan authority were clearly discriminatory and in violation of the AML. The same is true of the discriminatory exclusion of non-local producers from the provincial emergency medicine reserves by the Zhejiang authority. The legality of the other measure adopted by the Zhejiang authority depends on whether it constitutes a discriminatory qualification requirement. The local authority may genuinely prefer to work with drug producers that have won previous tenders and that have supplied the provincial authority before. However, if it turns out that a disproportionate number of the successful tenderers in the past were local producers, the requirement may be deemed to be

76 *Id*. at arts. 17-19.

77 四川、浙江省卫生和计划生育委员会及时纠正药品集中采购中违反《反垄断法》、排除限制竞争行为 [Sichuan and Zhejiang Provincial Health and Planning Commission Promptly Rectify Anticompetitive Conduct in Drug Procurement] (announced by Nat'l Dev. Reform Comm'n, Nov. 2, 2015), *available at* http://jjs.ndrc.gov.cn/gzdt/201111/t20111115_444599.html.

discriminatory. But in any case, the measures adopted by these two provincial authorities were much more clearly intended to favor local producers and thus more appropriately deemed abuses of administrative monopoly than those in the Anhui case.

3. Compulsory Licensing under the Patent Law

Article 50 of the PRC's Patent Law provides for the grant of a compulsory license on public health grounds.[78] The Patent Law does not explain what constitutes a public health ground for the purposes of a compulsory license. Nor do the implementing regulations of the law. Does public health refer to when an important drug is otherwise unavailable in the domestic market? Or when the drug is only available at a high price that puts it beyond the reach of most consumers? It is not clear thus far. In any case, as far as this Author is aware, this article has never been invoked to impose a compulsory license.

V. Future Enforcement Direction regarding the Pharmaceutical Industry under the AML

The next question to consider is how China should enforce the AML in the pharmaceutical sector. Antitrust enforcement in the pharmaceutical sector often implicates the patent-antitrust interface, under which there is a need to balance between the preservation of innovative incentives and the protection of consumer welfare. Patent protection generates innovation incentives by giving inventors a period of exclusivity, during which the inventor can charge supra-competitive prices. Patentees often attempt to maximize their profits from patent exclusivity through a variety of strategies, which in the pharmaceutical sector often consist of practices such as reverse payments, product hopping, and evergreening. Antitrust law prohibits these practices if they turn out to harm consumer welfare more than they enhance innovation.

In its enforcement against unreasonable patent exploitation, antitrust law tends to take the innovation incentives generated by patent law as a given. In other words, antitrust law tends to accept the basic premise of patent law that patent protection is necessary for generating innovation incentives. This is especially the case for the pharmaceutical sector, which has long been held out as the prime example of an industry in need of patent protection. Given the substantial R&D needed to produce a new drug and the significant probability of failure of pharmaceutical R&D projects, it has long been argued that patent protection is vital for continual innovation in the sector. The implication is that when dealing with patent practices in the sector, antitrust law should err on the side of caution lest the innovation incentives generated by the patent system be undermined to the detriment of future innovation.

For a developing country like China, it is important to be circumspect with respect to innovation incentive arguments. Innovation incentives are generated in the form of supra-competitive profit, which necessitates consumer welfare loss as consumers are forced to pay a higher price for a drug. Given that consumers

78 Zhuan li fa [Patent Law] (promulgated by the Standing Comm. Nat'l People's Cong., Mar. 12. 1984, effective Apr. 1, 1985, first amended Sept. 4, 1992, second amended Aug. 25, 2000, third amended Dec. 27, 2008), *available at* http://english.sipo.gov.cn/laws/lawsregulations/201101/t20110119_566244.html.

in developing countries are likely to be poorer, developing countries should be particularly careful when asked to sacrifice their consumers' welfare in order to generate innovation incentives for pharmaceutical manufacturers, especially when these manufacturers are foreign ones. Therefore, before jumping to the conclusion that the PRC's enforcement authorities should defer to patent policy when considering antitrust enforcement against patent practices in the pharmaceutical sector, it is important to critically evaluate the basic premise of this patent policy deference argument and to see whether China would actually benefit from emphasizing patent policy over antitrust policy.

1. Is Patent Protection Necessary for Securing Innovation?

a. An Overview

One striking feature of the discourse about the patent system is the incongruity between the general perception of antitrust practitioners about the system and academic opinions among economists. While it is almost an article of faith within antitrust circles that patent protection is needed to secure innovation, economists have long expressed considerable reservations about, if not outright hostility toward, patents.[79] Machlup, one of the pioneers in innovation economics, famously opined that: "If we did not have a patent system, it would be irresponsible, on the basis of our present knowledge of its economic consequences, to recommend instituting one. But since we have had a patent system for a long time, it would be irresponsible, on the basis of our present knowledge, to recommend abolishing it."[80] This observation was made in 1958. Despite half a century of further research, this skepticism about the patent system has not been dispelled.

Sharing this ambivalent attitude toward the patent system, Scherer asserts that, "It is almost impossible to conceive of any existing social institutions so faulty in many ways. It survives only because there seems to be nothing better."[81] He believes that the strongest justification for the patent system is to secure the kind of groundbreaking inventions that are rare, but redound a disproportionately great amount of social benefits. An example is the photocopying technology invented by physicist Chester Carlson and commercialized by The Haloid Corporation, which was subsequently renamed Xerox.[82] Xerography, as the technology is officially known, is generally regarded as a technology that would not have been successfully commercialized without patent protection.[83] Nevertheless, instances like Xerox where patent exclusivity is proven necessary for an innovation are rare. Piciotto notes that economists "have therefore always had difficulty finding adequate justification for these exclusive rights."[84] Boldrin and Levine have

---

79 For highly critical views of the patent system, *see generally* Michele Boldrin & David K. Levine, Against Intellectual Monopoly 68-92 (2008); Adam B. Jaffe & Josh Lerner, Innovation and Its Discontents: How Our Broken Patent System is Endangering Innovation and Progress, and What to Do About It 56-77 (2004); James Bessen & Michael J. Meurer, Patent Failure: How Judges, Bureaucrats, and Lawyers Put Innovators at Risk 1-28 (2008).

80 Fritz Machlup, An Economic Review of the Patent System, S. Doc. No. 85-15, at 80 (1958).

81 Frederic M. Scherer, *The Economics of the Patent System*, *in* Industrial Market Structure and Economic Performance 439, 454 (Frederic M. Scherer ed., 1980) [hereinafter Scherer, *Patent System*]

82 Frederic M. Scherer, *Technological Innovation and Monopolization* 42 (Am. Antitrust Inst. Working Paper No. 05-07, 2005).

83 *Id.* at 42-43. Carlson faced enormous difficulty convincing technology firms to commercialize the invention. Haloid might not have taken on the highly risky venture without patent protection for the invention.

84 Sol Picciotto, *Defending the Public Interest in TRIPS and the WTO*, *in* Global Intellectual Property Rights: Knowledge, Access and Development 224, 225 (Peter Drahos & Ruth Mayne eds., 2002).

even recently argued that intellectual property, including patents, is more appropriately called "intellectual monopoly" and should be abolished.[85] They assert that the patent system creates vastly more harm than good for society.

b. Empirical Evidence

Economics is replete with empirical studies indicating the industry variation of the importance of patent protection to innovation. The first systematic study of this issue was conducted in the United Kingdom. Using data from 27 firms, Taylor and Silberston found that about 60% of pharmaceutical R&D was dependent on patent protection.[86] This result has been subsequently confirmed by other studies in the United States.

A number of major studies on the relationship between patent protection and innovation were published in the United States in the 1980s, at a time when there was widespread anxiety that the country was losing its technological edge over other countries, most notably Japan. In 1981, Mansfield and his co-authors published the results of a study on the imitation time and costs in chemical, drug, electronics, and machinery industries for 48 product innovations.[87] They found that about 50% of the innovations in the sample would not have been introduced absent patent protection, with the bulk belonging to the pharmaceutical industry.[88] Leaving out innovations from that industry, the corresponding proportion falls to less than one-quarter.[89] All in all, they found that 90% of pharmaceutical innovations are dependent on patent protection.[90] Mansfield subsequently conducted another survey with an expanded scope, covering 100 firms in 12 industries. The survey produced results largely consistent with his 1981 study. He found that patent protection was only deemed to be important for the development and commercialization of over 30% of the innovations in the pharmaceutical and chemical industries.[91] These survey results led Mansfield to conclude that, "Despite the fact that the patent system generally is defended at least partly on the grounds that it increases the rate of innovation, the present study indicates that its effects in this regard are very small in most of the industries we studied."[92]

In one of the most authoritative studies on the topic, Levin and his colleagues at Yale conducted an extensive study of the appropriability conditions in more than 100 manufacturing industries. This survey has been sometimes referred to as the Yale survey. Focusing on the 18 most heavily sampled industries, they were able to establish "the limited effectiveness of patents as a means of appropriation. . . . In only one industry, drugs, were product patents regarded by a majority of respondents as strictly more effective than other means of appropriation."[93]

In fact, even the seemingly widely accepted view that the quasi-rent generated by patent protection is crucial to pharmaceutical innovations has been challenged by none other than Scherer. In the context of

---

85 *See generally* Boldrin & Levine, *supra* note 79.

86 Edwin Mansfield, *Patents and Innovation: An Empirical Study*, 32 Mgmt. Sci. 173, 174 (1986).

87 Edwin Mansfield, Mark Schwartz & Samuel Wagner, *Imitation Costs and Patents: An Empirical Study*, 91 Econ. J. 907 (1981).

88 *Id.*

89 *Id.*

90 Mansfield, *supra* note 86, at 174.

91 *Id.* The results were compiled from estimates provided by leading R&D executives in these 100 firms.

92 *Id.* at 180.

93 Richard C. Levin et al., *Appropriating the Returns from Industrial Research and Development*, 18(3) Brookings Papers Econ. Activity 783, 796 (1987).

an analysis of the global welfare from pharmaceutical patenting, Scherer rejects this benign account of the effect of the quasi-rent and argues that the pharmaceutical companies are better characterized as rent seekers.[94] He discovered a correlation between gross margins and R&D outlays: "When gross margins rise, so also do R&D outlays; when margins fall, R&D outlays fall virtually in tandem."[95] In other words, pharmaceutical firms increase their R&D when there is more cash flow at their disposal. Based on this empirical observation, Scherer argues that, "a competitive rent-seeking model better describes the relationship of pharmaceutical R&D spending to cash flows. Rising quasi-rent potentials are almost fully exhausted by the competitive escalation of costs—for R&D, marketing and implicit returns on R&D investment—leaving only small pure surplus for the stockholders of pharmaceutical companies."[96] Scherer's conclusion suggests that patent protection may not be entirely defensible even for the pharmaceutical industry. This view is shared by Boldrin and Levine.[97]

A number of studies focused specifically on whether the introduction of pharmaceutical patents led to increased innovation in the sector. Most of the studies focused on the introduction of pharmaceutical patents following the ratification of the TRIPS Agreement. One study also examined the case of Italy, which introduced pharmaceutical patents following a ruling by its constitutional court. These studies are discussed further below.

Pharmaceutical R&D did not experience any significant increase in any of the developing countries surveyed by economists following the TRIPS Agreement. Based on a number of economic studies from Lebanon, South Korea, and Argentina, Maskus concluded that pharmaceutical R&D in those countries was not expected to increase after patent protection was introduced.[98] Nogues conducted a detailed study of the Argentine pharmaceutical industry, and similarly "found no reason to expect an increase in domestic R&D in pharmaceuticals due to recognition of product patents. The main reason is that the development of new chemical entities is outside the reach of local companies in any developing country, since there are no firms in such countries big enough (in terms of total sales) to finance the high costs of pharmaceutical R&D."[99] Maskus shares a similar view, asserting that, "Few, if any, firms in developing countries are likely to find it attractive to engage in fundamental R&D in competition with the major international research-based pharmaceutical companies, which have expertise in research and marketing and benefit from significant economies of scale."[100]

Another natural experiment can be found in Italy,[101] which had not granted patent protection to pharmaceuticals prior to 1978, when the Italian Constitutional Court held that the denial of patent protection for pharmaceuticals was unconstitutional.[102] Up till then, Italy had boasted a vibrant generic pharmaceutical sector.[103] In response to the Court's decision, the Italian Parliament amended the patent law to include

---

94 Frederic M. Scherer, *A Note on Global Welfare in Pharmaceutical Patenting*, 27 World Econ. 1127, 1136 (2004).

95 *Id.*

96 *Id.*

97 *See generally* Boldrin & Levine, *supra* note 79, 212-42.

98 Keith E. Maskus, Intellectual Property Rights in the Global Economy 165 (2000).

99 Julio Nogues, *Patents and Pharmaceutical Drugs: Understanding the Pressures on Developing Countries*, 24 J. World Trade L. 350, 352 (1991).

100 Maskus, *supra* note 98, at 220.

101 Even though Italy is not a developing country, the innovative capacity of its pharmaceutical industry circa 1978 is not significantly different from that of today's Indian and Brazilian pharmaceutical industries. Therefore, the Italian experience is nonetheless relevant.

102 Frederic M. Scherer & Sandy Weisburst, *Economic Effects of Strengthening Pharmaceutical Patent Protection in Italy*, 26 Int'l Rev. Ind. Prop. & Copyright L. 1009 (1995).

103 *Id.*

pharmaceuticals.[104] Again, if pharmaceutical innovation boomed after the amendment, one may conclude that patent protection does spur innovation. The results of these natural experiments are particularly persuasive evidence on the relationship between patent protection and innovation because pharmaceuticals, at least in developed countries, are heavily reliant on patent protection. Therefore, one would expect the introduction of pharmaceutical patents to have a pronounced incentive effect.

Scherer found that after pharmaceutical patents became available in Italy, there was no significant increase in pharmaceutical R&D expenditures relative to world trends, no significant increase in the number of new drug entities introduced by Italian firms, and a sharp deterioration of the Italian balance of trade in drugs.[105] Export sales plummeted and multinational firms began to import many of their products into Italy from other European countries.[106] The domestic pharmaceutical firms were gradually taken over by multinational firms,[107] and generic production capacity moved from Italy to India.[108] Most tellingly, there was no emergence of significant domestic innovators in the industry. In short, the supposed dynamic efficiency benefits of patent protection did not materialize in Italy, just like in many developing countries following TRIPS.

The experiences recounted here reveal an important reality about innovation in developing countries: in some industries, innovation may be so technically complex or resource-intensive, or may require so much tacit knowledge, that developing countries simply do not have the capacity to innovate and compete globally. Moreover, even if innovation may be less demanding technologically or financially, the domestic industry may be so far behind the international technological frontier that innovation is again unattainable. In light of these arguments, Correa has concluded that, "With the exception of a few developing countries which have been able to build up a reasonable R&D infrastructure (such as the East Asian Tigers, India and Brazil), most developing countries are unlikely to substantially improve their innovative performance just on the basis of an expanded and stronger IPRs regime."[109]

As many industries in developing countries simply have no inventors who can take advantage of the innovation incentives generated by the patent system, the costs of a pro-patent policy are incurred in vain. This is corroborated by Stewart, Clarke, and Joekes' criticism of Jamaica's decision to exempt agreements related to intellectual property from the purview of antitrust law: "Yet, there is little or no innovation requiring conferring of industry property rights on locals, and there is ample historical evidence of firms using monopoly power derived from intellectual property rights to create barriers to entry by other [sic] or to divide up markets geographically."[110]

In conclusion, there is scant evidence that the extension of patent protection in developing countries will lead to increased innovation. When evaluating innovation-based claims in patent-antitrust cases, a developing country antitrust authority must be mindful of the limitations of the country's innovative capacity. No developing country would want to repeat Jamaica's mistake. In particular, the authority

---

104 *Id.*

105 *Id.* at 1020-23.

106 *Id.* at 1023.

107 Maskus, *supra* note 98, at 165.

108 Scherer & Weisburst, *supra* note 102, at 1023.

109 Carlos M. Correa, Intellectual Property Rights, the WTO and Developing Countries: The TRIPS Agreement and Policy Options 38 (2000).

110 Taimoon Stewart, Julian Clarke & Susan Joekes, Competition Law in Action: Experiences from Developing Countries 26 (2007).

should consider whether there is any innovative capacity in a particular industry, and if so, what kind of innovation it is capable of producing, e.g., product or process, novel or incremental.

2. Innovation Incentive Externalities

With the advent of globalization, the innovation incentives generated by a country's patent system are no longer confined within its borders. With increased trade and the possibility of foreign direct investment, these incentives may be felt by foreign inventors as well. Given that the market for many innovations is no longer domestic, but global, a multinational inventor will consider the innovation incentives provided by its various markets when making an investment decision. In short, innovation incentives spill over national boundaries and can have substantial externalities. When considering the impact of its decision in patent-antitrust cases, an antitrust authority may need to take these externalities into account.

The question is whether a developing country antitrust authority should pay heed to innovation incentive externalities. To formulate it slightly differently, the question is whether such an authority should consider the patentee reward accruing to foreign inventors when determining the legality of a patent practice. For a small developing country, the answer would seem to be negative. There are good reasons to doubt that a multinational firm will consider the innovation incentives provided by every market in which it operates. This is attested to by the fact that most innovations are only patented in a limited number of jurisdictions.[111] A multinational firm will focus on its larger markets, including the industrialized economies and the large developing countries.[112] For small developing countries, the profit potential from their domestic markets is so small that the technology investment decisions of multinational firms are unlikely to depend on it.[113] Even if one were to aggregate the profit potential generated by these small developing countries, it is unlikely to exceed a few percent of the global profit for a multinational corporation.[114] An invention that would have been abandoned with the loss of a few percent of profit potential is unlikely to be ground-breaking or a significant boost to global welfare. As Scherer noted, one wonders how much worse off society would be by foregoing such innovations.[115]

In contrast, the innovation incentives generated by large developing countries may have a substantial impact on technological investments on a global scale. This still does not mean that these countries should consider innovation incentive externalities in patent-antitrust cases. The provision of innovation incentives entails the transfer of welfare from consumers to inventors. In the global context, this transfer flows from developing country consumers to multinational firms. Given the impoverished state of consumers in many developing countries, such a tradeoff should not be lightly made. A developing country antitrust authority cannot be faulted for giving priority to the welfare of its downtrodden domestic consumers. If

111 Jeffrey Atik & Hans H. Lidgard, *Embracing Price Discrimination: TRIPS and the Suppression of Parallel Trade in Pharmaceuticals*, 27 U. Pa. J. Int'l Econ. L., 1043, 1058 (2006).

112 Mark V. Pauly, *Measures of Costs and Benefits for Drugs in Cost-Effectiveness Analysis*, *in* Pharmaceutical Innovation: Incentives, Competition and Cost-Benefit Analysis in International Perspective 212 (Frank A. Sloan & Chee-Ruey Hsieh eds., 2007) ("R&D often would be undertaken based on expected global sales, primarily in other [larger] countries, and the level of local sales need not appreciably affect R&D in small countries.").

113 In the context of pharmaceutical patenting, Scherer observed that, "legislators of many small and/or poor nations have viewed the addition to MNE profits resulting from their granting, as opposed to not offering, drug product patent protection within their borders as so small relative to the profits realized by MNEs in other parts of the world that their marginal impact on MNE research and testing is negligibly small." *See* Scherer & Weisburst, *supra* note 102, at 1012-13.

114 Jean O. Lanjouw, *A Patent Policy Proposal for Global Diseases*, Paper Presented at the 13th Annual World Bank Conference on Developmental Economics 7 (May 2001).

115 Scherer, *Patent System*, *supra* note 81, at 448.

an innovation is of sufficient global importance, developing countries are right to wonder whether they should be the ones to provide additional incentives through their patent systems.

Development economists have come up with a number of theoretical models that predict the effect of strengthening intellectual property protection in developing countries on innovation in developed countries. As far as innovation incentives are concerned, strengthening patent protection and loosening antitrust restrictions on patent exploitation have similar impacts. Surprisingly, and perhaps somewhat counter-intuitively, these models consistently show that innovation in developed countries will fall after developing countries raise their intellectual property protection. Based on the international product cycle, Parello constructed a model to study the impact of heightened intellectual protection in developing countries on the rate of innovation in developed countries and the rate of imitation in developing countries.[116] In the absence of foreign direct investment, Parello concludes that improved protection induces a short-run slowdown in the innovation rate in developed countries and impedes technology transfer by imitation.[117] Lai supplements Parello's analysis by examining the effect of enhanced protection in developing countries on the rate of innovation in developed countries when the means of technology transfer comprises both imitation and foreign direct investment.[118] When imitation is the only means of technology transfer, Lai's conclusions are similar to Parello's.[119] When technology transfer is accomplished through investment, Lai finds that both the rate of innovation and the rate of imitation rise in response to enhanced protection in developing countries.[120] Although his analysis is slightly more complicated, Helpman reaches the same result under the assumptions of no foreign direct investment and low imitation rate.[121] Lastly, a number of other theoretical studies corroborate the conclusions from Parello, Lai, and Helpman, with Maskus positing that, "if innovative firms expected slower loss of their technological advantages they could earn higher profits per innovation, reducing the need to engage in R&D."[122] In light of this considerable body of literature, there is even less reason for a developing country antitrust authority to consider innovation incentive externalities.

116 Carmelo Pierpaolo Parello, *A North-South Model of Intellectual Property Rights Protection and Skill Accumulation*, 85 J. Dev. Econ. 253 (2008).

117 *Id.* at 255, 265-66.

118 Edwin Lai, *International Intellectual Property Rights Protection and the Rate of Product Innovation*, 55 J. Dev. Econ. 133 (1998).

119 *Id.* at 135. The difference in results is due to the fact that, in the former case, heightened protection in developing countries will induce inventors in developed countries to invest in more innovation, raising their demand for skilled labor in their countries. Wages for these workers rise, lifting the costs of innovation. This increase in costs will in fact overwhelm any gains to the inventors from the enhanced intellectual property rights protection in developing countries, causing the overall rate of innovation to drop.

120 *Id.*

121 Elhanan Helpman, *Innovation, Imitation, and Intellectual Property Rights*, 61 Econometrica 1247, 1275 (1993).

122 Maskus, *supra* note 98, at 139. *See also* Keith E. Maskus, *The Role of Intellectual Property Rights in Encouraging Foreign Direct Investment and Technology Transfer*, *in* Intellectual Property and Development: Lessons from Recent Economic Research 41, 61 (Carsten Fink & Keith E. Maskus eds., 2005).

3. Lessons for China

It is clear from the foregoing discussion that, contrary to common belief, the case for the importance of patent protection for the pharmaceutical sector has been overstated. Development economists have demonstrated that extending patent protection to pharmaceuticals has not resulted in greater innovation in developing countries. In many developing countries, the capacity needed to generate pharmaceutical innovation simply does not exist, as illustrated by the experiences of Argentina, Lebanon, South Korea, and even Italy (even though Italy is not a developing country). In the absence of domestic innovative capacity, the need to preserve innovation incentives is much attenuated. Furthermore, the case for incurring consumer welfare loss to generate innovation incentives for foreign, developed country pharmaceutical manufacturers is highly questionable, especially in light of the economics literature reviewed in the previous section that suggests that raising patent protection in developing countries actually could reduce innovation in developed countries.

What this means for China is that unless and until there is clear evidence of sufficient domestic innovative capacity, which may very well emerge in the near future, to take advantage of the innovation incentives generated by the patent system and preserved by pro-patent antitrust rules, China should err on the side of protecting consumer welfare when dealing with a patent-antitrust issue in the pharmaceutical sector.[123] Therefore, with respect to practices such as reverse payments, product hopping, and evergreening, which seem to have questionable benefits in terms of innovation incentives but which inflict clear harm on consumer welfare, the PRC's enforcement authorities should take a hard line against them. Although these practices have been largely absent from China thus far, with the liberalization of the pharmaceutical sector in the country, and perhaps with the improved quality of the domestic generic manufacturers, it is entirely possible that they may arise in the future. The PRC's enforcement authorities should express fewer concerns for preserving innovation incentives when dealing with these practices.

VI. Conclusion

The pharmaceutical sector has thus far largely escaped scrutiny from the PRC's enforcement authorities. This is curious because the pharmaceutical industry features prominently in the enforcement agenda of other jurisdictions. This could be largely because of the unique domestic regulatory environment and industry structure in China that has obviated the need for branded manufacturers to expend considerable energy to forestall generic entry. This chapter has reviewed this unique regulatory environment facing the pharmaceutical industry in China and recent liberalization reforms, which is likely to create a sea change in the industry. It has also reviewed enforcement under the AML in the sector thus far and predicted possible future issues arising in the industry. Lastly, it has reviewed existing theoretical and empirical literature and suggested that for now, China should continue to emphasize consumer welfare when enforcing against patent practices in the pharmaceutical industry.

---

123 One may argue that domestic innovative capacity will not emerge unless there is strong patent protection. While this is certainly true, a developing country may be so far from the international technological frontier that no amount of innovation incentives will be able to spur worthwhile domestic innovation in the near future. Whether this is true of the domestic pharmaceutical industry in China will require a fairly extensive survey, which is beyond the scope of this book chapter. For now, I will argue that unless there is clear evidence of innovative capacity emerging in China, innovation incentives can still take a back seat vis-à-vis consumer welfare in the patent-antitrust interface in the pharmaceutical sector.

Implementing Effective Competition Law in the Pharmaceutical Industry in Mexico

Carlos Mena-Labarthe*

cmena@cofece.mx

Head of the Investigative Authority

Comisión Federal de Competencia Económica

Abstract

In the case of Mexico, the lack of precedents in competition and the complex legal framework that apply to the pharmaceutical sector have complicated the effective implementation of competition law. The competition authority has issued several recommendations in the sector; many of them were implemented and are currently delivering successful results. Some others have not been addressed yet, such as the asymmetries of information between doctors and patients and between doctors and manufacturers, which keep prices high and restrict the entry of generic medicines.

Undoubtedly, consumers and the pharmaceutical industry as a whole can benefit from more competitive markets but it is not easy to strike the correct equilibrium between the pursuit of complex, even antagonist public policies, and the interests of private firms. Thus the role of the competition authority in order to achieve this balance will be key. In doing so, the Mexican authority faces significant challenges in the promotion of a pro-competitive regulation and to encourage the discussion of intellectual property in pharmaceutical sector. Acknowledging the experience of other jurisdictions will be paramount for this task. In this sense, the Mexican authority must be aware of the emergence of new anti-competitive practices that are being investigated in other jurisdictions and that may be replicated in Mexico.

---

* I would like to thank Mónica Zegarra for their research assistance for this paper and Eduardo González Pier, Juan Carlos Burgos, Iker Arriola, and Jorge Kim for their valuable comments. Any errors are mine.

I. Introduction

Analyzing the pharmaceuticals industry from a competition perspective is one of the most complex but fascinating endeavors. Considering the analysis involves balancing issues such as incentives to innovate and perform research and development ("R&D"), intellectual property ("IP") rights, and healthcare policy and public budget concerns, the task is difficult for academic purposes and even more for public policy. During the past few years, competition law enforcement has proven to be an essential tool to increase access to pharmaceutical products and technologies around the world. Its importance arises especially from the fact that competition law allows authorities to impose broader remedies than with IP law. Additionally, as will be analyzed in this paper, advocacy efforts can be successful in removing regulatory barriers to entry that may be impeding new entrants and the efficient operation of the market. Consumers and the industry as a whole can benefit from more competitive markets but it is not easy to strike the correct balance. In this paper, I will analyze the case of Mexico in relation to many other jurisdictions around the world, especially developing countries, to reveal the main issues related to competition policy in the pharmaceutical industry.

In Mexico, competition policy applies across all industries, including pharmaceuticals, and to IP. However, conducting competition analysis in such fields is not an easy task for antitrust authorities, especially for young ones. A lack of precedents and experienced staff and the complex legal framework that applies to the pharmaceutical sector combine to create difficulties in the implementation of competition principles.[1] Moreover, many elements have to be considered in the analysis, as pharmaceutical firms usually will justify their anti-competitive practices with the existence of their lawfully granted exclusivity rights and the creation of dynamic efficiencies. Nevertheless, it has been widely recognized that even when the existence of an exclusive patent allows a pharmaceutical company to obtain enough profits to invest in the R&D required for new products, those same IP rights can also be used to unlawfully exclude competitors or foreclose markets.

The development of the competition policy in the Mexican pharmaceutical market is an important consideration. The first Mexican competition law was enacted 24 years ago. Since then, there have been important institutional and legal developments surrounding Mexican competition policy. Especially during the last 10 years, the Mexican competition authority, the Federal Economic Competition Commission ("COFECE"),[2] has been active in promoting competition law principles in many regulated markets, including in healthcare. This promotion has involved both advocacy and enforcement. Concerning advocacy, the authority has insisted on removing different barriers to entry caused by health and IP regulation in order to open markets. As I will review, many of those advocacy recommendations were implemented correctly and produced successful outcomes. Others lacked implementation or the policies did not produce the intended effects.

Regarding competition law enforcement, the COFECE has investigated and sanctioned firms in several cases involving bid-rigging in the pharmaceuticals industry. In addition, while the COFECE's experience with abuse of dominance cases in the industry to date is limited, it is expected that enforcement against such abuses will develop in the following years, as the agency has set healthcare as one of its priorities in its 2014-2017 Strategic Plan.

The aim of this paper is to elaborate on the market structure of the pharmaceutical industry in Mexico from a competition perspective, as well as on the actions that the Mexican competition authority has carried out to enhance competition in the industry, including both advocacy and enforcement.

---

1 Frederick Abbott et al., Using Competition Law to Promote Access to Health Technologies: A guidebook for low- and middle-income countries 8 (2014), *available at* http://ssrn.com/abstract=2439416.

2 All Mexican agencies will be referred to by their Spanish acronyms.

In the first section, I provide a brief description of the structure of the pharmaceutical industry in Mexico, including its historical evolution and function. In the next section, I outline the competition issues that have been found in the industry, classifying them into: i) those related to market characteristics, such as the regulatory framework, issues arising from the existence of asymmetric information, different business strategies, and the absence of countervailing buyer power; and ii) those issues derived from pharmaceutical companies' conduct. Finally, I share some thoughts about the prevailing competition concerns within the pharmaceuticals industry in Mexico.

II. Pharmaceutical Industry in Mexico

1. Evolution

The pharmaceutical market in Mexico has rapidly evolved during the last 20 years. In this period, there has been a significant increase in the production and distribution of generic drugs. Such increase can be traced back to 1984, when the Ministry of Health made its first significant effort to introduce generics, with the creation of a "basic framework" that established a list of the basic generic drugs to be prescribed in public healthcare institutions.[3] However, it was not until 1998, that generic drugs manufacturers made a serious attempt to enter the private market. Since that time, many efforts have been made to facilitate the development of the generics industry and the penetration of generic drugs in the Mexican market.[4]

The structure of Mexico's pharmaceuticals industry has also evolved. Ten years ago, the industry was compartmentalized between multinational firms focused on manufacturing innovative drugs and national firms focused on the production of generic drugs. This compartmentalization has blurred since that time. Currently, many multinational firms produce generic drugs in Mexico and many national firms have invested in the development and production of branded generic drugs.

2. Mexico as a Drug Manufacturer

Specifically concerning generic drugs, Mexico has become an important exporter. During the last two years, Mexico exported approximately 15 million units, 70% of which went to Latin American countries such as El Salvador, Ecuador, Peru, Chile, Costa Rica, Panama, and Colombia.[5]

The domestic generics industry in Mexico is represented by approximately 170 pharmaceutical firms.[6] Some of these are small family businesses, while others are backed by huge foreign investments, such as by the Israeli firm Teva,[7] the French firm Quifa-Perrigo,[8] the Indian firm Sun Pharma,[9] and the Canadian

---

3 Cori Hayden, *A Generic Solution? Pharmaceuticals and the Politics of the Similar in Mexico*, 48(4) Current Anthropology 475, 478 (2007), *available at* http://www.paho.org/hq/documents/events/ciess08/Pharmaceuticals_and_the_Politics_of_the_Similar_Mexico-Cori_Hayden.pdf?ua=1.

4 *Id.* at 478.

5 Alejandra Rodríguez, *México exportó US500 millones en genéricos*, El Economista, Apr. 24, 2015, http://eleconomista.com.mx/industrias/2015/04/24/mexico-exporto-us500-millones-genericos.

6 ProMéxico, Industria farmacéutica (2013), *available at* http://mim.promexico.gob.mx/work/sites/mim/resources/LocalContent/368/2/130820_DS_Farmaceutica_ESP.pdf.

7 *See* Teva México, http://www.tevamexico.com/ (last visited Dec. 28, 2015).

8 *See* Quifa-Perrigo, http://www.perrigo.com.mx/index.php/nosotros/quifa (last visited Dec. 28, 2015).

9 *See* Sun Pharma, http://www.sunpharma.com.mx/principales/acercade_pub.asp (last visited Dec. 28, 2015).

firm Apotex.[10] As has happened around the world, international pharmaceutical companies that wish to develop their global presence,[11] have bought regional Mexican drug manufacturers to expand their business. For instance, recently, Teva acquired the Mexican generics laboratory Rimsa in order to expand its operations in Latin America, which was considered an important move by Teva.

How well are generics penetrating the market in Mexico? According to the Federal Commission for Protection against Health Risks ("COFEPRIS") the volume of generic consumption increased from 54% in 2010 to 84% in 2015.[12] However, there are still pending issues in order to further increase penetration of generic drugs. According to a study by the Mexican Foundation for Health ("FUNSALUD")—and the chart below that is included in the study—by 2012 non-branded[13] and generics with denomination[14] already accounted for three quarters of the market volume and had 31%of the market value. Nevertheless, branded generics[15] and branded products (where the original drug is off-patent) still account for more than a half of total sales value and 23% of volume. This means that branded generics and branded products are seven times more expensive, on average, than non-branded generics.[16]

Table 1. Structure of the pharmaceutical market by drug type according to its source, 2012

Type of drug	Market share (%)	
	Value (%)	Volume (%)
Innovator on-patent (unique source)	15.2	1.5
Off-patent (multiple sources)	84.8	98.5
Non-branded generics[1]	14.0	42.7
Branded generics	20.5	9.5
Generics with denomination	17.4	31.9
Branded products	33.0	14.4
TOTAL	**100.0**	**100.0**

Source: FUNSALUD, Descripción de sector farmacéutico en México 2012 (2013), *available at* http://funsalud.org.mx/portal/wp-content/uploads/2013/08/DescripcionSF2012_Funsalud_vF-1401141.pdf.

10 *See* Apotex, http://www.apotex.com/mx/es/ (last visited Dec. 28, 2015).

11 For instance, Endo International (USA) acquired the Mexican Somar Group. Hetero Drugs (HUN) acquired Pharmaceutical Actives and Intermediate Chemicals.

12 Press Release, COFEPRIS, El gobierno de la república presenta avances de la política farmacéutica para la salud de los mexicanos (Mar. 26, 2015), *available at* http://www.cofepris.gob.mx/Documents/NotasPrincipales/26032015.pdf.

13 Generic versions sold under the generic name of the active substance.

14 Generic versions sold under a distinctive name without the support of a sales force to position the product. These are products whose distinctive name is the name of a brand laboratory, pharmacy chain, or supermarket.

15 Generic versions sold under a distinctive name and supported by a sales force that seeks to position the product.

16 FUNSALUD, Descripción de sector farmacéutico en México 2012 (2013), *available at* http://funsalud.org.mx/portal/wp-content/uploads/2013/08/DescripcionSF2012_Funsalud_vF-1401141.pdf.

For innovative drugs, the harmonization of IP regulations with our main commercial partners (the United States and Canada) has given immediate access to last-generation pharmaceutical solutions in the health system. Mexico is one the world's leading manufacturing centers considering that 14 out of the 15 main multinational pharmaceutical manufacturers own facilities in the country.[17] According to IMS Health, the innovative pharmaceutical companies with large sales in Mexico are Pfizer, Sanofi, Bayer HealthCare, Schering Plough, Boehringer Ingelheim, Pisa, Novartis, Johnson & Johnson, Merck, and Sanfer.[18]

3. Distribution and Retail

Another feature that is noticeable in the evolution of the pharmaceutical market in Mexico is the revamped distribution process after the purchase of Mexico's biggest medicine distributor last year, Saba Group, by the international Alliance Boots. In 2012, three distributors (Saba Group, Nadro, and Marzam) had more than a 60% of the market share.[19] Currently, with the arrival of international competitors, such as Alliance Boots, and the creation of joint ventures between pharmaceutical manufacturers and new pharmacy chains, the wholesale distributors' market power will change.

In 2009, independent pharmacies represented 59% of total sales, while pharmacy chains and supermarkets represented 40%.[20] By 2013, however, more than half of total sales in the private sector were made through pharmacy chains (including supermarket drugstores);[21] the rest were commercialized through traditional independent drugstores and generic-specialized pharmacies.[22]

The relatively recent growth of pharmacy chains and the sale of pharmaceutical products through supermarkets can be explained in part by the expansion of the generics market and the ability for supermarkets and pharmacy chains to directly purchase drugs from pharmaceutical manufacturers. Reforms in the regulation of generic drugs created incentives to develop private label products through strategic agreements with generic manufacturers.[23]

4. Demand and Countervailing Buyer Power

Derived from their operating size, pharmacy chains have exercised their purchasing power as they have begun to negotiate the supply of drugs in larger volumes and to leverage their control as the owners of retail shelf-space (for over-the-counter drugs or "OTCs"), which is the battlefield where pharmaceutical manufacturers fight for the best space to display their products.

Other players who have increased their buying power in the market for drugs are the public health institutions. Through the *Seguro Popular* program launched in 2003, Mexico has sought to achieve universal

17 ProMéxico, *supra* note 6, at 2-21.

18 *La revolución de los medicamentos genéricos*, Forbes México, Aug. 12, 2014, http://www.forbes.com.mx/la-revolucion-de-los-medicamentos-genericos/.

19 FUNSALUD, *supra* note 16, at 2-22.

20 OCDE, Recomendaciones para promover un marco regulatorio más favorable a la competencia en el mercado farmacéutico (2009), *available at* http://www.oecd.org/daf/competition/45048775.pdf.

21 Org. for Econ. Co-operation & Dev. [OECD], Competition Issues in the Distribution of Pharmaceuticals: Contribution from Mexico 7 (2014) [hereinafter OECD, Contribution from Mexico], *available at* http://www.oecd.org/officialdocuments/publicdisplaydocumentpdf/?cote=DAF/COMP/GF/WD(2014)49&docLanguage=En.

22 *Id*.

23 Some examples are Farmacias del Ahorro, Farmacias Benavides, Sanborns, Walmart, and Chedraui.

health insurance. This has substantially increased public expenditure on pharmaceuticals. Furthermore, to obtain better purchasing conditions in the acquisition of patented drugs, in 2008, Mexico created the Coordinating Commission for the Negotiation of Drug Prices, which defines the set of drugs that are subject to negotiations based on the requirements of various public institutions.

The involvement of the Commission in the purchase of drugs has provided a valuable counterweight to the pharmaceutical industry, especially in cases where the buying power of insurance companies is minor or absent. In Mexico, private insurers' major markets are middle-class individuals not covered under public programs, as well as individuals seeking supplemental insurance as a precaution.[24] The insurance sector's economic activity represented 2.1% of Mexico's GDP—an amount that is lower in comparison to other Latin American countries, where insurance sector activity averages 3.2%.[25] This situation derives from the fact that there is a low penetration rate of private medical insurance among the population. In 2012, only 7.6% of the population was covered.[26] Furthermore, private healthcare institutions are buying drugs at market prices, rather than through price control strategies.[27] However, 46% of drug purchases are acquired from wholesalers and 54% by alternative pharmaceutical manufacturers, thus wholesale purchasing could be acting as a countervailing buying power.[28]

5. Price Regulation

In Mexico, private sector healthcare expenditures are subject to maximum resale price regulation, which are applied only to pharmaceuticals with a valid patent. Price regulation comprises the international reference price ("PIR"), which is based on prices in the six countries where the product enjoys the highest sales penetration,[29] and a distribution margin, which integrates a reference price for public sale ("PMVP").[30] The PMVP is stamped on the package by the manufacturer and is verified by the Consumer Protection Agency ("PROFECO"), which monitors and sanctions pricing compliance. To date, PROFECO has sanctioned several cases in which the sales price exceeded the established maximum price.

6. Marketing Authorization

According to the General Health Law ("GHL"), the Ministry of Health exercises health regulation, control, and promotion through the COFEPRIS. In order to obtain approval for a pharmaceutical product, pharmaceutical companies must apply to the COFEPRIS. As part of its approval process, the Ministry can request information regarding marketing plans and make on-site inspection visits to manufacturing,

---

24 Deloitte, 2011 Survey of Health Care Consumers in Mexico: Key Finding, Strategies Implications 6 (2011), *available at* http://www2.deloitte.com/content/dam/Deloitte/mx/Documents/life-sciences-health-care/mx(es-mx)Mexico2011HelathCareSurvey.pdf.

25 Nat'l Council for Fin. Inclusion, Reporte de Inclusión Financiera 138 (2014), *available at* http://www.cnbv.gob.mx/Inclusi%C3%B3n/Documents/Reportes%20de%20IF/Reporte%20de%20Inclusion%20Financiera%206.pdf.

26 Ricardo Casares, *El reto del Seguro de Gastos Médicos en México*, PricewaterhouseCoopers México, http://www.pwc.com/mx/es/industrias/articulos-salud/gastos-medicos.html.

27 *See* Roberto Mendoza Zepeda, Canales de Distribución y Comercialización (2012), *available at* http://www.slideshare.net/bobyoriol/canales-de-distribucin-y-comercializacin-en-sector-farmacutico-en-mxico.

28 *Id.*

29 "The PIR is calculated as the weighted average of ex-factory prices from the previous quarter in the six countries where the product enjoys the highest sales penetration." *See* Pierre Moïse & Elizabeth Docteur, *Pharmaceutical Pricing and Reimbursement Policies in Mexico* 15 (OECD Working Papers, DELSA/HEA/WD/HWP(2007)1), *available at* http://www.oecd.org/mexico/38097348.pdf.

30 General Health Law, art. 31, *available at* http://www.diputados.gob.mx/LeyesBiblio/pdf/142_041115.pdf.

distribution, or storage facilities in order to verify that products meet requirements and do not represent a risk to the public health.

In addition, if the patent has expired or otherwise lost its validity, the COFEPRIS is empowered to authorize a generic drug. To do this, the COFEPRIS must verify that the generic drugs satisfy interchangeability criteria (efficiency, security, and quality) to protect consumers and to promote greater market penetration of generic drugs, which will be analyzed further below.

7. Intellectual Property Regulation

To prevent the grant of marketing authorizations that may infringe patent rights, there is a linkage system between the COFEPRIS and the Mexican Institute of Industrial Property ("IMPI"). Every six months the IMPI must publish a notice that includes the patents associated with allopathic drugs (known as the Gazette).

The IMPI was created in 1987 and is the institution responsible for managing the industrial property rights system in Mexico. This system has evolved gradually in Mexico. The Law on Inventions and Trademarks was amended in 1987, and in 1991 the Law on the Promotion and Protection of Industrial Property was published, in order to strengthen Mexico's IP framework.

Additionally, Mexico is a member of several international treaties relevant to the protection of trademarks, including: the Paris Convention for the Protection of Industrial Rights, the North American Free Trade Agreement, and the Agreement on Trade-Related Aspects of Intellectual Property Rights ("TRIPS"). In fact, according to the Global Intellectual Property Index, in 2014 Mexico was ranked as one of the Latin American countries with the greatest protection of IP rights.[31]

8. Competition Regulators

In Mexico, competition law applies to all industries. The COFECE is the authority in charge of enforcing competition policy across all the economic sectors, except for telecommunications and broadcasting.[32] Thus, concerning pharmaceutical and intellectual property matters, the COFECE is the body that guarantees their effective functioning. As part of its powers, the COFECE has the power to investigate cartels, abuse of dominance, mergers, and barriers to competition and essential inputs.

The following infographic describes the market structure of the Mexican pharmaceutical sector, highlighting the main actors in the different levels of the supply chain.

31 Global Intellectual Prop. Ctr., Unlimited Potential: GICP International IP Index 20-25 (3d ed. 2015), *available at* http://www.theglobalipcenter.com/wp-content/themes/gipc/map-index/assets/pdf/Index_Map_Index_3rdEdition.pdf.

32 The Federal Telecommunications Institute ("IFT") is in charge of competition matters in these markets.

Infographic A. Pharmaceutical Market in Mexico

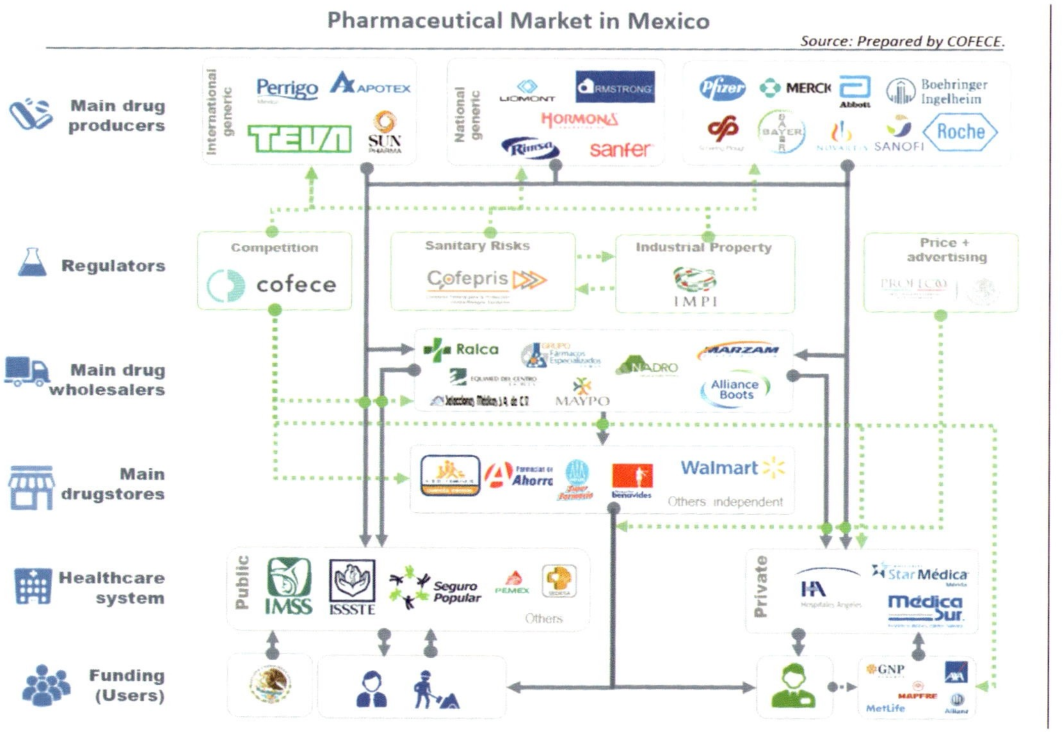

Source: Carlos Mena-Labarthe

III. Competition Issues

1. Issues Related to Market Characteristics

a. Regulatory Framework

The most important competition issue faced in the pharmaceutical sector is achieving a balance between several sensitive public policies that seek different, and even sometimes opposite, aims (i.e., health, competition, investment, and trade).

Regulation is an indispensable instrument of the government in achieving its public policy efforts. Moreover, since healthcare is established as a human right in the Mexican constitution, regulation in the healthcare sector is paramount. However, the government must be thorough when creating the rules that will manage an industry as complex as the pharmaceutical industry. A misplaced regulation may generate distortions in one or several of the markets that constitute the pharmaceutical sector and may impede the ultimate goal of providing optimal healthcare to Mexican citizens.

b. Allowing Foreign Manufacturing without a Local Plant

Previous legislation forced importers to have a factory or laboratory ("plant requirement") in Mexico so that their drug could be granted a marketing authorization. This was mainly done in order to promote investment in the pharmaceutical industry and secure sanitary control outside the country. This regulatory barrier was eliminated by amendment in 2008, and now pharmaceutical firms are only required to present a permit granted by the country of origin in order to be eligible for the marketing authorization. This amendment caused a major change in pharmaceutical markets. The amendment facilitated the entrance of imported drugs into Mexico, which increased competitive pressure, and eliminated burdens relating to the sharing of confidential information, while at the same time preserving control over health. In 2011, the COFEPRIS granted the first four drug licenses to a foreign manufacturer, three of which were for biotechnological drugs.[33]

c. Allowing Parallel Imports to Ensure Affordability

Parallel imports, also known as "gray market" drugs, occur when drugs produced under a patent commercialized in one country are then imported to another country without the authorization of the patent-holder.[34] Parallel imports are allowed by many countries because they give the local population the opportunity to buy more affordable drugs. The discussion about the ultimate benefits or harms from parallel imports revolves around the impact of gray markets on global R&D. However, some developing countries prefer promoting pharmaceutical affordability in their local market.[35] For instance, South Africa allows the import of patented drugs from other countries where they are cheaper than what is available locally.[36] In countries such as Peru, there is active discussion of whether parallel imports can promote price competition, as there is no proof that this practice will have short-run allocative efficiencies with small dynamic distortions.[37]

It is important to point out that the TRIPS agreement, to which Mexico is a party, explicitly states that this practice cannot be challenged under the World Trade Organization ("WTO") dispute settlement system. It therefore is a matter of national discretion.[38] It has been recognized that parallel imports may be a better solution than compulsory licensing in developing countries with low drug production technology.[39]

In the following table, there are some benefits and costs of parallel trading as identified in a Final Report to the World Intellectual Property Organization:[40]

---

33 These drugs involved the active ingredients panitumumab, darbepoetina Alfa, denosuma, and dexlansoprazo. *See* Press Release, Secretaría de Salud, México aprueba los primeros cuatro registros de medicamentos tras la eliminación del requisito de planta (Apr. 26, 2011), *available at* http://www.salud.gob.mx/ssa_app/noticias/datos/2011-04-26_5161.html.

34 Keith E. Maskus, Parallel Imports in Pharmaceuticals: Implications for Competition and Prices in Developing Countries 1-23 (2011), *available at* http://www.wipo.int/export/sites/www/about-ip/en/studies/pdf/ssa_maskus_pi.pdf.

35 *Id.*

36 *Id.*

37 Org. for Econ. Co-operation & Dev. [OECD], Competition Issues in the Distribution of Pharmaceuticals: Contribution from Peru 4 (2014), *available at* http://www.oecd.org/officialdocuments/publicdisplaydocumentpdf/?cote=DAF/COMP/GF/WD(2014)22&docLanguage=En.

38 Trade, foreign policy, diplomacy and health: Parallel Imports, http://www.who.int/trade/glossary/story070/en (last visited Dec. 29, 2015).

39 Krithpaka Boonfueng, *Parallel Imports in Pharmaceuticals: Increase Access to HIV Drugs*, Thai. L. Forum (2004), http://www.thailawforum.com/articles/hivdrugs1.html.

40 Maskus, *supra* note 35, at 1-22.

Benefits	Costs
Allows access to cheaper international drugs. It is expected that this reduction in price is passed on to patients.	Could raise the prices in exporting countries by reducing available supply there.
Provides health institutions negotiating power with original manufacturers to lower prices.	Transport costs and repackaging could represent a significant portion of any potential price advantages.
Could become a source of technology transfer.	Reduces R&D.
	Diminishes marketing investments to avoid freeriders.
	Slows global drug development.

In Mexico parallel trading of pharmaceuticals is neither expressly allowed nor prohibited. However, since the amendment of several customs regulations in 2014, which now require the approval of exclusive licensors in order to import products, it seems parallel imports are now discouraged.[41]

d. The Requirement of Bioequivalence to Stimulate Generic Competition

The bioequivalence requirement for generic drugs has been introduced gradually in developing countries. This requirement ensures the effectiveness, quality, and security of generic drugs are equivalent to that of the original patented drugs. The requirement thereby allows consumers and pharmacies to make informed consumption and supply decisions, ensuring the best choice and thus increasing demand sensitivity. Some countries have tried to implement bioequivalence as a measure to reduce the asymmetry of information in the market and to diminish healthcare costs, while at the same time ensuring the entry of generics into the market.

Within Latin America, Brazil[42] and Mexico are the countries with the highest number of bioequivalence studies on active substances. In the case of Brazil, all generics must prove their equivalence to the corresponding patented drugs. However, some products have a waiver from bioequivalence tests, like parenteral solutions or topical medications; in such cases the pharmaceutical equivalence is sufficient to guarantee interchangeability between generics and the original drugs.[43] Other countries that have incorporated bioequivalence tests as a requirement for generic entry are Argentina and Colombia.

In Mexico, the Bylaw for Health Inputs ("BHI") establishes the requirements to get an authorization for a generic drug. Pharmaceutical companies wishing to sell generic drugs must conduct technical and scientific tests to prove the identity and purity of the generic's components and the stability and the safety of the generic. The BHI also establishes that generic drugs will get a marketing authorization only when

---

41 Mauricio Jalife, *Medida aduanera borra esquema de importaciones paralelas*, El Financiero, July 16, 2014, http://www.elfinanciero.com.mx/opinion/borra-medida-aduanera-esquema-de-importaciones-paralelas.html.

42 Law No. 9,787 of Feb. 10, 1999 establishes the generic drug policy in Brazil. According to that law, generics can reach consumers only after passing the tests of pharmaceutical equivalence and bioequivalence.

43 Pró Genéricos, Institutional Profile 14 (n.d.), http://www.progenericos.org.br/pdf/Pro_generico_en.pdf.

they are interchangeable with the brand drugs[44] and the extension of the marketing registration is also subject to proving this feature.[45] The bioequivalence registration ensures the effectiveness, safety, and quality of generics. The regulation allows the commercialization (sale and/or marketing) of a generic drug either under a brand name or its generic denomination.[46]

An example of the effects of the lack of regulation of bioequivalence for generics is the Chilean market, where the lack of independently determined therapeutic equivalence has given doctors a justification to oppose legislation or regulations compelling them to prescribe generics. Consequently, consumers cannot legally substitute generic drugs at the point of sale, and generics have lost market share (-14.6% between 2008 and 2012).[47]

e. Medical Prescription

We can infer from the law that there are three relevant rules governing prescription practices in Mexico.[48] First, generics must be prescribed by the generic denomination (not the brand), although a preferred brand may be indicated. Second, non-generics (e.g., an off-patent drug) may be prescribed either by brand name or by generic denomination. Third, substitution of a generic for a branded drug is allowed only when the doctor has expressly authorized the substitution.

These provisions do not promote strong competition in pharmaceuticals. The first tends to favor recognized brands over unbranded generics, which are usually cheaper. The second and third discourage substitution of generics for their off-patent equivalents. A preferable alternative from the standpoint of promoting competition would be to allow the substitution of a generic drug unless expressly prohibited, once all generics are bioequivalent; nevertheless, a lack of trained personnel in pharmacies remains an issue.[49]

Pharmacies have incentives to promote brand-name drugs over generic ones, further hindering the entry and growth of generics in the market. In general, current Mexican regulations mirror regulations from other jurisdictions, such as the United Kingdom, where pharmacies may indicate a certain drug only if the doctor has not prescribed a specific brand. However, an important issue that can make a difference in the market is increasing the level of information available to patients in order to increase price-sensitivity and to allow informed consumers to make a better choice.

f. The Bolar Clause to Accelerate Generic Entry

In order to promote the entrance of generic drugs in the market, in Mexico the BHI introduced a Bolar-type clause.[50] This clause allows for the early filing of an application for the registration of a generic drug, the active substance of which is still subject to protection by a patent.

---

44 Mexican Bylaw for Health Inputs, art. 72.

45 Mexican Bylaw for Health Inputs, art. 190 bis 1.

46 Mexican Bylaw for Health Inputs, art. 24 § I-II.

47 OECD, Competition Issues in the Distribution of Pharmaceuticals: Contribution from Chile 3 (2014), *available at* http://www.oecd.org/officialdocuments/publicdisplaydocumentpdf/?cote=DAF/COMP/GF/WD(2014)3&docLanguage=En.

48 General Health Law, art. 226.

49 OCDE, *supra* note 21, at 15-16.

50 Mexican Bylaw for Health Inputs, art. 167 bis.

According to the Bolar clause, included in the 2003 regulation, patents with a lifespan under three years can be awarded to generic manufacturers. These manufacturers use the granted patents in order to carry out tests, studies, and experimental production, and they are potentially capable of introducing their generic drugs into the market at a time closer to the date of expiration of the patents. However, the marketing authorization for their drugs will not be authorized until the patents loses their validity.

Mexico joins other countries like South Africa, Brazil, Chile, Colombia, Uruguay, Peru, and Pakistan,[51] which also use Bolar provisions to allow generic manufacturers to conduct research and clinical trials before the patents have expired in order to accelerate their entry.

g. Data Exclusivity

In June 19, 2012, the COFEPRIS published an internal decree providing some recognition of data package exclusivity in accordance with Mexico's international treaties. The primary features of the internal decree are the following:

» Confidential information submitted in an application for sanity regulatory approval is protected against unfair commercial use and disclosure by the sanity authority;

» Five years of maximum protection of the clinical data following authorization; and

» During this timeframe, no one can make use of the information provided by the data holder in the authorization procedure.

The COFEPRIS will be able to grant approvals for generics only upon the completion of the five years of protection,[52] unless the generic manufacturer shows safety and efficacy of the new drug (chemical entity) independently. For this protection to apply, the requesting party must prove that the data was not disclosed prior to its submission before the health authority and that its generation necessitated a considerable effort, among other requirements.[53]

The COFEPRIS decree eliminated the conflicts between domestic legislation and international treaties, such as NAFTA and TRIPS. It also enhanced certainty and investment incentives for the firms engaging in clinical trials and the development of innovative drugs.

2. Trans-Pacific Partnership

In terms of intellectual property regulation, the Trans-Pacific Partnership ("TPP") presents special challenges regarding its implementation in the pharmaceutical sector. Issues related to the extended life of patents, as well as rights over reserved information, could interfere with access to drugs and, consequently, with the healthcare of citizens.

Even though the TPP contains mechanisms to prevent abusive practices, there could be major challenges for generic and emergent drug companies. The TPP provides 20 years protection to new patents, and it additionally grants five to eight years to reserve medical research carried out under the patent. Some of the main concerns arising from the TPP have to do with the extension of the parameters of patent licenses

---

51 Anthony Tridico, Jeffrey Jacobstein, & Leythem Wall, *Facilitating generic drug manufacturing: Bolar exemptions worldwide*, WIPO Mag., June 2014, *available at* http://www.wipo.int/wipo_magazine/en/2014/03/article_0004.html.

52 This applies to allopathic drugs.

53 *See* COFEPRIS Official Letter No. CAS/01/OR/896/2012.

and, with this, the possibility to reserve health information related to new drugs. According to specialists, this could defer the entrance of generic products and diminish access to drugs.

During the negotiation of TPP, economic and health sector experts, such as Joseph Stiglitz, have commented on the treaty's effect on the development of the pharmaceutical sector. In this regard, Stiglitz argued that "the proposed measures could promote monopolies on patented medicines and block 'biosimilar' competitors from introducing new medicines for years."[54] Additionally, countries such as India and Australia have argued that these measures would strain national healthcare budgets and keep life-saving medicines from patients who cannot afford them.[55]

Even though India is not a negotiating party to the agreement, nonetheless, it has pursued bilateral and regional trade agreements with Asian and South American countries that are part of the TPP. India also is negotiating economic partnership agreements with Australia and Canada. Therefore, TPP mechanisms and rules will impact most of the global pharmaceutical sector.

Mexican authorities have stated that even though the TPP could present them with some difficulties, Mexico's pharmaceutical sector could also benefit from the agreement. The head of the COFEPRIS affirmed that TPP conditions could attract foreign investment in the pharmaceutical sector. Therefore, consumers could have access to new drug brands, especially those applied to chronic and degenerative diseases.[56]

3. Asymmetric Information

In 2009, the Organisation for Economic Co-operation and Development ("OECD") considered that additional efforts were needed to increase demand sensitivity towards cost-effective alternatives in the pharmaceutical sector and to strengthen competition by generic drugs. Among the means proposed to accomplish these goals were the reduction of information asymmetries through awareness campaigns to consumers and doctors, establishing compulsory prescription by generic drug denomination, and allowing pharmacist substitution of generic drugs.[57]

There are some features in the pharmaceutical market that reduce the information required for effective competition, such as limits to the decision-making process of consumers, biases in physician prescriptions, and alterations in the pharmacies' recommendations and sales. Some of the identified issues in the market are discussed below.

a. Deceptive Information

The Federal Consumer Protection Law empowers the PROFECO to monitor and sanction deceptive or misleading information and advertising. In 2012, the PROFECO issued the *Guidelines for the Analysis and Verification of Information and Advertising*. Using its powers, the PROFECO has sanctioned some pharmaceutical companies for misleading advertising. For instance, in 2013, the PROFECO fined the

---

54 Joseph E. Stiglitz & Adam S. Hersh, *The Trans-Pacific Free-Trade Charade*, Project Syndicate, Oct. 2, 2015, https://www.project-syndicate.org/commentary/trans-pacific-partnership-charade-by-joseph-e--stiglitz-and-adam-s--hersh-2015-10#dMZUdYWOSuR2vTt2.99.

55 "Despite a compromise on the length of drug monopolies, a last-minute hitch over New Zealand's demands for access to dairy markets delayed an agreement." *See* Reuters, *TPP trade deadlock. Pacific countries near deal after biotech breakthrough*, The Guardian, Oct. 4, 2015, http://www.theguardian.com/business/2015/oct/04/tpp-trans-pacific-partnership-pacific-countries-pharmaceuticals.

56 Luis Miguel González, *Con TPP, certidumbre para genéricos e innovación*, El Economista, Oct. 14, 2015, http://eleconomista.com.mx/industrias/2015/10/14/tpp-certidumbre-genericos-e-innovacion.

57 OCDE, *supra* note 21, at 23-24.

manufacturers producing the drugs Xifen and Logan and ordered their removal from the OTC products market for containing misleading information as they were offered as OTC even when they did not have the authorization of COFEPRIS.[58] The COFEPRIS considered that both products contained components of risk, which should be prescribed by a specialist.

Also, under regulatory changes regarding health enacted in 2012,[59] pharmaceutical companies are required to file a notice to the Ministry of Health before advertising their product. Such preventive measures leave consumers in a better position to conduct a more informed decision-making process with regards to pharmaceutical products. Finally, one of the latest changes in the regulation of advertising was in 2014, when the COFEPRIS issued detailed guidelines regarding the approval of advertising for OTC drugs. The new guidelines are aligned with the Industry Codes of Practices (Code of Ethic and Transparency of the Pharmaceutical Industry).[60]

b. Disclosure—Principal-Agent Doctor

The principal-agent problem arises because the principal—the patient—lacks the knowledge necessary to choose the appropriate cure, while the agent—the doctor—possesses the necessary information but does not incur the expense associated with the cure. Thus, doctors are not motivated by the price-sensitivity of their patients (especially in decisions between branded and generic medicines and regarding alternative therapies).

Asymmetric information exists regarding the range of products currently available in the marketplace, including regarding, among other factors, their price and therapeutic effects. This means doctors prescribe drugs with partial and biased information, hindering a cost-effective substitution. The doctor may also be influenced by special offers of pharmaceutical companies designed to incentivize a less cost-effective treatment for the patient. There is evidence that financial arrangements (such as payments) can affect a doctor's decisions.[61]

As mentioned above in the section on prescriptions, the current regulation in Mexico indicates that once a doctor prescribes a drug via the brand name, pharmacies must provide that drug, even if there is an available generic version. This represents an opportunity for pharmaceutical manufacturers, who have created a system of incentives and rewards for doctors to favor their products when prescribing drugs and to limit the participation of their generic or lower-cost competitors.[62]

c. Advertising as a Barrier to Entry

Advertising strategies themselves can be barriers to entry. Although advertising might disseminate information, thereby increasing market size, and help consumers to make rational choices, it also might suggest to consumers that product differentiation exists where in fact it does not, as with a bioequivalent generic drug.

---

58 Ángel Pescador, *¿Por qué retira Profeco XIFEN y LOGAR?*, SDP Noticias, Aug. 13, 2013, http://www.sdpnoticias.com/columnas/2013/08/06/por-que-retira-profeco-xifen-y-logar.

59 *See* Reglamento de la Ley General de Salud en Materia de Publicidad, Jan. 19, 2012, *available at* http://www.salud.gob.mx/unidades/cdi/nom/compi/rlgsmp.html.

60 *See* Carla Bacchin de Moraes & Henrique Krüger Frizzo, Healthcare Enforcement & Litigation: Brazil (2015), *available at* https://gettingthedealthrough.com/area/80/jurisdiction/6/healthcare-enforcement-litigation-brazil/87.

61 OCDE, *supra* note 21, at 9.

62 Pelayo Vilar Puig, *La relación del médico con la industria farmacéutica*, *available at* http://www.facmed.unam.mx/sms/seam2k1/ultimos/03_ponencia.htm.

Strategies based on advertising are aimed at differentiating products and, as an intended consequence, at justifying higher prices for the advertised drug. As noted above, advertising also might persuade consumers that there is product differentiation even when there is not. For instance, when a therapeutic class faces few rivals and inelastic demand, competition does not take place in prices but in advertising and research and development. Both the manufacturers of off-patent drugs and branded generics will try to differentiate their products from cheaper, unbranded generics, through strong promotion and advertising strategies.

Advertising in the pharmaceutical industry also includes advertising addressed to physicians, which can be decisive for a generic firm's entry decision. In Mexico, advertising directed at physicians is allowed, but advertising drugs to the general public is prohibited, except for OTC products. It is possible that allowing direct advertising to the public might increase public information; however, as self-prescription and drug sales in the absence of a physician's prescription are both common in Mexico, advertising to the public could be more risky than intended.[63]

4. Absence of Buyer Power

a. Coordinating Commission for the Negotiation of Drug Prices

To establish a level playing field for drug pricing, some developing countries have created pricing commissions which help to create countervailing buying power *vis à vis* the pharmaceutical industry, especially for public sector procurement. Pricing commissions are particularly important in jurisdictions where the buying power exercised by insurance companies is minor or absent as a counterweight to pharmaceutical companies.

As mentioned at the beginning of the paper, to obtain better procurement conditions in patented drugs, as well as to increase the availability and access to drugs through public acquisitions, in 2008, Mexico created the Coordinating Commission for the Negotiation of Drug Prices. This Commission is integrated with the Ministries of Finance, Economy, and Health, as well as other public health institutions. Notably, the COFECE and the Ministry of Public Service (Secretaría de la Función Pública) are permanent advisors to the Commission. In brief, this Commission is in charge of negotiating on an annual basis the cost of on-patent drugs included in the Basic List and Input Catalogue ("CBIS") for public procurement.[64]

This negotiation strategy has been applied not only to patented drugs, but also to cases in which there is a single supplier of a product (including products for which there are no reasonable substitutes), such as pharmaceuticals and other health inputs. The Commission establishes the set of medicines and other health inputs in the CBIS that are subject to negotiations, based on the requirements of the public institutions of the National Health System and information on patents and marketing authorizations granted by the IMPI and COFEPRIS, the IP and health authorities, respectively. Despite this strategy, however, there are complex methods through which manufacturers generally will refuse to lower their prices, as, for instance, in the case of unique drugs without substitute therapies.

The Commission's negotiations are carried out directly with the producers and the settled price remains fixed for every healthcare institution participating in the negotiations, including hospitals, in the under-

63 OCDE, *supra* note 21, at 4, 14.

64 Comisión Coordinadora para la Negociación de Precios de Medicamentos y otros Insumos para la Salud, http://www.sidss.salud.gob.mx/contenidos/OrganosColegiados/ComisionCNPMIS.html (last visited Dec. 30, 2015).

standing that these are the same institutions participating in the consolidated bids for generic drugs. Through the Commission's negotiation power, the government prevents pharmaceutical firms from offering differentiated prices to different procuring public health institutions, which was what happened before the creation of the Commission.

The first annual negotiation obtained savings amounting to almost 5 billion pesos for purchases in 2009, equivalent to 50% of the previous year's expenditures. Agreements were reached with 10 out of 17 pharmaceutical manufacturers, impacting the 93 products most frequently used by health institutions. Discounts of up to 30% were attained by standardizing prices with lower cost drugs, regardless of inflation and exchange rates.[65]

Additionally, Mexico has managed to reduce the costs of generic drugs through consolidated public tenders. Mexico's healthcare institutions have achieved significant savings over retail prices. According to the OECD, due to this great volume and buying power created through consolidating public purchases, prices of drugs bought by the Mexican Institute of Social Security ("IMSS"), the main public health institution, are 80% lower than the established maximum prices.[66]

On average, public sector prices are a third of those observed in the private sector (retail). Better prices for the public sector may be explained by the larger volumes purchased, the government preference for unbranded generics, the improvements in bidding procedures and oversight of bids, and the negotiation of prices of patented or single-manufacturer drugs.[67] According to COFEPRIS, there was a 67% average drop in the price of the 31 drugs that lost their patents during the last five years, while the average drop was 68% in the public sector, where sales were carried out through public contract bids.

Last year, in the biggest public purchase in Mexico's history, 479 firms participated with proposals, 42 public institutions consolidated their needs in the bidding process, and more than 1,900 products were acquired with an expenditure of around 51 billion pesos (3 billion US dollars). According to the IMSS, total savings from the consolidated bid system during the last two years exceeded 8 billion pesos (460 million US dollars).[68]

b. Pharmacy Chains

Generic manufacturers have established strategic partnerships to produce drugs that will be commercialized under pharmacy chains' or supermarkets' own brands (e.g., Medimart–Walmart).[69] Pharmacy chains and supermarkets have incentives to promote patented drug substitution for generic drugs, even though regulation allows for replacement of a brand name drug with a generic drug only with express authorization from the doctor.[70] This has incentivized the entrance of generic products in spite of the existing regulation.

---

65 Mexican Health MinistryPress Release No. 047 on *Health Ministry* website, http://www.salud.gob.mx/ssa_app/noticias/datos/2009-02-14_3945.html, accessed September 30, 2015.

66 Mexican Institute for Competitiveness, Evaluación del Acuerdo de Trabajo IMSS-OCDE-CFC 7,57 (2012), *available at http://imco.org.mx/wp-content/uploads/2013/7/IMCO_Segunda_evaluacion_Acuerdo_OCDE-IMSS.pdf*

67 FUNSALUD, *supra* note 16, at 2-22.

68 Press Release, IMSS, Ahorro acumulado de casi 8 mil 300 millones de pesos en la Compra de Medicamentos y Material de Curación en la presente administración (Dec. 18, 2014), *available at* http://www.imss.gob.mx/prensa/archivo/201412/083.

69 Maribel R. Coronel, *Se les acaba el argumento a los genéricos*, El Economista, May 13, 2012, *available at* http://eleconomista.com.mx/columnas/salud-negocios/2012/05/13/se-les-acaba-argumento-genericos.

70 Claudia Tejeda, *Genéricos pegan a distribuidoras mayoristas*, El Economista, July 24, 2015, *available at* http://eleconomista.com.mx/industrias/2013/07/24/genericos-pegan-distribuidoras-mayoristas.

The enhanced presence of pharmacy chains is creating incentives for the vertical integration of generic manufacturers with retail outlets and pharmacies.[71] This could spur the strengthening of generic drugs' market position. In this regard, the change in retail supply may have strengthened generic manufacturers and increased the market share of their products.

5. Issues Related to Anticompetitive Behavior

Largely due to the advanced historical progress of competition policy in the United States and the European Union, developing countries have tended to adopt competition law models from these and other more developed jurisdictions.

As useful as this might appear at first, it is critical to understand that the ideal enforcement measures to address the aforementioned anticompetitive and abusive practices will not be found in a textbook, given that they arise from the rapidly evolving pharmaceutical market.

Moreover, some of the conduct remains the subject of debate and responses will develop on a case-by-case basis. Thus, in order to keep pace with the advancement of the pharmaceutical market, developing countries should not wait to import foreign legislation.

a. Price Fixing and Bid Rigging

In Mexico, the Commission has investigated various cases of bid rigging in the health sector. For instance, the previous Federal Competition Commission ("CFC") investigated and sanctioned a bid rigging case in medical equipment for the General Hospital of Mexico,[72] and settled a case of collusion in the vitamins market in 2002.[73]

In April 2015, the National Supreme Court of Justice ("SCJN") upheld the decision of the CFC issued in 2010, against the pharmaceutical manufacturers Baxter, Fresenius, Eli Lily, and Pisa for bid rigging in IMSS auctions of insulin and different types of serum. In this case, the Commission investigated bid offerings in tenders organized by the IMSS over the period from 2003 to 2006. The collusion consisted of agreements between those companies to coordinate bids in public auctions in order to allocate the contested markets. This was detected through an economic analysis regarding the outcomes of the tenders. The result of the cartel was an artificial price increase in insulin and serum. The coordination between competitors was facilitated by certain market conditions such as the homogeneity of the auctioned goods, the frequency of the invitations, the allocation of multiple agreements, the decentralization of the acquisition process, and the exchange of information between competitors.

The COFECE conducted an *ex-post* evaluation according to international best practices. The results suggest that the IMSS paid (on average) an overage of 2.9% in its serum purchases and 57.6% in human insulin during that period. This is equivalent to approximately 35 million US dollars. The fines imposed by the Commission reached 8.7 million US dollars.

In order to promote transparency, the COFECE adopted the *OECD Guidelines to Fight Bid Rigging in Public Procurement* and entered into several cooperation agreements with other institutions. In an advocacy

71 OECD, Contribution from Mexico, *supra* note 22, at 2-18.

72 Fed. Econ. Competition Comm'n, File DE-03-2000.

73 Fed. Econ. Competition Comm'n, File IO-09-99.

effort to spread and implement competition principles within public procurement, these agreements included ones aimed at capacity-building on the prevention and detection of collusion and corruption, as well as the issuance of reports with recommendations for public procurement regulation and practices.[74] Also, in 2014, the IMSS and COFECE signed a collaboration agreement to establish special mechanisms to promote public procurement international best practices among public servants.

In Brazil, CADE's enforcement history[75] contains two examples of cartel cases that illustrate the fines imposed by CADE on pharmaceutical companies:

» In 2007, companies were condemned for cartelization in the vitamins market and fined a total of over 3.7 million US dollars.

» In 2005, in the market for the manufacture of drugs in Brazil, CADE found evidence establishing unlawful agreements involving 20 companies to: fix conditions for sales and distribution of drugs in the market; create barriers to new entrants; and refuse to sell goods within the standard payment methods in order to boycott generics not manufactured by the manufacturers participating in the cartel.

In 2009, the Chilean Ministry of Economic Affairs, announced its findings that the FASA, Salcobrand, and Cruz Verde pharmacies fixed their prices between November 2007 and March 2008. These three pharmacies controlled 90% of the drug distribution market in Chile.[76] According to the Chilean Competition Tribunal, the extent of the damages caused by the conduct was particularly serious based on a number of factors, including the market power of the conspiring companies, the significant number of consumers affected throughout the country, and the finding that the agreement probably would have been maintained for longer and extended to other drugs but for the detection of the cartel.[77]

b. Excessive Pricing Investigations

Excessive pricing is not considered anticompetitive conduct in all jurisdictions. As a leading example, the US has not yet recognized the practice as anticompetitive. However, in those countries where the law treats excessive pricing as a violation,[78] the sanctions applied to the conduct have been limited. As Eleanor Fox has pointed out, there are two main concerns with prohibiting this practice. The first one is that limiting profits could hamper the incentives to become "successful" in the first place.[79] The second, is the difficulty in defining when prices become "excessive."[80] In spite of these considerations, this prohibition can be useful in pharmaceutical cases in developing countries where abusive practices can be particularly harmful to vulnerable sectors of the population.

Mexican competition law does not expressly prohibit excessive pricing, and, in consequence, there are no cases of excessive pricing in Mexico. There are, however, important examples from other developing countries. South Africa provides an example with its case against GlaxoSmithKline ("GSK") and

74 U.N. Conference on Trade & Dev., The role of competition in the pharmaceutical sector and its benefits for consumers 16 (2015), *available at* http://unctad.org/meetings/en/SessionalDocuments/tdrbpconf8d3_en.pdf.

75 Moraes & Frizzo, *supra* note 61, at 5-91.

76 *See* FNE, Requerimiento de la FNE en contra de Farmacias Ahumada S.A. y otros. Rol C N°184-08 (2009), *available at* http://www.fne.gob.cl/wp-content/uploads/2011/09/Minuta-alegato-caso-Farmacias.pdf.

77 Org. for Econ. Co-operation & Dev. [OECD], Competition Issues in the Distribution of Pharmaceuticals: Contribution from Chile 6 (2014), *available at* http://www.oecd.org/officialdocuments/publicdisplaydocumentpdf/?cote=DAF/COMP/GF/WD(2014)3&docLanguage=En.

78 The European Union is such a jurisdiction.

79 Eleanor M. Fox, Section 8(A) Threshold for "Excessiveness" as Lower for Necessities than Luxuries 1-3 (2003), *available at* http://keionline.org/sites/default/files/ER_Eleanor_Fox_NYU_Excessiveness_Necessities_20030828.pdf.

80 *Id.*

Boehringer Ingelheim ("BI"), most commonly known as the Hazel Tau case, which involves both refusal to deal and excessive pricing abuses.[81] South Africa is the largest consumer of anti-retroviral drugs ("ARV") in the world, and it imports all the ARVs consumed in the country. HIV/AIDS is a major health issue in South Africa, affecting 5.4 million infected people in the country.[82] In the Hazel Tau case, the complainants, a group of individuals infected with HIV, argued that GSK and BI charged excessive prices for their patent-protected ARV drugs. The South African Competition Commission additionally investigated GSK and BI for refusing to give access to competitors to an essential patent for HIV medications. Before the Commission, which accused the pharmaceutical manufacturers of abusing their dominant position, referred the case to the South African Competition Tribunal, GSK and BI agreed to voluntarily grant access to their patent to several generic companies, among other commitments.[83] During the investigation, the parties reached an agreement to grant licenses and maintain royalties below 5% of net sales. GSK and BI granted licenses to seven generic pharmaceutical companies in order to assist them in using the main formula to improve the combination of active ingredients and commercialize their own HIV treatments.[84] According to the South African Competition Commission, prices for ARV drugs reduced dramatically (between 60% to 80%) after the settlements.[84] This made HIV drugs available to vulnerable populations.

c. Refusal to Deal (from Drug Manufacturers)

In Mexico, the Industrial Property Law ("IPL") requires mandatory licensing in two situations. First, according to Article 70 of the IPL, the IMPI can grant licenses upon a party's request when a patent has not been exploited within 3 years after it was granted or 4 years after it was requested, except when the drug is imported. Secondly, according to Article 77, in cases of emergency or national security licenses may be granted, but only for as long as the emergency persists. As of 2007, no compulsory license had ever been granted, even though there had been many efforts to obtain one under Article 77 for HIV treatment. For instance, during the influenza crisis in 2009, the use of this article was debated.[85]

Almost all countries recognize some situations where compulsory licensing will allow third parties to manufacture a patented drug. The causes may differ in each country, but they often are related to exceptional circumstances. Compulsory licenses have been used recently to allow for domestic production of ARV drugs to treat HIV in Brazil, Ecuador, and Thailand.[86]

WTO members reached an agreement regarding IP right during the Doha Round in 2003. This resolution established that members could ease the import of cheaper generics through compulsory licensing provisions, especially in situations implicating public health crises.

---

81 Abbott et al., *supra* note 1, at 83.

82 OECD, Generic Pharmaceuticals: Note of South Africa 2 (2014), *available at* http://www.oecd.org/officialdocuments/publicdisplaydocumentpdf/?cote=DAF/COMP/WD(2014)68&docLanguage=En.

83 Treatment Action Campaign, *Competition commission settlement agreements secure access to affordable life-saving antiretroviral medicines*, December 2003 at 5, July 2015, *available at* http://www.tac.org.za/newsletter/2003/ns10_12_2003.htm

84 Statement of Complaint in Terms of Section 49b(2)(b) of the Competition Act 89 of 1998, Hazel Tau et al. vs. GlaxoSmithKline at 5, July 2015, *available at* http://www.section27.org.za/wp-content/uploads/2010/10/TauvGSKevidenceAndLegalSubmissions.pdf

85 Cacheaux, Cavazos & Newton LLP, *Licencias Obligatorias y Licencias de Utilidad Pública Para la Explotación de Patentes*, CCN Mexico Report, May 2009, *available at* http://mexicoreport.com/es/2009/05/Notas-en-Materia-de-Propiedad-Intelectual-Licencias-Obligatorias-y-Licencias-de-Utilidad-P-blica-Para-la-Explotaci-n-de-Patentes?aid=833.

86 Raymond A. Smith, Global HIV/AIDS Politics, Policy, and Activism: Persistent Challenges and Emerging Issues Vol. II: 8-9 (2013).

Furthermore, a notable example is Canada's compulsory licensing experience.[87] Canada's Access to Medicines Regime was implemented in 2004 and permitted Canada to use compulsory licenses to export generic versions of patented medicines to developing countries with major public health concerns. However, there has just been one case, which was during the Rwandan HIV crisis in 2007. Canada released its first compulsory license authorizing Apotex to import ApoTriavir, a three active component HIV treatment.[88]

Another example comes from the United States. In 2001, the United States Department of Health and Human Services faced an elevated anthrax threat in the wake of the September 11 attacks. Bayer owned the patent for the treatment of anthrax. The United States threatened the authorization of generic ciprofloxacin imports to enhance its stockpiles through an application of 28 U.S.C. §1498.[89] Even though compulsory licensing agreement ultimately was not pursued, the US government won concessions from Bayer, which agreed to a price of $1.83 per tablet, a 60.81% decrease from the usual price.[90]

Developing countries from Asia have also used compulsory licensing as an instrument of public policy.[91] For example, in response to the avian flu outbreak in Southeast Asia, between 2003 and 2006, compulsory licensing of Tamiflu was requested in many Asian countries, including Indonesia, India, Vietnam, and South Korea.[92] Likewise, in November 2005, Taiwan issued a compulsory license for Tamiflu to initiate local production of the drug's generic version. In response, Roche and Gilead, the main producers, insisted they could supply enough of their drug if the avian flu spread in Taiwan. Despite Roche and Gilead's insistence, under the compulsory license, Taiwanese drug firms could produce Tamiflu for domestic use. However, they could use it only when there was a shortage of supply from Roche and Gilead, and the compulsory licensing ended in December 2007.[93]

In the case of the Philippines, India, and Indonesia, Roche did not have patent protection for Tamiflu, and, after some time, the company agreed to cooperate with generic manufacturers for its production in the respective national markets. Additionally, after China pushed to impose a compulsory license, in 2006 Roche entered sublicensing agreements with a Chinese and an Indian generic drug manufacturer.

d. Other Anticompetitive Strategies

The COFECE faces the challenge of detecting potential anticompetitive conduct that can affect consumer welfare. The history of competition in the pharmaceutical sector around the world has revealed the existence of multiple strategies implemented by pharmaceutical companies to prevent the entry or to affect the business of competitors in the industry.

---

87 World Trade Organization, Ministerial Declaration of 1 September 2003, WT/L/540 and Corr.1, *available at* https://www.wto.org/english/tratop_e/trips_e/implem_para6_e.htm.

88 *Id.*

89 "Whenever an invention described in and covered by a patent of the United States is used or manufactured by or for the United States without license of the owner thereof or lawful right to use or manufacture the same, the owner's remedy shall be by action against the United States in the United States Court of Federal Claims for the recovery of his reasonable and entire compensation for such use and manufacture." *See* 28 U.S.C. § 1498, *available at* https://www.law.cornell.edu/uscode/text/28/1498.

90 Keith Bradsher & Edmund L. Andrews, *A NATION CHALLENGED: CIPRO; U.S. Says Bayer Will Cut Cost of Its Anthrax Drug*, New York Times, Oct. 24, 2001, http://www.nytimes.com/2001/10/24/business/a-nation-challenged-cipro-us-says-bayer-will-cut-cost-of-its-anthrax-drug.html.

91 Abbott et al., *supra* note 1, at 138-57.

92 Jerome H. Reichman, *Compulsory licensing of patented pharmaceutical inventions: evaluating the options*, 37(2) J.L. Med. Ethics 247 (2012), *available at* http://www.ncbi.nlm.nih.gov/pmc/articles/PMC2893582/#FN40.

93 *Id.*

Most of the strategies used by pharmaceutical companies are based on the use and abuse of the patent system in order to extend the exclusivity period of the drug. "Evergreening," "product hopping," and "pay for delay" are some of the most common schemes that have been used by pharmaceutical companies to prevent the entry of generic drugs in Europe and the United States.[94]

An important issue when considering these practices is the extent to which developing countries' legislation allows for findings of infringement even if the conduct does not necessarily constitute a clear-cut anti-competitive violation. Under Mexican law, both IP and the pharmaceutical industry are subject to Mexico's competition law. Despite this, there are few cases addressing these and other practices in the Mexican pharmaceutical sector.

The Commission has looked into two cases where generic manufacturers reported abuse of dominance by the original branded manufacturers. In 2003, Rimsa filed a complaint against Roche alleging anti-competitive practices in the distribution and commercialization of a drug called Filgrastim,[95] specifically arguing that Roche acted to raise its rivals' costs.

» The complainant argued that Roche intended to foreclose the generic commercialization of the product Filgrastim in two ways. First, by complaining to public health institutions during public procurement processes in order to drive the complainant out of the tender process. Second, Rimsa argued that, while the judicial procedure was still pending, Roche issued press releases stating that the complainant and other competitors were violating its IP rights.

» The previous Commission concluded that there was no undue pressure on public procurement institutions and that the press releases did not seek to exclude competitors from the market. The Commission also made clear that Roche was defending its IP rights, and that this could not constitute an abuse.

» In 2008, during an administrative appeal, the CFC established that, according to Article 5 of Mexico's competition law, the exclusive use of patents does not create monopolies.[96] In consequence, acts that are exclusively related to the exercise of the rights given by a patent cannot constitute conduct that violates the competition law.[97]

In 2004, generic manufacturers Landsteiner Scientific and PIHCSA accused Merck of abuse of dominance alleging that it had misleadingly been claiming to be the holder of a patent for the active pharmaceutical ingredient Alendronate.[98] On March 17, 2003, Merck requested the IMPI to take action against PIHCSA and Landsteiner for infringing its Alendronate patents. The requested measures were given effect two months later. Landsteiner, however, challenged these findings before the IMPI and won the case on June 17, 2003. Then, Merck filed an appeal against the IMPI for not granting it an extension on its patent. That case, however, was dismissed.

After the investigation, the Commission concluded that Merck had not violated competition law by lying about having the patent on another drug, Alendronato. Specifically, it found that Merck's actions were not for the purpose of eliminating competitors from the market, blocking their entry, or establishing

---

94 For examples of such cases, *see* OECD, Roundtable on Generic Pharmaceuticals 2-63 (2010), *available at* http://www.oecd.org/officialdocuments/publicdisplaydocumentpdf/?cote=DAF/COMP(2009)39&docLanguage=En.

95 Filgrastim is used to stimulate the production of granulocytes (a type of white blood cell) in patients undergoing therapy that will cause low white blood cell counts. This medication is used to prevent infection and neutropenic (low white blood cells) fevers caused by chemotherapy.

96 Fed. Econ. Competition Comm'n, Files DE-54-2003 and DE-013-2004.

97 Fed. Econ. Competition Comm'n, File RA-02-2008.

98 For a summary of the case, *see* OECD, Annual Report on Competition Policy Developments in Mexico: 2005 at 4-5 (2006), *available at* http://www.oecd.org/mexico/37028560.pdf.

exclusive advantages for a group of people. This was based on the fact that the patent nullification trial was being carried out at the same time, and in that case it was necessary to assume the patent was still effective. The case against Merck was thus closed.

In addition to these cases investigated by the Commission, there are indications that pharmaceutical manufacturers could be using litigation or other administrative processes to delay the entrance of generics. For instance, affected third parties can file a patent infringement claim with the IMPI, which is required to implement preliminary measures while investigating the infringement. These measures may include the recall of infringing drugs or the prevention of their circulation.[99]

In the case of patent litigation proceedings, the IMPI must consult with health and public procurement authorities to look for existing trials and, in certain cases, to prevent marketing authorizations or the granting of public contracts.[100] Some disputes arising from the IMPI's administrative process have resulted in Amparo proceedings.[101] These cases relate to the IMPI's refusal to extend patents and refusal to include in the Gazette notice of patents.

» In 2013, Merck challenged the IMPI's refusal to include in the Gazette the patent for *methods to induce terminal differentiation*.[102] The district court denied the challenge on the basis that an unfair practice would occur and that the fundamental right of access to drugs and treatments would be violated, thus harming patients in need of the relevant drug.[103]

» It was also determined that the asserted patent did not improve the active substance for cancer treatment. Thus, it would have only created an obstacle for other manufacturers to produce the substance, which is also important for fighting other diseases.

Disputes have also involved health authorities. The COFEPRIS is entitled to revoke marketing authorizations under certain circumstances: i) when the information or documents provided by the applicant are false; ii) when the reports provided by authorized third parties are false; and iii) when the products no longer possess the attributes or characteristics under which they were authorized or when they lose their preventive or therapeutic properties.[104]

Like most other agencies, the COFEPRIS holds its own administrative proceedings regarding the grant of marketing authorization for a drug, which are also subject to review at Amparo trials. In October 2011, Pfizer started an Amparo trial to suspend the granting of permits by the COFEPRIS to manufacture a generic version of Sildenafil, which is the active ingredient of Viagra. The Amparo trial commenced after 11 manufacturers began the process to apply for marketing authorization with the COFEPRIS.[105] As a result of the decision, the authorization of generic Sildenafil remained blocked during the pendency of the trial. It was not until November 2012 that three generic manufacturers obtained the marketing authorization for the production of Sildenafil.

---

99 *See* Industrial Property Law, Chapter VII, *available at* http://www.diputados.gob.mx/LeyesBiblio/pdf/50.pdf.

100 Internal Regulations of the Interinstitutional Commission for the Basic List and Catalogue of Health Inputs, art. 18 § VI.

101 Amparo proceedings are a Mexican legal institution (federal trial) that grants relief from authorities' actions that breach complainants' constitutional rights.

102 Mex. Fed. Judicial Auth., *Informative Note*, May 28, 2014, *available at* http://www.cjf.gob.mx/documentos/notasInformativas/docsNotasInformativas/2014/notaInformativa68.pdf.

103 Access to drugs is considered a fundamental right for healthcare.

104 General Health Law, art.380.

105 The manufacturers were Liomont, Siegfried Rhein, Pharmagen, Ranbaxy México, Serral, Grin Laboratories, Protein, Corne Laboratories, Sandoz, and Alpharma Laboratories.

III. Conclusions

Promoting competition principles and enforcing competition law in the pharmaceutical industry is one of the most complex but crucial tasks for ensuring the affordability of drugs in the present while fostering innovation for the future. In Mexico, as in other developing countries, competition authorities have used both advocacy and enforcement tools to achieve that purpose, but there is still very much to be done.

The penetration of generic drugs in the pharmaceutical industry is the cornerstone to reducing drug prices and should be a priority for governments in all jurisdictions. That is the reason why Mexico has taken measures to facilitate generic firms' access to the markets through modernizing its healthcare and IP regulatory frameworks. However, there are still additional issues that need to be addressed in order to further enhance competition, including addressing the significant information asymmetries between doctors and patients and between doctors and manufacturers, which keep drug prices high despite the existence of generics.

In Mexico, given the new challenges facing healthcare and IP policies, the regulatory framework that applies to the pharmaceutical industry has undergone numerous changes in an effort to maintain the balance between the different priorities of public authorities and private firms. In this regard, the Mexican competition authority should continue monitoring changes in the regulatory framework in order to prevent the creation of unanticipated incentives that reduce competition. Naturally, this is not a task that a competition authority can carry out on its own. Thus, the COFECE will continue to foster its inter-institutional relationships with sectorial regulators (IMPI, PROFECO, COFEPRIS) in order to carry out in-depth and joint analysis that will allow the quickest and most efficient detection of competition issues in the pharmaceutical industry.

There are still many challenges ahead concerning horizontal agreements, vertical restraints, and abuse of dominance. Generic drugs have just started to penetrate the Mexican market in the past few years, and they are already becoming important rivals for manufacturers of patented drugs. The Commission should be aware of the possible appearance of new anticompetitive practices designed to impede the entrance of generics, as well as other forms of abuse. The issue of collusion is an issue of its own and the authorities should have cartels as a priority in all markets, regardless of their form, but especially with bid rigging in the health sector. The effect of such bid rigging can have such immense consequences that both competition agencies and procurers should be involved in the detection, investigation, and sanctioning of this type of collusion.

Finally, authorities should always keep in mind that competition law encourages both allocative and dynamic efficiencies. It is only through considering both that competition policymakers and enforcers will help to ensure the affordability and availability of drugs, as well as the continued innovation that leads to better products. Therefore, competition law principles should also be reflected in the modernization of IP policies that will facilitate the achievement of these goals.

Annex 1. Competition Issues in the Pharmaceutical Industry

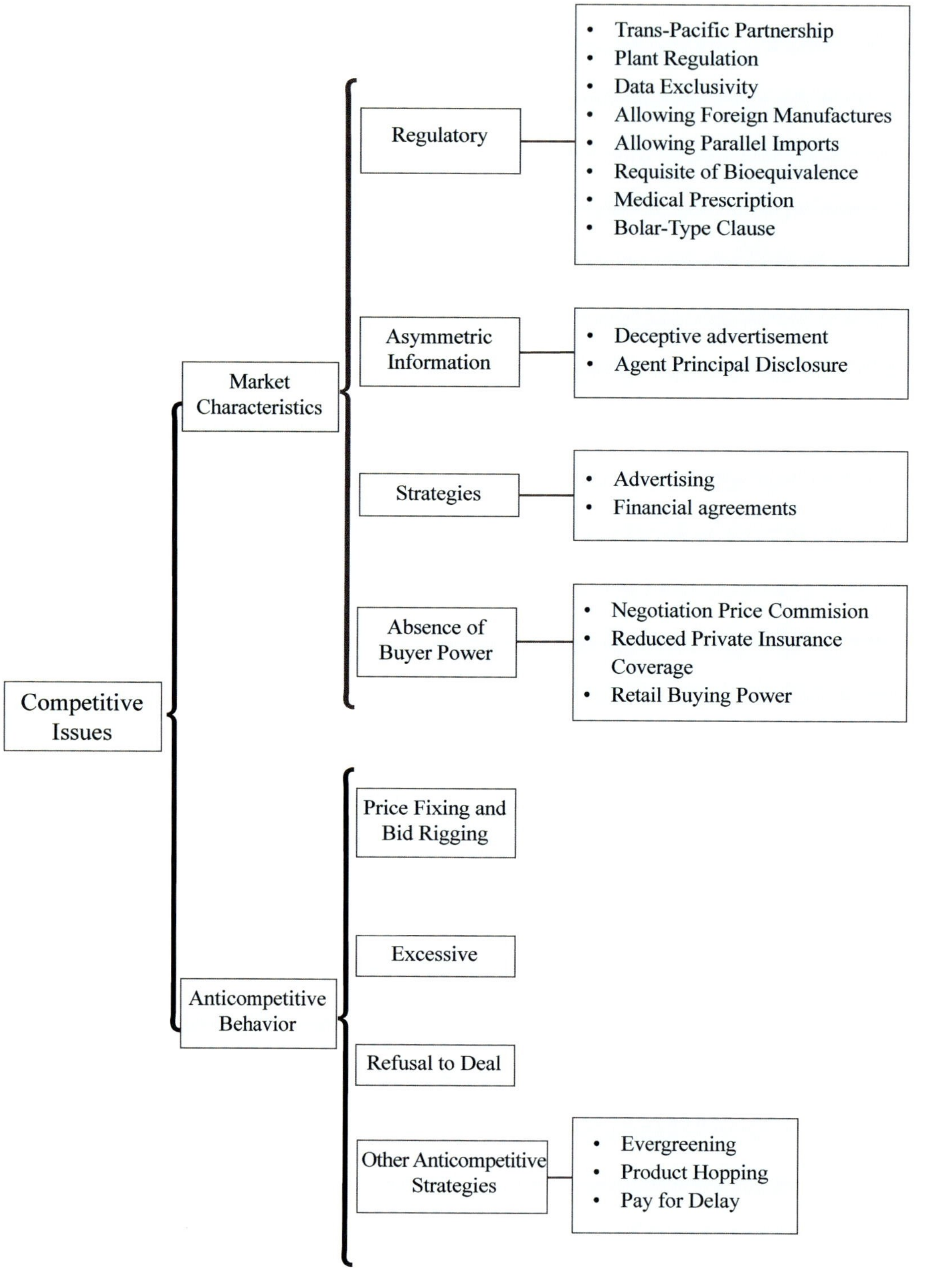

Source: Carlos Mena-Labarthe

1 Generic versions sold under the generic name of the active substance.

Too Many Gatekeepers? The Costs of Globalized Merger Control

George S. Cary

gcary@cgsh.com

Partner, Cleary Gottlieb Steen & Hamilton

Elaine Ewing

eewing@cgsh.com

Partner, Cleary Gottlieb Steen & Hamilton

Tara L. Tavernia

ttavernia@cgsh.com

Associate, Cleary Gottlieb Steen & Hamilton

Abstract

Over the last twenty years, an ever-growing number of jurisdictions have adopted merger control regimes. Although the global proliferation of merger control regimes has yielded some benefits, such as addressing competitive concerns in mergers with localized anticompetitive effects, it has also imposed substantial costs. These costs include, among others, at times significant delay in the ability to close a transaction and achieve anticipated efficiencies, the risk that an agency will improperly block a transaction or impose inefficient remedies, and the possibility that pro-competitive transactions will not be pursued in light of these concerns.

This article analyzes the costs and benefits of the global proliferation of merger control regimes and proposes steps that regulators can take to reduce the costs of globalized merger control without impairing their ability to address local competitive concerns.

One of the most striking changes in the antitrust world over the last two decades is the global proliferation of merger control regimes. Twenty years ago, companies seeking to merge could focus on the US agencies and the European Commission. Today, more than 100 countries have merger control regimes, with new jurisdictions joining the list each year. This expansion has yielded meaningful benefits—including the prevention of mergers with localized anticompetitive effects—but also has imposed significant costs that may well outweigh these benefits. Regulators and practitioners, however, can and should take steps to reduce these costs.

The global spread of merger control is widely heralded as a success. In a September 2015 speech, Margrethe Vestager, the European Commission's Commissioner for Competition, lauded the global proliferation of merger control as "good news . . . because many more people know that a competition watchdog will protect their interests if companies misbehave."[1] Certainly, there are many cases where the spread of merger control has protected consumers from local transactions generating local anticompetitive effects that might have gone unchecked 20 years earlier. For instance, in October 2015, Mexican authorities required that supermarket chain Soriana, in connection with its proposed merger with Comercial Mexicana, divest (or not acquire) grocery stores in 27 local markets in Mexico.[2] And in November 2015, Brazil's Council for Economic Defense ("CADE") conditionally cleared a transaction between two Brazilian dental products companies (Dabi Atlante and Gnatus), requiring divestiture of the Gnatus brand and the termination of exclusive distribution and service agreements.[3]

But, as we will discuss below, the global proliferation of merger control imposes real costs. In this respect, the global proliferation of merger control butts heads with another important trend of the last two decades—the shift away from the historical view that mergers are neutral at best and anticompetitive at worst. Today, there is widespread recognition that corporate transactions can have substantial pro-competitive benefits, including reductions in the marginal cost of production and the realization of research and development ("R&D") synergies. When the closing of a pro-competitive transaction is delayed while waiting for a dozen global clearances, so, of course, are its pro-competitive benefits.

In considering the costs of globalization, we draw a distinction between what we will term the "*internationalization*" of merger control and what we will term the "*globalization*" of merger control. The Soriana/Comercial Mexicana and Dabi Atlante/Gnatus cases exemplify internationalization—the phenomenon where the spread of global antitrust enforcement has allowed jurisdictions to prevent transactions that would otherwise cause local competitive harm.

"Globalization" is different. Globalization is the phenomenon whereby numerous agencies review the same global transaction and consider the same global effects. Rather than prevent anticompetitive transactions that would previously have proceeded unchecked, globalization layers additional bureaucracy, uncertainty, inefficiency, and costs onto transactions that were already being carefully reviewed and enforced, where appropriate. Rather than protect consumers, globalization effectively serves as a tax on major corporate transactions.

1 Margrethe Vestager, Comm'r, Eur. Comm'n, *Merger review: Building a global community of practice*, Presented at the ICN Merger Workshop (Sept. 24, 2015), https://ec.europa.eu/commission/2014-2019/vestager/announcements/merger-review-building-global-community-practice_en.

2 Press Release, COFECE, Condiciona COFECE concentración entre Soriana y Comercial Mexicana (Oct. 9, 2015), https://www.cofece.mx/cofece/index.php/prensa/historico-de-noticias/condiciona-cofece-concentracion-entre-soriana-y-comercial-mexicana.

3 Press Release, CADE, Cade aprova fusão da Dabi Atlante e Gnatus (Nov. 25, 2015), http://www.cade.gov.br/Default.aspx?4bfe0f1aeb21f73bcf7dce61fd5f.

To be fair, there is a fine line between internationalization and globalization. A global transaction may involve local markets and jurisdictions with unique competitive dynamics and isolated problems. For example, in 2013, several jurisdictions conditionally cleared Nestlé's acquisition of Pfizer's nutrition business. Among others, South Africa[4] and Australia[5] required Nestlé to license Pfizer's infant formula products to another company in order to maintain existing local competitive dynamics. In late 2013 and early 2014, the purchase of the Slovenian food retail chain Mercator by Agrokor, a Croatian food production and retail group, was reviewed by several European countries and ultimately cleared, subject to conditions in Serbia[6] and Croatia[7] to address local competitive concerns. And in the Holcim/Lafarge transaction, CADE[8] and the Competition Commission of India[9] required the divestiture of certain local plants in order to remedy potential competitive harm in specific regional markets.

In thinking about the proliferation of merger control, then, the challenge becomes ensuring that the desire to catch these few cases does not impose an undue burden on the dozens or hundreds of global transactions that do not pose unique competitive harms in a handful of jurisdictions.

Finding the appropriate balance is difficult because of the "lowest common denominator" problem posed by merger control. In most contexts, even in antitrust, globalized enforcement means parallel regimes with effects specific to each jurisdiction. For example, the global spread of cartel enforcement largely involves jurisdictions individually assessing conduct and imposing penalties without any spillover effect in other jurisdictions. But in the merger review context, a decision made by any given jurisdiction has repercussions in every other country.

Before discussing the costs imposed, it may be instructive to review some data regarding the extent of global merger control.

Broadly, the global proliferation of merger control means that major international transactions may require filings in a dozen or more jurisdictions. While not a complete list, recent examples of transactions requiring 10 or more filings include: GSK/Novartis (21 jurisdictions); Lafarge/Holcim (20); Microsoft/Nokia (17); TRW Automotive/ZF Friedrichshafen (14); Nestlé/Pfizer Nutrition (13); Medtronic/Covidien (13); Lenovo/IBM (13); DuPont/Mitsui/DKK (13); Continental/Veyance (11); Eaton/Cooper (10); and Baxter/Gambro (10). Even smaller transactions may require half a dozen filings. Recent examples include Coca-Cola's sale of its energy drink business to Monster, which required six filings; 3M's acquisition of Capital Safety, which also required six filings; Onex's acquisition of Kraussmaffei's companies, which required seven filings; and Platform Specialty Products' acquisition of Alent, which required nine filings.

---

4 Competition Trib. of S. Afr., Decision, Case No. 65/LM/Jun12 (015248) (Mar. 18, 2013), *available at* http://www.comptrib.co.za/assets/Uploads/65LMJun12-015248.pdf.

5 Press Release, Austl. Competition & Consumer Comm'n, ACCC to not oppose acquisition by Nestlé of Pfizer Nutrition (Nov. 22, 2012), https://www.accc.gov.au/media-release/accc-to-not-oppose-acquisition-by-nestl%C3%A9-of-pfizer-nutrition.

6 Comm'n for the Protection of Competition, Decision, No. 6/0-02-466/2013-199 (Dec. 25, 2013), *available at* http://www.kzk.org.rs/kzk/wp-content/uploads/2014/01/466-%D0%A5%D0%A5%D0%A5.pdf.

7 Press Release, Croatian Competition Agency, Agrokor-Mercator merger conditionally approved (Apr. 14, 2014), http://www.aztn.hr/en/agrokor-mercator-merger-conditionally-approved/.

8 Press Release, CADE, CADE approves with restrictions Holcim/Lafarge merger (Oct. 12, 2014), http://www.cade.gov.br/Default.aspx?81b445d42ce136fd0835065ffd44.

9 Competition Comm'n of India, Decision, No. C-2014/07/190 (Mar. 30, 2015), *available at*http://www.cci.gov.in/sites/default/files/C-2014-07-190_0.pdf.

Comparing the number of notifications filed in each jurisdiction reveals that certain jurisdictions are far more active than others. For example, in 2014, merging parties filed over 2,000 notifications in Russia,[10] around 1,000 notifications in Germany,[11] 781 notifications in the Ukraine,[12] 571 notifications in South Korea,[13] 423 notifications in Brazil,[14] 321 notifications in Austria,[15] 289 notifications in Japan,[16] 262 notifications in China,[17] 244 notifications in Canada,[18] 215 notifications in Turkey,[19] and 200 notifications in France.[20]

As you would expect, the number of filings reflects each jurisdiction's filing thresholds. Of the jurisdictions listed above, Ukraine offers an extreme example of low filing thresholds, requiring parties to file if their combined global assets or turnover exceeds €12 million, each party has at least €1 million in global assets or turnover, and at least one party has €1 million in Ukrainian assets or turnover.[21] While Germany requires the parties to have a combined global turnover of €500 million, the German-specific thresholds are quite low—one party must have €25 million in German turnover, and the second only needs to have €5 million in German turnover. Not surprisingly, these jurisdictions receive hundreds of filings per year. In contrast, France has rather high thresholds for French turnover, requiring each party to have at least €50 million in French turnover (in addition to €150 million in global turnover), and thus receives far fewer filings.

Notwithstanding these thousands of filings, the globalization of merger control has resulted in limited additional enforcement of global transactions. The instances where foreign-to-foreign transactions are subject to conditions or entirely blocked are few and far between. In France, 10 transactions were conditionally cleared in 2014, and none were foreign-to-foreign transactions.[22] In 2014, the German

---

10 Alexander Viktorov, *Russia: Merger Control*, Getting the Deal Through (Sept. 8, 2015), https://gettingthedealthrough.com/area/20/jurisdiction/26/merger-control-russia/.

11 Evelyn Niitväli & Marc Reysen, *Germany: Merger Control*, Global Competition Rev. (n.d.), http://globalcompetitionreview.com/reviews/72/sections/249/chapters/2923/germany-merger-control/.

12 Sergey Denisenko & Denis Lysenko, *Ukraine: Merger Control*, Global Competition Rev. (n.d.), http://globalcompetitionreview.com/reviews/72/sections/270/chapters/2957/ukraine-merger-control/.

13 Sanghoon Shin & Seong-Un Yun, *Korea: Merger Control*, Getting the Deal Through (Sept. 8, 2015), https://gettingthedealthrough.com/area/20/jurisdiction/35/merger-control-korea/.

14 CADE, Balanço do triênio da Lei 12.529/11 (May 2015), http://www.cade.gov.br/upload/Balan%C3%A7o%203%20anos%20nova%20lei-atualizado.pdf.

15 Sarah Fürlinger & Theodor Thanner, *Austria: Federal Competition Authority*, Global Competition Rev. (n.d.), http://globalcompetitionreview.com/reviews/72/sections/240/chapters/2901/austria-federal-competition-authority/.

16 Akinori Uesugi & Kaori Yamada, *Japan: Merger Control*, Getting the Deal Through (Sept. 8, 2015), https://gettingthedealthrough.com/area/20/jurisdiction/36/merger-control-japan/ (reporting data for fiscal year 2014, which covers the period from April 1, 2014 through March 31, 2015).

17 Press Release, Ministry of Commerce of the People's Republic of China ("MOFCOM"), 2014 Business Review XVIIII: Carry out Anti-monopoly Work According to Law and Maintain a Market with Fair Competition (Feb. 5, 2015), http://english.mofcom.gov.cn/article/zt_businessreview/news/201503/20150300912159.shtml.

18 John Pecman, *Canada: Competition Bureau*, Global Competition Rev. (n.d.), http://globalcompetitionreview.com/reviews/74/sections/276/chapters/2992/canada-competition-bureau/.

19 Gönenç Gürkaynak & Ayşe Güner, *Turkey: Merger Control*, Global Competition Rev. (n.d.), http://globalcompetitionreview.com/reviews/72/sections/269/chapters/2956/turkey-merger-control/.

20 Bruno Lasserre, *France: Competition Authority*, Global Competition Rev. (n.d.), http://globalcompetitionreview.com/reviews/72/sections/248/chapters/2914/france-competition-authority/.

21 Ukraine also has a share threshold that requires filing where the combined entity will have a 35% or greater share in a relevant market.

22 Autorité de la Concurrence, *Le Contrôle des Concentrations*, http://www.autoritedelaconcurrence.fr/user/tableaudcc.php?dt=2014.

authority blocked one transaction[23] and granted conditional clearance to a second;[24] both of these transactions were domestic. In Turkey, no transactions were blocked in 2014, and of the three transactions that were cleared conditionally, only one was a foreign-to-foreign transaction, involving two European companies, Bekaert and Pirelli.[25] In Brazil, from 2012 to May 2015, 20 transactions were conditionally approved or blocked, and only five were foreign-to-foreign, all of which were conditionally approved.[26] In two of these five cases (Munksjö/Ahlstrom and Mach/Syniverse), the remedies imposed by CADE duplicated those imposed by European authorities. In Munksjö/Ahlstrom, Ahlstrom was required to divest a plant in Germany that the European Commission also required it to divest.[27] In Mach/Syniverse, Mach was required to divest assets related to certain services provided in Europe that the European Commission also required it sell.[28] In a third case, Continental/Veyance, CADE's remedy included the divestiture of a plant in Mexico that the US Department of Justice ("DOJ") also required the parties to divest.[29] Similarly, in Medtronic/Covidien, the Canadian consent decree requiring global divestiture of a pipeline product was near verbatim to the consent decree required by the US Federal Trade Commission ("FTC").[30]

China's antitrust authority in charge of reviewing mergers, MOFCOM, offers a stark contrast to those jurisdictions that focus on domestic transactions. Since 2008, MOFCOM has imposed remedies upon or blocked 28 transactions—23 of which were foreign-to-foreign.[31] Rather than focus on local effects, MOFCOM seems inclined to use the antitrust process to influence global industrial policy and to do so in furtherance of protectionist aims. In several cases, MOFCOM has imposed remedies on global transactions that exceeded the scope of any remedies imposed by other regulators, and has done so without a solid economic rationale. In Gavilon/Marubeni, Glencore/Xstrata,[32] ThermoFisher/Life, and Merck/AZ Electronic, MOFCOM imposed behavioral remedies related to pricing and supply in China that seem aimed at ensuring that Chinese customers receive products on particularly favorable terms. MOFCOM has also required merging parties to license their patents in China on favorable terms, including in Merck/AZ Electronic and Microsoft/Nokia—transactions that were unconditionally cleared by other global

23 Fed. Cartel Office, Decision, B3-135/13 (May 14, 2014), *available at* http://www.bundeskartellamt.de/SharedDocs/Entscheidung/DE/Entscheidungen/Fusionskontrolle/2014/B3-135-13.pdf?__blob=publicationFile&v=2.

24 Fed. Cartel Office, Decision, B6-98/13 (Apr. 25, 2014), *available at* http://www.bundeskartellamt.de/SharedDocs/Entscheidung/DE/Entscheidungen/Fusionskontrolle/2014/B6-98-13.pdf;jsessionid=CEB145CD6BF4344178A2F1CFAC5D0C0A.1_cid378?__blob=publicationFile&v=2.

25 Gönenç Gurkaynak, M. Hakan Özgökçen & Esen Ergül, *Turkey: An Overview on the Turkish Competition Board's Recent Phase II Decisions*, Mondaq, June 24, 2015, http://www.mondaq.com/turkey/x/406954/Trade+Regulation+Practices/An+Overview+On+The+Turkish+Competition+Boards+Recent+Phase+Ii+Decisions.

26 The enforcement of foreign-to-foreign transactions is rare in many other jurisdictions as well. *See, e.g.*, Denmark ("Only on rare occasions have remedies been necessary in foreign-to-foreign mergers,"); Israel ("To date, only in a few cases of foreign-to-foreign mergers have remedies been required."); Norway (since the current Competition Act came into effect in 2004, the Norwegian Competition Authority has intervened in 35 merger cases and only four involved foreign-to-foreign transactions). *See* Getting the Deal Through (John Davies ed., 2015), https://gettingthedealthrough.com/area/20/merger-control/.

27 Press Release, CADE, Cade celebra primeiros Acordos em Controle de Concentrações (May 22, 2013), http://www.cade.gov.br/Default.aspx?3ff2031 6ef25fb071320300256fe; Eur. Comm'n, Decision, Case M.6576 (May 24, 2013), *available at* http://ec.europa.eu/competition/mergers/cases/decisions/m6576_20130524_20600_4231067_EN.pdf.

28 Press Release, CADE, Cade celebra primeiros Acordos em Controle de Concentrações (May 22, 2013), http://www.cade.gov.br/Default.aspx?3ff20316ef25fb071320300256fe; Eur. Comm'n, Decision, Case M.6690 (May 29, 2013), *available at* http://ec.europa.eu/competition/mergers/cases/decisions/m6690_4017_2.pdf.

29 CADE, Decision, Proceeding No. 08700.004185/2014-50 (Jan. 29, 2015), *available at* http://sei.cade.gov.br/sei/institucional/pesquisa/documento_consulta_externa.php?a6_-38uSff0w6rlBdBW1VVbWwvvmOW7xmF6zCMe31m3573IKEOhklTV5V-ygvN_CoXd99Ef5asXC2rXTNHyGDg; DOJ, Decision, Case 1:14-cv-02087 (Mar. 30, 2015), *available at* http://www.justice.gov/file/492816/download.

30 Can. Competition Trib., Decision, Case CT-2014-008 (Nov. 26, 2014), *available at* http://www.ct-tc.gc.ca/CMFiles/CT 2014 008_Registered%20Consent%20Agreement_2_38_11-26-2014_7467.pdf; FTC, Decision, Case No. 1410187 (Jan. 21, 2015), https://www.ftc.gov/system/files/documents/cases/150121medtroniccovidiendo.pdf.

31 MOFCOM, Announcements, http://fldj.mofcom.gov.cn/article/ztxx/?.

32 MOFCOM also required the parties to divest a copper mine in Peru and ultimately approved its sale to a Chinese buyer.

authorities. Finally, while less clearly protectionist, MOFCOM's remedies in Western Digital/HGST and Samsung/Seagate, which required the hard disk drive companies to hold separate and independently operate their existing and acquired businesses, prevented the full realization of the pro-competitive benefits of those transactions.

I. What are the costs of globalization?

At its worst, globalization can prevent or destroy pro-competitive transactions. A single jurisdiction can destroy the pro-competitive benefits of a deal by blocking the transaction entirely or imposing a remedy that prevents the realization of the transaction's anticipated efficiencies, like some of the MOFCOM examples discussed above.

Improperly blocked transactions and inefficient remedies are, fortunately, uncommon. Far more common is the scenario where additional reviews dramatically extend the timeline of the antitrust review of a transaction, resulting in significant delay in its closing. This too is a serious concern. Delay in a single jurisdiction can delay the realization of substantial efficiencies globally. Moreover, the extent of such delays is likely greater than is immediately apparent because merging parties (and authorities) are influenced by the known timing of other jurisdictions. For instance, if a transaction requires a full-form filing with MOFCOM, all involved understand that there will be a four- to seven-month (or longer) review process in China, which can reduce the incentive to move things along more quickly in the United States and elsewhere.

Such delay imposes real costs. Since the 1970s, when the US Hart-Scott-Rodino Antitrust Improvements Act was passed, economic knowledge about the effects of corporate transactions has exploded.[33] While there was once skepticism that mergers could generate significant efficiencies, more recent economic work has concluded that mergers often reduce costs and increase efficiency, resulting in increased innovation, greater output, and lower prices.

It is now widely recognized that corporate transactions are often a pro-competitive improvement on the pre-transaction status quo.[34]

Mergers can also lead to reduced costs of production and/or distribution by allowing parties to shift manufacturing from higher-cost assets to lower-cost assets, or by optimizing distribution networks to reduce transportation costs.[35] And mergers that increase the parties' scale (production volume) and/or scope (range of products produced) can also lead to lower costs.[36]

Mergers can also generate important R&D efficiencies. Indeed, there are several ways in which mergers can enhance innovation. For example, where the merging parties have complementary R&D assets,

---

33 Notably, the 1982 Merger Guidelines were highly skeptical that efficiencies should even be considered in merger analysis, restricting their consideration to "extraordinary cases." U.S. Dep't of Justice, Merger Guidelines (1982), *reprinted in* 4 Trade Reg. Rep. (CCH) ¶ 13,102.

34 *See, e.g.*, William J. Kolasky & Andrew R. Dick, *The Merger Guidelines and the Integration of Efficiencies into Antitrust Review of Horizontal Mergers*, 71 Antitrust L.J. 207, 240 (2003) (describing how "the US courts and antitrust agencies have made substantial progress . . . in learning how to integrate efficiencies into their evaluation of potentially anticompetitive mergers").

35 *See, e.g.*, Joseph Farrell & Carl Shapiro, *Scale Economies and Synergies in Horizontal Merger Analysis*, 68 Antitrust L.J. 685, 695 (2001) (noting that mergers may generate "re-optimization" by optimizing distribution networks and production across facilities).

36 *See, e.g.*, Kolasky & Dick, *supra* note 34, at 244, 246 (2003).

innovation may accelerate when they are combined post-transaction.[37] More broadly, mergers can increase the incentive to innovate because a larger firm can benefit from spreading new innovations across a larger base of sales.[38] Moreover, any merger-generated increase in innovation can spur competitors to innovate themselves to keep up with the merging parties, further benefitting customers and consumers.[39]

Mergers and acquisitions are also part of another means to efficiency: a robust market for corporate control. Corporate transactions allow investors to identify poorly managed companies and bid to take them over. Post-takeover, underperforming management can be improved or replaced, allowing the company to operate more efficiently to the benefit of shareholders and customers.[40] Even the threat of a potential takeover drives efficiency within corporations; if managers underperform, they may be replaced by new ownership.[41]

A delay in closing is, by definition, a delay in the realization of these efficiencies and benefits. Where these efficiencies are significant, a delay in their realization can have a serious detrimental effect on consumers. Such delays are particularly concerning in high-technology industries, where markets evolve rapidly. A delay of even a few months in realizing R&D synergies can prevent merging parties from keeping pace with industry change and put them permanently behind competitors.

Moreover, it is widely recognized that the pendency of a corporate transaction has a negative impact on the companies' operations. This concern is particularly acute at the target where, given gun-jumping concerns and interim operating covenants, there can be paralysis in terms of corporate decision-making. Even if the target is contractually able to make major changes to its business, it may be unwilling to do so while its acquisition is pending. At the same time, at either company, there is also a risk that the company takes action that is in its best interest as an independent company but that is inefficient for the combined company. Once again, the stakes are higher in high-tech industries, where a few months of paralysis or delay can mean falling far behind in R&D. More generally, there is significant uncertainty for customers, suppliers, and employees, all of whom may be tempted to jump ship during the pendency of a transaction. Finally, across industries, delay also imposes basic financial costs: the need to secure additional or more expensive financing or pay additional interest.

Corporate executives, of course, recognize these issues and factor them in when deciding whether to pursue a corporate transaction (and what price to offer or accept). Essentially, these risks function as a tax on otherwise pro-competitive corporate transactions. In extreme cases, this tax may deter companies from pursuing transactions altogether. As Daniel Cooperman, former General Counsel of Oracle, explained, "[w]hether delay results from procedural overload or duplication, or from the sincere regulatory pursuit of an aggressive but unverifiable theory of competition, the additional time spent in the regulatory process may be the largest and most important transactions cost of all—and the one that thwarts the most potentially

---

37 *See, e.g.*, Gary L. Roberts & Steven C. Salop, *Efficiencies in Dynamic Merger Analysis*, 19(4) World Competition L. & Econ. Rev. 5, at 8 (1996).

38 *See, e.g.*, *id.*

39 *See, e.g.*, *id.* ("Mergers can also lead to diffusion of cost savings over time through the broader process of inducing competitive innovation. Competitive pressure may spur rival firms to increase their independent investments in order to keep up with the newly merged entity.").

40 *See, e.g.*, Henry Manne, *Mergers and the Market for Corporate Control*, 73 J. Pol. Econ. 110, 113 (1965) ("As an existing company is poorly managed—in the sense of not making as great a return for the shareholders as could be accomplished under other feasible managements—the market price of the shares declines relative to the shares of other companies in the same industry or relative to the market as a whole . . . the lower the stock price, relative to what it could be with more efficient management, the more attractive the take-over becomes to those who believe that they can manage the company more efficiently.").

41 *See e.g.*, *id.*; Lucian Arye Bebchuk, *Why Firms Adopt Antitakeover Arrangements*, 152 U. Pa. L. Rev. 713, 720 (2003).

procompetitive transactions."[42] These considerations also may be a factor when sellers are evaluating which buyer to sell to—sellers may make decisions based in part on filing requirements and their resulting implications for deal timing, rather than best strategic fit or best return to shareholders.

Even where transactions are not deterred or unduly delayed, the expansive regulatory process results in substantial administrative costs that should not be ignored. Preparation of filings is costly and time-consuming. Merging parties must retain counsel in individual filing jurisdictions and, in most cases, must collect substantial information about the business in each jurisdiction. Often, particularly in smaller jurisdictions or jurisdictions where the parties are minimally active, the required information simply does not exist in the ordinary course of business. Companies do not invest in the competitive intelligence needed to track product level shares in jurisdictions where they have tens of thousands of dollars in sales, yet many jurisdictions ask for exactly this information. The cost of gathering this information is particularly high because the people best positioned to collect it are typically businesspeople in the overlap product areas, who must be diverted from the important work of integration planning, which is critical to the success of a merger. (The fact that this information does not exist and must be estimated in many cases also raises the question of how useful this information is to the authorities.)

Several jurisdictions also have significant filing fees. For example, the Common Market for Eastern and Southern Africa ("COMESA") requires a filing fee of up to US$200,000 (down, in response to international outcry, from US$500,000); in the UK, filing fees can be as much as £160,000; and in Germany, filing fees can be as much as €100,000 for significant cases. Such fees function as yet another tax on pro-competitive transactions and create a perverse incentive for jurisdictions to lower their thresholds and increase the number of transactions reviewed, regardless of whether there is any real risk to competition.

This system does not serve consumers well, and this tax on global transactions can be reduced without jeopardizing them. But developing a system that can identify and resolve local problems without imposing undue burden and delay on global transactions will require significant international coordination that goes well beyond the formal and informal cooperation that many authorities undertake today.[43] Moreover, successfully reducing this tax will require acknowledging that having a dozen decision-makers review the same transaction simply cannot be efficient and, worse, has the potential to seriously undermine economic efficiency and consumer welfare.

Unfortunately, there may be little appetite within any particular jurisdiction to move toward a coordinated regime: regulators face a perverse incentive from collecting filing fees, regulators and practitioners depend on filings for their livelihood, and the culture of the international competition community rewards activism over passivity.

It is time for the international competition community to consider whether, notwithstanding its worthy goals, the globalization of merger enforcement has gone too far. We sketch out below proposed initial steps that individual regulators can take to reduce the costs of global merger control without interfering with their ability to step in when a transaction is truly anticompetitive. While insufficient to remedy all

---

42 Daniel Cooperman, Senior Vice President, Gen. Counsel & Sec'y, Oracle Corp., Testimony before the Antitrust Modernization Commission, at 1 (Nov. 8, 2005), http://govinfo.library.unt.edu/amc/commission_hearings/pdf/Statement_Cooperman.pdf.

43 There is no doubt that extensive cooperation among agencies is a reality of the antitrust world today. For example, the DOJ reports that it worked with other enforcers in 40% of its merger challenges over the last five years. *See* Bill Baer, Assistant Attorney Gen., Dep't of Justice, *Cooperation, Convergence, and the Challenges Ahead in Competition Enforcement*, Remarks at the Ninth Annual Global Antitrust Enforcement Symposium (Sept. 29, 2015), http://www.justice.gov/opa/speech/assistant-attorney-general-bill-baer-delivers-remarks-ninth-annual-global-antitrust. And the European Commission reports that it worked with agencies outside the EU in 58% of its complex merger investigations. *See* Eur. Comm'n, Report on Competition Policy 2014 at 17 (2015), http://eur-lex.europa.eu/legal-content/EN/TXT/PDF/?uri=CELEX:52015DC0247&from=EN.

of the problems we have identified, we hope that these measures can serve as first steps toward realizing the goals of antitrust laws: enhancing efficiency, promoting economic growth, and benefitting consumers.

1. *Establish clear and thoughtful thresholds.* A simple first step towards getting merger control under control is for individual jurisdictions to take a hard look at their filing thresholds.[44]

To start, thresholds must be clear. Though this seems obvious, in some jurisdictions, companies cannot readily determine whether a filing is required. Market share thresholds in jurisdictions such as Spain, Portugal, and Taiwan require the parties to determine an antitrust relevant market and then estimate their own shares within that jurisdiction. And other jurisdictions have components of their thresholds that are far from clear—e.g., assessing the value of the "Mexican portion of the transaction" is a component of the Mexican filing threshold.

Thresholds must also require that a transaction have a clear nexus to the filing jurisdiction. To this end, we would prescribe a focus on the target's revenues or assets, requiring filings only where the target has more than *de minimis* turnover and/or assets in the jurisdiction. While there may be some exceptions, it is quite uncommon that a transaction will lead to competitive harm in a jurisdiction where a target has no or minimal presence. Yet many jurisdictions require filings where the target has a *de minimis*—or less—presence in the jurisdiction. In several countries, including Macedonia, a filing may be required even where one party has *no sales* in the country. Many more countries have thresholds that can be satisfied by only a *de minimis* local presence (e.g., Slovenia, which requires only €1 million in local target turnover, and Ukraine, which requires just €1 million in local turnover or assets by either party).[45]

2. *Create a "fast track" mechanism allowing for quick clearance.* While not eliminating the costs of notification, creating a "fast-track" process where parties can be confident that transactions that do not raise competitive concerns will be cleared quickly, eliminates some of the uncertainty and related problems associated with the merger control process. (Of course, this depends on having a fair, economically sound review process with no non-competition issues distorting the process.)

In order for a fast-track process to work, several conditions must be met: First, the form itself must not be so onerous that just completing it will require weeks of effort. Second, there must be a firm timeline that begins when a filing is submitted—meaning no "pre-consultation" period like those in the EU, China, Romania, and the Ukraine. And finally, the review period must be short—ideally, 30 days or less. The timeline should be the rule, not a guideline, as even where clearances are in practice granted quickly (as is often, but not always, the case in Brazil), the prospect of a protracted review process leads to uncertainty even where no competitive concerns are ultimately identified.

3. *Focus on local transactions.* Where multi-national deals are reported in individual jurisdictions, regulators should recognize that most global deals need not be enforced in each and every jurisdic-

44 We would also propose ensuring that the agency determining the thresholds is independent from the agency that receives the fees so as to reduce the incentive to set low thresholds in order to collect additional filing fees.

45 When we prescribe a focus on the "target," we mean the business that is actually being acquired. Certain jurisdictions, including Brazil and, in some transactions, South Korea, look at *target group* turnover rather than *target* turnover. As a result, transactions involving minimal (or no) sales in those jurisdictions may still need to be notified. In February 2015, for example, the global acquisition of semiconductor manufacturer Lantiq Holdco S.A.R.L. by Intel Corporation required notification in Brazil—where the target had negligible Brazilian sales and accounted for less than 1% of the Brazilian market—because the target group's turnover, including sales by companies who had a common controlling shareholder and the companies in which they had an interest of 20% or more, exceeded the Brazilian turnover thresholds. *See* CADE, Merger Case No. 08700.000486/2015-95.

tion. Instead, in cases where the relevant markets are global and the required divestitures are not local, jurisdictions should coordinate with and defer to other jurisdictions imposing remedies (particularly those most directly affected, which often will be the EU and United States) rather than impose a "me too" consent decree, as Canada required in Medtronic/Covidien and Brazil required in Munksjö/Ahlstrom and Mach/Syniverse.

4. *Pursue (at least) "soft convergence."* A standardized merger filing that multiple jurisdictions could accept—perhaps requiring basic corporate information, market shares, top customers globally and in each triggered jurisdiction, and the 4(c)/(d)-type documents required in the United States and by the European Commission—should replace the hodgepodge of forms required by the multitude of jurisdictions.[46] The aim would be a "soft," voluntary convergence that could evolve further, while increasing efficiency and certainty for companies in the meantime.

We are, of course, quick to recognize that the United States is not immune to many of the criticisms raised above. The US filing thresholds pick up a tremendous number of transactions that raise no competitive issues. In fiscal year 2014, only about 3% of notified transactions (51 of 1,618) reviewed by the US competition authorities received a Second Request,[47] and only 33 transactions were ultimately challenged or cleared with a remedy.[48] And over 80% of requests for early termination were granted.[49] Clearly, a significant number of US merger filings involve transactions that raise no competitive concerns, and it is worth considering how the United States could revise its rules to eliminate many of these filings and the accompanying filing fees (as high as US$280,000) and delay. (It seems to us that optimizing the notification requirements based on real-world experience would be a worthy project for the FTC's economists.)

One possibility would be to exempt transactions where there is objectively no overlap between the merging entities, e.g., no horizontal overlap at the six-digit NAICS code level. While this would not capture vertical transactions, the competition concerns they raise are typically addressed with conduct remedies that can be implemented post-closing. To the extent that some small number of transactions that raise horizontal concerns (e.g., potential competition transactions) were not captured, the US agencies would still have jurisdiction to investigate and even sue to block those transactions, just as they can do today with transactions that fall below the filing threshold.

Relatedly, it is also worth considering whether the US thresholds should be raised further than the typical annual adjustment for inflation (a mechanism we would urge other agencies to adopt), especially given the agencies' continued ability to enforce transactions valued below the threshold. This approach would be consistent with FTC and DOJ practice, where investigations are heavily weighted toward high-dollar value transactions. In fiscal year 2014, transactions valued over US$1 billion constituted just 14% of total transactions notified in the United States, but represented 49% of Second Requests issued.[50] In contrast, transactions valued below US$200 million constituted 40.8% of transactions notified, but represented just 11.8% of Second Requests issued.[51]

---

46 For those in the United States, this could be viewed as akin to the "Common Application" completed by college applicants.

47 Fed. Trade Comm'n & Dep't of Justice, Hart-Scott-Rodino Annual Report: Fiscal Year 2014 30, *available at* https://www.ftc.gov/system/files/documents/reports/federal-trade-commission-bureau-competition-department-justice-antitrust-division-hart-scott-rodino.s.c.18a-hart-scott-rodino-antitrust-improvements-act-1976/150813hsr_report.pdf.

48 *Id.* at 2. This figure includes challenges to transactions that were below the notification threshold.

49 *Id.* at 22 (noting that early termination was granted in 1,020 transactions of 1,618 transactions in which a Second Request could have been issued; early termination was only requested in 1,274 of those transactions).

50 *Id.* at 30.

51 *Id.*

Another shortcoming of the current US model is that both state and federal agencies can enforce transactions. Like their global counterparts, "me too" consent decrees with state attorneys general in cases that have been enforced by the FTC or DOJ add little protective value, but add sometimes significant administrative cost and potential for delay. For example, in 2009, the FTC investigated the acquisition of Morton International by K+S Aktiengesellschaft in response to concerns that the proposed transaction would harm competition in the market for bulk road salt in Maine and Connecticut. The FTC ultimately required divestitures in those states.[52] The Connecticut Attorney General conducted a parallel investigation, which was resolved by an agreement to divest the same set of assets—and pay US$40,000 toward the costs of the state investigation.[53] In the 2015 Safeway/Albertsons case, the FTC required the divestiture of 168 grocery stores in eight states.[54] State attorneys general in Nevada, Washington, and California each required a subset of the FTC divestitures.[55] Safeway was required to pay attorneys' fees and costs to the state agencies.[56] Though the mechanisms for practical implementation might be challenging, we would strongly support reforming the US system such that state attorneys general only have jurisdiction over mergers with purely intrastate effects.

* * *

We should note that there are some encouraging signs that the international community is aware of and responding to these concerns. For example, effective January 1, 2014, the European Commission implemented measures aimed at simplifying the EU merger regime, including by, among other things, expanding the scope of transactions that can be reviewed under the Commission's simplified procedure, reducing the amount of information required in the notification form (particularly under the simplified procedure), and making it easier for companies to seek a referral to or from a member state.[57] MOFCOM introduced a simplified process in February 2014 for cases with combined market shares below 15%. In the first year that MOFCOM's simplified process was in place, simple cases were reviewed in an average of 29 days after MOFCOM accepted the filing, though the pre-acceptance review period still takes several weeks and introduces significant uncertainty.[58] More recently, MOFCOM has introduced additional reforms aimed at continuing to streamline the merger review process.[59] While there is reason to be skeptical about these proposals, the response to international concern is encouraging.

But there is still work to be done. Though the economic paradigm has shifted to acknowledge that corporate transactions can in fact be pro-competitive, and though many agencies have recognized this in

---

52 Fed. Trade Comm'n, Decision and Order, No. C-4273 (Nov. 13, 2009), *available at* https://www.ftc.gov/sites/default/files/documents/cases/2009/11/091113mortonsaltdo.pdf.

53 Press Release, Conn. Office of the Attorney Gen., Attorney General Announces Agreement Preserving Competition in Connecticut's Deicing Road Salt Market (Nov. 20, 2009), http://www.ct.gov/ag/cwp/view.asp?A=2341&Q=451152.

54 Fed. Trade Comm'n, Decision and Order, No. C-4504 (July 2, 2015), *available at* http://www.ftc.gov/system/files/documents/cases/150702cerberusdo.pdf.

55 Press Release, Safeway, Albertsons and Safeway Receive U.S. FTC Clearance for Proposed Merger (Jan. 27, 2015), http://investor.safeway.com/phoenix.zhtml?c=64607&p=irol-newsArticle_pf&ID=2010943.

56 *See Washington v. Cerberus Institutional Partners V., L.P.*, 2:15-cv-00147-JCC (W.D. Wash. Jan. 30, 2015), Consent Decree (awarding US$28,000 in attorneys' fees and costs); *Nevada v. Cerberus Institutional Partners V., L.P.*, 2:15-cv-00176-JAD-NJK (D. Nev. Feb. 3, 2015) (awarding US$90,000 in attorneys' fees and costs).

57 Press Release, Eur. Comm'n, Mergers: Commission cuts red tape for businesses (Dec. 5, 2013), ec.europa.eu/rapid/press-release_IP-13-1214_en.pdf.

58 Cleary Gottlieb Steen & Hamilton LLP, Asian Competition Quarterly Report: January – March 2015 at 1 (2015), http://www.cgsh.com/files/Publication/f4e5265f-253d-422c-a966-1b234abe9d3b/Presentation/PublicationAttachment/84297c26-73c1-4a00-8a3c-1b7c16ebab67/Asian_Competition_Report_1Q_2015.pdf.

59 Melissa Lipman, *Chinese Merger Reviews May Move Faster After Changes*, Law360, Sept. 18, 2015, http://www.law360.com/articles/703033/chinese-merger-reviews-may-move-faster-after-changes.

their substantive standards, regulators have been slow to reflect this paradigm shift in their procedural requirements. Further work is needed to encourage regulators, particularly those in emerging jurisdictions, to recognize that their role of preserving and promoting competition means not only preventing anticompetitive transactions but also facilitating prompt clearance of the many transactions that affirmatively benefit consumers.

Public Interest Industrial Policy and Remedies: The South African Experience

D.M. Davis

dennis_davis22@hotmail.com

President, South African Competition Appeal Court

Professor, Cape Town University

Abstract

South Africa included within its Competition Act which was passed in 1998 a specific set of provisions which enjoined the competition authorities to take account of a set of public interest considerations in the assessment of a merger.

This paper examines the way in which the principle adjudicators, the Competition Tribunal and the Competition Appeal Court, have sought to reconcile these public interest considerations with cognizable competition concerns in the assessment of mergers. The paper analyses the key cases that have been decided and, in particular the difficulty in grounded the balancing exercise on the basis of sound economic evidence.

The paper concludes in the view that, notwithstanding the evidential problems posed in the exercise mandated by the Act, the stark levels of inequality and poverty which continue to plague South African society makes it necessary to pursue this project.

A legislature has a menu of options in dealing with public interest criteria in a merger chapter to be included in competition legislation. It can avoid public interest criteria entirely, it may include public interest within a substance test for assessing the competitive effects of a merger, it can assign a public interest exception to the substantive test, or it may develop sector specific policies to deal with certain mergers.

The South African Competition Act of 1998 chose to formulate a substantive test in which public interest considerations were incorporated into the heart of the formulation. Hence, the public interest enquiry is not dependent upon a separate decision taken by a ministerial authority.

The introduction of the public interest provisions followed a report by the Department of Trade and Industry ("DTI") entitled *Proposed Guideline for Competition Policy*. In this document the DTI argued that a coherent competition policy would lead to more competitive and efficient economic outcomes, including lower costs along the value chain, enhance the attractiveness of South Africa to foreign investors, allow for a more balanced regional economy, stimulate entrepreneurial activity, promote the international competitiveness of South African firms, and, through its influence on production processes, assist in the furtherance of the government's overall socio-economic policy.

Three particular sets of legislative provisions relate to public interest. The preamble of the Act canvasses the context and purposes for enacting the Act. Public interest is directly referred to therein, particularly in the provision that "the economy must be open to a greater spread of ownership," in particular to historically disadvantaged South Africans. The Act seeks to promote an efficient, competitive environment balancing the interest of workers, owners, and consumers and focuses on development which will benefit all South Africans.

Section 2 of the Act, the purpose section, sets out a range of objectives, several of which are directly related to public interest concerns. These include the promotion of employment, the advancement of the "social and economic welfare of South Africans," the expansion of opportunity for South African companies in world markets, the provision of equitable opportunities for small and medium sized enterprises, the promotion of a greater spread of ownership, particularly with respect to historically disadvantaged individuals.

The public interest concept is most luminously illustrated in the provisions dealing with mergers. These provisions are directly relevant to a consideration of whether a merger should be approved. Section 12A provides that, in addition to competition and efficiency considerations traditionally considered by competition authorities, it is necessary to assess whether a merger can or cannot be justified on substantial public interest grounds by assessing a range of factors, set out in Section 16A(3), which provides thus:

> When determining whether a merger can or cannot be justified on public interest grounds, the Competition Commission or the Competition Tribunal must consider the effect that the merger will have on—
>
> (i) a particular industrial sector or region;
>
> (ii) employment;
>
> (iii) the ability of small businesses or firms, controlled or owned by historically disadvantaged persons, to become competitive; and
>
> (iv) the ability of national industries to compete in international markets.

I. The Initial Reaction

In his extremely thoughtful book on the history and early development of competition jurisprudence in South Africa,[1] Lewis writes that the inclusion of public interest grounds in merger review, in particular, elicited huge controversy. He notes further "that no matter how controversial and no matter how much business community in particular would have preferred the omission, everyone involved in the negotiating process recognised that no major piece of socio-economic legislation would have passed muster without incorporating job creation and BEE (black economic empowerment) into the overall objectives of the policy and statute."[2]

In reflecting on the first decade of the Competition Act, and the jurisprudence that developed, Lewis contends that, textbook orthodoxy notwithstanding, public interest issues can be incorporated credibly into a core competition evaluation without doing violence to the principal objectives of a competition agency, namely the promotion of competition. He argues that this has been done principally in two ways: the Competition Tribunal resisted extravagant expansions of the ambit of public interest; and, because the public interest criteria had been incorporated into the Act, it was possible for the competition authorities to achieve a balance between traditional cognizable competition considerations and public interest criteria.

II. The Key Public Interest Merger Cases

In *Metropolitan Holdings Limited / Momentum Group Limited*,[3] the Competition Tribunal gave considerable attention to the scheme of Section 16A. The Tribunal held that initially it was required to determine the competition effects of a merger. If a merger was not likely to substantially prevent or lessen competition, the Tribunal was still required to consider its effect on the public interest.

The Tribunal was required to decide the question of what was to occur once a substantial public interest ground had been raised and, accordingly, whether the merging parties faced an evidential burden of justification. It held that, "once a prima facie ground has been alleged that a merger may not be justifiable on substantial public interest grounds, the evidential burden will shift to the merging parties to rebut it."[4] In the filing of the relevant documents in the *Metropolitan* case, the merging parties indicated that "as a worst case scenario," the merger could lead to a net amount of 1000 retrenchments.[5]

This was the backdrop to a consideration of public interest questions in this case, in particular employment. Employment losses were of a considerable magnitude and the short term prospect of reemployment for a substantial section of this effected class was extremely limited. It was fair to presume that the merger would have a potentially substantial adverse effect in respect of the public interest goal of protecting employment.

---

1 David Lewis, Thieves at the Dinner Table: Enforcing the Competition Act: A Personal Account (2012).

2 *Id.* at 188.

3 [2010] 2 PCLR 337 (CC).

4 *Id.* ¶ 68.

5 *Id.* ¶ 61.

An evidential burden lay upon the merging parties, which according to the Tribunal was required to satisfy two criteria:

(1) a rational process has been followed to arrive at the determination of the number of jobs to be lost, i.e. that the reason for the job reduction and the number of jobs proposed to be shed are rationally connected; and

(2) the public interest in preventing employment loss is balanced by an equally weighty, but countervailing public interest, justifying the job loss and which is cognisable under the Act.[6]

The Tribunal held that, even if the merging parties made good on efficiency arguments in respect of job losses, the efficiency argument in a case where the job losses were as substantial as in this case, had to be justified on a ground that was public in nature in order to gainsay the public interest in preserving jobs.[7] As an example of a justification that the Tribunal was not prepared to accept, it cited an employment loss caused by cost saving, justified solely by ensuing benefits to the shareholders. Hence, it took the view that purely private efficiency gains could not be taken into account as countervailing factors to a lessening of a competition.

Significantly, the Tribunal acknowledged that what was required in terms of the section was a balancing exercise, in this case, between the private interests of shareholders and what was referred to as "the weightier public interest" in preventing employment loss as a result of the merger. In this balancing exercise, other aspects of public interest would have to be taken into account. For example, if it was found that the merger had an adverse effect on employment, in circumstances where the maintenance of a factory was at stake in a region that suffered from considerable unemployment, this would be a countervailing factor which could trump an argument raised on public interest considerations to refuse the merger or to impose particular conditions.

In this case, the Tribunal found that there were no countervailing public interest considerations which would represent an obstacle to the imposition of conditions. For this reason the Tribunal approved the merger, subject to a moratorium on all merger related retrenchments for a period of two years, excluding senior employees as defined in the order.

In *Minister of Economic Development and others v. Wal-Mart Stores Inc. and others*, both the Competition Tribunal and, on appeal, the Competition Appeal Court held that the merger of Wal-Mart and Massmart Holdings Ltd, a company which had an African footprint on a vastly smaller scale but similar to Wal-Mart, raised no adverse competition issues. The merger nevertheless prompted certain public interest concerns which the parties urged the Court to deal with by way of the imposition of conditions. The Tribunal and the Court were in agreement that Wal-Mart raised no cognizable competition considerations. Wal-Mart had not competed in South Africa prior to the merger and its only presence in the country was a procurement arm which did no more than purchase South African produce for an export market.

Two sets of public interest considerations were triggered by this transaction. In the first place, the relevant trade union contended that 574 of its workers, who had been dismissed prior to the merger, had lost their jobs in anticipation of the merger and accordingly reinstatement was justified in terms of Section 16A(3). Further, in regard to labor matters, the question arose as to the future of the rights of the relevant unions in terms of agreements which had been entered into with Massmart prior to the merger.

6 *Id.* ¶ 70.

7 *Id.* ¶ 68-71.

These labor issues were dealt with by way of a range of concessions that were offered by the merging parties. The second public interest consideration raised a far more difficult question, namely, the argument that as a result of the merger there would be a significant shift in purchasing away from South African manufacturers towards low-cost Asian producers which, in turn, would have a significant impact upon small and medium size businesses in South Africa and a consequent loss of jobs.

The Tribunal concluded, notwithstanding a clear concern with regard to the effect of the merger upon local producers and jobs, that the possible losses which flowed therefrom had to be weighed against the consumer interest in lower prices and job creation at Massmart. As consumers would benefit from the lower prices associated with the merger and these likely were low income consumers or consumers without any means of support of their own, being the poorest of the poor in South Africa, it followed that a public interest in lower prices was compelling.

At both the Tribunal and the Court, the argument was raised about the introduction of certain procurement conditions. These were rejected. In order to impose procurement conditions, there would have to be a determination of the local procurement levels of Massmart premerger, followed by a requirement to hold Massmart to these levels for some period in the future. This would clearly be difficult to implement and, in addition, would be a discriminatory practice, unless similar procurement conditions were imposed upon Massmart's competitors, in particular, large supermarket chains that operate in South Africa and beyond.

One of the great challenges facing the Competition Appeal Court was that the cost advantages that Wal-Mart was able to secure depended, to a large degree, on the way it manages its own value chain globally. Wal-Mart's coordination of its "global purchasing operations and superior infrastructure for exploiting global value chains" would result in an inevitable importation of goods which could offer considerable benefits by way of cheaper products for local consumers, as well as greater choice. In short, the national competition authority was faced with a significant public interest problem of a clear threat to local manufacturing caused by the broader consequences of globalization and the rapid expansion of global value chains. Within this context, the Court required further evidence to find some meaningful set of conditions having decided, as had the Tribunal, that it could not disallow the merger on the traditional grounds of increased prices or reduced output.

In its initial finding, the Court ordered the reinstatement of the 503 workers who had been retrenched in 2009 and 2010 and further ordered the merged entity to honor existing labor agreements, including the recognition of the existing trade union and its right to represent the bargaining units for at least three years from the date of the transaction.

It further ordered the merging parties to commission a study to determine the most appropriate means, together with a mechanism, by which local South African suppliers could be empowered to respond to the challenges posed by the merger and hence participate in the benefits thereof. The study was to be conducted by three experts, one to be appointed by the union, another by the merging parties, and the third by the three government ministers who had opposed the merger.

The experts prepared two reports, which were not unanimous. Having considered these reports, the Court decided to create a fund in the amount of R 250 million which was designed to ensure the integration of small and medium sized South African businesses from historically disadvantaged communities into Wal-Mart's global valuc chain, a task which would be done by way of technical assistance by Wal-Mart using its expertise and the necessary funds.

Within the first year of the fund's inception, 164 small scale South African farmers had been successfully linked to Massmart's fresh produce supply chain and 337 farmers were trained to link into the supply chain. Furthermore, 514 tons of goods were supplied to Massmart by small scale farmers.[8]

III. Conclusion

One of the difficulties experienced in the few public interest cases that have been brought before the Tribunal and the Court concerns the manner in which to assess the competing arguments; that is, on the one hand, arguments in favor of allowing a merger and, on the other, the disadvantages which may fall within the public interest provision.

In assessing the record, James Hodge, Sha'ista Goga, and Tshepiso Moahloli observe, with regard to the public interest enquiry, that economic evidence may well be helpful:

> While other public-interest considerations have units of analysis (like jobs) that may be difficult to compare with potential price and output changes, economists' ability to both quantify and determine the incidence of different effects may still prove useful in reaching a decision. For instance, if faced with a substantial employment gain from a potentially anticompetitive transaction, it would be useful to understand both the magnitude of the price effect and the incidence on different groups of consumers who may themselves hold different weightings in public interest. Indeed, the incidence of public-interest costs as against potential beneficiaries was a feature of the economic debate in both the Metropolitan/Momentum and Wal-Mart/Massmart mergers.[9]

The decision in *Walmart* was not accepted without critical demur. Staples, Holland, and Rossouw argue that the "labour condition" imposed upon Walmart represented the construction of "a competition bridge too far."[10] The core of the criticism is captured in the following paragraph:

> By imposing a condition that extends beyond their public interest mandate, the competition authorities have created the potential for a number of negative consequences to arise from the Walmart condition.
>
> An economic analysis of the impact of the Walmart condition indicates that, to the end that SACCAWU's entrenched position affords it additional bargaining power, the net effect could be detriment to employment when the merged entity grows, or when employees are lost through natural attrition. In these circumstances, the objectives of the Competition Act would not be supported (in so far as these include the promotion of employment).
>
> In addition, the Walmart condition raises significant concern in that it does not provide for the possibility of a change in SACCAWU's position within the emerged entity or for altering the merged entity's obligations in these circumstances. This could prejudice both the interest of the employees and the merged entity's business.[11]

---

8 Sithembiso Sangweni, *Wal-Mart's R200m fund develops local farmers*, GetBiz, Oct. 17, 2014, http://www.getbiz.co.za/index.php/biz-news/retail/78-wal-mart-s-r200m-fund-develops-local-farmers.

9 James Hodge, Sha'ista Goga & Tshepiso Moahloli, *Public-interest considerations in the South African Competition Act: A critical review*, *in* The Development of Competition Law and Economics in South Africa (Kasturi Moodaliyar & Simon Roberts eds., 2013).

10 J. Staples, M. Holland & J. Rossouw, *Taking Public Interest Too Far: Walmart Stores Inc v Massmart Holdings Ltd*, 25(1) S. Afr. Mercantile L.J. 94at 101 (2013).

11 *Id.* at 106.

There is merit in this observation. Contrary to the predictions placed before the Court, Massmart has not become a dominant player in the relevant market. Its competitors, particularly the powerful national chains, Shoprite Checkers and Pick'n Pay, continue to maintain market share and are not subject to similar restrictive conditions.

Notwithstanding these reservations, the Competition Commission has published a set of draft guidelines in respect of the public interest component of the merger enquiry, which indicates a determination to vindicate the Act's ambition.

In terms of these draft guidelines, the Commission in general will adopt the following steps in undertaking the public interest inquiry:

1. Determine the likely effect on the public interest;
2. Determine whether the alleged effect on a specific public interest is a result of that merger or is merger specific. In other words, is there a sufficient causal nexus between the merger and the alleged effect;
3. Determine whether these effects are substantial;
4. Consider whether the merging parties can justify the likely effect on the particular public interest; and
5. Consider possible remedies to address any likely negative effect on the public interest.[12]

In the application of these principles, the Commission says that in the first line of public interest enquiry following from a negative competition finding, the Commission will consider what the effects are. If there are positive public interest effects, the Commission will assess whether the claimed positive effects are merger specific and substantial such that the claimed positive effects could outweigh the negative competition effects. In this case, the merging parties will have to justify the substantial positive effects on public interest grounds. This will be followed by a balancing of the negative competition effects and the positive public interest effects.

If however, if the public interest effects are negative, the Commission will proceed to determine whether these are merger specific, substantial, and justifiable. Where the public interest effect is neutral, the Commission will consider what the negative and positive effects are and balance these. The Commission will also determine whether these are merger specific and substantial.

The draft guidelines reveal a clear commitment on the part of the Commission to incorporate the public interest factors specified in Section 16A(3) into an holistic enquiry concerning the effect upon competition in the relevant market, should the merger be permitted to proceed.

Given the history of South Africa, which is felt in many of the key sections of the Competition Act, it is understandable that the public interest factors would play a significant role in a merger enquiry. The challenges concerning a false positive or negative are, arguably, more extreme in these cases as is the mandated proportionality enquiry, which poses significant challenges to competition regulators.

However, the socio-economic arguments in favor of the system set out in Section 16 of the South African Competition Act are so compelling that their rejection may place the competition enterprise in some deficit

---

12 S. Afr. Competition Comm'n, Draft Guidelines on the assessment of public interest provisions in merger regulation under the Competition Act No. 89 of 1998 (as amended) 9 (2015), *available at* http://www.compcom.co.za/wp-content/uploads/2015/01/Final-Public-Interest-Guidelines-public-version-210115.pdf.

of legitimacy. Recently, in an admittedly broader context, Baker and Salop have drawn attention to the relationship between competition policy and inequality. Manifestly in a country with the worst reported Gini-coefficient in the world, this issue is of pressing importance. In particular, the authors state the following:

> We recognize that implementing this approach in practice for mergers, which we will use as an example, would require undertaking a detailed distributional analysis. The difficulty of determining the downstream effects of price increases on intermediate inputs often would make this type of distributional analysis challenging. Thus, in application, the approach likely would focus primarily on mergers in markets for consumer products. Even in dealing with mergers in markets for final goods, moreover, it would be necessary to formulate rules for making tradeoffs among groups of buyers. Should harms to the poor count more than harms to the middle class? Can gains to the wealthy ever outweigh losses to those less wealthy—for example, if the gains are large and the losses small? If inequality is adopted as an antitrust goal, these will be important issues to debate.[13]

Baker and Salop, of course, are writing within the context of US antitrust law. But, given the implications for the public interest, as set out expressly in the South African Competition Act, this challenge is one which raises a significant possibility for a developing jurisprudence within a country which has disturbing levels of inequality, together with government policy which manifestly has not done enough to deal with this problem.

13 Jonathan B. Baker & Stephen C. Salop, *Antitrust, Competition Policy, and Inequality*, 104 Geo. L.J. 1, 25 (2015), *available at* http://georgetownlawjournal.org/files/2015/04/BakerSalop-AntitrustCompetitionPolicyandInequality2.pdf.

Public Interest, Industrial Policy, and Remedies in Merger Control in India

Samir Gandhi
samir.gandhi@azbpartners.com
Partner, AZB Partners

Abstract

The pharmaceutical industry is a strategically important industry for the Indian government. The government has made it a public policy priority to ensure that pharmaceuticals are provided equitably and at affordable prices. This paper argues that the Competition Commission of India may be using merger remedies in the pharmaceutical sector to further this public policy goal. The paper first provides an historical overview of the merger control regime in India. It then describes India's public policy regarding the pharmaceutical sector. Finally, the paper demonstrates how the Competition Commission of India is using merger remedies in its review of pharmaceutical mergers to ensure that pharmaceuticals remain affordable in India.

I. Introduction

Competition law has only recently been introduced in India. The enforcement of the merger control provisions of the Competition Act, 2002 ("Competition Act") by the Competition Commission of India ("CCI") commenced in June 2011. In this short period of time, the CCI has developed a reputation as an independent and efficient competition authority. The CCI has also demonstrated that it can deal with contentious transactions through the design of effective remedies to address competition concerns. It also has become evident that industrial policy has to date, at least in part, driven the CCI's approach to remedies in mergers and acquisitions that were otherwise likely to result in an appreciable adverse effect on competition. While merger remedies are typically looked at in isolation with respect to resolving the specific competition concerns arising from a given merger transaction, public interest and industrial policy do play an important role. Public policy considerations with respect to merger control remedies are not merely theoretical and academic issues, but are necessary considerations for business and antitrust practitioners in devising appropriate merger control remedies. In recent years, this has been nowhere more apparent than in the pharmaceutical industry in India. The history of the merger control regime and this interplay between the Government of India's ("GoI") long-standing policy to make medicines affordable and widely available and the formulation of remedies in merger control matters will be examined in this paper.

II. Competition Law and Merger Control in India

1. The History of Antitrust and Merger Control in India

Prior to the introduction of the Competition Act, the Monopolies and Restrictive Trade Practices Act, 1969 ("MRTP Act") regulated business activities. This competition regime included a quasi-judicial body for investigating cases of unfair and restrictive trade practices, the Monopolies and Restrictive Trade Practices Commission ("MRTP Commission"). The MRTP Act contained provisions that implicitly dealt with mergers and acquisitions (commonly referred to as "combinations" in present Indian antitrust law). Specifically, Sections 20 to 26 of the MRTP Act dealt with combinations. Notably, these sections were subsequently repealed by the MRTP (Amendment) Act, 1991.

Prior to the amendment, Section 23 of the MRTP Act was the most significant provision with respect to combinations. It mandated that no combination could take place without the sanction and express approval of the Central Government.[1] These sections gave the Central Government significant power to prevent combinations which would lead to the concentration of economic power, and the MRTP Act was framed in a manner that ensured that the jurisdiction of the Central Government over combinations overrode the jurisdiction of the MRTP Commission.[2]

---

1 *See* Aditya Bhattacharjea, *Of Omissions and Commissions: India's Competition Laws*, 45(35) Econ. & Pol. Wkly (2010).

2 Tanaya Sanyal & Sohini Chatterjee, *Combination Control: Strengthening the Regulatory Framework of Competition Law in India*, 5 NUJS L. Rev. 425, (2012).

The liberalization of the Indian economy led to the restructuring of the entire financial system in India. This also led to Indian antitrust policy evolving from an anti-monopoly to a pro-competition approach. Legislation in the form of the Competition Act was enacted to mirror this changed dynamic.[3] This was followed by the creation of an independent competition authority—the CCI).[4]

2. The Merger Control Regime in India

As part of its mandate, the CCI now regulates combinations.[5] Provisions relating to combinations (being mergers, amalgamations, or acquisitions) are set out in Sections 5 and 6 of the Competition Act. These combinations provisions are augmented by the Competition Commission of India (Procedure in regard to the transaction of business relating to combinations) Regulations, 2011 ("Combination Regulations").

The provisions of the Competition Act regulating combinations seek to prohibit combinations that are likely to have an appreciable adverse effect on competition ("AAEC"), prior to any harm/violation actually occurring. Similar to other merger control regimes, the idea is to work *ex ante*. The Competition Act's aim is to prevent combinations, which if consummated, will have an AAEC. This function complements the provisions of the Act that prohibit anticompetitive agreements and cases of abuse of market power that arise *ex post*.

Consistent with the liberalization of the Indian economy, the Competition Act does not require every transaction to be notified. Nonetheless, the regulation of corporate transactions is the key tool of *ex ante* competition regulation and it is necessary to capture transactions of significance that are likely to cause an AAEC (i.e., change in market structures such that their competitive nature is harmed significantly). A failure to do so would likely result in less efficient markets in which enterprises would be less customer-oriented and innovative, even in the absence of contraventions of competition law.[6] Therefore, a balance must be found whereby the formation of entities with significant market power is prevented while still maintaining an open economy that does not unnecessarily interfere in business transactions. This balance is also essential in a developing economy like India, where scarce government resources must be applied with maximum effect and efficiency to ensure positive economic outcomes.

The Competition Act sets out certain asset and turnover thresholds that, if satisfied, will qualify a merger, amalgamation, or acquisition as a "combination." These thresholds are calculated on the basis of assets and turnovers of either the parties (buyer and target enterprise) or groups to which the parties will belong post-combination.[7] Schedule I to the Combination Regulations provides the categories of combinations that are ordinarily not likely to cause an AAEC in India and need not normally be notified with the CCI.[8] Additionally, transactions where the target enterprise (i.e., the enterprise whose shares or assets are being acquired) either has assets of less than INR 2,500 million (approximately USD 40 million) in India, or has a turnover of less than INR 7,500 million (approximately USD 125 million) in India, are currently exempt from the mandatory pre-notification requirements.[9]

---

3 The Competition Act was given Presidential assent in January 2003.

4 The CCI commenced operations in 2003, and enforcement of Sections 3 and 4 of the Competition Act commenced from May 1, 2009.

5 Enforcement of Sections 5 and 6 of the Competition Act commenced on June 1, 2011.

6 Sanyal & Chatterjee, *supra* note 2.

7 *See* Competition Act § 5.

8 Schedule I to the Combinations Regulations sets out 11 circumstances where a combination need not normally be notified.

9 Notification by the Ministry of Corporate Affairs, dated Mar. 4, 2011, read with Corrigendum, dated May 27, 2011.

In the Indian context, it appears that the GoI has found the right balance between regulation and freedom to do business. In particular, the CCI has cleared more than 250 transactions and now is reviewing a significantly increased volume of transactions (almost a 100% increase in notified transactions from 2013-14 (43) to 2014-15 (87)).[10] It has cleared these transactions within the statutory timeframe under the Combination Regulations.

The substantive factors that the CCI is required to consider are in line with those set out in more mature jurisdictions. While the CCI does not typically expressly identify economic theories of harm that may arise from a transaction, the CCI does consider factors such as market shares, barriers to entry, imports, and vertical integration in its analysis.[11] Notably, the Competition Act also provides the CCI the flexibility to consider public policy/interest matters. These factors also include issues relating to economic development and the balancing of benefits of a given merger.[12]

The GoI has also given the CCI the power to require remedies to overcome competition concerns arising from mergers. In particular, Section 31 of the Competition Act enables the CCI to propose modifications (merger remedies) that it believes could effectively eliminate concerns that a merger will have an AAEC.[13] Despite the short history of merger control in India, last year the CCI approved its first two combinations subject to structural "remedies." Notably, the first combination approved subject to remedies related to the pharmaceutical sector. This is perhaps because of the importance of the pharmaceutical sector in ensuring access to medicine in a developing and low-income country like India.

III. India's Public Policy Approach to the Pharmaceuticals Sector

The crafting of policies in sectors involving intellectual property law and competition law is a balancing exercise, as these policies will have to adequately balance the interests of different players who may have opposing interests. Although both disciplines share the same goal of innovation, the means through which they implement it are different. The pharmaceutical sector is a prime example of this tension, and the GoI has the formidable task of ensuring that the right balance is struck.

Although produced by private companies, the GoI has had a long-standing policy to maximize access of affordable medicines to as many Indians as possible. In this context, India's pharmaceutical industry has a unique history. For more than 30 years, India did not recognize pharmaceutical patents.[14] This contributed

10 Nicholas J. Franczyk, *India Competition Law Developments, The Year in Review: June 1, 2014 – May 31, 2015*, Paper Presented at Sixth Annual Chicago Forum on International Antitrust Issues (Jun. 8-9, 2015). Additionally, the CCI received 21 merger filings (for approval) in October 2015, the highest number of filings in a month since 2011. *CCI gets 21 merger filings in October, highest in four years*, The Econ. Times, Nov. 25, 2015, http://articles.economictimes.indiatimes.com/2015-11-25/news/68560794_1_filings-mergers-and-acquisitions-cci-chairman-ashok-chawla.

11 Section 20(4) of the Competition Act sets out what the CCI is to consider in assessing whether a combination is likely to have an AAEC.

12 *See* Competition Act §§ 20(4)(m)-20(4)(n).

13 Subsections 31(4) to 31(9) of the Competition Act provide powers to the CCI including the power to propose modifications (i.e., propose remedies), as well as allow parties to a transaction to submit amendments to the modifications proposed by the CCI.

14 *See* Suhrith Parthasarathy, *Adverse Reaction: India's radical challenge to the global patent regime*, The Caravan, Jun. 1, 2013, http://www.caravanmagazine.in/reportage/adverse-reaction.

to domestic firms becoming very capable at reverse engineering to produce cheap generic medicine.[15] However, after joining the World Trade Organization ("WTO") in 1995, India changed its patent laws. This led to the introduction of significant amendments to the Patents Act, 1970. This new regulatory regime, in place since 2005, includes special protections for both patent holders and generic manufacturers. For example, the law does not recognize patents that only provide for minor changes to existing drugs, a practice known as "evergreening."[16] While these drug reformulations are often used to extend patents elsewhere, they get no protection in India. India also has broad criteria for "compulsory licensing."[17] India's intellectual property rules give the GoI and its agencies the power to compel patent holders to, under certain circumstances, license a patented drug to a generic company.[18]

In keeping with this broad pharmaceutical policy, certain amendments to the Competition Act were proposed in 2012 ("Proposed Amendments"). These were proposed after the Maira Committee suggested that the industry would be better regulated by providing the CCI with more teeth to regulate M&A activity in the pharmaceutical sector as opposed to making amendments to foreign direct investment laws. Some of the Maira Committee's recommendations included introducing public interest criteria for merger clearance.[19] This recommendation would have drawn from the experience in South Africa, for example, the case of Clicks Pharmaceutical Wholesale Ltd and New United Pharmaceutical Distributors, wherein the transaction was also reviewed for its impact on the public interest and when none was found it was cleared. Another recommendation included giving merger approvals on conditions like China has done for six mergers since its newly constituted Anti-Monopoly Law in 2008.[20] The Proposed Amendments ultimately did not become law. However, they demonstrated the GoI's desire to pay particular attention to mergers in the pharmaceutical industry. Reflecting such concerns, the GoI's Foreign Direct Investment policy, although permitting up to 100 percent foreign direct investment in existing and new ventures in the pharmaceutical industry, states that the approval of the Foreign Investment Promotion Board is required for investment in brownfield ventures.[21]

While the Proposed Amendments did not become law, the GoI's consideration of the Maira Committee's recommendations may well have signaled to the CCI the GoI's sensitivity towards the pharmaceutical sector. Arguably, this has meant that the CCI has conducted more rigorous reviews of mergers in the pharmaceutical sector. As a result, this has led to a greater focus on merger remedies in this sector.

---

15 Between 2010 and 2020, the size of the pharmaceutical industry in India is expected to increase from $12 billion to $74 billion. *See Taking pains: Indian patent rules infuriate Big Pharma*, The Economist, Sept. 8, 2012 [hereinafter *Taking pains*].

16 Amy Kazmin, *India: Patents and precedents*, The Fin. Times, May 15, 2013.

17 Parthasarathy, *supra* note 14.

18 *Taking pains*, *supra* note 15.

19 Natasha Nayak, Competition Impediments in the Pharmaceutical Sector in India 25 (2011), *available at* http://circ.in/pdf/Pharmaceuticals_Sector.pdf.

20 *Id.*

21 Press Release, Ministry of Commerce & Indus., FDI Policy in Pharmaceutical Sector (Mar. 13, 2015), *available at* http://pib.nic.in/newsite/PrintRelease.aspx?relid=116994.

IV. Remedies as a Tool to Enforce Public Policy? An Examination of Mergers in the Pharmaceutical Sector

Merger remedies aim to prevent competitive harm while encouraging benefits such as efficiencies, cost reduction, and innovation that are likely to arise from a transaction. Remedies are, by definition, case-specific. Broadly speaking, depending on the competition concerns in question, remedies are either: (i) structural, i.e., some form of structural change in the form of divestitures of business assets or shareholdings to unlink competitors or access and IP-based remedies; or (ii) behavioral, i.e., enabling measures that adjust commercial dealings and/or control outcomes such as the imposition of price caps. While structural remedies are primarily used to restore the balance of competition in the relevant market, behavioral remedies are designed to modify or constrain the behavior of merging firms for a certain period.[22] The CCI's preference is for structural remedies and this approach has been demonstrated in the two, and to date only, clearances the CCI approved subject to remedies, being the Sun Pharma-Ranbaxy[23] and Lafarge-Holcim decisions.[24]

In arriving at these decisions, the CCI appears to have considered several economic principles in designing the remedies. The decisions appear to support the view that the CCI seeks to ensure that the businesses divested are viable competitors.[25]

Sun Pharmaceutical's US$4 billion acquisition of rival drug company, Ranbaxy Laboratories, was the first transaction to be conditionally approved by the CCI after a detailed inquiry. The CCI's approval was conditional on the parties divesting seven active pharmaceutical ingredients ("APIs") within six months, so as to create a "viable, effective, independent and long term competitor."[26]

In its analysis, the CCI defined the relevant product market at the molecular level, i.e., that medicines and formulations based on the same APIs may be considered to constitute a separate relevant product market. The CCI determined that the primary competition concern arising out of the merger was the "possibility of vertical integration between the Parties as the APIs manufactured and sold by one Party could be used as raw material for the formulations produced by the other."[27] Therefore, the CCI opined that the transaction was likely to have an AAEC in India for seven formulations, and accordingly required modifications to

---

22 For a detailed discussion on merger remedies including structural and behavioral remedies, *see* Int'l Competition Network, The Merger Remedies Review Project: Report for the fourth ICN annual conference (2005), *available at* http://www.internationalcompetitionnetwork.org/uploads/library/doc323.pdf.

23 Combination Registration No. C-2014/05/170, approved by way of order dated 5 Dec. 2014 [hereinafter Sun/Ranbaxy Order]. It is relevant to note that the CCI has passed two orders in relation to the Sun-Ranbaxy merger: the first order, dated December 15, 2014, directed the divestiture of seven formulations. In a follow-on order, dated March 17, 2015, the CCI approved Sun and Ranbaxy's identification of a pharmaceutical company, Emcure Pharmaceuticals Limited, as the purchaser of the products divested. Any references in this article to the Sun-Ranbaxy merger are to the first order.

24 The CCI decided and explicitly stated that a divestiture of Lafarge's (i) Jojobera plant in Jharkhand and (ii) the integrated unit at Sonadih in Chhattisgarh would be required to avoid a likely AAEC from arising and the divestiture of these assets would be "most effective" in eliminating competitive concerns. *See* Combination Registration No. C-2014/07/190 approved by way of order dated Mar. 30 2015, ¶ 17.4.

25 In both cases involving structural remedies, the CCI sought to ensure that the businesses divested were viable competitors post-combination. *See id.* ¶ 17.5(ii); Sun/Ranbaxy Order, *supra* note 23, ¶ 39.

26 *Id.* ¶ 39(a).

27 *Id.* ¶ 28.

the transaction. In particular, this involved Sun Pharma divesting two formulations and Ranbaxy divesting five formulations.

Although the CCI had unconditionally approved close to 200 transactions in the first three years of the existence of the Indian merger control regime, and had appeared to be reluctant to exercise its divestiture powers, a major merger in the pharmaceutical industry appears to have compelled it to take action. The text of the Sun/Ranbaxy order does not itself refer to public policy concerns. However, the GoI's medicines policy may have influenced the CCI's desire to ensure healthy competition in the pharmaceutical sector.

The CCI's interventions with respect to the pharmaceutical sector are not limited to interventions through formal merger control remedies. While the Maira Committee's recommendations were not implemented, the sentiments behind the recommendations have been acted upon by the CCI. For example, in Orchid/Hospira,[28] the parties argued that the non-compete clause restricting research, development, and testing by the seller and its promoters was standard industry practice. The Business Transfer Agreement ("BTA") contained non-compete clauses that restricted Orchid and Mr. K. Raghvendra Rao (its promoter) from (among other things) researching, developing, and testing the APIs. Both Orchid and Hospira contended that non-compete clauses were standard in such transactions and were an essential safeguard for Hospira, as Orchid and Mr. K. Raghvendra Rao possessed the experience, technical knowhow, and the ability to establish an independent business that could in effect undermine Hospira's entire investment. However, the CCI asked the parties to justify the non-compete clauses in greater detail, and was of the view that if non-compete clauses were indeed necessary to be incorporated in any agreement, such clauses should be reasonable, particularly in respect of (i) the duration of restraint and (ii) the business activities, geographical area, and persons on whom such restraint is applicable, so as to ensure that such obligations do not cause any AAEC in the relevant market. In response to the CCI's observations, the parties agreed to modify the BTA to: (i) limit the non-compete period to four years in relation to the domestic market in India; and (ii) to allow Orchid to conduct research and development on such new molecules, which would result in the development of APIs that do not currently exist.

Finally, the CCI's sensitivity to the pharmaceutical sector is also demonstrated by a number of cases that arise in the context of cartels. The CCI has aggressively pursued alleged cartels in the pharmaceutical sector, both at the manufacturer[29] and retail levels.[30]

V. Conclusion

The first instance of the CCI requiring structural remedies to overcome competition concerns to clear a corporate transaction related to a transaction in the pharmaceutical sector. This example, in addition to intervention by way of the shortening of non-compete clauses occurring in the pharmaceutical sector, as well as several instances of the CCI cracking down on trade associations in the pharmaceutical sector, indicate the CCI's inclination towards a closer and stricter scrutiny of the pharmaceutical sector.

Despite being an independent statutory authority, recent examples indicate that the CCI is not immune to the GoI's public policy agenda. The CCI's decisions in transactions involving pharmaceutical companies

28 Combination Registration No. C-2014/09/ /9 approved by way of order dated Dec. 21, 2012.

29 Case No. 26/ 2013 – Bio Med Private Limited vs. Union of India & Others.

30 Case No. 30/2011– M/s Peeveear Medical Agencies, Kerala vs. All India Organisation of Chemists and Druggists & Others, and Case No. 41/2011 - M/s Sandhya Drug Agency vs. Assam Drug Dealers Association & Others.

support a view that public policy concerns in India indeed influence merger control decisions and the design of remedies by the CCI. This is illustrated by the first formal remedies involving a transaction in the pharmaceutical sector, a sector that has been a priority for successive governments. Other interventions by the CCI in the pharmaceutical sector have further supported this view. Antitrust practitioners negotiating merger control remedies should take heed of this and also consider the impact of the GoI's public policy objectives when proposing remedies in relation to specific merger transactions that give rise to competition concerns.

The Emergence of Due Process following the Growth of International Antitrust Enforcement

J. Mark Gidley*

mgidley@whitecase.com

Partner and Chair, Global Competition Group, White & Case
Former Acting Assistant Attorney General, US Antitrust Division (1992-93)

Maxwell J. Hyman

maxwell.hyman@whitecase.com

Associate, White & Case

Abstract

The phenomenal spread of antitrust law to developing nations has spurred discussion of whether and how poor countries can benefit from it. Proponents tout antitrust law's potential to foster free and competitive market economies. But one of the most significant contributions of competition law's spread to developing legal systems, as well as in developed countries, is less direct: the international proliferation of antitrust law has been quietly strengthening legal institutions in developing countries and hastening the spread of due process.

Developing nations adopt antitrust law in the hope of stimulating growth. And because fair legal systems attract investment, developing nations are also motivated to ensure that their competition systems respect

---

* The views expressed herein are strictly made for academic purposes, and do not necessarily reflect the views of White & Case LLP, its partners, or its clients. The authors thank Matthew P. Bernstein for his assistance.

property and due process rights. Antitrust cases have already generated landmark due process opinions that reinforce fairness concepts in other areas of law involving government enforcement. As recent litigation in developed and in developing nations concerning fairness in competition proceedings indicates, antitrust law will serve a similar function for developing legal systems.

The spread of antitrust laws to developing nations may contribute to the advancement of due process in other areas of these nations' legal systems and thereby strengthen the rule of law. Institutional-economics theory holds that this subtle benefit promises significant rewards for developing nations.

I. Introduction

Although modern antitrust laws date back as far as 125 years,[1] the last 30 years have witnessed a remarkable spread of competition laws throughout the globe.[2] Many of these antitrust regimes were first enacted in a single decade, the 1990s,[3] and a majority of antitrust newcomers are developing countries.[4] Today, over 125 agencies in over 100 countries enforce competition laws. Developing nations have been attracted to antitrust law's ability to stimulate and enable economic growth when it is informed by sound economic principles.[5]

The phenomenal spread of antitrust law to developing nations has spurred discussion of whether and how poor countries can benefit from it. Proponents tout antitrust law's ability to foster free and competitive markets,[6] or even to reduce levels of perceived corruption among developing populations.[7] But this article suggests that one of the most significant contributions of competition law's spread to developing legal systems is less direct: the international proliferation of antitrust law has the potential to strengthen institu-

---

1 Canada adopted the world's first antitrust law, the Canadian Anti-Combines Act of 1889, and the United States followed with the Sherman Act a year later. *See* Charles Paul Hoffman, *A Reappraisal of the Canadian Anti-Combines Act of 1889*, 39 Queen's L.J. 127, 128 (2013) (describing the Anti-Combines Act as "the world's first modern competition statute").

2 Jerg Gutmann & Stefan Voigt, *Lending a Hand to the Invisible Hand? Assessing the Effects of Newly Enacted Competition Laws*, Presented at the Inaugural Workshop of the Centre for Competition and Regulation 2 (Feb. 8, 2014), http://ssrn.com/abstract=2392780 ("Between 1890 and 1990, only very few countries introduced competition laws . . . . [B]y 2012 this number has increased to 115."); D. Daniel Sokol & Andreas Stephan, *Prioritizing Cartel Enforcement in Developing World Competition Agencies*, *in* Competition Law and Development 137, 13940 (D. Daniel Sokol et al. eds., 2013).

3 *See* Niels Petersen, *Antitrust Law and the Promotion of Democratic and Economic Growth*, 9 J. Competition L. & Econ. 596, 601 (2013) (showing, in Figure 1, the incredible rise in introductions of antitrust law in the 1990s); *id.* at 620–36 (listing dates in which states enacted antitrust laws, many occurring in the 1990s); Abbott B. Lipsky, Jr., *The Global Antitrust Explosion: Safeguarding Trade and Commerce or Runaway Regulation?*, 26 Fletcher F. World Aff. 59, 60–61 (2002) ("Until 1990, perhaps only a half-dozen other developed nations had functional antitrust regimes."); Mark R.A. Palim, *The Worldwide Growth of Competition Law: An Empirical Analysis*, 43 Antitrust Bull. 105, 109 (1998) (noting that, at the end of 1996, 61% of countries with antitrust regimes enacted competition law after 1990, and 79% of them passed the law during or after 1980).

4 Diane R. Hazel, *Competition in Context: The Limitations of Using Competition Law as a Vehicle for Social Policy in the Developing World*, 37 Hous. J. Int'l L. 275, 276 n.1 (2015) (collecting sources).

5 For example, the newly enacted Philippine Competition Act was intended to increase internal and foreign investment. *See Mabini Dialogue Focuses on Philippine Competition Law*, Foreign Ser. Inst. (Oct. 6, 2015, 12:47 A.M.), http://www.fsi.gov.ph/mabini-dialogue-focuses-on-philippine-competition-law/ (summarizing remarks of Geronimo L. Sy, Assistant Secretary of the Philippines Office for Competition, stating that the Act "significantly supports the Philippine government's economic agenda of achieving inclusive growth").

6 Some studies suggest that introduction of sound competition law principles results in notable positive economic effects in developing nations. For example, some studies show that competition law adoption may free up imports needed by developing nations lacking the means to produce certain goods on their own; it can increase the amount of internal investment by as much as four percentage points; and it has the potential to aid the free market in efficiently allocating resources. *See* Gutmann & Voigt, *supra* note 2, at 16 ("[I]ntroduction of competition legislation is followed by increases in overall investment between three and four percentage points."); *see also* Chadwick Teo, Trade Ministry of Trade & Indus. (Sing.), *Competition Policy and Economic Growth*, Paper Presented at the ASEAN Conference on Fair Competition Law and Policy in the ASEAN Free Trade Area 4-5 (Mar. 4-8, 2003), https://www.jftc.go.jp/eacpf/04/singapore_p.pdf (explaining particular benefits of sound competition law for developing nations). Indeed, one study concluded that an "antitrust institution that exists for ten years increases the GDP per capita by 2.6 percent." *See* Petersen, *supra* note 3, at 19. Of course, cross-country comparisons are difficult, and some research has come to contrary conclusions, as discussed below.

7 *See* Gutmann & Voigt, *supra* note 2, at 16.

tions in developing countries and hasten the spread of due process. Viewed from the perspective of institutional economics—a theory associated with the scholarship of Douglass North and Frank Cross—this subtle benefit promises significant rewards for developing nations.[8] Part I demonstrates that success in closing the gap between poor and rich nations does not depend upon geographic location, better distribution of natural resources, or trade flows. Rather, the presence of sound legal institutions is key.[9]

The global spread of antitrust law has the potential to strengthen developing legal institutions for two reasons.

First, as shown in subpart II.A, there is an active movement to ensure that antitrust laws and procedures respect fundamental due process rights. A significant focus of this effort is on motivating developing nations to enact sufficient procedural safeguards. The arguments for these protections are based in sound economics. Firms are more likely to invest in economies that employ fair rules, that have legal constitutions that protect due process rights, and that respect private property. Several developing nations have acted upon these economic incentives and have introduced due process protections into their competition regimes.

And second, subpart II.B argues that antitrust litigation pioneering fairness concepts may spread to other legal institutions in the country. As markets globalize, developing nations will pursue antitrust enforcement actions against sophisticated parties with the resources and will to advocate for fair proceedings. Recent judicial opinions from the United States, European states, and Australia demonstrate that, when those countries' judicial supervision has been effectively triggered, antitrust cases give rise to developments in fundamental rights such as privacy and due process that apply outside the antitrust context. When legal institutions are in place to protect property rights and due process, the spread of antitrust laws and the exercise of enforcement powers may spread due process protections to other areas of the country's legal system and, thereby, strengthen the rule of law.

This article takes the long-term optimistic view of the effect that antitrust law's spread to the developing world will have on the advancement of due process rights. But it also notes that several established competition regimes are rife with procedural shortcomings that render these systems inadequate to protect rights of the accused. And the trend of ever-rising fines and criminal sanctions demonstrates the growing need to address these shortcomings.[10]

In their pursuit of economic growth through sound competition law, most antitrust newcomers have adopted regimes that resemble those of the United States or European Union.[11] However, adopting substantive antitrust enforcement regimes modeled after the American or European systems is not in and of itself a sufficient guarantee of procedural due process protections. Even these far more developed competition systems contain lamentable due process failures. Inadequate procedural protections undermine the strength of any antitrust institution and can threaten to counteract the economic benefits that nations hope to achieve through competition law. Part III shows that, although strong legal institutions contribute

8 *See generally* Frank B. Cross, *Law and Economic Growth*, 80 Tex. L. Rev. 1738 (2002); Douglass C. North, Institutions, Institutional Change and Economic Progress 16 (1990).

9 *See* Part I, *infra* (discussing institutional-economics theory).

10 *See* Christopher B. Hockett, *Antitrust and Due Process*, 28 Antitrust 1, 3 (2014) ("Penalties for competition infractions have also increased dramatically. . . . Jurisdictions outside the U.S. and EU are following the upward trend in penalties for competition violations, with India assessing a $1.1 billion fine in 2012 against a cement cartel (albeit a domestic one), and Brazil, Japan, Korea, South Africa, Taiwan, and Turkey each assessing fines in excess of $100 million on individual cartels in 2013, most of which set new records.").

11 *See* Maher M. Dabbah, *Competition Law and Policy in Developing Countries: A Critical Assessment of the Challenges to Establishing an Effective Competition Law Regime*, 33 World Competition 457, 461 (2010) (noting that "the vast majority" of new competition laws enacted by developing nations are modelled on "competition rules and standards" designed by UNCTAD or on the EU or US laws).

to economic growth, weak institutions hamper economic growth.[12] Indeed, nations that fail to lay a strong institutional foundation for economic growth are often overtaken by those that do.

Whether antitrust law's global spread will positively impact economic growth and development depends on a number of factors. Antitrust laws and enforcement policy must be based on sound economics; antitrust law has the potential to damage a nation's economic growth and global competitiveness if it is written or interpreted improperly. The agencies that enforce competition law must be competent, well-funded, and free of parochialism, cronyism, and nationalism.[13] And the antitrust adjudicator must be independent from the national competition authority, free from corruption, and must possess tools for effective judicial review and fact-finding.[14] Accused should have notice of charges, access to the evidence, and the ability to summon witnesses and to cross-examine government witnesses.

This article will highlight some contemporary due process issues and how these deficiencies impede economic growth, bearing in mind that a sound competition regime may take years to form; after all, the United States' antitrust laws have developed over a hundred of years of litigation and gray areas still remain. The article will then offer some suggestions for reform. The Appendix provides a list of key due process rights that must be protected in antitrust enforcement regimes.

II. Institutional Economics: Due Process and Respect for Property Rights

The problem of wealth disparities between poor and rich countries has long perplexed economists. Are human-capital issues like education and training the issue? Is wealth mostly a function of a country's access to foreign markets? Or do endowments, such as a country's natural resources, make the difference? And what role does law play? Two economic models, neoclassical economics and institutional economics, have attempted to provide answers.

The neoclassical economics model predicts that developing nations, which are often labor-rich, will grow faster than developed nations, which are capital-rich but face diminishing marginal returns.[15] Neoclassical

---

12 Cross, *supra* note 8, at 1739 ("It is now generally recognized that government institutions and the law are relevant to increasing economic growth.").

13 *See* Hockett, *supra* note 10, at 4 ("[T]here may be some jurisdictions in which competition law is . . . invoked as a means to pursue other goals—such as protecting domestic industries, pursuing national industrial policies, or advancing perceived national security interests."); Eleanor M. Fox & Michael J. Trebilcock, *The Design of Competition Law Institutions and the Global Convergence of Process Norms: The GAL Competition Project* 16 (N.Y.U. L. & Econ. Working Papers, Paper 304, 2012), http://lsr.nellco.org/nyu_lewp/304?utm_source=lsr.nellco.org%2Fnyu_lewp%2F304&utm_medium=PDF&utm_campaign=PDFCoverPages ("Shortfalls in [competition agency] expertise are especially likely in younger and resource-starved jurisdictions. . . . Some jurisdictions suffer from lack of reasoned decision-making, lack of publication of decisions, and lack of independence from political interference at some or all stages—investigative, enforcement, and adjudicative.").

14 William E. Kovacic, *Getting Started: Creating New Competition Policy Institutions in Transition Economies*, 23 Brook. J. Int'l L. 403, 420-21 (1997) ("Some judicial systems are deeply infected with corruption, and outcomes in litigated disputes often hinge on the payment of bribes to judges and court administrators.").

15 *See* Matthew A. Cole & Eric Neumayer, *The Pitfalls of Convergence Analysis: Is the Income Gap Really Widening?* 2 (LSE Research Online Working Paper, 2003), http://eprints.lse.ac.uk/archive/00000603 (discussing the neoclassical model's assumptions); Stephen Knack & Phillip Keefer, *Why Don't Poor Countries Catch Up? A Cross-National Test of an Institutional Explanation*, 35 Econ. Inquiry 590, 590-91 (1997) ("Since 1952 scholars have advanced the hypothesis that poorer countries should grow faster than richer ones. Some have derived this hypothesis from the assumption of diminishing returns to physical capital, which should cause more advanced countries to grow more slowly than less advanced countries").

economics hypothesizes that capital will flow from rich to poor countries through a series of mutually beneficial transactions and that the natural force of the "invisible hand" will eventually force worldwide growth rates to equalize.[16] From the neoclassical perspective, the wealth gap is only temporary and may be narrowed with more trade; laws are less important because the economy "will correct initially incorrect models, punish deviant behavior, and lead surviving players to the correct models."[17]

Unfortunately, "[g]reat and persistent disparities in wealth remain, and countries have often shown a divergence . . . of economic welfare."[18] Another camp of economists devised the institutional-economics model in response. "The fundamental theory of institutional economics is straightforward. It begins with the assumption that individuals will invest for economic growth when they can capture the returns from their investments. . . . To achieve optimality requires the existence of '[p]erfectly specified and costlessly enforced property rights.'"[19] Institutional economics accepts the neoclassical model's premise that people will invest when doing so is in their interest,[20] but recognizes that, "in the real world . . . carrying out a transaction is associated with costs" that get in the way of optimally efficient exchanges.[21] Transaction costs, generally understood as costs actually or potentially incurred in achieving the transaction,[22] can arise from various sources including distrust, information deficits, the absence of the rule of law, and, especially, uncertainty.[23]

Because transaction costs are inherent, optimally efficient conditions often can only be achieved with the help of *institutions*—broadly defined "as a set of humanly devised behavioral rules that govern and shape the interactions of human beings . . . by helping them to form expectations of what other people will do."[24] It is the protection of property rights through institutions that has led to investment and economic growth. "The 'establishment of secure and stable property rights' was a 'key element in the rise of the West and the onset of modern economic growth.'"[25]

---

16 Cross, *supra* note 8, at 1740 n.9 (citing Michael J. Trebilcock, *What Makes Poor Countries Poor? The Role of Institutional Capital in Economic Development*, *in* The Law and Economics of Development 16 (Edgrado Buscaglia, William Ratliff & Robert Cooter eds., 1997)) (noting that the neoclassical theory predicts that "levels of economic development should steadily converge among nations, ultimately equalizing wealth, at least roughly").

17 North, *supra* note 8, at 16. *See also* Werner Lachmann, *The Development Dimension of Competition Law and Policy* 8 (UNCTAD Ser. on Issues in Competition L. & Pol'y, 1999), http://unctad.org/en/Docs/poitcdclpm9.en.pdf ("Most developing countries operate inside a production possibility curve which is backward in terms of technology. Since technical innovation in the developed nations is pushing the technological frontier outward at a rapid rate, the gap with developing countries is widening over time.").

18 Cross, *supra* note 8, at 1741 (alteration in original). *See also* Knack & Keefer, *supra* note 15, at 590 (noting "the persistence, and even growth, of the gap between the world's rich and poor nations").

19 Cross, *supra* note 8, at 1741. *See also id.* at 1742 ("Another Nobel laureate, Mancur Olson, has identified 'the conditions necessary for economic success' as including 'secure and well-defined rights for all to private property and impartial enforcement of contracts.'")

20 *Id.* at 1741.

21 Frank Bickenbach, Lars Kumkar & Rüdiger Soltwedel, *The New Institutional Economics of Antitrust and Regulation* 2 (Kiel Inst. World Econ. Working Paper No. 961, 1999), http://ssrn.com/abstract=315742.

22 *See* Ronald H. Coase, *The Nature of the Firm*, 4 Economica 386, 390-91 (1937) (introducing the concept of transaction costs into institutional-economics theory).

23 *See* Oliver E. Williamson, *Transaction-Cost Economics: The Governance of Contractual Relations*, 22 J.L. & Econ. 233, 239, 252-54 (1979) (listing "uncertainty" as among the "critical dimensions for characterizing transactions," and observing that uncertainty causes firms to seek a governance structure or to withdraw from the market through a process of vertical integration).

24 Dani Rodrik, *Institutions for High-quality Growth: What They are and How to Acquire Them* 2 (Nat'l Bureau of Econ. Research, Working Paper 7540, 2000); *see also* Cross, *supra* note 8, at 1741 ("Throughout human history, 'growth has been more exceptional than stagnation or decline,' which suggests that the circumstances enabling growth are not inevitable or natural but require thought and effort." (footnote omitted) (quoting North, *supra* note 8, at 7)).

25 Cross, *supra* note 8, at 1742. *See also id.* ("North's tour de force through history begins in the ancient world but keys on the Industrial Revolution . . . . England and the Netherlands surpassed France and Spain during the seventeenth century, in large part because of the effective recognition of property rights.").

Institutions take several forms, including an independent judiciary and formal legal rights such as the rights to property and to due process of law.[26] Institutional economists theorize that, "institutional capital may be a more important determinant of economic development than financial capital, physical capital, human capital, or technological capital."[27] And nations that do not lay strong institutional groundworks ahead of time cannot take full advantage of opportunities for economic growth when they arise.[28] Cross notes:

> The World Bank has embarked upon a major research program on the importance of the rule of law, including a private sector survey of over 3800 enterprises in 73 countries. They produced a general government credibility indicator for variables such as political instability, the security of persons and property, the predictability of judicial enforcement, and corruption. When the credibility indicator was disaggregated into its components, the most robust predictor of growth was the predictability of judicial enforcement, which was significant in every regression. The rule of law appears to be particularly important to entrepreneurial enterprises.[29]

Data support the institutional-economics theory that high-quality legal institutions are the most important determinant of economic growth and demonstrate the theory's particular relevance for developing nations. After examining three samples of 64, 79, and 137 nations, one study found that "the quality of institutions trump[ed]" other determinants of economic growth, including exposure to foreign trade and geographical location (which is correlated with natural resources and agricultural productivity).[30] The study established that high-quality institutions are "the only positive and significant determinant of income levels."[31] Other research found "that when good institutions are absent," the wealth gap between rich and poor nations widens, and that "[i]n extreme cases, poor countries with institutions that are excessively deficient are found to grow more slowly than wealthy countries, even when other factors, including investments in human and physical capital, are taken into account."[32] That study concluded that the "poor getting poorer" phenomenon "appears to be a direct consequence of the institutional environment in those countries."[33]

The economic power of high-quality institutions is well-established; the challenge is in identifying which institutional qualities have positive effects on development. One such quality, which is statistically

---

26 *See* Christopher Clague, *Introduction* to Institutions and Economic Development: Growth and Governance in Less-Developed and Post-Socialist Countries 1 (Christopher Clague ed., 1997) (discussing the broad definition of "institution"); Rodrik, *supra* note 24, at 5 (listing "regulatory institutions" as important parts of an ideal institutional mix).

27 Cross, *supra* note 8, at 1741 (quoting Michael J. Trebilcock, *What Makes Poor Countries Poor? The Role of Institutional Capital in Economic Development*, *in* The Law and Economics of Development 16 (Edgrado Buscaglia, William Ratliff & Robret Cooter eds., 1997)).

28 *See* Lachmann, *supra* note 17, at v ("Historical experience, including in countries which are now developed and in newly industrialized countries, has shown that the comparative advantages of today are mostly the results of the successful governmental intervention of yesterday, and that infant industry policies can increase efficiency and competitiveness."); Cross, *supra* note 8, at 1742 (summarizing Douglass North's historical analysis, which proved that the most successful economies implemented strong institutions prior to the onset of growth).

29 Cross, *supra* note 8, at 1768-69.

30 Dani Rodrik, Arvind Subramaniam & Francesco Trebbi, *Institutions Rule: The Primacy of Institutions over Geography and Integration in Economic Development*, 9 J. Econ. Growth 131, 135 (2004). A 1995 study of Ghana's transition from "communal" to "individual" property rights revealed a marked increase in investment activity, in part due to reduced fears of expropriation. *See* Timothy Besley, *Property Rights and Investment Incentives: Theory and Evidence from Ghana*, 103 J. Pol. Econ. 903, 936 (1995) ("The findings . . . were quite supportive of the idea that better land rights facilitate investment.").

31 Dani Rodrik & Arvind Subramanian, *The Primacy of Institutions (and what this does and does not mean)*, Fin. & Dev., June 2003, at 31, *available at* https://www.imf.org/external/pubs/ft/fandd/2003/06/pdf/rodrik.pdf.

32 Knack & Keefer, *supra* note 15, at 591.

33 *Id.*

significant, is fairness.[34] Fair and consistent rules and outcomes incentivize investment by permitting firms to act according to a set of normal expectations.[35] Indeed, because "the perceived fairness of social rules and institutions can increase or decrease welfare in ways that cannot be replicated through the redistribution of money,"[36] the most successful legal institutions feature protections for the rule of law,[37] such as "independent judiciaries, . . . well-defined administrative procedures, [and] transparent decision making."[38] On the other hand, arbitrary decisions and expropriations are hallmarks of low-quality institutions that create insecurity and transaction costs.[39]

Although the concept of "due process" has many manifestations, including the right to a hearing before a neutral adjudicator and the right to confrontation, its essential purpose is to guarantee fair and consistent treatment. Therefore, while due process protections are an end in and of themselves, they are also a common quality of strong institutions and are vitally important to achieving stable economic growth. The economic underpinnings of particular due process protections are discussed in further detail in Part III.

III. Strengthening Legal Institutions through Creation of Due Process Standards for Antitrust Enforcement

A movement led by organizations of national antitrust agencies to improve due process protections in antitrust law has followed in the wake of the global wave of antitrust enforcement.[40] The movement argues that fair antitrust laws and procedures create more predicable outcomes and, therefore, make an economy more attractive to investment.[41] There is evidence that foreign investors are attracted to stable

---

34 Rodrik, *supra* note 24, at 12 ("Healthy societies have a range of institutions that make . . . colossal coordination failures less likely. The rule of law [and] a high-quality judiciary . . . are examples of such institutions. What makes these arrangements function as institutions of conflict management is that they entail a double 'commitment technology': they warn the potential 'winners' of social conflict that their gains will be limited, and assure the 'losers' that they will not be expropriated. They tend to increase the incentives for social groups to cooperate by reducing the payoff to socially uncooperative strategies.").

35 *Id.*

36 Lee Anne Fennell & Richard H. McAdams, *Fairness in Law and Economics: Introduction* 3 (Coase-Sandor Inst. L. & Econ., Working Paper No. 704 (2d Series), 2014), http://chicagounbound.uchicago.edu/cgi/viewcontent.cgi?article=1935&context=public_law_and_legal_theory. *See also* Bickenbach et al., *supra* note 21, at 10 ("Antitrust and regulation may add confidence and the expectation of being treated fairly and may thus help contain transaction costs more effectively than private agreements on the basis of contract law and court enforcement alone.").

37 *See* Rodrik, *supra* note 24, at 2 ("A clearly delineated system of property rights, a regulatory apparatus curbing the worst forms of fraud, anti-competitive behavior, and moral hazard, . . . *the rule of law* and clean government—these are social arrangements that economists usually take for granted, but which are conspicuous by their absence in poor countries." (emphasis added)).

38 Knack & Keefer, *supra* note 15, at 591.

39 *See id.* at 593-94 (listing, as a measure of institutional quality, the rule of law and constraints on executive power). *See also id.* at 594 ("Arbitrary administrative decisions undermine the legal bases upon which the security of property and contractual rights in a country rests.").

40 Paul O'Brien, Krisztian Katona & Randolph Tritell, *Procedural Fairness in Competition Investigations: U.S. FTC Practice and Recent Guidance from the International Competition Network*, CPI Antitrust Chron., July 2015, at 7 ("Procedural fairness is a necessary and beneficial ingredient of effective competition enforcement. . . . Regardless of the chosen enforcement framework, there are specific investigative practices that can promote transparency and better outcomes."); U.N. Conf. on Trade & Dev [UNCTAD], Model Law on Competition 69 (2010), *available at* http://unctad.org/en/Docs/tdrbpconf7d8_en.pdf ("[I]t is indispensable . . . that in the process of investigation, the general principles and rules of due process of law . . . be duly observed.").

41 Ass'n of Se. Asian Nations [ASEAN], ASEAN Regional Guidelines on Competition Policy 1 (2010), www.asean.org/storage/images/2012/publications/ASEAN%20Regional%20Guidelines%20on%20Competition%20Policy.pdf (establishing guidelines for competition policy "to help in the process of building stronger economic integration in the region" and stressing that "[b]usinesses engaged in the same or similar lines of activity should be subject to the same set of legal principles and standards to ensure fairness, equality, transparency, consistency and non-discriminatory treatment under the law"); Int'l Competition Network [ICN], ICN Guidance on Investigative Process 1 (2015), http://www.internationalcompetitionnetwork.org/uploads/library/doc1028.pdf ("Effective enforcement tools, procedural safeguards, and consistency

regulatory frameworks that employ due process protections reflecting international norms.[42] These safeguards ensure that decisions are founded on law, rather than other considerations, and help to guarantee predictable outcomes. Foreign investment, therefore, is encouraged when a country's antitrust enforcement regime provides procedural protections during investigations and effective judicial review.[43] Several developing countries, persuaded by these arguments, have enacted safeguards for fair and transparent proceedings.

The first cases challenging antitrust enforcement actions are now beginning to make their way through the domestic courts of these developing countries. As new competition agencies increase their enforcement efforts, as penalties rise, as sophisticated parties enter emerging markets and confront enforcement proceedings, and as defense counsel challenge the status quo, some disputes will inevitably hinge on these due process protections. Although these disputes will arise in "antitrust" cases, their impact will not be so limited. Published legal opinions stemming from antitrust cases that advance fundamental rights—especially if those rulings rest on constitutional foundations—may be invoked in myriad other contexts. When the right of privacy against searches is protected in competition cases, that precedent can protect individuals in their own homes. In this way, the due process safeguards developing nations put in place in order to attract foreign investment will eventually help to strengthen other institutions. Even in some countries that have yet to enact sufficient due process protections into their antitrust regimes, parties have cited the movement toward due process to press for more adequate protections.[44] Because quality institutions are the most important determinant of long-term economic growth,[45] this broader benefit of antitrust law's spread to the developing world should be recognized as one of the most important.

1. The Spread of Antitrust Enforcement Has the Potential to Advance Due Process in Developing Nations

Although significant reform is still needed to ensure that competition proceedings respect the fundamental principle of fairness, efforts to achieve progress on due process protections have met some success. Developing nations, responding to the economic incentives of fair and substantively sound antitrust law,

---

of process and procedures within an agency contribute to efficient, effective, accurate and predictable enforcement by competition agencies. The credibility of a competition agency and, more broadly, of the overall mission of competition enforcement are closely tied to the integrity of the agency's investigative process"); ICN, Competition Agency Transparency Practices 10 (2013), http://www.internationalcompetitionnetwork.org/uploads/library/doc892.pdf ("[R]espondents recognized a public interest and value in publishing specific agency decisions . . . as a central tool to provide transparency about the agency's likely enforcement approach to similar facts and more generally"); ICN, Investigative Process Project Issues Paper and Mandate 1 (2012), http://www.internationalcompetitionnetwork.org/uploads/library/doc799.pdf (noting that effective antitrust enforcement relies on "the integrity of the process of conducting competition investigations and how this is perceived") [hereinafter ICN, Investigative Process Project]; Org. Econ. Co-operation Dev. [OECD], Procedural Fairness and Transparency Key Points 23 (2012), http://www.oecd.org/competition/mergers/50235955.pdf ("[T]ransparency and fairness are not only essential requirements for the parties involved in a competition proceeding, but are also a key part of efficient and effective case management by the competition authority").

42 *See* Working Grp. on the Relationship between Trade and Inv., *Communication from the European Community and its Member States*, WTO Doc. WT/WGTI/W/63 ¶ 11 (Nov. 12, 1998) ("A stable framework of competition rules will attract foreign investment by strengthening the regulatory fabric of the economy and confidence in the stability of policy."). *See also* Daniel A. Crane, *Substance, Procedure, and Institutions in the International Harmonization of Competition Policy*, 10 Chi. J. Int'l L. 143, 146-47 (2009) (explaining the transaction costs that inconsistent procedural requirements impose).

43 *See* Working Grp., *supra* note 42, ¶ 11.

44 *See infra* notes 94–96 and accompanying text (discussing the Botswana *Panel Beaters* and *Sugar Beans* cases).

45 *See supra* notes 30-34 and accompanying text (reviewing the institutional-economics theory and its empirical support).

have enacted procedural safeguards into their competition law systems.[46] Competition agencies have a natural, institutional self-interest in due process because due process protections provide legitimacy to the agency's actions.[47] As former Chairman of the US Federal Trade Commission William Kovacic has written, "An additional dimension of process-oriented institution building is to establish agency policies that ensure that agency employees execute their responsibilities honorably and that the agency is perceived externally as a firm but fair champion of the nation's competition laws."[48] Consequently, fairness is "a necessary and beneficial ingredient of effective competition enforcement" that "can promote transparency and better outcomes."[49]

The following section reviews the progress that countries have made through international and regional organizations to promote due process in antitrust proceedings. It then showcases some developing nations that have enacted fairness guarantees into their competition regimes in an attempt to stimulate investment and economic growth.

a. Efforts of International and Regional Organizations to Advance Due Process

In 2010, ASEAN published its *Regional Guidelines on Competition Policy*, which noted that a "[s]ound institutional framework and due process are fundamental in ensuring the effective application of competition law"[50] and that "[b]usinesses engaged in the same or similar lines of activity should be subject to the same set of legal principles and standards to ensure fairness, equality, transparency, consistency and non-discriminatory treatment under the law."[51] It prodded member states to consider common competition related provisions "that effectively address anti-competitive behaviours, [sic] based on principles of transparency [and] due process."[52] Along these lines, it set forth a detailed eight-part framework for fair and transparent proceedings,[53] and required ASEAN member states to enact a compliant competition law "by 2015."[54] The *Regional Guidelines* are addressed to the 10 ASEAN member states: Brunei Darussalam, Cambodia, Indonesia, Laos, Malaysia, Myanmar, the Philippines, Singapore, Thailand, and Vietnam. In December 2015, the Asian Competition Forum held an annual conference devoted to further improving due process and transparency in Asian competition law systems.[55]

46 Other explanations for the trend towards due process include the obvious efficiency of borrowing from some aspects of an already highly evolved system instead of developing competition policy from the ground up. Some authors also argue that the spread of competition law is due in large part to pressure applied by international organizations. See, e.g., Thomas K. Cheng, Convergence and Its Discontents: A Reconsideration of the Merits of Convergence of Global Competition Law, 12 Chi. J. Int'l Law 433, 460 (2012).

47 *See* Clifford Chance, *Early experiences of the new COMESA Competition Regime*, Briefing Note, July 2013, at 1, http://www.cliffordchance.com/briefings/2013/07/early_experiencesofthenewcomesacompetitio.html (Alastair Mordaunt, Director and Chief Executive Officer of the Common Market for Eastern and Southern Africa's Competition Commission, suggested that, "there is a need for us as a new regional regulator to be accepted, and the only way you can be accepted is to be consistent, to be transparent and to have due process."); Fox & Trebilcock, *supra* note 13, at 74 ("[M]ost [competition agencies] seem to aspire to a higher standard, and, in any event, increasing transparency of shortfalls through global competition journalism, published peer reviews, and word-of-mouth may produce gentle pressure to address the weaknesses.").

48 Kovacic, *supra* note 14, at 435.

49 O'Brien, Katona & Tritell, *supra* note 40, at 7.

50 ASEAN, *supra* note 41, at 34.

51 *Id.* at 6.

52 *Id.* at 44.

53 *Id.* at 35-37.

54 *Id.* at 1.

55 *See* Conference Invitation, Asian Competition Forum 11th Annual Conference, Asian Competition Forum, http://www.asiancompetitionforum.org/conference-invitation.html (last visited Jan. 13, 2016).

Other international organizations have also been steadily pressing for accountability and due process in competition proceedings. In 2010, the Organisation for Economic Co-operation and Development's ("OECD") Competition Committee held roundtable discussions with more than 30 participating members on procedural fairness and due process rights in competition proceedings. These discussions culminated in published OECD guidelines entitled *Procedural Fairness and Transparency: Key Points*.[56] These OECD guidelines noted several essential features of fair competition proceedings, including: (1) transparency in the decision-making process; (2) accessible and timely notice of charges; (3) opportunities for parties to respond, to present evidence, and to confer with agency officials;[57] (4) consideration of exculpatory evidence by the decision-maker; (5) a defined duration for investigations; and (6) publication of decisions.[58]

In 2012, the International Competition Network ("ICN"), which is composed of representatives from nearly every competition authority in existence,[59] established a working group dedicated to investigative processes employed by competition regimes.[60] This ICN working group noted that, "the credibility of competition agencies and of the general mission of competition enforcement is linked to the integrity of the process of conducting competition investigations and how this is perceived."[61] In 2013, the ICN released a guide entitled *Competition Agency Transparency Practices*.[62] And in 2015, it issued the *Guidance on Investigative Processes* ("*Guidance*").[63] The *Guidance* noted that, "there is broad consensus among ICN members regarding the importance of transparency, engagement and protection of confidential information within different legal and institutional frameworks that impact the choice of investigative process and how these fundamental procedural fairness principles are implemented."[64] In response to surveys on the subject, the *Guidance* identified principles of fair antitrust enforcement that were common among the member competition authorities, including: (1) defining the government's investigatory powers in a legal framework with clear substantive and procedural requirements; (2) refraining from using investigatory tools to impose burdens on parties; (3) providing transparent legal standards and policies governing enforcement; (4) disclosing charges and their bases; (5) providing opportunities to present rebuttal evidence and arguments; (6) and respecting applicable legal privileges.[65]

---

56 OECD, Procedural Fairness and Transparency: Key Points (2012), http://www.oecd.org/competition/mergers/50235955.pdf [hereinafter OECD, Procedural Fairness].

57 The opportunity to meet with agency staff is not enough; the meeting must serve as an opportunity for meaningful dialogue between the government and the party. Unfortunately, practitioners observe that meetings with government officials in antitrust investigations around the globe often are not satisfactory or meaningful. *See* Hockett, *supra* note 10 at 4 (summarizing a survey of nearly 100 attorneys "conducted on transparency and due process" safeguards: "55 percent stated that the meetings [with government officials] were either untimely or not meaningful, or both"; additionally, 41 percent responded that "they were not given a meaningful opportunity to challenge the evidence against them or to cross-examine witnesses during the agency process").

58 *Id.* at 9-21.

59 Alden F. Abbott, *Competition Policy and Its Convergence as Key Drivers of Economic Development*, 28 Miss. C. L. Rev. 37, 46 (2008) (citing Sheridan Scott, Comm'r of Competition, Competition Bureau (Canada), Remarks at the 7th Annual ICN Conference 3 (Apr. 14, 2008)).

60 ICN, Investigative Process Project, *supra* note 41, at 1.

61 *Id.*

62 ICN, Competition Agency Transparency Practices (2013), http://www.internationalcompetitionnetwork.org/uploads/library/doc892.pdf.

63 ICN, ICN Guidance on Investigative Process (2015), http://www.internationalcompetitionnetwork.org/uploads/library/doc1028.pdf.

64 *Id.* at 1.

65 *Id.* at 2-7.

b. Developing Nations Implementing Antitrust Due Process Protections

Developing nations eager to spur economic growth and to attract foreign investment are responding to the economic incentives of establishing fair procedures that mirror international norms, and several have imported due process measures into their antitrust regimes.

The Philippines enacted its first comprehensive antitrust regime, the Philippine Competition Act,[66] in July 2015. It is reported that economic considerations motivated the Philippines to incorporate due process safeguards into its competition law and, in fact, that these protections substantially facilitated negotiation of a fair trade agreement with the European Union.[67] The Philippine Competition Act provides that the Philippine Competition Commission, after receiving a complaint or making a preliminary finding of anticompetitive activity, may[68] issue a "show cause order" detailing the "business conduct complained of" and a summary of the evidence underlying the order.[69] The party under scrutiny then has an opportunity to respond to the show cause order.[70] The Act mandates "due notice and hearing" before the Philippine Competition Commission imposes any penalties,[71] and requires that the Commission publish its final decisions and rulings online for public review.[72]

When Botswana's Competition Act[73] entered into force in 2011, one of its primary objectives was to "provide a transparent, predictable and reliable investment environment to both domestic and foreign investors."[74] The Act created the independent Botswana Competition Authority and Botswana Competition Commission, and established certain due process protections. The Botswana Competition Authority is the primary antitrust enforcer and possesses the power to police and prosecute allegedly anticompetitive activities. The Botswana Competition Commission is an administrative body that both adjudicates cases and provides the Botswana Competition Authority with policy direction and administrative supervision, including on hiring matters.

---

66 An Act Providing for a National Competition Policy Prohibiting Anti-Competitive Agreements, Abuse of Dominant Position and Anti-competitive Mergers and Acquisitions, Establishing the Philippine Competition Commission and Appropriating Funds Therefor, Rep. Act. No. 10667, *available at* http://www.gov.ph/2015/07/21/republic-act-no-10667/ [hereinafter Philippine Competition Act].

67 *See* Richmond S. Mercurio, *Competition Act boosts bid for free trade deal with EU*, PHIL. STAR, Sept. 12, 2015, http://www.philstar.com/business/2015/09/12/1498653/competition-act-boosts-bid-free-trade-deal-eu (reporting that enactment of the Philippine Competition Act's "provisions on due process [and] procedural fairness" enabled negotiation of a free-trade agreement with the European Union); *see also* Phil. News Agency, *Competition Act to boost Philippine competitiveness, says NEDA chief*, INTERAKSYON, July 1, 2015, http://www.interaksyon.com/business/113419/competition-bill-to-improve-ph-footing-in-global-economy----neda (reporting that, according to the Director-General of the Philippines' National Economic and Development Authority, the Philippine Competition Act was enacted "to improve the country's business climate").

68 The Philippine Competition Act conditions the issuance of a show cause order on the Commission's discretionary determination that the order would not harm the "interest of the public." *See* Philippine Competition Act § 37(b).

69 *Id.*

70 *Id.*

71 *Id.* §§ 12 (d), 29 (a), 31 (b).

72 *Id.* § 52.

73 An Act to Provide for the Establishment of the Competition Authority, its Mandate, the Regulation of Competition in the Economy, and Matters Incidental Thereto, No. 17 of 2009, http://www.wipo.int/edocs/lexdocs/laws/en/bw/bw009en.pdf [hereinafter Competition Act, 2009].

74 MINISTRY OF TRADE & INDUS. (BOTSWANA), NATIONAL TRADE POLICY FOR BOTSWANA 4 (2009), http://www.mti.gov.bw/sites/default/files/files/policies/trade_policy_july_2009.pdf; *see also* AECOM INT'L DEV., REPORT: ANALYSIS OF BOTSWANA'S TRADE RELATED STRATEGIES AND POLICIES 12 (2009), http://pdf.usaid.gov/pdf_docs/Pnadu570.pdf (summarizing Botswana's competition policy and noting that it emphasizes "fair and transparent competition practices[,] policies and laws to increase investor confidence"); MINISTRY OF TRADE & INDUS. (BOTSWANA), NATIONAL COMPETITION POLICY FOR BOTSWANA 6 (2005), http://www.wipo.int/edocs/lexdocs/laws/en/bw/bw010en.pdf (listing, among the guiding principles of Botswana's competition law, "[u]niversal and transparent application of competition rules . . . [that leads] . . . to efficiency in the allocation of resources").

Before conducting a search, by statute, the Botswana Competition Authority's inspectors must first secure a warrant from a separate magistrate court by proving they have "reasonable grounds" to believe an antitrust violation has occurred.[75] When an inspector first enters a premises to conduct a search, he or she must provide "the owner or person in control of the premises" with a copy of the warrant and proof of the inspector's identity.[76] If no one is present during the search, then the inspector must "affix a copy of the warrant to the premises in a prominent and visible position."[77] Once the Botswana Competition Authority refers a complaint to the Botswana Competition Commission for adjudication, parties are entitled to lodge their objections in a hearing before a four-member panel.[78] The Botswana Competition Commission is empowered to compel witnesses to provide oral or written testimony.[79] Following this hearing, the Botswana Competition Commission provides parties with written notice of its proposed decision, which sets forth the reasons supporting its preliminary judgment.[80] Parties are then afforded another opportunity to present their views to the Commission.[81] If a party appeals the Botswana Competition Commission's final decision to the Botswana High Court, then it remains nonbinding until the appeal is adjudicated.[82]

Bulgaria passed its 2008 Protection of Competition Act "to ensure that the parties' due process rights were fully respected" and to mirror the processes employed by the European Commission.[83] Bulgaria requires its competition authority to file a "Statement of Objection" describing the basis of charges and notifying parties of their right to access the case file.[84] Parties are given an opportunity to respond to the Statement of Objection with their own evidence within 30 days.[85] Poland,[86] Mexico,[87] and Chile[88] have adopted similar reforms with the encouragement of their US and EU trading partners.

The international movement toward assuring procedural protections for due process rights in competition proceedings is active. Enthusiasm for attaining competition law's perceived economic benefits and desire to attract foreign investment is motivating some developing countries to adopt protections for due process rights in antitrust proceedings. In this way, the global spread of antitrust law is helping to lay due process foundations in developing nations. The next section discusses how these due process protections may strengthen other legal institutions.

---

75 Competition Act, 2009 § 36(3).

76 *Id.* § 36(5)(a).

77 *Id.* § 36(5)(b).

78 *Id.* § 39(1), 40(3).

79 *Id.* § 40(5).

80 *Id.* § 41(2).

81 *Id.* § 42.

82 *Id.* § 67.

83 OECD, Procedural Fairness, *supra* note 56, at 51.

84 *Id.* at 51-52.

85 *Id.* at 15.

86 *Id.* at 65 (enhancing transparency by adopting express guidelines on the leniency program and for the imposition of fines).

87 *Id.* at 17 (implementing an electronic filing system that allows full simultaneous access to all information included in a case file).

88 *Id.* at 66 (adopting the Transparency Act, which obliges the competition agency to publish all acts and resolutions that affect third parties, such as the closing of an investigation or the settlement of a case).

2. Antitrust Cases Advance Due Process Rights Applicable in Other Contexts

Although developing nations may adopt due process protections with the goal of attracting foreign investment, implementing these safeguards will help advance due process rights more generally and, therefore, strengthen developing legal institutions. Particularly with respect to cartel actions, antitrust matters present due process issues that transcend subject matter categories. As developing nations ramp up their competition enforcement efforts,[89] they will inevitably hear cases that prominently feature due process issues. For example, in the years when the European Commission imposed relatively low fines, procedural due process issues escaped judicial review. However, when fines rose dramatically in the 1990s, so too did challenges to enforcement procedures.

Even today, as the United States and Europe and other developed nations come to grips with the due process issues inherent in aspects of their enforcement efforts, developing countries are just now confronting due process issues. Parties have already raised due process issues in high-profile cases before developing competition authorities. Some have prevailed. In a 2013 ruling, India's Competition Appellate Tribunal dismissed the Competition Commission of India's finding that the Board of Cricket Control abused its dominant market position, holding that the Commission violated "principles of natural justice" when it relied on information outside the record to define the relevant market without providing the accused with an opportunity to contest that evidence.[90] And in a 2015 ruling, the Competition Appellate Tribunal threw out a decision by the Competition Commission of India to fine a hospital 38.1 million rupees over an alleged abuse of dominance, calling it "wholly erroneous and unsustainable," for overlooking key evidence, for holding preconceived notions that the hospital violated Indian competition law, and for failing to take testimony from a central figure in the matter.[91]

Only two years after Botswana's Competition Act entered into force, the respondents in *Panel Beaters*, a bid-rigging case, lodged a due process challenge against the Botswana Competition Commission's dual role as both the adjudicator of competition cases and as the Botswana Competition Authority's governing body.[92] They argued, albeit unsuccessfully, that "[t]his institutional arrangement . . . [was] likely to lead to a perception of bias . . . in the adjudication process"[93] and that the Competition Commission's structure does not comply with international norms.[94] The respondents appealed to the Botswana High Court but

---

89 *See* Dina I. Waked, *Do Developing Countries Enforce their Antitrust Laws? A Statistical Study of Public Antitrust Enforcement in Developing Countries*, Paper Presented at the ZEW Conference on Economic Methods in Competition Law Enforcement 88 (June 24-25, 2011), http://ssrn.com/abstract=2044047 (demonstrating that developing countries are carrying out regular enforcement activities that are increasing over time). *But see* Michal S. Gal, *Antitrust in a Globalized Economy: The Unique Enforcement Challenge Faced by Small and Developing Jurisdictions*, 33 Fordham Int'l L.J. 1, 15-25 (2009) (arguing that developing jurisdictions rarely tackle international antitrust issues).

90 *See Bd. of Control for Cricket in India v. Competition Comm'n of India*, Appeal No. 17 of 2013, ¶¶ 23, 27 (observing that "the appellant was not given a fair chance to defend itself").

91 Tom Webb, *Indian court overturns stem cell abuse of dominance decision*, Global Competition Rev., Jan. 6, 2016, http://globalcompetitionreview.com/news/article/40246/indian-court-overturns-stem-cell-abuse-dominance-decision/.

92 See Thula Kaira, Botswana: Competition Authority, Global Competition Rev. (n.d.), http://globalcompetitionreview.com/reviews/59/sections/204/chapters/2321/botswana-competition-authority/ (discussing the Panel Beaters case). This arrangement has also drawn fire from African legal scholars—including the Botswana Competition Commission's current chairman. See Zein Kebonang, Towards a Tipping Point: The Botswana Competition Act and the Nemo Judex Rule, 59 J. Afr. L. 178, 183, 191 (2014) (arguing that "procedural fairness demands that investigative and adjudicative functions must be kept separate" and that reform is necessary to eliminate the Botswana Competition Commission's "duality of roles").

93 Kaira, *supra* note 92.

94 Mark Griffiths & Wiri Gumbie, *Due Process Arguments Come to the Fore as the Botswana Competition Authority Gears Itself for Enforcement*, AfricanAntitrust.com, Dec. 16, 2013, http://africanantitrust.com/2013/12/16/due-process-arguments-come-to-the-fore-as-the-botswana-competition-authority-gears-itself-for-enforcement/.

voluntarily withdrew their appeal to resolve the issue out of court.[95] And in the *Sugar Beans* case, decided in July 2015, appellants successfully lodged a jurisdictional challenge against the Botswana Competition Authority's allegations of collusive bid rigging. The Competition Commission dismissed the case for lack of jurisdiction because the Competition Authority failed to refer the case for adjudication within one year after opening its investigation.[96]

Antitrust cases expounding upon due process rights may become an important resource for the accused in countries that do not provide representation or that generally have emerging justice systems. Cases from the United States, Europe, and Australia, presented below, demonstrate that antitrust rulings spawn published decisions that may be invoked to advance due process rights in other contexts.

a. Australia: No Anonymous Witnesses in Government Antitrust Cases

In *Australian Competition and Consumer Commission v. Prysmian Cavi E Sistemi Energia S.R.L.*,[97] the Federal Court of Australia expanded the circumstances in which the government must disclose the identity of witnesses in cases it brings in court, in order to protect rights of the accused. In order to receive first-to-report immunity, a participant in an alleged bid-rigging and price-fixing cartel provided information to the Australian Competition and Consumer Commission ("ACCC") on the alleged conduct. It was claimed that the ACCC had assured the witness that he would remain anonymous. Relying on information from this anonymous witness, which they named "Mr A," the ACCC filed suit in open court without naming the anonymous witness, merely describing alleged cartel conduct by the defendants with "Mr A."[98] In the *Prysmian* case, Nexans SA, one of the civil penalty defendants, asked the court to order disclosure of Mr. A's identity and all communications he made with the ACCC.[99] Nexans invoked basic principles of fairness: the right to confront witnesses and the right to search for facts for its defense. It is a basic principle of human rights that knowing the identity of the accuser is the first essential step in confronting the evidence against the accused.[100] To prepare a defense to price-fixing, a firm needs to know the person or persons who have alleged that the firm had participated in a cartel. This information permits defense witnesses to be interviewed and documents to be searched. Nexans naturally argued that this information was essential to contesting the underlying basis of the ACCC's asserted prima facie case.

The court ordered the ACCC to reveal Mr A's identity. Although the propriety of disclosure is nominally determined on a case-by-case basis,[101] prior Australian precedent had required disclosure where the

---

95 *Id. See also* Botswana Competition Auth., Annual Report 2014/15 22 (2015), http://www.competitionauthority.co.bw/sites/default/files/Annual%20Report%202014-15.pdf. Some sources report that planned reforms will separate the Botswana Competition Authority's adjudicative and investigative functions. *See, e.g.*, Portia Nkani, *Competition Commission, Competition Authority to separate*, Botswana Gazette, July 10, 2014, http://www.gazettebw.com/?p=8331.

96 *See Competition Auth. v. Creative Bus. Sols.* (*Sugar Beans*), No. CC-CR/01/A/15 I, ¶¶ 122, 124, 151-52 (2015).

97 [2011] FCA 938.

98 *Id.* ¶ 34. Before granting leave to serve a foreign defendant, Australian law requires the court to determine that the plaintiff "has a prima facie case for all or any of the relief claimed . . . in the proceeding." *Id.* ¶ 57 (quoting *Federal Court Rules* (Cth) O 8 r 3(2)(c)).

99 *Id.* ¶ 72. As recently as 2012, commentators have noted the "relative paucity of competition litigation in Australia . . . and thus limited guidance from the case law on a range of important procedural and substantive questions." *See* Fox & Trebilcock, *supra* note 13, at 60

100 In US jurisprudence, the right to confront witnesses is governed by the Confrontation Clause of the Bill of Rights. *See* U.S. Const. Amend. VI ("In all criminal prosecutions, the accused shall enjoy the right . . . to be confronted with the witnesses against him."). International human rights law also recognizes confrontation as a minimum guarantee of fair proceedings. *See* International Covenant on Civil and Political Rights (ICCPR) art. 14(3)(e), Dec. 19, 1966, 999 U.N.T.S. 171 (entered into force Mar. 23, 1976) (providing a party the right "[t]o examine, or have examined, the witnesses against him" as a "minimum guarantee").

101 *Prysmian*, [2011] FCA 938, ¶ 185.

informant provided material information and where revealing the informant's identity tended to prove the defendant's innocence or was necessary to fight the government's case.[102] But the *Prysmian* Court rested its decision, in part, on a different ground. The outcome depended on whether keeping the informant's identity secret would generally interfere with the defendant's ability to make strategic decisions based on the strength of the government's claims, including the decision to not combat the government's case.[103] Mr. A was the only natural person with whom the defendants had allegedly conspired. Consequently, the Court required the ACCC to disclose Mr. A's identity and the surrounding materials, including the ACCC's interview materials for Mr. A.

Permitting the defense to cross-examine witnesses at trial is necessary to weed out false testimony. And the right to confront witnesses—starting with revealing their identity to the defense—will deter the use of weak witnesses in the first place.[104]

b. Europe: Protections from Search and Seizure in European Dawn Raids—Nexans and the Right of Privacy

In *Nexans SA v. European Commission*, the European Union's General Court held, for the first time, that a warrantless "dawn raid" violated the fundamental right to privacy because the government did not have "reasonable grounds" to conduct it.[105]

Some time prior to 2009, the European Commission's Directorate-General for Competition ("DG Comp") received information pertaining to anticompetitive activity involving the sale of high-voltage underwater cables. The DG Comp then conducted a dawn raid at Nexans' offices. When it initiated the dawn raid, the DG Comp claimed—as was its routine practice— that it was entitled to conduct an exceedingly broad search—in that case, a search embracing any material associated with "the supply of electric cables."[106] After the DG Comp executed the search, Nexans brought suit before the European Union's General Court against the DG Comp in 2009, arguing the search was defective in that it was overbroad and violated its right to privacy.

The General Court held in 2012 that the DG Comp had indeed violated Nexans' privacy rights. Although European procedures do not currently provide for the General Court to conduct pre-dawn raid review of the DG Comp's requested search, the General Court made clear for the first time under EU law that the European Convention of Human Rights empowers it to conduct post-search judicial review of the underlying

---

102 *See, e.g.*, *Haydon v. Magistrates' Court of South Australia* (2001) 87 SASR 448 ¶ 13, 70, 71 (requiring disclosure of an informant's identity where doing so would aid the defense at trial); *Jarvie v. Magistrates' Court of Victoria* (1995) 1 VR 84 ("[T]he overriding need for a fair trial must mean that in no circumstances can the identity of a witness be withheld from a defendant if there is good reason to think that disclosure may be of substantial assistance to the defendant in combating the case for the prosecution.").

103 *See Prysmian*, [2011] FCA at ¶ 208 ("*The fact is, without the documents and knowledge of Mr A's identity, . . . Nexans would find it difficult to assess the strength of the ACCC's claim.*") (emphasis added).

104 *See, e.g.*, *Melendez-Diaz v. Massachusetts*, 129 S.Ct. 2527, 2537 (2009) (concluding that "of course, the prospect of confrontation will deter fraudulent analysis in the first place," and forcing prosecutors to bring to court lab technicians who produce lab reports to face cross-examination, under the Confrontation Clause of the US Sixth Amendment, rather than permit prosecutors to stand at trial on a hearsay lab report).

105 Case T-135/09, *Nexans v. Comm'n*, 2012 E.C.R. I-000, ¶¶ 39-46, *available at* http://curia.europa.eu/juris/document/document.jsf?text=&docid=129701&pageIndex=0&doclang=EN&mode=lst&dir=&occ=first&part=1&cid=224723 ("[T]he Commission . . . must . . . identify the sectors covered by the alleged infringement with which the investigation is concerned with a degree of precision sufficient to enable the undertaking in question to limit its cooperation to its activities in the sectors in respect of which the Commission has *reasonable grounds* for suspecting an infringement of the competition rules, justifying interference in the undertaking's sphere of private activity, and to make it possible for the Court . . . to determine, if necessary, whether or not those grounds are sufficiently reasonable for those purposes." (emphasis added)).

106 *Id.* ¶ 3.

"reasonable grounds" for the DG Comp's searches and to annul those searches if they exceed the permissible scope.

The General Court compared the allegations made in the pre-search leniency statements with the DG Comp's scope of search. The Court concluded that, although the DG Comp possessed a reasonable basis to inspect Nexans' premises for materials relating to the sale of high-voltage underwater electric cables, it had no grounds to search for any materials relating to the sale of electric cables in general, such as low-voltage cables. Therefore, the DG Comp's search exceeded its alleged basis for conducting the investigation.[107] Because the DG Comp searched for documents to detect possible competition infringements in *all* of Nexans' activities, and did not limit its search to information related to the "reasonable grounds" justifying the search—i.e., anticompetitive activity in high-voltage cables—the DG Comp search amounted to a "fishing expedition" and its actions were "incompatible with the protection of the sphere of private activity of legal persons, guaranteed as a fundamental right in a democratic society."[108] Therefore, the General Court ordered the DG Comp, for the first time, to provide the Court with the leniency statements that were the purported basis for the search.

Nexans not only impacted the investigation in question, which was limited to only considering the specific products for which the DG Comp had "reasonable grounds" to search, it also paved the way for others to challenge the DG Comp's investigatory practices.[109] The case has changed the entire climate of EU investigations and has given others the fortitude to make similar challenges.

In a 2015 case,[110] the German Regional Court of Bonn restricted the Federal Cartel Office's use of an "imminent danger" exception to the ordinary court-order requirement for evidentiary seizures. Under German law, antitrust investigators must ordinarily secure a court order before seizing material uncovered during a lawful search. A statutory exception to this rule is available for evidence that would be in "imminent danger" of being lost if the government was forced to wait for a decision; this "imminent danger" exception embraces circumstances where the evidence obtained is so voluminous that the reviewing judge could not make a seizure determination remotely. The applicant complained that the government was routinely claiming that the quantity of evidence it seized was so vast as to make judicial review impractical but that the government was not supporting these assertions. Although the Court did not pass judgment on whether the government was invoking the "imminent danger" exception mechanically, it required the government "in future proceedings" to specifically state the efforts it made to analyze the evidence and why the exception therefore applied.

---

107 *Id.* ¶ 67, 91.

108 *Id.* ¶ 35, 66. The General Court's decision in *Nexans* has prompted comment on whether the European Convention for the Protection of Human Rights requires EU and national courts facing objections to government searches to hear these issues during the preliminary investigation stage, or whether aggrieved parties must first await a final decision by the DG Comp. The General Court concluded that it did not possess jurisdiction over Nexans' claims that the DG Comp improperly copied its corporate records for later examination at the DG Comp's Brussels office. *See Nexans*, 2012 ECR I-000, ¶ 131. This ruling seems to be at odds with other EU decisions. *See* Ingeborg Simonsson, *Digital Evidence Gathering in Dawn-Raids, Judicial Review: Up-Front or Retrospective?*, Presented at the 20th St. Gallen Int'l Competition L. Forum ICF 1–4, 7–11 (Apr. 4 5, 2013), http://ssrn.com/abstract=2327122 (noting that, on the question of the timing of relief, the *Nexans* Court relied on inapplicable cases and "that there would have been support for the opposite outcome[] in *Nexans*," and identifying advantages to reviewing such claims at the preliminary investigation stage).

109 *See, e.g.*, Joined Cases T-289/11, T-290/11 and T-521/11, Deutsche Bahn AG and Others v. Comm'n, 2013 E.C.R. II-0000, *available at* http://curia.europa.eu/juris/document/document.jsf?text=&docid=140725&pageIndex=0&doclang=EN&mode=lst&dir=&occ=first&part=1&cid=964210.

110 Landgericht Bonn [LG Bonn] [Bonn Regional Court], Sept. 21, 2015, No. 29 Qs 7/15.

c. United States: Stolt-Nielsen and the Enforcement of Government Amnesty Promises

In 1993, the Antitrust Division of the US Department of Justice ("DOJ") announced its corporate amnesty and leniency programs for antitrust violations. Similar programs have since been adopted in more than 50 other nations. By the early 2000s, more than 100 firms had signed written amnesty agreements with the DOJ.

In 2003, the DOJ decided for the first time to revoke a signed amnesty agreement in the *Stolt-Nielsen* cases.[111] In exchange for a promise by the DOJ "not to bring any criminal prosecution . . . for any act or offense it may have committed prior," Stolt-Nielsen disclosed evidence of its participation in a cartel.[112] At the time, the DOJ knew that Stolt-Nielsen had not independently investigated the anticompetitive conduct by its employees, had not reported past antitrust violations, and at least one of its employees "had been accused publicly of ongoing antitrust violations."[113] The DOJ materially relied on the information Stolt-Nielsen provided in its successful prosecution of other cartel co-conspirators.[114] Based on a co-conspirator's allegations, the DOJ concluded that Stolt-Nielsen failed to take "prompt and effective action" to terminate participation in the cartel activity it reported and thus the DOJ decided to revoke the amnesty agreement.[115] When the DOJ arrested a senior Stolt-Nielsen executive, Stolt-Nielsen and the executive promptly sought an injunction against further criminal prosecution in order to enforce their rights under the amnesty agreement.[116]

After a two-day evidentiary hearing, the district court enforced the agreement, directing the DOJ to make good on its promises to the company and its executives.[117] The court granted the injunction against the DOJ's criminal prosecution—the first injunction of its kind granted against the DOJ.[118] The DOJ, however, appealed and the Third Circuit reversed.[119]

The DOJ proceeded to indict two Stolt-Nielsen executives and the company so they moved to dismiss the indictment. In respect to the indictments, the district court explained:

Non-prosecution agreements are binding contracts. *United States v. Castaneda*, 162 F.3d 832, 835 (5th Cir. 1998).

---

111 The *Stolt-Nielsen* case generated two distinct court opinions that are relevant here: the original action, *United States v. Stolt-Nielsen S.A.* (*Stolt-Nielsen I*), 352 F. Supp. 2d 553 (E.D. Pa. 2005), and the dismissal of the DOJ's indictment, *United States v. Stolt-Nielsen S.A.* (*Stolt-Nielsen II*), 524 F. Supp. 2d 586 (E.D. Pa. 2007) (findings of fact and conclusions of law), and 524 F. Supp. 2d 609 (E.D. Pa. 2007) (memorandum opinion).

112 *Stolt-Nielsen I*, 352 F. Supp. 2d at 558.

113 *Stolt-Nielsen II*, 524 F. Supp. 2d at 621.

114 *See id.* at 614 ("Without Stolt-Nielsen's cooperation, the Division did not have sufficient evidence to sustain a conviction of any company in the parcel taker industry.").

115 *Id.* at 614-15.

116 *Stolt-Nielsen I*, 352 F. Supp. 2d at 559.

117 *Id.* at 555 ("[Stolt-Nielsen] performed its obligation under the agreement when it supplied DOJ with self-incriminating evidence that led to the successful prosecution of [the company's] co-conspirators. Because DOJ got the benefit of its bargain, it cannot avoid fulfilling its promise based on an understanding it contends the parties intended during negotiations but is not clearly defined in the integrated agreement"). *See also id.* at 560 ("Because due process is implicated, the government cannot unilaterally declare an immunity agreement void. Instead, due process demands that the government first obtain a judicial determination that the defendant breached the agreement.") (citations omitted).

118 *Id.* at 562-63.

119 *Stolt-Nielsen II*, 524 F. Supp. 2d at 615 (two-judge panel).

> While general principles of contract law guide interpretation of non-prosecution agreements, 'such agreements are unique and are to be construed in light of 'special due process concerns'. *United States v. Baird*, 218 F.3d 221, 229 (3d Cir. 2000).[120]

The court heard each of the DOJ's witnesses and concluded that there was "no credible evidence" that Stolt-Nielsen broke the agreement.[121] Examining the DOJ's evidence witness-by-witness, the court found that the DOJ's witnesses provided statements that were riddled with "inconsistencies" and "misstatements of fact."[122] Ruling again for Stolt-Nielsen, the court enforced the amnesty agreement and dismissed the indictment. The court held that, "as a matter of fundamental fairness," the DOJ "may not . . . revoke the [a]greement on the basis of facts known to it at the time it entered into the [a]greement."[123] The court further explained:

> It ill behooves government agents and prosecutors to enter into agreements of transactional immunity with mid-level co-conspirators, milk them of substantial leads and information that literally make the government's case . . . then, at the last moment, rely on some technical or relatively minor deficiency in performance to pull the rug out from under the cooperating informant by claiming a breach and proceed to prosecute him in a slam-dunk case based largely on his own revelations. Yet, this is precisely what we perceive to have happened here, and due process cannot abide such behavior.[124]

The *Stolt-Nielsen* decision is the first court decision to enforce an amnesty promise against the government and reaffirms that independent judiciaries perform an important check on the power of antitrust enforcement agencies.

3. Sustained Growth: An Important Benefit

Developing countries have attempted to adopt antitrust policy in the hope of stimulating economic growth through free markets. But protections for free markets, and the economic benefits that they entail, will not be the only potential value of antitrust law's spread to the developing world. Several developing nations have responded to economic incentives and have implemented procedural fairness measures as part of a comprehensive antitrust law. Litigation involving these safeguards may produce legal developments that can have a positive effect on other fields of law, including traditional criminal prosecutions. As due process values emerge, legal institutions will strengthen. Because high-quality institutions are the key to closing the gap between rich and poor nations, antitrust law's role in furthering due process values is perhaps the most important economic benefit that antitrust law can offer to the developing world.

---

120 *Id*. at 606 (omitting paragraph numbers).

121 *Id*. at 628.

122 *Id*. at 625.

123 Id. at 621. The DOJ chose not to appeal the district court's comprehensive findings of fact and conclusions of law. See Scott Hammond on Stolt-Nielsen, Global Competition Rev. (May 1, 2008), http://globalcompetitionreview.com/features/article/800/scott-hammond-stolt-nielsen/ ("In January, the US Department of Justice announced that it would not appeal against a court's reinstatement of Stolt-Nielsen's leniency arrangement.").

124 *Stolt-Nielsen II*, 524 F. Supp. 2d at 628 n.25 (enforcing the amnesty agreement).

IV. Three Examples of Urgent Due Process Issues in Antitrust Regimes

The methods that developing nations employ to enforce their antitrust laws carry economic consequences even if they rest on sound policies. Therefore, it is not sufficient for an antitrust regime to be built on sound economic principles; *fair* enforcement is a necessary condition for attaining the economic growth that countries expect from sound antitrust regulation. Fairness is "a necessary and beneficial ingredient of effective competition enforcement" that "can promote transparency and better outcomes."[125]

Legal institutions that are unfair, and therefore unpredictable, discourage investment by imposing transaction costs that are not present in other jurisdictions.[126] Therefore, just as the conditions for economic growth require thought, effort, and support through sound governmental institutions, deficient legal institutions "may in fact produce perverse policies, [and become] the source of man-made economic decline."[127] Even as experience in the United States has crossed the 100 year mark, there is still room for improvement in the US antitrust laws. For a cogent example, one need only look to Shughart and Tollison's 1991 study on the US economy after 125 years since passage of the Sherman Act, which demonstrates just how sensitive markets can be to methods of antitrust enforcement. The study found that mere "unanticipated rises" in antitrust enforcement from 1932 to 1981 were responsible for a net loss of jobs over that period.[128]

Due process guarantees are designed to ensure that firms are protected from the arbitrary decisions, abuses of power, and political influence in adjudications that are a common feature of weak legal institutions.[129] With respect to competition enforcement in particular, the need for adequate due process protections is even more pressing in light of the notable rise in criminal sentences and civil fines imposed for antitrust violations.[130] Compounding matters, inadequate protections in one jurisdiction may leave parties at

---

125 O'Brien, Katona & Tritell, *supra* note 40, at 7.

126 *See* Rodrik, *supra* note 24, at 12 (observing that lack of respect for the rule of law results in coordination failures); Lachmann, *supra* note 17, at 22 (noting that "weak rule of law" has often functioned as [an] obstacle[] to growth"); Knack & Keefer, *supra* note 15, at 594 (tying arbitrary decision-making to measures of low institutional quality); World Trade Org., *supra* note 42, ¶ 11 (noting that stable and predictable competition policy attracts investment).

127 Cross, *supra* note 8, at 1742.

128 William F. Shughart II & Robert D. Tollison, *The Employment Consequences of the Sherman and Clayton Acts*, 147 J. Inst. Theoretical Econ. 38, 50 (1991).

129 *See* Rodrik, *supra* note 24, at 12 (observing that lack of respect for the rule of law results in coordination failures); Lachmann, *supra* note 17, at 22 (noting that "weak rule of law" has often functioned as [an] obstacle[] to growth"); Knack & Keefer, *supra* note 15, at 594 (tying arbitrary decision-making to measures of institutional quality).

130 *See* Bill Baer, Assistant Attorney Gen., Antitrust Div., US Dep't of Justice, *Cooperation, Convergence, and the Challenges Ahead in Competition Enforcement*, Remarks as Prepared for the Georgetown Law 9th Annual Global Antitrust Enforcement Symposium 2-3 (Sept. 29, 2015), http://www.justice.gov/opa/file/782361/download ("In 2014 alone, at least 19 different jurisdictions levied criminal fines or administrative penalties against cartel conduct totaling more than $6.5 billion."). The United States has continued to secure record fines and increasingly long prison sentences. In 2014, the Antitrust Division collected US$1.8 billion; already by the middle of 2015, it had collected US$2.7 billion against cartel members. *See* Allen & Overy, Global Cartel Enforcement: 2015 (Mid-Year) Report 2 (2015), http://www.allenovery.com/SiteCollectionDocuments/Global_Cartel_Enforcement_2015_Mid-Year_Report.PDF. US antitrust actions are resulting in record-breaking fines—some as high as US$1.6 billion. *See* Douglas H. Ginsburg, Judge, D.C. Cir., *Due Process in Competition Proceedings*, Keynote Address at the International Competition Network Roundtable on Investigative Process 4 (Mar. 25, 2014), http://www.internationalcompetitionnetwork.org/uploads/library/doc958.pdf. In 2012, 78 percent of individuals sentenced in US competition cases received jail time. *See id.* at 4. *See also* US Dep't of Justice, *Criminal Program Update*, U.S. Dep't Just. (Aug. 12, 2015), http://www.justice.gov/atr/public-documents/division-update-spring-2013/criminal-program. In 2013, the European Union imposed fines amounting to US$2 billion, which was over double the United States' haul that year. *See* Jacquelyn MacLennan & Christopher Curran, *Standing in the antitrust firing line*, Insight, July 1, 2015, http://www.whitecase.com/publications/insight/standing-antitrust-firing-line. In 2014, Japan raked in US$398.5 million against cartels, up from US$225.4 million the year prior. *See* Allen & Overy, Global Antitrust Enforcement: 2014 (Mid-Year) Cartel Report 2 (2014), http://www.allenovery.com/publications/en-gb/Pages/Global-Antitrust-Enforcement--2014--Mid-Year--Cartel-Report.aspx.

significant risk of liability in several other jurisdictions as antitrust authorities increasingly conduct coordinated cross-border and transnational investigations.[131]

Industrialized and developing nations alike should, therefore, be especially sensitive to whether their competition enforcement procedures are offering sufficient protection. This section discusses three due process issues of particular importance, explaining how they protect firms' expectations and highlighting some deficiencies in current competition systems. Readers will observe that many of the most serious procedural shortcomings in competition regimes are found in the developed world.[132] Nevertheless, developing nations can benefit from the lessons learned slowly in the litigation of due process rights in the US and Europe. The Appendix provides a detailed list of suggested features for fair competition proceedings.

1. Prosecutors and Agencies Limiting Access to the Evidence at Trial

Requiring the government to disclose the basis for its enforcement actions, and any exculpatory evidence it possesses, discourages government actors from using public power for personal gain or other nefarious purposes.[133] As such, mandatory and automatic disclosure of the government's evidence helps to ensure that antitrust laws are applied according to the nature of the alleged acts, which allows firms to use less time (and money) wringing their hands over how to avoid unfair treatment and to instead focus on more economically beneficial tasks, like making deals. Yet several countries still impose restrictions on disclosure that threaten to weaken institutions and expose firms to unnecessary transaction costs.

In the United States, criminal prosecutors are only required to disclose evidence that they deem material and favorable to the defense, also known as *Brady* material.[134] The current *Brady* doctrine, which delegates the decision of whether evidence is "relevant" and subject to disclosure to the prosecutors, places prosecu-

---

131 Damien Gerard, *Regulation 1/2003 (and beyond): Balancing Effective Enforcement and Due Process in Cross-border Antitrust Investigations*, *in* International Antitrust Litigation: Conflict of Laws and Coordination 368, 369 (Jürgen Basedow, Stéphanie Franq & Laurence Idot, eds. 2012) (explaining how, in the EU context, multijurisdictional differences in due process rules combined with rules unconditionally permitting competition agencies to share evidence functionally alter defendants' rights).

> Practically, according to Article 22 [of Regulation 1/2003], ECN members can request each other to carry out inspections and any other fact-finding measures on each other's behalf and for each other's benefit. Any information collected pursuant to Article 22, or otherwise in the context of national proceedings, including confidential information, may then be communicated by the 'transmitting authority', ie the ECN members that gathered the information to the 'receiving authority', ie the ECN members that requested the information, in accordance with Article 12. The information may then be used as evidence by the receiving ECN member 'for the purpose of applying Article 101 or 102 of the Treaty[on the Functioning of the European Union] and in respect of the subject matter for which it was collected by the transmitting authority'. Limitations apply in relation to the prosecution of individuals: information can be 'used in evidence' by the receiving authority only if the law of the transmitting authority 'foresees sanctions of a similar kind' for individuals or applies the 'same level of protection in the rights of defence' of individuals than under the law of the receiving authority.

Id. (footnotes omitted).

132 For example, only recently did the US Department of Justice, under Assistant Attorney General Bill Baer, end its practice of publicly announcing that it was "carving" out certain persons from the protection of a corporate plea bargain. *See* Bill Baer, Assistant Attorney Gen., Antitrust Div., US Dep't of Justice, Statement of Assistant Attorney General Bill Baer on Changes to Antitrust Division's Carve-Out Practice Regarding Corporate Plea Agreements (Apr. 12, 2013), http://www.justice.gov/opa/pr/statement-assistant-attorney-general-bill-baer-changes-antitrust-division-s-carve-out. The publicly carved-out executives almost invariably lost their jobs and ability to earn a living in their industry—despite the complete absence of any finding of guilt or due process. In the *Air Cargo* cases, more than 80 airline executives were "carved out" of corporate plea agreement protections—less than a quarter were ever indicted. The reform was long overdue.

133 *See* William J. Brennan, Jr., *The Criminal Prosecution: Sporting Event or Quest for Truth?*, 1963 Wash. U. L.Q. 279, 280 (1963) ("We have forgotten that these safeguards, while they do indeed make harder the conviction of an accused, were not provided for that purpose . . . . These safeguards are checks upon government—to guarantee that government shall remain the servant and not the master of us all.").

134 *Brady v. Maryland*, 373 U.S 83, 87 (1963). *See also* Bennett L. Gershman, *Reflections on* Brady v. Maryland, 47 S. Tex. L. Rev. 685, 703-07 (2006) (discussing the favorability and materiality requirements).

tors in inherent conflicts of interest.[135] Not surprisingly, "[t]here is an epidemic of *Brady* violations abroad in the land,"[136] and much (if not most) *Brady* evidence is never disclosed.[137] To avoid these conflicts, some individual US Attorney's Offices have adopted an "open-file" policy that permits the accused access to all evidence in the prosecutor's possession.[138] However, many Offices have decided against an open-file policy and, at this writing, the DOJ Antitrust Division has no such written policy.[139] This situation is a human rights disgrace as antitrust evidence is often subtle and the legitimacy of actions may require the surrounding context. The *Stolt-Nielsen* trial demonstrated that isolated snippets of evidence can be misread to suggest a violation, when the full context demonstrates completely legitimate joint venture activity. Currently, rights of the accused may depend on the government's choice of forum or the choices made by prosecution teams. The adversary system is completely undermined when access to the evidence is denied.

To make matters worse, in many high-profile antitrust prosecutions, much of the evidence is overseas and the leniency applicants may be tempted to, or even are encouraged to, cherry-pick only the "bad" documents from overseas files. As a result, the full files are not brought into the United States. This is one of the moral hazards of a program that permits one competitor to turn in its rivals for crippling punishments (forcing jail sentences on opposing executives and steep fines). Cherry picking of overseas files leaves defendants with little overseas discovery recourse to confront witnesses sufficiently.

Some recent precedent has extended *Brady* protections, but true reform awaits the DOJ's adoption by rule of open files, or a judicial response. The Sixth Circuit applied the *Brady* rule in a civil extradition case in part because "[t]he consequences of denaturalization and extradition *equal or exceed those of most criminal convictions*."[140] The Fourth Circuit recently cited this case as illustrating the "rare instance" in which *Brady* obligations may apply to a civil case brought by the government.[141]

Japan's Anti-Monopoly Act and its attendant regulations have also drawn increasing scrutiny. The Japan Fair Trade Commission ("JFTC") is neither obligated to disclose the evidence obtained during an investigation nor the underlying basis for its administrative findings of anticompetitive activity until the first court hearing; at that point, the JFTC has already issued an "enforceable court order."[142] The JFTC also conducts custodial interrogations without allowing access to counsel and compels written witness statements in custodial interrogations—as discussed below. The JFTC even retains the power to refuse inspection

---

135 *See* Douglas H. Ginsburg & Taylor M. Owings, *Due Process in Competition Proceedings*, 11 Competition L. Int'l 39, 44 (2015) ("[B]oth US agencies as well as DG Comp tout the amount of fines they collect as a measure of their success").

136 *Olson v. United States*, 737 F.3d 625, 626 (9th Cir. 2013) (Kozinsky, J., dissenting from denial of petition for rehearing en banc).

137 *See* Bennett L. Gershman, *Litigating* Brady v. Maryland: *Games Prosecutors Play*, 57 Case W. Res. L. Rev. 532, 536 (2007) ("[I]t is commonly believed that most *Brady* evidence never gets disclosed; rather, it remains buried in drawers, boxes, and file cabinets in the offices of the prosecutor, the police, and other law enforcement and government agencies connected to the case.").

138 *See* Andrew Smith, Note, Brady *Obligations, Criminal Sanctions, and Solutions in a New Era of Scrutiny*, 61 Vand. L. Rev. 1935, 1963 (2008) (explaining the divergent policies among US Attorney's Offices).

139 For background, see Anthony Barkow & Beth George, *Prosecuting Political Defendants*, 44 Ga. L. Rev. 953, n.286 (2010) (noting the DOJ declined to implement an open-file policy).

140 *Demanjanjuk v. Petrovsky*, 10 F.3d 338, 354 (6th Cir. 1993) (emphasis added).

141 *See Fox ex rel. Fox*, 739 F.3d 131, 138-39 (4th Cir. 2014). Ginsburg and Owings note that the European Court of Human Rights, the European Court of Justice, and the Supreme Court of Canada have held that large civil fines may amount to criminal penalties, thus implicating greater procedural safeguards. *See* Ginsburg & Owings, *supra* note 135, at 41 (noting, for example, the Supreme Court of Canada's *Wigglesworth* decision, in which the court held that Section 11 of the Canadian Charter of Rights and Freedoms applies to a person facing a civil fine because Section 11 "is intended to provide procedural safeguards in proceedings which may attract penal consequences even if not criminal in the strict sense").

142 Am. Chamber of Comm. in Japan, *Assuring Due Process: Central to AMA Reform*, ACCJ Viewpoint, Mar. 2015, at 4 [hereinafter *Assuring Due Process*] (on file with author).

targets the right to copy *their own documents* that the JFTC obtained, for example, during a dawn raid, and has refused these requests in the past.[143]

2. Lack of a Neutral Decision-Maker; Failure to Separate the Investigatory and Adjudicatory Roles

The decision-maker in a competition agency must be legally independent from the investigator. Without a layer of separation maintaining distance between the adjudicatory and investigatory roles, the investigator is asked to determine whether its efforts have borne fruit—indeed, whether its existence is justified.[144] Such "integrated agencies . . . raise systemic concerns that the integration of investigation, enforcement, and adjudicative functions create bias or lack of objectivity ('confirmation bias'), or the appearance of it, in the discharge of the adjudicatory functions vested in the agencies may render the agencies 'judges in their own cause.'"[145] This increases the risk that antitrust authorities will emphasize ends over means, especially where the ends are measured in the aggregate total of yearly fines accruing to the government. Therefore, the risk of unfair proceedings is enhanced, and economic growth is impeded,[146] unless investigations and adjudications are carried out by two independent bodies.[147]

In the European Union, the officials who investigate a case also determine if a violation has occurred.[148] After charges are brought, parties are not provided a hearing in front of the adjudicator before a verdict is rendered.[149] As Ian Forrester has observed: "the procedures of the European Commission in determining guilt or innocence under the competition rules, and in imposing sanctions, manifestly do not correspond to the standards established by the [European Convention on Human Rights]."[150] The adjudicatory panel is staffed with political appointees who do not attend hearings and do not participate in drafting the order.[151] Similar issues exist under Japanese law. The same body that conducts the investigation, the JFTC, also decides whether a violation occurred.[152]

---

143 *Id.*

144 Ginsburg & Owings, *supra* note 135, at 45 ("Competition cases brought by an enforcement agency in which the same official(s) direct or authorise the staff to undertake the investigation, direct or authorise the staff to prosecute a case based upon the evidence turned up in that investigation, and then decide whether the evidence is sufficient to show an infringement, might reasonably be thought to have an interest in the outcome; for them to say the evidence is insufficient is to say the entire undertaking was a waste of resources for which they are responsible. The potential for unfairness is self-evident.").

145 Fox & Trebilcock, *supra* note 13, at 12-13.

146 Daniel M. Klerman, *Legal Infrastructure, Judicial Independence, and Economic Development*, 19 Pac. McGeorge Glob. Bus. & Dev. L.J. 427, 427-28 (2007) (arguing that "economic theory supports the idea that judicial independence facilitates economic growth").

147 *See* Kebonang, *supra* note 92, at 178-79 (making this argument against the relationship between the Botswana Competition Authority and Competition Commission).

148 Ian S. Forrester, *Due process in EC competition cases: A distinguished institution with flawed procedures*, 34 Econ. L. Rev. 817, 818, 823 (2009).

149 *Id.* at 823 ("The hearing gives the accused company the chance to restate its case to the case team which is accusing it, but not to argue before a neutral judge, hearing officer or other person who will decide on guilt or innocence.").

150 *Id.*

151 Forrester, *supra* note 148, at 822 ("[T]he decision . . . is taken by a college of 27 political appointees who take such a decision collectively by a majority vote. No competition agency on earth takes decisions this way, nor does any criminal instance in any democratic country. There is the institutional possibility that political considerations will influence—pollute is perhaps too strong—the decision making."); Martin Möllmann, *Due Process in Antitrust Proceedings Before the European Commission: Fundamental Rights are Not Enough*, CPI Antitrust Chron., June 2014, at 2.

152 *Assuring Due Process*, *supra* note 142, at 5.

3. Preventing an Effective Defense: Limited Access to Counsel and Insufficient Time to Prepare

Fair legal proceedings place the defendant on equal footing with his or her accuser. Both the International Covenant on Civil and Political Rights and the European Convention for Human Rights hold this principle to be a fundamental guarantee of a fair trial.[153] The right to counsel at stages affecting legal interests and the right to adequate time and facilities for preparing a defense are particularly crucial to ensuring a fair dispute between the government and the accused.[154] Involvement of counsel is needed to ameliorate the often-coercive interrogation environment.[155] And defendants cannot have a meaningful opportunity to be heard unless provided with sufficient time to formulate a reasoned response to charges (on the other hand, depending on the relevant statute of limitations, the government often has several years to compile its case).[156] These rights, by guaranteeing that the defense has the same opportunity to present its evidence, impose a check on executive power—they force the government to rely on the strength of its case rather than any weaknesses it can exploit from the defense. This enables enforcement according to the written or common laws that inform firms' expectations and, therefore, yields economic benefits.[157] Yet some competition authorities block parties under investigation from seeking the assistance of attorneys during key investigatory phases. Others permit little time to prepare a response. Further, some competition authorities do not allow themselves any time to really consider the arguments of the defense but rather proceed immediately to the adoption of their final decision, literally minutes or hours after the defendant gave evidence and made specific arguments in writing or at an oral hearing. In these jurisdictions, the ability to meaningfully mount a defense is significantly undermined and the risk of unfair enforcement is heightened.

In Japan, the presence of an attorney is not guaranteed at dawn raids and the JFTC will not wait for even a reasonable amount of time for the company's attorney to arrive before starting an unannounced inspection.[158] In cases where the company's attorney is present during the inspection, the JFTC may revoke the right to counsel if it deems that the attorney's presence "affect[s] the smoother implementation of the

---

153 *See* ICCPR, art. 3 ("In the determination of any criminal charge against him, everyone shall be entitled to the following minimum guarantees, in full equality"). Although this provision of the ICCPR is expressly limited to criminal trials, exceedingly high civil antitrust fines may amount to penalties that implicate rights applying to criminal cases. *See* Ginsburg & Owings, *supra* note 135, at 41 (citing *A Menarini Diagnostics SRL v. Italy*, Judgment of 27 September 2011, 43509/08, paras. 58-67).

154 *See* ICCPR, art. 3(b), (d) (listing, among other minimum guarantees of fair trial, the right "[t]o have adequate time and facilities for the preparation of [a] defence," and the right "[t]o have legal assistance assigned to him, in any case where the interests of justice so require").

155 1 U.S. Inst. of Peace, Model Codes for Post-Conflict Criminal Justice: Model Criminal Code art. 71 cmt. (2007) ("The presence of counsel during interview not only facilitates the right of the suspect or the accused to defend himself or herself . . . but also helps to protect the accused's right to freedom from coercion, duress, threat, torture or cruel, inhuman, or degrading treatment.").

156 *See* Human Rights Comm., *Marais v. Madagascar*, Comm. No. 49/1979, ¶ 17.3, U.N. Doc. CCPR/C/OP/2 (1990) (finding that Madagascar infringed the defendant's right to a fair trial under Article 14(3) of the ICCPR by failing to provide him with adequate time to prepare a defense). In the United States, the statute of limitations for criminal conspiracies, including antitrust cartels, is five years. *See* 18 U.S.C. § 3282. Japan imposes the same limitation. *See* Etsuko Hara & Hideto Ishida, *Japan: Cartels*, Global Competition Rev. (n.d.), http://globalcompetitionreview.com/reviews/69/sections/235/chapters/2753/japan-cartels/.

157 *See* Thomas W. Wälde, *"Equality of Arms" in Investment Arbitration: Procedural Challenges*, *in* Arbitration Under International Investment Agreements: A Guide to the Key Issues 161 (Katia Yannaca-Small ed., 2010) (observing that the "self-restraint" required to implement the principle of equality "is difficult for some governments," especially if the investment dispute is politically charged, or if the government is accustomed to influencing investigations and adjudications, and no separation of powers is in place); *cf.* Knack & Keefer, *supra* note 15, at 591 n.2 ("Even if the entrepreneur's expectation is that, on average, the policies of today will prevail tomorrow, the possibility of large deviations from today's policies—which is higher when institutions are deficient—is sufficient to induce slower investment and less efficient production.").

158 *See* Japan Fair Trade Comm'n, Report Issued by the Advisory Panel on Administrative Investigation Procedures Under the Anti-Monopoly Act (Summary) ¶ 1(a) (2014), http://www8.cao.go.jp/chosei/dokkin/finalreport/brief-english.pdf ("[C]ompanies may not refuse an on-the-spot inspection on the grounds that the attorney has not arrived.") [hereinafter JFTC Report].

on-the-spot inspection."[159] The right to legal representation during witness interviews is even further restricted. At these closed-door custodial interviews, attorneys are not permitted to accompany interviewees, note-taking and audio or video recording is outlawed, and court reporters are prohibited.[160] In civil investigations, witnesses must answer all questions under penalty of perjury—Japanese law does not recognize a privilege from self-incrimination in administrative proceedings.[161] Once the interview is complete, the JFTC prepares a statement, which the witness is expected to sign out of the presence of counsel,[162] but the JFTC does not provide the witness with a copy.[163] Compounding matters, "confessions . . . form the basis of nine-tenths of [all] criminal prosecutions" in Japan.[164]

In 2014, under mounting criticism for its disregard of the right to counsel in antitrust investigations, the JFTC created an advisory panel to review its investigation procedures. Unfortunately, the advisory panel recommended no significant changes.[165] Allowing another opportunity for reform, the JFTC issued draft guidelines on administrative investigation procedures and called for public comment.[166] Several organizations, including the Japan Federation of Bar Associations, the National Federation of Small Business Associations, and the Japan Business Federation, noted that the draft guidelines still failed to remedy due-process and right-to-counsel issues.[167] As of the date of publication of this paper, the JFTC has not released a final version of the guidelines.

India's antitrust laws provide a prime example of a system that does not afford parties sufficient time to prepare their cases. After filing its recent findings relating to Google's alleged anticompetitive modification of search results, the Competition Commission of India gave the global internet behemoth 10 days to respond with evidence and arguments tailored to Indian law.[168] Google asked for an extension on September 8th, 2015.[169] Previously, in March 2014, the Commission had fined Google 10 million rupees after determining Google failed to show cause for failing to provide requested information despite being granted several extensions.[170] Google protested that it was not given sufficient time to comply.[171]

---

159 *Id.* ¶ 1(b).

160 *Id.* ¶ 3(b).

161 *See* Mel Marquis & Shingo Seryo, *Japan's Consolidated Anti-Monopoly Act: Recent Developments and Non-Developments*, Competition Pol'y Int'l, Oct. 2015, at 7, https://www.competitionpolicyinternational.com/assets/Asia-Column-October-Full.pdf (noting that although "Article 38(1) of Japan's Constitution provides for a right against self-incrimination where the party testifying may be held criminally liable," that privilege does not extend to "the context of . . . normal administrative investigations").

162 The Anti-Monopoly Act does not contain an express right for witnesses to refuse to sign the statement. *See* Shiteki-dokusen no Kinshi oyobi Kōseitorihiki no Kakuho ni Kansuru Hōritsu [Dokusen Kinshihō] [Anti-Monopoly Act], Act No. 54 of 1947, art. 111, *available at* http://www.jftc.go.jp/en/legislation_gls/amended_ama09/amended_ama15_12.html.

163 *Assuring Due Process*, *supra* note 142, at 6.

164 *Criminal justice in Japan: Forced to confess*, The Economist, Dec. 5, 2015, at 16.

165 *See* JFTC REPORT, *supra* note 158, at 1-3; Faaez Samadi, *JFTC escapes stronger due process commitments*, Global Competition Rev. (Jan. 5, 2015), http://globalcompetitionreview.com/news/article/37692/jftc-escapes-stronger-due-process-commitments/.

166 *See* Japan Fair Trade Comm'n, Guidelines on Antitrust Review Procedures (2015), *available at* http://www.nichibenren.or.jp/library/ja/opinion/report/data/2015/opinion_150724.pdf (Japanese language).

167 Yuri Nagano, *Japanese industry lobbies may object to new administrative investigation guidelines*, PaRR (Sept. 17, 2015), http://app.parr-global.com/intelligence/view/1303780 (on file with author).

168 Mark Briggs, *Indian report puts Google on alert*, Global Competition Rev. (Sept. 1, 2015), http://globalcompetitionreview.com/news/article/39393/indian-report-puts-google-alert/.

169 Deepali Gupta, *Google search bias case: Company seeks extension deadline*, Times of India, Sept. 8, 2015, http://timesofindia.indiatimes.com/tech/tech-news/Google-search-bias-case-Company-seeks-extension-deadline/articleshow/48864899.cms?.

170 Pratibha Jain, *Google's failure to show cause to CCI costs Rs. 10 Million*, Lexology (Apr. 8, 2014), http://www.lexology.com/library/detail.aspx?g=8b8d7383-99b1-4caa-a8ef-616eee99369f.

171 *Id.*

Lastly, Russia's Federal Antimonopoly Service recently adopted an infringement decision for an alleged concerted practice against major international container shipping companies without allowing them the opportunity and time to present economic evidence in a meaningful way.[172] There were reportedly two short hearings on December 7 and 14, 2015, and the infringement decision was announced right at the end of the second hearing, notwithstanding the fact that during the hearings the defendants presented additional evidence.[173] Surely, the arguments of the defendants were arguably made in vain if the authority had already been inclined to issue the infringement decision in this case. Apparently, this unacceptable procedural sequence is not something unique to Russia. For example, Lithuania had followed a similar approach, although now the law has been changed to give the authority sufficient time to consider the parties' arguments.[174] There is no doubt that such amendments are not only a matter of due process but also of ensuring quality of enforcement.

V. Concluding Remarks and Suggestions

The international proliferation of antitrust law—when based on sound economics—offers developing economies something more than an opportunity for economic growth through free markets. Because firms are more likely to invest in nations that have fair and clear procedures and sound legal institutions, the lure of foreign investment is pushing developing nations to incorporate into their antitrust regimes higher levels of due process guarantees in accordance with international standards. Continued progress will also be expected to be made in developed countries, where due process rights are not fully observed or practiced today. Across the globe, the independent judicial branch has been key to this growth of due process (along with, at times, enlightened antitrust enforcers making procedural changes to their own rules and procedures), and there is an emerging consensus among jurists that many current competition agency enforcement practices do not comport with fundamental due process rights. The growth of global competition studies, comparative studies of competition systems, and even the rankings of global competition agencies also play a role in driving countries to reform, improve, and refine the due process accorded to the accused. Due process is an important determinant not only of firms' confidence for investment, but also of the legitimacy of government institutions. When due process is assured, competition agency outcomes will improve. Due process reforms will in turn inspire other competition agencies to follow suit and will provide parties with an opportunity to advance due process rights outside the antitrust context. The result will be stronger legal institutions, which are proven to be the most important determinant of economic growth.

---

172 The decision is now under appeal. *See* Janet Porter, *Maersk to appeal Russian antitrust decision on GRIs*, Lloyd's Loading List (Jan. 15, 2016), http://www.lloydsloadinglist.com/freight-directory/news/Maersk-to-appeal-Russian-antitrust-decision-on-GRIs/65359.htm#.VrfQZ7IrJpg.

173 *Compare* Ginsburg & Owings, *supra* note 135, at 43 (describing potential shortcomings of administrative decision-making including the tendency that officers may serve only as a "rubber stamp" of staff recommendations and observing, as "the US Supreme Court put it: 'the fundamental requirement of due process is the opportunity to be heard at a meaningful time and in a meaningful manner.'") (quoting *Mathews v. Eldridge*, 424 U.S. 319, 333 (1976)).

174 Šarunas Pajarskas, Head of Administration, Competition Council of the Republic of Lithuania, *New Developments in Competition Policy in Lithuania After the Accession to the European Union*, http://kt.gov.lt/en/index.php?show=cases_other&other_doc=other_20040602 (last visited Feb. 2, 2016) ("[T]he time period for the Competition Council to take a final decision has also been liberalized - it has been prolonged for one month (in addition to the previous four months period) if the companies so request the Council.").

Sound competition policy takes years to form. In comparison, enhancing due process protections and affording fair procedures in competition cases is a relatively simple and straightforward—but powerful—fix. All competition authorities, whether they are old or new, should place emphasis on the adequacy of due process protections in competition proceedings.

VI. Appendix

The following is a partial listing of fundamental rights that every competition regime should afford targets of their investigations in order to respect due process rights and the rule of law:[1]

1) Ascertainable, written, transparent rules for competition
2) Effective access to legal counsel at all stages of the proceedings
   2a) Right to counsel during interrogations
3) Conduct of investigations
   3a) Right to remain silent
   3b) Right to have privileged communications with counsel remain privileged
   3c) Search and seizure—probable cause standard, pre-search judicial review, privacy rights respected
   3d) Written and public agency rules for the conduct of investigations
   3e) Protections for maintaining confidential business data and trade secrets[2]
4) A meaningful right and opportunity to assert defenses[3]
   4a) Notice of the specifics of charges (no anonymous witnesses) and sufficient time to respond
5) Independence of judiciary from prosecutorial function: separation of powers
6) Impartial and meaningful judicial review of agency actions at the trial court level
   6a) Trial rights—the opportunity to subpoena witnesses and documents
   6b) The right to present evidence and legal arguments
   6c) Freedom from reliance on anonymous or absent witnesses
   6d) Defendants have a fundamental right to question government witnesses that the government presents "live" at trial[4]

---

1 *See also* Christopher B. Hockett, *Antitrust and Due Process*, 28 Antitrust 1, 4 (2014) (listing 7 norms for antitrust due process).

2 *See New York v. Actavis, plc*, Civ. No. 14-7473, 2014 WL 5353774, at *3 (S.D.N.Y. Oct. 21, 2014) (compelling New York Attorney General to seal portions of complaint to protect confidential business information; "courts grant confidential treatment under circumstances where trade secrets and material that would place a party at a competitive disadvantage are being used in public filings."); William E. Kovacic, *Getting Started: Creating New Competition Policy Institutions in Transition Economies*, 23 Brook. J. Int'l L. 403, 435 (1997) ("For example, before the agency begins collecting business records, it must institute safeguards to ensure that such records can be retrieved readily and that confidential information will not be disclosed. A lapse in such safeguards early in the agency's existence could raise fatal doubts about its competence.").

3 The authors are aware of many agencies around the world—including in Europe—that spend many months if not years developing a list of alleged violations of law (e.g., 300, 500, or 800 paragraphs of detailed factual assertions) and then provide the defense a meaninglessly short period of time to respond—15, 30, or 60 days. Such a short response period precludes any meaningful opportunity to investigate the charges, marshal the evidence, and present a factual and legal response. *See Mathews v. Eldridge*, 424 U.S. 319, 333 (1976) ("the fundamental requirement of due process is the opportunity to be heard at a meaningful time and in a meaningful manner.").

4 *See Melendez-Diaz v. Massachusetts*, 557 U.S. 305 (2009).

6e) Access to the evidence possessed by or within the power of the government agency (e.g., open file access, access to a leniency applicant's files, etc.)

7) The sanctity of amnesty promises is upheld

8) The right and ability to obtain overseas evidence

9) The right to appellate review.[5]

5 Eleanor M. Fox & Michael J. Trebilcock, *The Design of Competition Law Institutions and the Global Convergence of Process Norms: The GAL Competition Project* 17 (N.Y.U. L. & Econ. Working Papers, Paper 304, 2012), http://lsr.nellco.org/nyu_lewp/304?utm_source=lsr.nellco.org%2Fnyu_lewp%2F304&utm_medium=PDF&utm_campaign=PDFCoverPages ("A right of appeal to a panel of decision-makers who can set aside decisions based on error is a recognized right of defense.").

Competition and Development: Insights into Building Institutions from the Kenyan Experience

Francis Wang'ombe Kariuki

fwkariuki@cak.go.ke

Director-General, Competition Authority of Kenya

Simon Roberts

simonjonroberts@gmail.com

Professor of Economics, University of Johannesburg

Abstract

The Competition Authority of Kenya is a relatively young institution which has successfully developed internal capacity while promoting a competition culture. The paper reviews the challenges faced and draws lessons for developing country authorities. It highlights the strategic approach adopted taking into account the concentrated markets in Kenya, widespread anti-competitive practices on the part of trade associations and legacy of extensive government intervention in the economy. The paper considers the analytical challenges of merger evaluation and abuse of dominance cases and observes the need to take account of dynamic considerations of incentivising investment alongside static competition concerns. Lastly, the importance of engagement with stakeholders and key interest groups which goes beyond advocacy is emphasized as part of building an understanding of competition.

I. Introduction

Kenya has a relatively new competition authority, established under the Competition Act No. 12 of 2010 ("Competition Act"). In this paper we review the Kenyan experience in terms of strategic planning and across the main areas of competition enforcement (mergers, cartels and abuse of dominance). We highlight important cases in each of these areas. From this we address three main issues that are critical to the evolution of competition in developing countries.

The first issue is about how a competition culture is built, rather than imposed, in the context of concentrated markets and a history of far-reaching government regulation. This relates to the prioritization of the authority as well as the enforcement challenges it faces given the capacity of a young authority.

The second issue is how a young competition authority engages with the analytical challenges required for merger evaluation and competition enforcement, taking into account considerations such as the availability of data, the size of the informal sector, and the need to incentivize investment.

Our third main concern is how developing country authorities understand and relate with stakeholders and key interest groups. This includes the communication strategies adopted, as well as how competition issues are articulated in relation to conceptions of the public interest and the government's industrial policies and development strategy more broadly.

II. Building Institutions: The Role of Prioritization and Strategic Planning

Kenya enacted its new Competition Act in 2010 and it came into effect on August 1st, 2011. The Act establishes the Competition Authority of Kenya ("CAK"), which acts as the regulatory institution, and the Competition Tribunal, to which appeals can be made. The CAK has the mandate to investigate alleged restrictive trade practices and abuses of dominance and also to evaluate all proposed mergers and acquisitions. It further acts as a government advisor in regard to competition matters. It also has a consumer protection mandate, which is not dealt with in this paper. The CAK is headed by the Director-General and the Board makes determinations pursuant to the investigations and analysis.

It is important to highlight that the Kenyan Government was motivated to enact the new law since it intends to use, among others things, competition policy to promote and sustain long-term economic growth, innovation, and productivity, as envisioned in the report entitled *Kenya Vision 2030: A Globally Competitive and Prosperous Kenya* ("*Kenya Vision 2030*").[1] The change of government in 2002 brought a sharp focus on the part of key members of the political class, as well as policymakers, on the need to address the dismal economic growth the country had experienced for the previous two decades.[2]

---

1 Gov't of Kenya, Kenya Vision 2030: A Globally Competitive and Prosperous Kenya (2007).

2 *See* David O. Ong'olo (2016), "*The New Competition Act for Kenya: Contextual Background and Implementation Challenges Ahead*", in Mehta, P (ed.), Evolution of Competition Laws and their Enforcement, Vol. II, (London: Routledge, 2016 forthcoming).

The Government's *Economic Recovery Strategy for Wealth and Employment Creation* (often called *ERS*),[3] was the Government's initial short-term approach to the low growth phenomenon in the economy. The *ERS* led to *Kenya Vision 2030*, which is a long-term development plan.

Kenya Vision 2030 underscores that the growth process is hinged on the healthy functioning of the domestic and external market system. *Kenya Vision 2030* sets out that a market-based economy, oiled by fair competition, will be a means of facilitating growth in all sectors of the economy. Consequently, the medium-term plan for *Kenya Vision 2030* committed to fast-tracking the review of Kenya's competition law.[4] This commitment led to the enactment of the Competition Act and positioned the CAK as an integral institution in driving the Government's current economic agenda. In late 2010, this was buttressed by the then President in his Memorandum to the Speaker of the National Assembly, dated 26th August, 2010, when refusing to assent to the Price Control and Essential Commodities Bill. In the Memorandum, the President stated that price controls go against the country's general economic policy and therefore he urged the Parliament to hasten the passage of the Competition Act, which was then in the Second Reading.

After the enactment of the Act, the CAK changed from the Monopolies and Prices Department in the National Treasury, which had the mandate of enforcing the previous law, the Restrictive Trade Practices, Monopolies and Price Control Act of 1988. Some of the staff from the Department, after undergoing competency and soft skills interviews, were absorbed into the CAK. This in effect meant that the impetus behind the new legislation was carried into the CAK, including the first (and current) Director-General, who was the former Head of the Monopolies and Prices Department.

In order to concretize the impetus behind the new legislation, the CAK developed and launched its 1st Strategic Plan on December 10, 2010. The Strategic Plan aimed at articulating the mandate of the CAK as part of the development of a market economy in Kenya.[5] The Plan prioritized the key areas that the Authority had to focus on, premised on the resources available, an assessment of the sector's contribution to the Kenyan economy, and the demonstrable achievement of the Government's transformational agenda, as envisaged in *Kenya Vision 2030*.

On the above basis, the Plan prioritized the CAK's activities in sectors that are key to the reduction of poverty and inequality, since this was a key priority of the Government. These activities included increasing agricultural productivity as the agriculture sector contributes 25% of the country's GDP. The Plan also is alive to the fact that the speed of private-sector growth will be determined by the acceleration of the Government's current efforts to address infrastructure and other logistical bottlenecks and, particularly, the business regulatory framework. In order to improve the business regulatory framework and enhance the business environment, various guidelines on merger analysis and the handling of restrictive trade practices have been developed and published.

The CAK has also entered into cooperation frameworks with some sector regulators, specifically the Central Bank of Kenya and the Communications Authority of Kenya, with the objective of easing the sharing of information, analysis, and decision-making concerning competition matters within the sectors. As an attempt to further the Government's initiatives of minimizing regulatory bottlenecks in various sectors, such as transport, banking, retail, and telecommunications, the CAK prioritized the finalization of the Product Market Regulation study. The study is aimed at benchmarking Kenya's regulatory regimes

3 Gov't of Kenya, Economic Recovery Strategy for Wealth and Employment Creation (2003).

4 Gov't of Kenya, First Medium Term Plan, 2008 – 2012 78 (2008).

5 The importance of competition in the Government's policy framework is highlighted by the fact that the Cabinet Secretaries to the National Treasury and the Ministry of Industrialization and Enterprise Development attended the launch of the CAK's Strategic Plan.

with the regimes of developed countries within the Organisation for Economic Co-operation and Development and at advising on the measures to be undertaken in order to facilitate achievement of *Kenya Vision 2030*.

In regard to the agenda of increasing agricultural productivity, with the aim of reducing poverty, the CAK has prioritized market inquiries in the seed, pyrethrum, artificial insemination, and tea sectors. These inquiries are aimed at identifying competition issues that may be affecting the efficient allocation of resources in these sectors to the detriment of productivity and consumer welfare. The prioritization of cases was also based on the need to positively impact poor households. As a result, the CAK has quickly enforced cases in sectors involving mobile money transfers and retail.

In an attempt to support the Government's agenda of easing the investment climate in Kenya, the CAK has directed its resources to assisting initiatives aimed at bringing down interest rates in the banking sector. Towards this, the CAK is focusing on banking by conducting inquiries aimed at identifying the markets that may be exhibiting anticompetitive tendencies and also at identifying any regulatory changes that could improve the banking sector. The CAK has also focused on the insurance industry, especially the actions of industry associations that may be acting as an impediment to effective competition and hence negatively affecting consumers.

To deepen its visibility and at the same time develop a culture of competition, the CAK has adopted a proactive approach to the press, holding annual workshops for journalists, which both explain the role of competition law and also provide information on the reasons behind the CAK's decisions and its future work and priorities. In this way, the CAK has sought to frame the national debate on the role of competition. It has focused attention on the real harm to consumers from anticompetitive conduct, as well as the ways in which state restraints or government actions have had detrimental effects on competition. A good example is in the pyrethrum sector where a state-created monopoly has led to farmers abandoning pyrethrum growing due to poor prices and, as a result, Kenya's market share declining from 85% of the world market in the 1980s to its current share of 5%.

The Authority has also focused on motivating the universities to conduct research and introduce courses relevant to supporting competition regulation in Kenya. This has been done through conducting public lectures by the Authority's staff and inviting speakers from other competition agencies. This is supplemented by the CAK sponsoring an essay writing competition based on competition issues. This essay competition will be held annually and it targets undergraduate and postgraduate students who are interested in conducting research in the field of competition.

The CAK, jointly with the University of Johannesburg's Centre for Competition, Regulation and Economic Development, has been conducting annual training on competition policy and law for legal practitioners in Kenya and in the region. The training is aimed at motivating corporations to adopt internal measures to ensure that their actions are compliant with the Competition Act and to minimize the time and costs of engaging with the CAK, especially for merger applications, which involve extensive back-and-forth discussions between the Authority and corporations.

The above initiatives elucidate a clear intention of the CAK to prioritize its activities to support the Government's economic agenda, while at the same time being efficient, transparent, and accountable in its decision-making. This is also coupled with efforts to ease the investment climate in the economy by advising the Government, through informed research, on removal of obstacles, specifically state restraints, to a well-functioning market economy. The alignment of the CAK's priorities with the national economic agenda has resulted in positive reciprocation by the National Treasury in terms of tripling the Authority's budget in the span of three years. This has enabled the CAK to increase its staff capacity by 150% and to deepen its operational infrastructure.

III. Mergers—The Discipline of Defining Markets

From the outset, the most prominent area of work for the CAK was merger review. This is attributed to the provisions of the Competition Act that create a suspensory regime for all mergers. The Kenyan experience is consistent with the argument put forward by David Lewis that merger review has a particularly important role in the early years in the development of a competition institution, in terms of the analytical framework for assessing markets and firm behavior, and in establishing a reputation for objective assessments.[6] In this section, we review two mergers that raised important issues for the CAK and that, in particular, illustrate issues for developing countries in defining and analyzing markets.

1. Acquisition of Buzeki Dairy Limited ("Buzeki") by Brookside Dairy Limited ("Brookside")

The acquisition of the business and assets of Buzeki by Brookside was a horizontal merger. The merger represented the largest dairy processing company in Kenya acquiring the fifth largest (measured in terms of the production of pasteurized fresh milk). The CAK approved the merger after finding that the market included mini-dairies and informal trade in fresh milk that accounted for around 50% of milk sales. This included sales through the national supermarket chains where "milk bars" allow consumers to bring their own container and purchase fresh milk from a dispenser. The merger also raised issues about the economies of scale required for investment in expanded capacity for products such as powdered milk in which Kenya competed against imports and in a wider regional market.

In terms of the parties' business activities, Brookside had operations in Kenya, Tanzania, and Uganda and also had a large farmers' network and milk collection and storage capacity in the region. The company processed various milk products, specifically fresh milk, fermented or cultured milk, butter and ghee, long life milk or ultra-high-temperature ("UHT") processed milk, yoghurt, flavored milk, and cream. Meanwhile, Buzeki processed fresh milk, fermented or cultured milk, butter and ghee, UHT long life milk, yoghurt, and UHT flavored milk.

According to data provided by the Kenya Dairy Board (the sector regulator), it was found that Kenya produced about 4.1 billion liters of milk. Out of this, 2 billion liters (48%) is retained at the household level while the rest of the milk (52%) is marketed through formal and informal channels. Dairy processors account for about 24% of the milk that is marketed and the other channels account for 76%. In addition, the data showed that liquid milk accounts for more than 90% of the sales of milk processors.

---

6 David Lewis, Thieves at the Dinner Table: Enforcing the Competition Act: A Personal Account, (Jacana Media, Auckland Park South Africa) at pages 76-77 (2012).

The CAK therefore concluded that there were overlaps between the merging parties in respect of the following:

i. Buying of milk from farmers;

ii. The processing and marketing of fresh milk; and

iii. The production and marketing of UHT milk (long life milk), yoghurt/fermented milk and butter and ghee.

The relevant product market was defined as the market for milk that included milk marketed through formal and informal channels.[7] The marketed milk market included both processed and unprocessed milk (raw milk). Processed and unprocessed milk was found to be substitutable in terms of homogeneity and purpose, among other factors. This market definition was further informed by the imposition of a 16% value-added tax ("VAT") by the Government on formal processed milk in September 2013. The 16% VAT was used as a proxy for a SSNIP[8] test. The data obtained from one of the largest retail chains in the country showed that milk sales for all formal processors declined for fresh and long life milk. Fresh milk sales declined by an average of 17.4% for all processors whereas for Brookside it declined by 18.1% and for Buzeki by 8.05%. Sales for long life milk declined by an average of 11.3%. The decline in sales implies that consumers substituted to milk sold through informal channels (as the volume of fresh milk being produced is assumed not to have changed).

This indicates that the raw milk marketed through informal channels was easily substitutable for the processed milk and hence that the relevant product market was larger than the processed milk market alone. It was also noted that milk processing firms face stiff competition from mini-industries, cottage industries, milk bars, producers, dairy cooperatives, and informal traders. In the relevant product market, the marketed milk market, the market share of Brookside was 7.35% while Buzeki's share was 1.44%. Post-merger, the market share of Brookside would be 8.79% of the marketed milk market.

In addition, the Authority considered that the merger would generate efficiencies and this would increase the ability of Brookside to compete locally and internationally, especially since the merger would help Brookside to invest in the production of powdered milk.

The Brookside-Buzeki merger highlights some of the key variables that may exert competitive pressure and that are important to consider in developing countries when defining markets, and that may not be a factor in developed countries. The informal sector plays a key role in defining relevant markets in Kenya and the key challenge is accessing data regarding the sector. This is also one reason why the CAK is investing a lot of resources in conducting market inquiries and motivating universities to conduct research so as to arrive at optimal market definitions based on informed analysis.

7 The Authority considered this market alone because liquid milk accounts for more than 90% of the sales of dairy processors.

8 Small but Significant Non-transitory Increase in Price.

2. Acquisition and Sale of Six Ukwala Supermarkets ("Ukwala") by Tusker Mattresses Limited ("Tuskys")

The Tuskys-Ukwala merger also highlights important debates with regard to market definition. This merger involved two national supermarket chains and turned specifically on a number of stores in the Central Business District ("CBD") of Nairobi. In this case, the merging parties argued that the geographic market was wide, covering the whole of Nairobi, while the CAK, with reference to store location and shopping patterns, found that a narrower market limited to the CBD was warranted, and thus prohibited the acquisition of the CBD stores based on this market definition[9] (the merger also involved the acquisition of other stores outside the market that was approved).

Tuskys engaged in retail business with a chain of supermarkets spread all over the main urban centers in Kenya and Uganda. Ukwala, the target undertaking, was a private limited company that engaged in retail business with a chain of supermarkets spread across the main urban centers in Kenya. The transaction involved the acquisition of the supermarket business and all the assets of Ukwala's six Nairobi branches. The transaction included all stock, inventories, equipment, goodwill, records, and leases. Since the parties' activities were comparable, the transaction between Tuskys and Ukwala was a horizontal merger.[10]

The CAK carefully considered the nature of the parties' retail activities as supermarkets and defined the relevant product market as the Secondary/Top Up market for the retail of branded groceries and household goods.[11] The Tuskys and Ukwala branches that were relevant to this transaction were located within the CBD where conditions such as parking and population density per square meter were unfavorable for one-stop shopping. The relevant geographic market therefore was defined as the Nairobi CBD.[12]

Given that the relevant market was defined as the Secondary/Top Up market for the retail of branded groceries and household goods within the Nairobi CBD, the market shares of the retailers were calculated in terms of the number of stores within the CBD. The number of stores that a supermarket chain operates was used as a proxy of the market share for the purpose of the analysis.[13] It was found that if approved, **the proposed transaction would increase Tuskys' market share from 39.3%** to 57.2%. Given that the dominance threshold is recognized as having over 50% market share, in effect Tuskys would become the dominant retail firm in the relevant market as established in Section 23 of the Competition Act as a result of the proposed transaction.

In addition to the creation of dominance, the CAK found that the pre-merger Herfindahl-Hirschman Index ("HHI") index of 2450 indicated that the branded retail market within the CBD was highly concentrated and that the proposed transaction would further aggravate the level of concentration within this market by increasing the HHI by 1403 to 3853.

The limited space available within the CBD for retail supermarkets was found to mean that significant barriers to entry existed. This is evidenced by the fact that for Eastmatt (the newest entrant) to enter the

9 All the Ukwala Stores have since been taken over by a new entrant in the Kenyan market.

10 Both parties were listed in the international standard industrial classification system as retailers by the Kenya Association of Manufacturers.

11 The relevant product market was delineated by considering store and customer characteristics, the prices of a selected basket of goods, and the *Brown Shoe* criteria. This analysis was informed by FTC v. Whole Foods Market, Inc., 502 F.Supp. 2d 1 (D.D.C. 2007).

12 This conclusion was made in light of the nature of the product offerings made by the supermarkets, the current geographic purchasing trends, and the role of bus route proximity to the geographic market.

13 The merging parties sought to reference the national shares of the major market players in the supermarket industry, which were as follows: Nakumatt Holdings Ltd (28%), Tuskys Ltd (16%), Uchumi Ltd (7%), Naivas Ltd (8%), Ukwala (2%) Ltd, and Eastmatt Supermarket (3%).

branded retail market within the CBD Tuskys had to vacate one of its previous premises. The limitation of available space arguably also constrains expansion by the existing players. In this regard, the limitation of space was a significant barrier to entry that would have preserved and subsequently enhanced any market power that Tuskys would enjoy as a result of the transaction.

Based on the above competition assessment, the Authority determined that the acquisition would:

a. Likely prevent or lessen competition in the Secondary/Top Up market for the retail of branded groceries and household goods within the Nairobi CBD;

b. Lead to a significant change in concentration in the Secondary/Top Up market for the retail of branded groceries and household goods within the Nairobi CBD;

c. Mean that Tuskys would become the dominant branded retailer in the Nairobi CBD and thus would possess market power; and

d. Maintain and enhance the market power enjoyed by Tuskys post-merger because of the significant barriers to entry.

This assessment led to the CAK approving the transaction subject to the condition to exclude the business and assets of five Ukwala supermarket branches in the Nairobi CBD from the transaction.[14]

IV. Restrictive Practices and Market Inquiries—Addressing Entrenched Coordinated Business Practices

The Competition Act addresses restrictive practices under Sections 21 and 22, which cover both horizontal and vertical practices. The main focus of the Act has been on how to address the widespread coordination by competitors, including through trade associations. These practices had in many cases developed under the auspices of previous government policies that were oriented toward encouraging collective action by firms at different levels of the supply chain. Powerful interests could control rents at different stages in production and marketing that had the overall impact of making the economy very uncompetitive. Access to economic activities was also dependent on lobbying organizations controlled by "insider" interest groups. The Competition Act anticipated the prevalence of anticompetitive conduct on the part of trade associations by explicitly setting out in Section 22 the types of arrangements that trade associations could not engage in, as well as stipulating that any arrangements under the auspices of a trade association would be understood to be arrangements entered into by all of its members.

We highlight the challenges facing a young competition authority in addressing cartel conduct in the context of pervasive coordination by tight-knit business groupings and the extensive involvement of government in different markets. This situation starkly illustrates the problems with a "hard enforcement" approach typically advocated in international antitrust circles. The prevalence and general acceptance of coordinated arrangements means that severe penalties, whether financial and/or penal sanctions as found

14 The purpose of the condition was to mitigate against the potentially significant competition issues raised. The excluded stores were selected based on their proximity to the Tuskys supermarkets in the CBD.

in the Kenyan Competition Act, are simply not realistic, especially given the poor awareness and understanding of competition principles on the part of judges. In fact, the Competition Act has weak administrative penalties alongside a criminal regime with provision for imprisonment.

1. Early Cases of Coordination

The first decided case involving coordinated conduct effectively illustrates the challenges with establishing a competition culture and addressing coordinated conduct. The case concerned arrangements entered into between Tuskys and Ukwala prior to their proposed supermarket merger, which was discussed above. Under the arrangement Tuskys agreed to run the stores of Ukwala in the Nairobi CBD before possibly agreeing to acquire them, which was referred to by the parties as testing a "proof of concept." The parties argued strongly that the proof of concept in itself did not constitute an acquisition; however, they were apparently oblivious to the fact that this arrangement was a straightforward prevention of competition between them (by object). This conclusion was not altered by the fact that other supermarkets in the CBD were not part of the arrangement.[15]

The second case related to the Association of Kenya Reinsurers ("AKR") sending a communication to its members that set a minimum rate for a particular client. In April 2015, the CAK fined the AKR KSh 721,000 (around US$7000) for setting minimum rates to reinsurance companies (its members) for group life insurance offered to the National Intelligence Service ("NIS") and its employees. The companies claimed to have the support of the Insurance Regulatory Authority ("IRA"). According to an article in the *Business Daily*:

> Increased competition has seen insurance companies resort to undercutting—charging lower than minimum set premiums—as a strategy to woo customers and increase the uptake of their products.
>
> The IRA said the practice of undercutting is rampant and poses a "serious threat" to the profitability and attractiveness of Kenya's insurance sector. Twelve insurers reported underwriting losses in 2013.[16]

Similar conduct amounting to naked coordination around minimum prices was undertaken by companies responsible for outdoor advertising. An association meeting attended by the companies was used to set minimum prices for standard roadside billboards in Nairobi and other major towns and cities. What is more surprising is that the association members jointly signed a letter that was sent to customers to inform them of the decision regarding minimum prices.

Assessments by the CAK suggest that despite the Competition Act having been in force for four years and extensive advocacy activities having been undertaken, conduct that contravenes the Act is still quite common. In effect, trade associations and firms do not understand why their practices are in breach of competition law when these practices were previously business norms. Note, these are not secret price fixing arrangements. The practices appear to be viewed by the associations as part of their responsibility to "organize" their markets, as had been encouraged by prior government policies. As well as highlighting

15 After agreeing to a settlement with the CAK where the parties admitted their coordination, they continued with the proposed merger. When this was only approved with the condition that the stores in the CBD be divested, the parties lodged an appeal, which has since been withdrawn.

16 Mugambi Mutegi, *Anti-competition fine by CAK alarms insurance firms*, Bus. Daily, Apr. 15, 2015, http://www.businessdailyafrica.com/Corporate-News/Anti-competition-fine-by-CAK-alarms-insurance-firms/-/539550/2686964/-/l66uey/-/index.html.

the role of government policies, this situation illustrates the challenges with regard to establishing the values of competition in a market economy.

To address the practices of trade associations, the CAK adopted a novel and innovative compliance process through two inquiries. These inquiries are discussed in the next section.

2. Inquiries into Trade Associations in Agro-processing and Financial Services and the "Special Compliance Process"

In early 2015, the CAK decided to pursue a program called the Special Compliance Process ("SCP") for trade associations. The SCP was motivated by the realization that, notwithstanding the Competition Act having a number of specific provisions that apply to trade associations, many trade associations continue to have rules, practices, and procedures that likely contravene the Act. It appeared that the associations and their members simply had not internalized the implications of the Act nor had they made the required changes to the business culture. The practices and rules of trade associations may also have been encouraged by past government policies and have been undertaken in the spirit of the collective development of industries and sectors. The practices are likely to continue to have considerable support within government departments where officials have been used to issuing licenses and maintaining price controls.

In line with the provisions of the Competition Act that provide that the functions of the CAK include the promotion and enforcement of compliance with the Act (under Section 9) and gives the CAK powers to address restrictive practices and anticompetitive conduct, the CAK is using the inquiry provisions to assess the prevalence of restrictive practices and to allow for voluntary disclosures and compliance undertakings on the part of trade associations and their members. The inquiries are being conducted in the financial services and the agriculture and agro-processing sectors. The inquiries are being undertaken under Section 18 of the Act and were published in the official gazette in mid-2015. The result of an inquiry is a report that draws conclusions and may make recommendations for further action. The reports from the inquiries will likely recommend investigations of conduct where it is found that parties have not fully disclosed the rules, practices, and procedures that may raise competition concerns, and/or have not taken steps to properly address and rectify such rules, practices, and procedures. If the inquiries conclude that the conduct has been disclosed and properly addressed then no further action would be required.

As such, the inquiries provide a *process* for the CAK to set out its expectations regarding the substantial compliance of trade associations and their members with the Competition Act. The CAK also recognizes that compliance involves a cultural change that is embodied in practical reforms within organizations. An alternative remedial approach where specific contraventions are identified would require the CAK to open an investigation in each case and to evaluate each type of conduct and practice, and would also mean parties could be subject to possible damages claims, which may encourage them to engage in litigation to slow the investigation and contest any findings.

The core objectives of the SCP under the two inquiries are the following:

» to facilitate the identification and rectification of past conduct;

» to increase awareness and to foster better practices in the future; and

» to address and resolve inadvertent contraventions without requiring in-depth investigations (under Section 31 of the Competition Act), thus reducing the costs of compliance for trade associations and their members and the burden of investigations on the CAK.

The inquiries do not immunize associations and their members from future investigation and prosecution if they do not rectify their conduct or they engage in other conduct. The inquiries target conduct under the auspices of trade associations and may include long-standing practices that are not expressly covered by the written rules or procedures of trade associations. The SCP does not cover conduct that is the subject of an already ongoing investigation or other conduct by some or all members of a trade association that is not under the auspices of an association. The financial services and agricultural sectors were selected because the CAK has good cause to believe that there are competition issues associated with the rules, practices, and procedures of the trade associations in those sectors.

In terms of the inquiries' procedures, trade associations are requested to provide all relevant documents as well as to identify arrangements and practices that may lessen or distort competition and to make representations as to how these are to be remedied. Such representations demonstrate good faith cooperation and are evidence of attempts at compliance, notwithstanding possible contraventions. The inquiries will not recommend that an investigation be initiated into conduct that has been properly disclosed and remedied by the parties involved. If, however, trade associations and their members do not cooperate in voluntarily making representations and, furthermore, do not respond fully to requests for information, then an adverse inference may be drawn about their activities. Based on the evaluation of information obtained in the inquiry process, whether from the trade associations or from other sources, each inquiry may recommend the initiation of formal investigations.

Trade associations and their members may decide it is preferable to make changes without providing details of their past conduct to the CAK and therefore may not respond fully to the information requests made. This means that they would still be subject to investigations and adverse findings and thus also potentially to damages claims.

In essence, by going the inquiry route the CAK is incentivizing the disclosure of information. The aim is to obtain information from trade associations and market participants regarding the extent of the potentially anticompetitive arrangements under the auspices of trade associations. The process also lays the basis for investigations because if the CAK assesses that trade associations and their members have not provided full and proper disclosure to the inquiry, it is likely to conclude that an investigation is required.

The inquiries are currently underway, with the first deadline for the submission of information on the rules, regulations, procedures, and practices of trade associations being at the end of September 2015. Initial indications are that a number of associations have taken the opportunity afforded by the inquiry to properly review their practices.

V. Abuse of Dominance—Competition Enforcement to Foster Dynamic Rivalry

Abuse of dominance is generally regarded as the most complex area of competition enforcement. While developing countries such as Kenya have concentrated markets, which suggests a high probability of abuse as well as substantial harm from such conduct, there is also a need to incentivize investment and innovation. These challenges are exemplified in the case of Safaricom, the main mobile network operator in Kenya.

In 2007, Safaricom launched a new mobile phone based payment and money transfer service known as M-Pesa (Pesa is Swahili for money).[17] The service allows users to make transfers using their cell phones. This service works through users being able to use a network of agents to load money on their cell phones and to make transfers to other users who can then cash-out at an agent. The service includes the ability to make payments to sellers of goods and services. Users are charged a small fee for sending and withdrawing money using the service. Since 2007, the mobile money transfer system in Kenya has grown rapidly to become the most successful in the world.

Mobile money transfer ("MMT") is an example of combining technologies to provide a new product that meets the needs of the majority of the population that do not have a bank account. Critical to understanding the implications of MMT is the offering of new services based on an existing network and the competition implications that may arise.

It is well recognized that network effects can raise barriers to entry and, in this case, Safaricom has been dominant in mobile telephony, sustaining a market share in excess of 70% of subscribers. The M-Pesa service represents a major innovation initially in the form of enabling money transfers between two Safaricom subscribers and was later extended to mobile payments and mobile banking (which required partnering with registered banks). While MMT was targeted at the unbanked, the extension of the service to payments and loans, as well as to the sale of related products such as insurance, has taken the innovation into the realm of competition in financial markets.

In the roll-out of the money transfer system, Safaricom signed up agents on an exclusive basis. These agents would typically be retailers who would be handling money as part of their day-to-day activities and thus be well positioned to do the cash-in and cash-out functions. Airtel, who is the main rival to Safaricom in mobile telephony and had its own MMT service, lodged a complaint that the agent exclusivity arrangements were anticompetitive. The complaint argued that the ubiquity of Safaricom's M-Pesa meant that actual and potential agents would not want to sign-up to Airtel as it had very few active users. And, without an agent network, Airtel could not be an effective competitor. It was evident that, despite having significantly lower money transfer charges, Airtel had failed to make in-roads. Safaricom claimed that Airtel was just seeking to freeride on the investments it had made in the agent network. It should also be noted that there was no inter-operability of the money transfer systems, and instead each one operated as a standalone closed system.

---

17 M-Pesa was based on work supported by the UK's Department for International Development together with Vodafone. Vodafone is also a shareholder in Safaricom.

The case thus relates to the balancing of encouraging investment in new services with the potential competitive harm that can result from first mover advantages. While these issues are complex, a new agency nevertheless has to engage with these challenges. It is especially important as the legacy of state involvement and regulation of the economy means that, while some sectors have tight-knit oligopolies, it is not uncommon for sectors with scale economies to have a single and entrenched dominant firm.

The CAK reached a settlement with Safaricom in 2014 that removed the agent exclusivity but that resulted in no penalty or admission of a contravention. In reaching the settlement, the CAK had to balance the evidence of harm to competition with the risks of over-enforcement and the chilling of investment and innovation. With regard to the exclusivity requirement, it was telling that in major urban areas the big supermarkets had resisted exclusivity and so it was not clear the extent to which it was required. Safaricom had also already obtained substantial returns from its investments in M-Pesa, thus rewarding the investments it had made. In addition, for Airtel to sign up agents, including those who were also agents for Safaricom, it would have to install its own system and conduct the required training. Moreover, Safaricom was in an overwhelmingly dominant position and had all the advantages that this dominance brings, meaning competition in the market was weak.

The decision thus opened up the market to competition. Soon after the decision, Safaricom cut its transfer rates to below those of Airtel, thus bringing substantial gains to consumers from what appeared to be more vigorous competition on the merits. It does not appear, however, that Airtel has significantly grown its market share. There are a number of other issues related to competition in the sector that continue to be examined by the CAK.

VI. Conclusions

A number of insights can be drawn from the Kenyan experience. The over-arching theme we wish to emphasize is how a competition culture is built, rather than imposed, in the context of concentrated markets and a history of far-reaching government regulation. This is most clearly illustrated in cases of coordination. A much more nuanced approach needs to be adopted by young authorities in this area than is commonly recommended. And, the emphasis on criminalization in the international debates on cartels is misdirected and potentially damaging in a developing country such as Kenya, where such conduct is normal business behavior rather than being viewed as akin to racketeering or fraud, and there is little, if any, credible threat of imprisonment. The powerful interests and prevailing views against the criminalization of cartels mean that the CAK will not have many influential allies if it simply steams ahead with enforcement.

Second, the Kenyan case illustrates how a young authority with limited capacity engages in the necessary evidence gathering and market definition assessments, and makes judgment calls balancing likely harm to competition with efficiencies and procompetitive investments that expand the production of goods and services. In an area such as merger evaluation, requiring detailed empirical economic analysis would mean a regime run by foreign consultants. Instead, an appreciation of the realities on the ground is at least as important. The assessment of routes to market for fresh milk in the Brookside-Buzeki merger highlights these concerns.

The investments in value-added products that were made pursuant to the Brookside-Buzeki merger further indicates the importance of understanding competition in relation to industrial policy. Industrial policy and competition policy can and should be complementary and mutually reinforcing. It is trite to observe that competition requires competitors, which in turn means the development of productive capabilities and investment in facilities that falls within the realm of industrial policy. In developing countries such as Kenya it is important to *generate* competitive local markets. They do not simply exist in the absence of government restrictions.

Our third main concern is how developing country authorities understand and relate with stakeholders and key interest groups. This goes beyond communication strategies. It involves building the capacity and understanding of the media. For example, the CAK has held an annual workshop with the main media companies to review cases and conduct training on the principles and methodologies used in competition assessments. In terms of the government, the CAK has worked to ensure that competition policy is incorporated into the government agenda and that the CAK's strategic planning is aligned with government's priorities. In this regard, it is not the case that public interest concerns will override competition priorities but rather that it is important for competition authorities to win over opinion through engagement and analysis. Effective analysis, transparency, and well-founded decision-making will mean the institution is respected as a center of expertise and will protect its operational and functional independence. A strong reputation also means buy-in from stakeholders and provides a base for attracting support and funding from development partners.

The experience of Kenya demonstrates that building a competition culture and values is an incremental process. A relatively modest institution can start working and addressing concrete issues in competition cases. This creates interest and demand for further action through engagement with stakeholders. The growing process includes learning and reflection. An advantage in Kenya, as in several other countries such as South Africa, is that those responsible for developing the competition law are then charged with taking the competition institutions forward, meaning that there is clear direction from the beginning.

International Cooperation & Convergence to International Best Practices: The Brazilian Experience

MARIANA TAVARES DE ARAUJO

mtavares@levysalomao.com.br

Partner, Levy & Salomão

Abstract

Brazil's competition law regime over the past 20 years has modernized by adopting international best practices. This development of Brazilian competition law has produced several benefits, such as increased efficiency and better enforcement. This paper provides an overview of how Brazilian competition law reflects international best practices. First, it discusses the historical development of Brazilian competition law up to 2012. Second, it describes the changes that were introduced by the new competition law in 2011. Lastly, it discusses how international best practices influenced the new competition law.

I. Introduction

The present article discusses Brazil's efforts towards convergence to international best practices and the rewards it has reaped along the way. During the past 20 years, convergence on substance and procedure has set the path to modern competition law enforcement in the country, while also ensuring the most efficient use of its scarce resources.

Brazil's experience is not unique. Competition agencies in developed and developing countries alike have strong reasons to pursue further cooperation and convergence: Over 120 jurisdictions have competition laws and agencies, and approximately 90 of such jurisdictions have merger control systems.[1] Merger and conduct cases are increasingly multinational due to globalization. Case dockets grow every year, while government resources in most countries do not follow suit.

Joining forces through international cooperation is therefore the only possible way to achieve consistency, efficient outcomes, and predictability in competition enforcement. It is also a promising tool to minimize (although perhaps not eliminate entirely) clashes among the different systems.

The second section of this paper reviews the institutional and legal framework in place up to 2012 and summarizes the key measures adopted by Brazilian antitrust authorities up till then in an effort to comply with international best practices. Section 3 describes the most relevant changes introduced by the 2011 law. Section 4 discusses the role international best practices and convergence played in this process. Section 5 concludes.

II. The Transition into the Current System

The first Brazilian competition law dates from the 1930s, but it was only in the mid-1990s when antitrust rules effectively gained space in Brazil as the country shifted to a market-based economy. In 1994, Congress enacted Law No. 8,884, which governed Brazil's administrative antitrust law and policy until May 2012, as part of several reforms derived from the Washington Consensus. In May 2012, the current antitrust statute entered into force in Brazil, introducing significant changes to the country's institutional and legal framework. The new statutory provisions follow successful examples from more mature jurisdictions and international best practices on merger review, on anticompetitive conduct enforcement, and on the organization of an antitrust authority.

The 1994 Law established the Administrative Council of Economic Defense ("CADE")[2] as an independent agency responsible for issuing final decisions at the administrative level in connection with all merger and anticompetitive conduct cases. CADE was comprised of six Commissioners, a Chairman, and two independent legal officers: (i) CADE's Attorney General, who represented it in court; and (ii) the Federal Public Prosecutor. Both officers had the duty of ensuring that procedural fairness would guide the decision-making process, and over time both would also render opinions in all cases pending decision at the administrative level, ultimately adding to the inefficiency of the system. All of CADE's decisions were subject to judicial review.

---

1 *See* Int'l Competition Network [ICN], The ICN Factsheet and Key Messages (2009), http://www.internationalcompetitionnetwork.org/uploads/library/doc608.pdf.

2 All acronyms of government agencies and departments will refer to the Portuguese spelling.

Under Law No. 8,884/94, the Secretariat of Economic Law of the Ministry of Justice ("SDE") and the Secretariat of Economic Monitoring of the Ministry of Finance ("SEAE") were responsible for investigating anticompetitive practices and issuing non-binding reports in connection with merger reviews. Together with CADE, the agencies were jointly referred as the "Brazilian Competition Policy System" (*Sistema Brasileiro de Defesa da Concorrência*).

From 1994 to 2003, the Brazilian antitrust authorities focused primarily on merger review, and substantial resources were devoted to the review of competitively innocuous mergers.[3] The post-merger review system introduced in 1994 proved to be very inefficient: CADE reviewed around 8,000 transactions, and only very few cases were approved with remedies or ultimately blocked.[4]

During this time, the agencies implemented several changes through regulations to work around the relevant legal and institutional limitations set forth by the statute. All of the changes took into account well-tested experiences from more mature jurisdictions. Technical assistance from agencies such as the US Department of Justice and the Federal Trade Commission and international organizations such as the Organization for Economic Co-operation and Development ("OECD") were also crucial in all these steps.

The SDE and SEAE reorganized its activities through internal protocols so that the SDE could concentrate on anticompetitive conduct investigations, with special focus on anti-cartel enforcement, and the SEAE could focus on merger analysis.

Relevant measures to conform merger review to international best practices included: (i) the introduction of a "fast track" procedure for simple cases; (ii) the possibility of CADE entering into consent decrees (*Medida Cautelar*) or agreements with the parties (*Acordo para Presevar a Reversibilidade da Operação* or *APRO*) that prevented complex transactions from being closed prior to CADE adjudicating the case; and (iii) the ability of CADE to issue binding interpretations of law with the purpose of ensuring legal certainty regarding the notification thresholds (*Súmulas*).

On conduct enforcement, as of 2003, the SDE started to use the enhanced investigation tools granted by the Brazilian Congress in 2000 (such as dawn raids and leniency), and CADE began imposing record fines (up to 22.5 percent of the company's gross turnover in the year preceding the initiation of the investigation) on companies and executives found liable for anticompetitive conduct. Cooperation between the SDE and state and federal prosecutors on cartel prosecution generally increased legal certainty regarding the use of the leniency program, enhanced the authorities' detection abilities, and allowed for stricter sanctions.

---

3 The 1994 Law established a post-merger control system. Article 54 of the Law provided that any act that could limit or otherwise restrain competition must be submitted to CADE for review. Under §3 of Article 54, the acts for which this submission was required included transactions aimed at any form of economic concentration, whether by means of mergers or acquisitions, by the incorporation of companies for the purpose of controlling other companies, or by any form of corporate grouping, which caused any participating company or group of companies to achieve at least a 20 percent market share of a relevant market, or in which any of the participants has posted annual gross revenues equivalent to at least BRL 400 million. A few years after the introduction of the 1994 merger review system, a new law was passed providing for a merger filing fee (Law No. 9,781, of Jan. 19, 1999).

4 The blocked transactions were the following: the proposed joint venture between asbestos producers Brasilit and Eternit (Case No. 06/94, adjudicated in 1996), the proposed joint venture between Brasil-Álcool and Bolsa Brasileira do Álcool which had the goal of serving as a joint selling agency for all of the output of the parties (Case No. 08012.002315/99-50, and Case No. 08012.004117/99-67, adjudicated in 2000), and the merger between chocolate makers Nestlé and Garoto (Case No. 08012.001697/2002-89, adjudicated in 2004), in which CADE ruled that the transaction had to be unwound, notwithstanding the fact that the transaction had closed two years earlier. The decision is now being challenged in court. Only in cases involving high concentrations in the Brazilian market and a lack of efficiencies resulting from the transaction has CADE imposed restrictions in order to approve the transaction (e.g., Case No. 12/94, Rhodia/Sinasa (the Case No. 27/94, Kolynos / Colgate-Palmolive; Case No. 16/94, Siderúrgica Laisa/Grupo Korf Gmbh, "Gerdau Case"); Case No. 58/95, Brahma/Miller; Case No. 83/96, Antarctica/Anheuser Bush). Although CADE has imposed conditions on approximately 3.4 percent of transactions for the period 2000-2005, structural requirements directing the sale or utilization of assets were imposed only in four cases. *See* ORG. FOR ECON. CO-OPERATION & DEV. & INTER-AMERICAN DEV. BANK, COMPETITION LAW AND POLICY IN BRAZIL: A PEER REVIEW 31 (2005).

III. Brazil's Current Competition Law

1. Institutional Framework

Law No. 12,529/2011 (the "Competition Law") entered into force in May 2012 and consolidated the investigative, prosecutorial, and adjudicative functions of the Brazilian competition authorities into one autonomous agency. CADE was restructured to include: (i) an administrative Tribunal composed of six commissioners and a chairman responsible for adjudicating complex merger and antitrust cases; (ii) a Directorate General for Competition ("DG" or *Superintendência-Geral*) responsible for conducting antitrust investigations, reviewing merger cases, and issuing final decisions on non-complex merger cases; and (iii) an Economics Department responsible for providing economic support both to the Tribunal and the DG. All of CADE's decisions are subject to judicial review by non-specialized judicial courts.

The DG, appointed by the President of the Republic and confirmed by Congress for a two-year term, performs the former functions of the SDE's Antitrust Division and the SEAE, thus combining the roles of an investigator and a prosecutor. The SEAE continues to exist but deals exclusively with "competition advocacy" before the Brazilian regulatory agencies and other governmental bodies. It is particularly important that this function continues to be performed by the SEAE, since its position as part of the powerful Ministry of Finance affords it access to many other government bodies. Now divested of its other responsibilities, the SEAE may be in a better position to promote competition standards within the government.

The creation of an Economics Department within CADE is an indication of the increasing weight that economic analysis has been playing in competition matters over recent years. This is a trend that began under the previous statute and that is expected to continue in every important abuse of dominance and merger case under the current regime.

Another important development was the provision for 200 permanent positions in CADE. Until 2012, the most serious problem confronting Brazil's competition authorities has been its lack of resources, compounded by a high rate of employee turnover that adversely affects its institutional memory. While to date CADE has only hired around 50 new officials, consolidation of the three agencies has alone helped mitigate understaffing, which had led to a large backlog of investigations.

2. Merger Control

After almost 25 years of a post-merger review system being in place in Brazil, the 2011 Law introduced a mandatory pre-merger notification system.[5] The maximum period to conduct a merger review is 330 calendar days from the date of filing or from the date CADE considers the filing to be complete. Simple cases can be cleared solely by the DG without the need for review by the Tribunal. The few complex

5 Law No. 12,529/2011 provides for minimum-size thresholds, expressed in total revenues derived in Brazil, for two merging parties. The 20 percent market share test in the 1994 Law was eliminated in the new Competition Law, following international best practices that recommend that notification thresholds should be clear and understandable, based on objectively quantifiable criteria. The Law also introduced a claw back provision that allows CADE to review transactions that fall outside the merger thresholds within one year of their closing. Fines for "gun jumping" range from BRL 60,000 to BRL 60 million. Violations can occur even if the parties to the transaction do not compete in the same markets. In cases involving competitors, coordination of competitive activities or detailed information exchanges can also lead to a cartel violation, subjecting the parties to fines from 0.1 to 20 percent of a company's (group of companies' or conglomerate's) gross revenues generated in the "sector of activity" affected by the infringement in the year prior to the initiation of the investigation.

cases that require the adoption of remedies to address antitrust concerns, or transactions that have to be blocked, need to be reviewed by CADE's Tribunal.[6] This rearrangement of roles between the prosecutorial and adjudicative agencies has brought more efficiency to Brazil's competition system and has freed-up resources of the Tribunal so it can focus on the review of complex cases.

The Competition Law provides for minimum transaction size thresholds for merger reviews that are calculated by looking at the total Brazilian revenues derived in the last fiscal year by at least two parties to the transaction. The Ministries of Finance and Justice Joint Resolution No. 994/2012 establishes that one party must have Brazilian revenues in the last fiscal year of at least BRL 750 million and the other party of at least BRL 75 million—both acquirer and seller, including the whole economic group,[7] should be taken into account. The Competition Law also sets forth an effects test, according to which only transactions that have potential effects in the country are reportable. Such thresholds take into account several recommendations by the International Competition Network ("ICN"), in particular by eliminating the market share test that existed in the previous statute.[8]

The average review period in 2015 has been 20 calendar days for simple cases and 84 calendar days for complex transactions,[9] which is fully aligned with international best practices.

From a substantive perspective, while Brazil's competition law does not contain language specifically setting forth the substantive standard to be employed in reviewing mergers, CADE's interpretation of the law indicates that the standard applied in Brazil contains both a dominant position test and a lessening or restriction of competition test.[10]

3. Prosecution of Anticompetitive Behavior

Article 36 of the Competition Law deals with all types of anticompetitive conduct. The new legislation did not change the definition or the types of anticompetitive conduct that could be prosecuted in Brazil under the previous law. The Law prohibits acts "that have as object or effect:" to (i) limit, restrain, or in any way cause injury to open competition or free enterprise; (ii) control a relevant market of a certain good or service; (iii) increase profits on a discriminatory basis; or (iv) engage in market abuse. Article 36 § 30 contains a lengthy but not exclusive list of acts that may be considered antitrust violations provided

---

6 For complex cases, Brazil's competition law allows the Reporting Commissioner to authorize the parties to close the transaction before receiving CADE's clearance, subject to conditions such as the limitations on the freedom of the acquirer to liquidate assets, integrate activities, dismiss workers, close stores or plants, terminate brands or product lines, and alter marketing plans.

7 Pursuant to CADE's Resolution No. 2/2012 (as amended by CADE's Resolution No. 9/2014), the following entities shall be considered as part of the same "economic group" for the purposes of calculating the group's revenues: (i) entities subject to common control; (ii) all the companies in which any of the entities subject to common control holds, directly or indirectly, at least 20 percent of the voting or total capital stock. In transactions involving private equity funds, the turnover of the following entities shall be taken into account for the purposes of determining whether a filing is mandatory: (i) the economic group of each investor holding, directly or indirectly, 50 percent or more of the fund directly involved in the transaction, either individually or by means of an agreement with other investors; and (ii) the portfolio companies that are controlled by the fund directly involved in the transaction, as well as the portfolio companies in which such fund holds, directly or indirectly, an interest of 20 percent or more. In case of joint ventures, the entirety of the joint venture's turnover shall be considered for the purposes of turnover calculation for all the parties holding a stake of at least 20 percent in it. *See* Merger Filing No. 08700.001525/2013-18.

8 *See* ICN, Recommended Practices for Merger Notification Procedures 3-4 (2002), http://www.internationalcompetitionnetwork.org/uploads/library/doc588.pdf.

9 *See* CADE's website, www.cade.gov.br

10 The Merger Guidelines, which were issued under the previous 1994 statute, employ traditional merger analysis and describe five steps in the review process: (i) Step 1: Defining the relevant product and geographic markets; (ii) Step 2: Determining whether the market share of the merged entity is sufficiently large to permit the exercise of market power; (iii) Step 3: Assessing the probability that market power will be exercised post-merger; (iv) Step 4: Examining the efficiencies generated by the transaction; and (v) Step 5: Evaluating the net effect of the transaction on economic welfare. Historically, whenever CADE reaches Step 5, the transaction is either blocker or subject to substantial remedies. Furthermore, no case has been approved based solely on efficiencies arguments.

they have as an object, or produce, the above-mentioned effects. The listed practices include various types of horizontal and vertical agreements and unilateral abuses of market power.

Law No. 12,529/2011 also modified Brazil's Leniency Program.[11] The 2000 rule that leniency was not available to a "leader" of the cartel was eliminated. The elimination of the disqualification of the leader as an applicant in the law does not necessarily mean that the authority will disregard the role played by a cartel participant in determining whether to grant leniency or not—Article 86 of Law No. 12,529/2011 provides that the authority *may* grant leniency if the program requirements are fulfilled. Therefore, the authority is no longer required to address arguments that a leniency applicant must be disqualified for having been a leader in a conspiracy, but this will most likely not be followed by policy changes resulting in immunity from sanctions independent of the role played by each party. Further, a grant of leniency previously extended to criminal liability under the Federal Economic Crimes Law but not to other possible crimes under other criminal statutes, such as fraud in public procurement. The 2011 Law broadened the leniency grant to extend to the latter crimes as well.

These amendments had the purpose of enhancing transparency and legal certainty regarding the Program's rules in line with successful experiences in more mature jurisdictions and with the recommendations set forth in chapter 2 of the ICN's 2009 *Anti-Cartel Enforcement Manual*, which covers the drafting and implementing of an effective leniency program.[12] Recently, in November 2015, CADE put out for public consultation draft guidelines for the Leniency Program. The draft provisions shed light on CADE's enforcement practice regarding important developments of the leniency program during the past 5 years (e.g., leniency "plus," the interface between leniency for cartels and leniency for corrupt practices, etc.) and overall show CADE's commitment to further convergence to international best practices.

Changes to the criminal sanctions applicable to anticompetitive conduct were also introduced by Law No. 12,529/2011. The previous provision in the Federal Economic Crimes Law set forth jail terms of 2 to 5 years *or* the payment of a criminal fine. The new Competition Law amended that provision and established that anticompetitive behavior may be punished with a jail term of 2 to 5 years *plus* the payment of a criminal fine. Criminal prosecution continues to be solely against individuals, and state- and federal-level prosecutors are the ones in charge of prosecuting the conduct.

Finally, as for procedure, both the previous Law and the current Law grant court-like due process protections. In the balance between agency effectiveness and rights of defense, the Law prioritized the latter, thus aligning with provisions of Brazil's constitution.

---

11 Brazil's Leniency Program follows the general lines of the US Leniency Program and adopts a winner-takes-all approach. It has the following general features: (i) full or partial immunity from administrative sanctions for the first company and/or individual to apply for a leniency agreement; (ii) immunity from criminal sanctions, provided that the individual(s) sign the agreement along with the company; (iii) full confidentiality of the application; (iv) requirement for immediate cessation of the applicant's involvement in the alleged or investigated violation; and (v) the applicant must effectively and permanently cooperate with the investigation. Full or partial administrative immunity for companies and individuals depends on whether the DG was previously aware of the illegal conduct at issue. If the DG was unaware, the party may be entitled to a waiver from any penalties. If the DG was previously aware, the applicable penalty can be reduced by one- to two-thirds, depending on the effectiveness of the cooperation and the "good faith" of the party in complying with the leniency agreement. In the leniency agreement, the DG states whether it was previously aware of the conduct and makes a recommendation to CADE, which will apply the grant of leniency while adjudicating the case.

12 *See* ICN, Anti-Cartel Enforcement Manual at ch. 2 (2009), http://www.internationalcompetitionnetwork.org/uploads/library/doc341.pdf.

IV. The Role of International Best Practices and Convergence

International best practices have been a crucial resource for Brazilian antitrust authorities for the past two decades, during which the economy has gone through significant changes, and all the measures discussed above were implemented. During this time, guidance from more experienced jurisdictions has been particularly welcome in two situations: (a) when the authorities are confronted with issues for the first time; and (b) when the authorities need to convince other stakeholders (e.g., government agencies, the bar, Congress, the courts, etc.) of the need for specific measures (e.g., introducing changes to existing rules, arguing a complex case in court, etc.).[13]

A hardcore cartel, abuse of dominant position, or anticompetitive merger have similar effects on consumer welfare regardless of whether they take place in a developed or developing jurisdiction, a small market or large economy, or in a national or regional market. Antitrust rules, on the other hand, control the creation and uses of economic power and so help markets work for the benefit of the people (buyers, sellers, and firms competing on the merits) rather than for the benefit of a privileged and powerful few. As a result, having an effective antitrust system based on rules that have been tested elsewhere during the past century has been critical for Brazil and arguably for other countries at a comparable level of economic development and facing similar challenges.

Convergence allows agencies around the world to potentially reach similar answers regarding comparable challenges when reviewing cases that often have the same elements. But most antitrust rules contained in best practices are general in nature, while market structure and other elements of a case are specific to each jurisdiction, so agencies around the world will continue to reach different outcomes regardless of the degree of convergence achieved on the legal and economic theories they apply. Therefore, the critiques that best practices are based on experiences in the developed world and thus may not be as useful for developing countries, while in theory could be a potential challenge, may not prove a problem in practice.[14]

In a multi-jurisdictional merger, for example, when agencies work closely together, differences in the products affected by the merger and the market structures in the different jurisdictions will lead to potentially different outcomes, which ideally will not lead to the respective investigations coming into conflict. International best practices can make this interaction easier. Conversely, since agencies increasingly investigate the same matters, without convergence, this process tends to become burdensome for the agencies and parties involved.

Furthermore, the traditional approach of imposing structural remedies with horizontal transactions and conduct remedies with vertical integrations is being replaced by a growing inclination toward hybrid solutions, which may be a good option to have in the enforcement toolkit. In this context, agencies are being encouraged to be creative in devising remedies. The effort to ensure proportionality in antitrust intervention, which is the idea behind spurring creativity, is key from a procedural fairness perspective

13 For example, the OECD's *Recommendation on Effective Action against Hard Core Cartels* and the ICN's *Recommended Practices for Merger Notification & Review Procedures* are two popular sets of best practices that Brazilian authorities have resorted to in the past in order to introduce key changes to its laws and policies. Both have been key resources for these changes, and powerful assets for winning support.

14 *See* Rachel Brandenburger et al., *Global Antitrust Policies: How Wide is the Gap?*. 1 Concurrences Competition L.J. 3 (2012), *available at* http://www.justice.gov/sites/default/files/atr/legacy/2012/05/04/282930.pdf.

as well. However, creativity in devising merger remedies can easily lead to conflicting decisions in global deals, particularly in cases involving relevant markets broader than a local market.[15]

In order to craft proportionate and effective remedies, parties must be given the opportunity to respond to the evidence and agency concerns regarding competition issues affecting the specific jurisdiction, and to propose possible solutions. Close coordination among the agencies in the jurisdictions potentially affected by the transaction is also important for crafting remedies. From a practical standpoint, this may be the only way for remedies to be implemented throughout the globe.

In Brazil, merger parties can negotiate undertakings with CADE to remedy perceived competition issues, which can be offered from the day of filing up to 30 days following the DG's challenge of the transaction before the Tribunal. It has been increasingly common for the DG to engage in international cooperation for complex transnational merger cases, usually following a waiver issued by the parties. In the Mach/Syniverse[16] and Ahlstrom Corporation/Munkjö AB mergers, global transactions also subject to the review of the European Commission, CADE accepted the same divestiture package that was offered abroad, allowing for an efficient divestiture process. Later, in the review of the Lafarge/Holcim merger that was filed in 20 jurisdictions, although the case involved locally-defined markets (and, therefore, local divestiture packages) CADE was open to considering the uniform remedy that had been proposed by the parties to other key authorities reviewing the case.[17] This result would not have been possible if Brazil and the EU did not have similar rules, standards, and methods of analysis that facilitate communication and help in avoiding systemic clashes.

With cartel enforcement, both the potential rewards and challenges are perhaps even greater. The proliferation of anti-cartel regimes with strong detection and sanctioning tools is welcome news and creates opportunities for joint actions that will likely lead to increased deterrence. But agencies worldwide are now confronted with the difficult question of where deterrence ends and over-punishment begins. At the backdrop of this question lies the need to preserve parties' rights while also allowing antitrust authorities to fulfill their duty to prosecute and punish international conspiracies that harm consumers in their jurisdiction.[18]

Brazil has been increasing its cooperation with foreign antitrust agencies in cartel cases over the years. In February 2009, Brazil's administrative and criminal authorities launched a simultaneous dawn raid in connection with an international cartel investigation together with the US Department of Justice and the European Commission. Brazil's antitrust authorities have executed cooperation agreements with the US Department of Justice, the European Commission, as well as with the competition agencies in Canada, Portugal, Argentina, Chile, and Russia. The Brazilian authorities have in a number of instances requested the assistance of foreign authorities to conduct an investigation and, more recently with the increasing number of dawn raids, foreign authorities have become interested in evidences seized in Brazil.

At the same time, defendants in the Air Cargo investigation that did not settle in Brazil were fined approximately US$80 million by CADE—and one of the individuals was sentenced by a criminal court

---

15 *See* Ana Paula Martinez & Mariana Tavares de Araujo, *Merger Remedies in Transnational Mergers: When Less is More*, 1 CPI Antitrust Chronicle (Dec. 2014), *available at* http://www.levysalomao.com.br/files/publicacao/anexo/20141217140852_merger-remedies.pdf.

16 Merger Case No. 08700.006437/2012-13 (Syniverse Holdings, Inc. and WP Roaming III S.A.R.L.), cleared in April 2013. Mach/Syniverse was filed under the previous statute and involved the market for the sale of roaming technology to mobile operators. CADE was concerned over the elevated concentration that would arise from the transaction in the markets for GSM data clearing and near real-time roaming data exchange. Consequently, the parties offered commitments to divest a significant part of Mach's assets that adequately addressed CADE's concerns and the transaction was subsequently cleared.

17 *See* Footnote 16.

18 *See* John Terzaken & Peter Huizing, *How Much Is Too Much? A Call For Global Principles To Guide The Punishment Of International Cartels*, Allen & Overy, Spring 2013, http://awards.concurrences.com/IMG/pdf/how_much.pdf.

judge to serve jail time for 10 years and 3 months, in addition to paying a separate criminal fine. The fine could seem low compared to other sanctions imposed by CADE in recent cases if one did not consider the fact that many of the same defendants had been sanctioned in approximately 10 other jurisdictions also. Fairness in sanctioning is also an important policy to consider. Over-punishment weakens competition by potentially reducing the number of companies in a market, which ultimately harms consumers. This is certainly an area where coordination will increasingly matter.[19]

Finally, international best practices was an important influence on the Brazilian government and Congress when they passed the 2011 Competition Law. Resorting to best practices in different ways had a significant impact in speeding up congressional review and ensuring that representatives and senators did not get carried away and introduce too many of their own ideas into the Competition Law, which would have not necessarily led to the best outcome for Brazilian consumers.[20]

V. Conclusion

International best practices have been key resources. However, when deciding which route to take on implementation, Brazilian authorities have been mindful of what would be appropriate under the legal system and/or the specifics of each case. This combination has proven to be a successful recipe for effective enforcement in Brazil, which now has an effective cartel program in place, and an admittedly far from perfect but significantly improved merger system.

Harmonization on key elements of merger review and cartel enforcement in particular has allowed Brazil's antitrust agencies to effectively cooperate with their counterparts in more mature jurisdictions. This has improved Brazil's reputation as a strong antitrust enforcer, both domestically and internationally.

While cooperation and convergence are powerful tools for enforcement that allow for the efficient use of scarce government resources, participating in antitrust networks such as the ICN and OECD involves real commitment. Often, the case-handlers that are fluent English speakers and that are involved in key enforcement roles at the Brazilian antitrust agencies are the same ones in charge of attending international meetings and participating in projects, such as drafting submissions. This has been the case in Brazil for a number of years.

Additional consideration on how to involve newer agencies in the international antitrust networks without straining their limited resources may be an area that can benefit from further work. The investment has most certainly paid off for Brazil, but it was not always easy. Facilitating participation may expand and further improve these global networks.

19 In May 2014, CADE's Tribunal issued a final ruling on the cement cartel investigation. Sanctions include a record-fine of roughly US$1.3 billion, plus other ancillary sanctions, such as the divestiture of assets and a ban on carrying out transactions in the cement and concrete sector for five years. It was the first time that CADE resorted to this type of sanction, which is relatively unusual in cartel cases. The second highest fine imposed by CADE in connection with a cartel case was roughly US$1 billion for an industrial gases cartel in 2010.

20 ICN representatives met with important congressional representatives and senators and a letter from the chair of ICN's steering committee supported the changes. Further, the OECD's Competition Committee Secretariat met with key members of Congress to lobby for the reform and conclusions from the OECD peer review were shared with them.

International Competition Technical Assistance: The Federal Trade Commission's Experience and Challenges for the Future

Timothy T. Hughes

thughes@ftc.gov

Counsel for Competition Technical Assistance, US Federal Trade Commission

Russell W. Damtoft

rdamtoft@ftc.gov

Associate Director, Office of International Affairs, US Federal Trade Commission

Randolph W. Tritell[*]

rtritell@ftc.gov

Director, Official of International Affairs, US Federal Trade Commission

Abstract

The FTC's technical assistance program contributes to economic growth in developing and emerging economies by helping to build institutions that enforce competition laws based on sound economic principles convergent with internationally recognized standards. While researchers have found it difficult to measure how much competition law enforcement contributes to growth, they have found demonstrable benefits

---

* The views expressed are the authors' own and not necessarily those of the Federal Trade Commission or its Commissioners.

from policy reforms that introduce competition into economies and sectors of economies previously insulated from competition. When based on sound economic principles, competition law enforcement helps to facilitate and accelerate the economic gains from these market-oriented reforms.

During a jurisdiction's transition to a more market-oriented economy, the FTC's technical assistance program addresses fundamental questions. FTC attorneys or economists that serve as long-term resident advisors in the agency or have worked with recipient jurisdictions for many years acquire the familiarity with local practice and issues needed to train new agency staff how to distinguish legitimate aggressive competitive behavior from anti-competitive conduct. When a jurisdiction becomes more experienced, the content of the FTC's technical assistance increases its focus on sophisticated analytic issues and economic tools for investigation. The objective throughout is to build institutions capable of maintaining an environment in which competition law, applied in a manner that is convergent with international best practices, can foster economic growth.

I. Introduction

Competition law enforcement in all jurisdictions aspires to contribute at least indirectly to economic growth. For a competition authority to contribute, it must be able to identify industry structures and firm behavior that enhance or harm competition, distinguish anticompetitive from pro-competitive or competitively neutral behavior, and deploy policy and enforcement resources to address harmful behavior effectively. Building institutions and staff with this capability is not an easy or quick task. For competition enforcement authorities and policymakers in developing and emerging economies this task is particularly urgent and challenging.

The US competition agencies help newer agencies develop the capacity to meet these challenges through their technical assistance programs, in which they offer the analytical framework and practical skills that they have learned over many years to be most helpful in promoting economic growth. As the International Competition Network ("ICN") has noted,

> Successful enforcement of a competition law requires not only technical knowledge, but experience and judgment. In developed countries, this comes from on-the-job experience and institutional knowledge of the process of trial and error that led to past failures and successes. Technical assistance is the process by which a newer competition agency can take advantage of the experience of others as it develops that experience and judgment on its own.[1]

Supported in many cases by funding from the US Agency for International Development ("USAID") and other institutions, the Federal Trade Commission ("FTC"), frequently in partnership with the Antitrust Division of the Department of Justice ("DOJ"), has been working to meet this need for over 25 years.[2] Through their technical assistance programs, the US competition agencies share and advance the long-term goals of US assistance including poverty reduction, economic growth, and development.

---

1 Int'l Competition Network [ICN], Findings Related to Technical Assistance for Newer Competition Agencies 1 (2007), http://www.internationalcompetitionnetwork.org/uploads/library/doc366.pdf.

2 Fed. Trade Comm'n & Dep't of Justice, U.S. Federal Trade Commission's And Department of Justice's Experience With Technical Assistance For The Effective Application of Competition Laws 2 (2008), https://www.ftc.gov/sites/default/files/attachments/international-assistance-program/ftcdojtechnicalassist.pdf.

This article examines the role that economic development has played in the motivation, history, methods, and content of the FTC's technical assistance program. It also discusses the lessons learned from our experience and the challenges that we foresee in tailoring the program to the level of experience of the competition authority and the stage of economic development of the recipient jurisdiction.

II. Goals of the FTC's Technical Assistance Program

The FTC's technical assistance program has two principal goals: (1) building the capacity of competition authorities and policymakers to use competition to promote economic development; and (2) fostering convergence toward standards of competition law enforcement that enhance consumer welfare. The FTC pursues both goals at every stage of assistance.

1. Economic Development

During the early years of a jurisdiction's transition toward a market economy, policymakers and the public often question the ability of competition law enforcement to contribute to economic growth. This is also the period during which competition law enforcement—and therefore technical assistance—can be an important factor in implementing competition policies with a positive and measurable effect on economic development.

While studies in developed economies have tried to measure the extent to which implementation of competition law and policy contributes to economic growth,[3] several studies in less developed economies have demonstrated the measurable benefits that the introduction of competition policies contribute to economic growth, development, and poverty reduction.[4] The link between robust domestic competition as a means of promoting growth and development is increasingly well-established. As one scholar noted, "the growth rate of living standards essentially equals the growth rate of domestic productivity. Even though world trade is larger than ever before, national living standards are overwhelmingly determined by domestic factors rather than by competition for world markets."[5] The McKinsey Global Institute undertook a 12-year study, beginning in 1991, to determine why some nations remain wealthy while others remain stagnant or poor, even after years of international aid. In his book describing the lessons

---

3 *See, e.g.*, Jonathan Baker, *The Case for Antitrust Enforcement*, 17 J. Econ. Persp. 27 (2003); Robert W. Crandall & Clifford Winston, *Does Antitrust Policy Improve Consumer Welfare? Assessing the Evidence*, 17 J. Econ. Persp. 3 (2003); Hiau Looi Kee & Bernard Hoekman, *Imports, Entry and Competition Law as Market Disciplines* (World Bank Policy Research Working Paper 3031, 2003) (finding insignificant direct effect, but indirect effect on equilibrium mark-ups by promoting larger number of domestic firms); Simon J. Evenett, Links Between Development and Competition Law In Developing Countries (2003) (finding no positive impact on foreign direct investment); Casey Lee & Bernadine Zhang Yuhua, *SMEs, Competition Law and Economic Growth* (APEC Policy Support Unit, Issues Paper No. 10, 2015).

4 *See, e.g.*, Mark A. Dutz, & Maria Vagliasindi, *Competition policy implementation in transition economies: An empirical assessment*, 44 Eur. Econ. Rev. 762 (2000); Wendy Carlin, Mark Shaffer & Paul Seabright, *A minimum of rivalry: evidence from transition economies on the importance of competition for innovation and growth* 2 (The Davidson Inst. Working Paper Series, No. 670, 2004) (finding that in Eastern Europe and countries of the Commonwealth of Independent States, "Firms facing between one and three competitors had sales growth of nearly 11% over the three years to 1999, while monopolists saw real sales decline by over 1% and firms facing more than three competitors had sales growth of under 2%."); Michael W. Nicholson, *An Antitrust Law Index for Empirical Analysis of International Competition Policy*, 4 J. Competition L. & Econ. 1009 (2008); Godius Kahyarara, *Competition Policy, Manufacturing Exports, Investment and Productivity: Firm Level Evidence from Tanzania Manufacturing Enterprises*, *in* Competition, Competitiveness & Development: Lessons from Developing Countries 264, 285 (2004) (finding in Tanzania, "firm-level productivity in the post-competition policy era is about 50 per cent higher than the productivity effect in the pre-competition policy period.").

5 Paul Krugman, Pop Internationalism 9 (1997).

learned from that study, the Institute's founder, William Lewis, explained that, "economic progress depends on increasing productivity, which depends on undistorted competition. When government policies limit competition . . . more efficient companies can't replace less efficient ones. Economic growth slows and nations remain poor."[6] In its 2005 World Development Report, the World Bank noted that, "Barriers to competition benefit some firms but deny opportunities and increase costs to other firms and to consumers. They also weaken incentives for protected firms to innovate and improve their productivity. Increasing competitive pressure can increase the probability of firm innovation by more than 50 percent."[7] Furthermore, recent studies based on developments in Mexico, for example, have shown that the burden of restrictions to competition falls disproportionately on the poor,[8] and that eliminating restrictions on competition in the supermarket industry can improve consumer welfare by 7% per household.[9]

Improved domestic competitive conditions can also enhance international competitiveness. Michael Porter, in his seminal work, *The Competitive Advantage of Nations*, wrote that, "Few roles of government are more important to the upgrading of an economy than ensuring vigorous domestic rivalry. . . . Firms that do not have to compete at home rarely succeed abroad."[10] In addition, modernizing the whole range of commercial laws is needed to keep and attract the domestic and foreign investment needed to grow domestic markets.

Given that FTC technical assistance typically begins when the trust and competency of competition authorities are in the process of being established, and that studies have demonstrated that having competent and trusted competition authorities intensifies competition that leads to economic development, early assistance makes a particularly valuable contribution to economic growth.[11]

2. Convergence

Convergence toward best practices in the design and implementation of competition laws is a key goal of the FTC's international antitrust program.[12] Now that over 130 countries have competition laws, the risk to global commerce posed by inconsistent standards of antitrust adjudication is significant. For example, as a former FTC Chairman noted, in a world of multiple arbiters, the one with the most restrictive rules can effectively set the standard for all.[13] The FTC works bilaterally and through multilateral organizations, such as the ICN, the Organisation for Economic Co-operation and Development ("OECD"), and the United Nations Conference for Trade and Development ("UNCTAD"), to build consensus around

---

6 William W. Lewis, The Power Of Productivity: Wealth, Poverty, And The Threat To Global Stability 103 (2004).

7 World Bank, World Development Report 2005: A Better Investment Climate for Everyone World Development Report 15 (2005).

8 *See* Carlos M. Urzúa, *Distributive and Regional Effects of Monopoly Power*, 22(2) Economía Mexicana NUEVA ÉPOCA 279 (2013).

9 *See* David Atkin, Benjamin Faber & Marco Gonzalez-Navarro, *Retail Globalization and Household Welfare: Evidence from Mexico* 32 (NBER Working Paper 21176, 2015).

10 Michael Porter, The Competitive Advantage of Nations 662 (1990).

11 *See, e.g.*, R. Shyam Khemani, *Competition Policy and Promotion of Investment, Economic Growth and Poverty Alleviation in Least Developed Countries* (Foreign Investment Advisory Services, Occasional Paper No. 19, 2007) (finding a positive impact the more effective the law: (1) the less that dominant firms influence markets; (2) the higher the ranking on the Business Competitiveness Index; and (3) the greater the intensity of competition in local markets); Tay-Cheng Ma, *The Effect of Competition Law Enforcement on Economic Growth*, 7(2) J. Competition L. & Econ. 301 (2011); Niels Petersen, *Antitrust Law and the Promotion of Democracy and Economic Growth*, 9(3) J. Competition L. & Econ. 593 (2013).

12 Randolph Tritell & Elizabeth Kraus, The Federal Trade Commission's International Antitrust Program 2 (2015), https://www.ftc.gov/system/files/attachments/international-competition/the_ftcs_international_antitrust_program_may_2015.pdf.

13 Timothy Muris, *Merger Enforcement in a World of Multiple Arbiters*, Prepared Remarks for the Brookings Institution Roundtable of Trade and Investment Policy 10 (Dec. 21, 2001), https://www.ftc.gov/sites/default/files/documents/public_statements/merger-enforcement-world-multiple-arbiters/brookings.pdf.

sound, economically-grounded legal principles and transparent and fair procedures that support pro-competitive outcomes. This effort has been remarkably successful since the ICN was established in 2001.[14]

One of the goals of the FTC's technical assistance program is to promote the implementation of those consensus principles by developing competition agencies. Through its technical assistance program, the FTC promotes understanding and analysis of these principles and the skills needed to apply them. This begins with the program's first contacts with the legislators and competition authorities engaged in drafting new competition laws and regulations and continues through the period of institution building and implementation. The program takes on special importance during the early stages of implementing competition policy, when the effects of competition policy have not yet taken firm root and the public and political bodies may not yet appreciate its value. While the further development of skills is critical at this stage, it is equally important to help the agencies continue on the path of convergence even in the face of pressures to regulate prices or protect local incumbents. Finally, the FTC seeks to assist maturing competition agencies to apply increasingly sophisticated tools that enable them to more finely discern anticompetitive conduct from procompetitive commercial behavior.

In addition to its overall goal of increasing consumer welfare, the FTC's program promotes convergence as a way of fostering a business-enabling environment that is needed for economic growth. The business community has noted the potential for competition legislation both to improve the business climate and to misdirect enforcement and degrade the climate. Convergent and transparent competition laws and application support the commercial objectives of predictable and sound enforcement by reducing risks, facilitating planning, and avoiding undue burdens and delays for cross-border transactions and business activity. Application of rules based on sound economics also prevents discriminatory application. Appreciation of a culture of competition spurs greater domestic entrepreneurship and greater willingness to permit foreign companies access to business opportunities that can benefit the domestic economy. For these reasons, both the US Chamber of Commerce and the Antitrust Modernization Commission have supported antitrust technical assistance.[15]

---

14 *See, e.g.*, Hugh M. Hollman & William E. Kovacic, *The International Competition Network: Its Past, Current and Future Role*, 20 Minn. J. Int'l L. 274 (2011); Russell W. Damtoft & Ronan Flanagan, *The Development of International Networks in Antitrust*, 43 Int'l Law. 137 (2009); Alden F. Abbott, *Competition Policy and its Convergence as Key Drivers of Economic Development*, 28 Miss. C. L. Rev. 37 (2008-2009).

15 US Chamber of Commerce, Building Open and Competitive Markets 4 (2010), https://www.uschamber.com/sites/default/files/legacy/grc/Senate%20Brieifing%20-%20May%207th.pdf; Antitrust Modernization Comm'n, Antitrust Modernization Commission: Report and Recommendations viii (2007), http://govinfo.library.unt.edu/amc/report_recommendation/amc_final_report.pdf.

III. Evolution of the FTC Technical Assistance Program

The FTC and DOJ technical assistance program has evolved from a program funded by USAID and targeted to a few jurisdictions needing assistance with basic skills to implement a competition law to a substantial program funded by several sources to provide assistance to dozens of jurisdictions with varying levels of experience and an array of issues and challenges.

1. Origins and Early Stage of the Program

The FTC and DOJ began conducting technical assistance in the 1990s in the transitioning economies of Central and Eastern Europe and in a few Latin American countries. At the time, competition law and policy were in their infancy in those countries. During the 1990s, at any given time, two or three Central or Eastern European countries or former Soviet republics and two or three Latin American countries were receiving USAID-funded technical assistance provided by the FTC and DOJ. Assistance consisted of helping to write laws and regulations and instructing staff in the basics of analyzing and investigating competition cases, typically by placing FTC and DOJ staff as long-term advisors in developing agencies.[16]

At that time and until about 10 years ago, the FTC and DOJ provided technical assistance to jurisdictions and competition authorities that were in the early stages of moving to a market economy. Passage of a competition law and creation of a competition authority often coincided with other policy reforms that included introducing competition into the economy as a whole or into sectors that had previously been subject to extensive government intervention, regulation, or planning. The assistance was provided when the agencies were just beginning to draft competition laws and regulations and to develop the analytical and investigational skills needed to enforce the law in accordance with international best practices that support these competition policies.

Competition agencies were among the institutions that provided policymakers the support and comfort to make market-oriented reforms. New competition laws and institutions also enabled governments to prevent unregulated private enterprises, many of which were recently privatized state-owned firms, from abusing their power, and to address other practices that harmed consumers and impeded growth. Competition law enforcement regimes completed the package needed to support competition policies and the transition to a market economy. They also helped prevent governments from intentionally or unintentionally retrenching on market reforms.

Technical assistance can enable young agencies to enforce competition laws based on sound economic principles in a way that helps achieve the benefits of liberalization. These benefits can have a particularly significant impact on the lives of the poor and near poor. The benefits to development and poverty reduction during the early years of introducing competition to an economy or major sectors can have dramatic results, as demonstrated in the US airline and telecommunications sectors.[17] As sectors such as

---

16 *See* Fed. Trade Comm'n & Dep't of Justice, *supra* note 3, at 2.

17 *See generally* Robert Crandall & Jerry Ellig, Economic Deregulation and Customer Choice: Lessons for the Electric Industry (1997), *available at* http://mercatus.org/sites/default/files/publication/MC_RSP_RP-Dregulation_970101.pdf.

electricity, cable television, and pharmaceuticals open to competition and the benefits to economic growth from competition spread to them, competition law enforcement can play an important role by ensuring that the benefits of liberalization are passed on to consumers.

The first stage of introducing competition policies and law enforcement is typically a long process, frequently lasting 10 or more years. Political developments can cause the process to stall or to fail and require restarting. During this stage, whether and how quickly to continue with privatization and deregulation is often an open question. There can also be considerable misunderstanding about the characteristics of a competitive market and what kind of structures and behaviors should follow from the policy decision to introduce competition to a whole economy (e.g., Eastern Europe) or major sectors of the economy (e.g., Vietnam).

The FTC's technical assistance work, especially during the first 10 years of the program, was in jurisdictions that were just establishing the foundational commercial laws governing contracts, banking, corporate law, bankruptcy, securities, and of course the institutions needed to enforce these laws. That work continues in some jurisdictions. Building an effective competition policy and law enforcement system is not necessarily the first priority among the countries implementing new commercial legal systems, but it is nevertheless a necessary building block. The aim of FTC technical assistance in such jurisdictions was, and in some jurisdictions remains, to build the basic capacity to enforce the competition laws effectively and to contribute that one piece to creating a market economy and reducing poverty. FTC attorneys and economists who serve as resident advisors and the attorneys specifically assigned to the FTC's technical assistance program become familiar with the major policy initiatives taking place in the economies in which they work and the difficulties that young competition authorities encounter in implementing a law effectively in that context. They also become familiar with local procedural rules and typical investigational methods. Their familiarity with these issues is vital to the FTC program's ability to promote both economic development and convergence.

2. Assistance Evolves as Recipients Mature

The FTC's technical assistance work focused largely on the basics until 2008 because the program was almost completely dependent on USAID for funding and, as a result, was motivated by USAID's commitment to poverty reduction and economic growth.[18] USAID's funds and focus, however, were not sufficient to address the competition technical assistance needs arising around the world. By 2008, many jurisdictions in which USAID had made a significant investment and in which the FTC had invested its time and manpower in technical assistance had become fairly experienced. Nevertheless, they still lacked the ability to use more sophisticated economic tools or to address more intricate problems, such as measuring efficiencies, designing and applying divestiture remedies, analyzing the antitrust/intellectual property interface, or dealing with two-sided markets. Their economies had become more market oriented, and thus had "graduated" from USAID programs, but the competition agencies still needed assistance. As a senior official from one such agency told one of the authors, "We are good, but we are not as good as the world thinks we are." It became clear that the FTC technical assistance program needed greater freedom and flexibility to work where the foundations for competition law and policy had largely already been laid.

18 A small percentage of the funds during this period also came from the US Department of Commerce's Commercial Law & Development Program, typically for technical assistance in Egypt and the Middle East, from the US Trade Development Agency for technical assistance in Mexico and later in China, or in unusual cases from the FTC's own funds.

Responding to express encouragement from Congress in 2007[19] and supported by additional funding, the FTC began to make much greater use of FTC appropriated funds for technical assistance. Beginning in 2008, the FTC began or continued work in several jurisdictions where USAID and other donor agencies had not worked or no longer worked on competition matters.[20]

As a result, the types of economies and the competition environment in which the technical assistance program currently operates are quite different from those in the early 1990s. The number of jurisdictions with young competition authorities has vastly increased, and the degree to which they have well-functioning competitive marketplaces has become quite diverse. As a result, the types of assistance needed and requested have also expanded. In 2014, several dozen jurisdictions received FTC technical assistance, ranging from in-country seminars to participation in webinars.[21] The economies in which the program operates now range from some of the least developed countries of sub-Saharan Africa to the robust economies of Mexico and India. While many jurisdictions still request technical assistance for basic capacity building, the requested assistance usually ranges from intermediate-stage issues to sophisticated issues, such as training economists on the use of economic modeling to assess competitive effects.

While USAID-funded assistance had been largely driven by USAID's development goals, FTC-funded assistance focuses more on the FTC's convergence goals. Most recently, the largest recipient of FTC-funded assistance has been the Competition Commission of India. In addition, the FTC, with DOJ, expanded its cooperation with the US Trade and Development Agency to provide technical assistance to China's new competition agencies,[22] and the FTC expanded its cooperation with the US Department of Commerce's Commercial Law Development Program ("CLDP") in the Middle East.

Thus, the FTC's self-funded assistance often builds on earlier USAID-funded work. The goals of poverty reduction and economic development are compatible and are inherent in all competition authority work, only to a greater degree in less developed economies.

IV. Selection of Priority Jurisdictions

With the freedom to conduct technical assistance without regard to USAID funding priorities came the question of how the FTC should determine priorities. This is an important question because FTC funding and access to its expert attorneys and economists are limited. Several factors influence how priorities are set, including: relevance to FTC convergence goals and enforcement interests; relevance to larger US government objectives; size of the jurisdiction's economy; absorptive capacity of the recipient agency; focusing training on a specific area; maintaining a balance between reaching new agencies and maintaining relationships with historical partners; matching FTC expertise and the requested assistance; the availability of other sources of assistance; and resource considerations such as travel and related costs.

---

19 154 Cong. Rec. H16054 (daily ed. Dec. 17, 2007), *available at* http://frwebgate.access.gpo.gov/cgi-bin/getpage.cgi?position=all&page=H16054&dbname=2007_record.

20 The additional funding also allowed the FTC to begin technical assistance in support of its consumer protection mission, which had been only occasionally supported by USAID.

21 *See* Fed. Trade Comm'n, FTC Office of International Affairs: FY2014 Technical Assistance Report (2014), https://www.ftc.gov/system/files/documents/reports/ftc-office-international-affairs-technical-assistance-report-fy2014/fy2014oiatarpt.pdf.

22 *See* Fed. Trade Comm'n, FTC Office of International Affairs: FY 2013 Technical Assistance Report 4 (2013), https://www.ftc.gov/system/files/documents/reports/ftc-office-international-affairs-technical-assistance-report-fy2013/fy2013oiatarpt.pdf. USAID is prohibited from providing government-to-government assistance in China due to restrictions imposed in the wake of the 1989 Tiananmen Square events. *See* Dianne E. Rennack, China: Economic Sanctions 2 (2006), https://www.fas.org/sgp/crs/row/RL31910.pdf.

Requests from jurisdictions like Mexico, India, or China that frequently review antitrust transactions in common with the FTC, or regions with significant commercial ties to the United States are more likely to be considered for technical assistance than those whose antitrust or commercial ties are remote. Some agencies are also more prepared to absorb technical assistance than others because they have started investigating cases and already have staff who are ready to absorb assistance—i.e., they are at a "teachable moment." A potential recipient that can articulate a clear purpose for a particular assistance mission, such as market definition or ramifications of a recent statutory amendment, is also more likely to receive assistance.

The size of the economy is also relevant. Some jurisdictions like India and Indonesia are a priority because they have large economies in whose economic performance the United States has a substantial interest and where poverty reduction is a major objective. Countries that are just now establishing competition agencies and need basic capacity building, however, often have very small economies. Yet some of these small economies, such as those in the Caribbean or Central America, are neighbors with close economic and other ties with the United States and are therefore higher priority recipients than their size might suggest.

Agencies in some jurisdictions have had a particularly strong historical technical assistance relationship with the FTC, such as those in Central and Southeastern Europe. While our assistance in the latter region predates the accession of these States to the European Union ("EU"), it now makes sense for the EU to play the lead role in providing assistance to the region given the availability of EU resources and the mandate that those countries adapt their laws to the EU framework. Nevertheless, limited US involvement may be appropriate.

Sometimes agencies other than the FTC are better suited to provide technical assistance in certain areas. For example, the FTC has received requests from agencies interested in assistance in topics, such as anti-cartel enforcement, telecommunications, and state aids, that the FTC is not well placed to provide.

Finally, airfares and travel time to some countries are high relative to the other criteria that they may satisfy and may tip the balance unless the assistance can be part of a regional program (e.g., Cambodia, Laos, and some African countries).

There is no mechanical formula for weighing these various criteria, and their relative importance varies from year to year.

V. Methods of Delivery and Content

A competition technical assistance program's ability to contribute to a jurisdiction's economic growth is only as great as its ability to affect the recipient enforcement entities and policymakers. This, in turn, hinges on both the means of delivery and the content delivered. The FTC developed successful methods of delivery through experience in the early years of its program. These methods have been reinforced by an ICN survey and imitated by many other donors. While these methods have remained stable over the years, the substantive content of the program has evolved. The program now covers a much broader array of issues and in much greater depth in jurisdictions with which the program has worked for several years. As explained above, in the early stages of establishing a competition regime, economies are generally in the process of making broad policy changes and assistance is directed to fundamental issues such as distinguishing between pro-growth aggressive competitive behavior and anti-growth exclusionary behavior.

At later stages, the competition authority typically requests assistance with specific refinements to laws, regulations, procedures, or other more technical issues.[23]

1. Methods of Delivering Technical Assistance

One of the greatest challenges in delivering technical assistance is determining how to convey practical and analytical knowledge in a usable and sustainable way. Two days of PowerPoint presentations by experienced academics, practitioners, and agency officials in a conference room of a luxury hotel do not do the job. The ICN conducted an empirical study of the kinds of programs that have worked well and those that have not.[24] It found that: project design requires active collaboration between recipient, funder, and provider; a needs assessment is critical; assistance activities should be related closely to the goals; knowledgeable providers, especially those with competition agency experience, are essential; the absorptive capacity of agency staff must be considered; and different circumstances dictate whether long-term and/or short-term interventions are best employed.[25] These findings largely mirror the FTC's experience. The challenge is how to convey analytical frameworks and practical tools in an effective and sustained manner, and to design effective institutions that will take root and be sustainable.

The FTC delivers technical assistance in five ways: resident advisors; short-term missions; consultations and written comments from FTC staff in Washington, DC; regional conferences and internships in the United States for foreign personnel; and informal email and telephone consultations. The blend and frequency with which it uses these methods depends on the state of development of competition law and institutions in the recipient jurisdiction.

a. Long-Term Advisors

For developing competition authorities that have just begun operation, the most effective capacity-building tool is the use of resident advisors who work directly in the office of the new authority for several months. Investigation and analysis are best learned in the context of actual cases in the local context. Advisors are thus in place when a case presents the proverbial "teachable moment" that cannot be replicated in a scheduled seminar. Advisors build relationships of trust and rapport as colleagues, which results in their advice being more readily sought, accepted, and applied. Their regular presence permits insights about case selection, internal procedures, the fairness of processes as actually applied in investigations, and priority setting that are generally not apparent to short-term advisors.

b. Skills Workshops

The next most useful assistance tools are interactive investigative skills workshops, and thus a significant focus of the technical assistance program involves conducting training for competition authority staff on specific methods of competition analysis, investigative techniques, and prosecutorial or enforcement skills and procedures. In these workshops, the FTC and DOJ use hypothetical but realistic cases that present

23 *See* Timothy T. Hughes, *Designing Technical Assistance for Different Stages of Institution Building*, Remarks before the 4th APEC Training Program On Competition Policy 11-12 (Aug. 3-6, 2004), http://www.jftc.go.jp/eacpf/05/APECTrainingProgramAugust2004/usa.hughes.pdf.

24 ICN, Assessing Technical Assistance: Preliminary Results (2005), http://www.internationalcompetitionnetwork.org/uploads/library/doc365.pdf.

25 *Id.* at iii-iv.

issues typically found in monopolization, cartel, or merger cases.[26] FTC professionals, frequently in conjunction with DOJ staff, guide participants through interactive role-playing designed to help them learn to identify issues, develop an investigational plan, interview witnesses, gather and analyze documents, evaluate results, and devise an appropriate remedy. This allows participants to watch a real investigation unfold, but with the facts tailored to those that they might encounter in their work.

c. Internships

In 2006, the FTC received Congressional authority to allow foreign agency staffs to have access to nonpublic information, which enabled them to work alongside FTC staff to learn how the FTC conducts investigations and analyze cases.[27] In response, the FTC established an International Fellows Program[28] through which foreign agency case handlers come to the FTC for periods of approximately three months. Fellows are assigned to a division in one of the FTC Bureaus and participate in all aspects of an investigation. While the confidential information they may see remains protected, they bring the skills and analytical techniques they learned home with them. Their experience also facilitates cooperation between the FTC and the Fellow's home agency.

d. Informal Consultations and Webinars

One of the by-products of using career enforcers to conduct technical assistance is that personal relationships that FTC staff develop with their international counterparts through working on projects together often lead to ongoing relationships through which recipients engage in follow-up consultations and maintain regular contact with the US agencies via telephone or e-mail.

In addition, technology sometimes allows the FTC to use new tools to provide technical assistance. For example, the FTC participates in and helps coordinate a monthly Spanish-language webinar among Latin American competition agencies, and has from time to time, when language and time differences permit, conducts webinars with newer agencies. The webinars tend to be most valuable when they supplement in-person assistance, as assistance is more likely to be internalized when delivered by a person with whom a relationship of trust has been established.[29]

e. Building Relationships

To be effective, assistance must take into account the needs, resources, and experience of the recipient. Special challenges exist in developing countries that sometimes require adjusting ways of thinking about "best practices." Understanding the local economy and having a feel for the context in which recipient agencies operate is also important. This requires an ongoing relationship built over time. Consultants that "parachute in" for a week lack this local knowledge. On the other hand, resident advisors or FTC

---

26 For examples of such hypothetical cases, *see* Training Materials, https://www.ftc.gov/policy/international/international-assistance-program/training-materials (last visited Jan. 12, 2016).

27 Undertaking Spam, Spyware, And Fraud Enforcement With Enforcers Beyond Borders Act of 2006, (Public Law 109-455, Dec. 22, 2006, 120 Stat. 3372 (codified in scattered sections of 15 U.S.C. Chapter 2). This statute applies only to the FTC.

28 *See* International Fellows Program, https://www.ftc.gov/internationalfellows (last visited Jan. 12, 2016).

29 The FTC leads the ICN's Training on Demand Project, in which competition agency staff and non-government advisors create online training modules directed at newer competition agencies. The topics of the modules produced to date include, among others, market power, market definition, competitive effects, fundamentals of mergers, leniency, planning investigations, interviewing techniques, and competition advocacy. *See* ICN Training on Demand, http://www.internationalcompetitionnetwork.org/about/steering-group/outreach/icncurriculum.aspx (last visited Jan. 12, 2016).

attorneys who work with a jurisdiction over years, commenting on drafts of laws and regulations and conducting training workshops, can make the adjustments needed to be most useful for an agency. These relationships often last years after the end of formal technical assistance programs.

f. Building Judicial Capacity

Depending on the specific features of the competition law system, judges may hear and decide competition cases, enforce the agency's orders, and adjudicate appeals of agency decisions. To fulfill these roles, judges must understand the purpose and methods of antitrust analysis. In many countries, however, there is seldom training available to judges and, as a result, judges sometimes forego substantive review of orders in favor of parsing competition agency rulings on narrow procedural grounds. To help judges reach sound interpretations of competition law and ensure the effectiveness of competition agency orders, programs to assist judges have proven quite helpful. Because judges often prefer dialogue with fellow judges to instruction from government functionaries, the FTC taps into the willingness of several current and former federal judges to help conduct judicial workshops.

g. Leveraging Resources

Co-teaching with recent recipients of technical assistance can also aid in delivering technical assistance. For example, the FTC has partnered with the Mexican antitrust agency to deliver technical assistance in Central America and with agencies from the Baltic States to deliver assistance to an agency in the Caucasus region. While FTC staff may have a relative advantage on antitrust law and economics, the partner agencies have a greater understanding of the economic and political context in countries that in some ways resemble their own. Both the FTC and recipient authorities have found these partnerships to be quite valuable.

2. Substantive Content of Technical Assistance Programs

The substantive content of a particular program is driven largely by the recipient agency's level of experience and sophistication in implementing its competition law.

a. Early Stage Content

The FTC's technical assistance is likely to have its greatest impact during the early years of a jurisdiction's transition to a market economy. As discussed above, many of the issues that typically confront an agency during its early years involve the difficulties that arise from the major government policy decision to move toward a competition driven market and the inevitable "creative destruction" that accompanies that move. For example, to what extent should the displacement of workers that privatization or modernization of production or distribution facilities cause be a concern of the competition authority? To what extent should the power of large buyers and sellers to reduce profit margins of small, local suppliers and competitors be a concern? Frequently, a genuine competition law enforcement concern is present and addressing the concern in a market oriented way is possible.

Competition authorities should be concerned with privatizations that merely transfer monopoly power from a publicly controlled monopoly that may be somewhat responsive to the poor to a private party that may be concerned solely with profit. A competition authority should be involved to help structure the privatization in a way that will avoid the abuse of power. In mergers or joint ventures that seem likely to result in the displacement of labor, competition authorities have a role in determining if the displacement arising from modernization is the result of genuine efficiencies or simply from a reduction in output resulting from increased market power. When the entry of large buyers and sellers tempt small businesses to form cartels, competition authority experts can offer alternatives such as encouraging efficiency enhancing cooperatives and joint ventures. In other words, competition agency staff are taught how to distinguish harm to competitors from harm to competition.

On a more practical level, staff are taught skills such as what line of questioning and which witnesses will likely be most fruitful in assessing competitive effects, and what kind of remedies are best for deterrence and restoring competition to the market. The goals of technical assistance at this stage are to help ensure that enforcement is consistent with international norms of good practice such as the ICN Recommended Practices and that the institution and staff are capable of investigating conduct and applying the law.

These issues are not unique to developing and emerging economies, but they are more common and often have much greater political and social ramifications than in developed economies. It may not be enough to say that the social displacement resulting from competition is a creative, destructive force that will in the long term lead to increased consumer welfare. Nor is it realistic to suggest that a competition agency ignore powerful political pressures and pass on to other ministries the problems of the displaced. The FTC's technical assistance program and the experts involved are sensitive to these issues and work with their counterparts to find market-oriented, competition-compatible ways of addressing these problems. Economies generally do not move quickly from planned, regulated, or crony capitalist systems to open and competitive ones. During the transition, an effective competition authority, assisted by experienced experts sensitive to the issues of a developing economy, can help the transition to move forward as smoothly as possible.

b. Later Stage Content

After 10 years of receiving capacity building technical assistance—assuming that an agency has been bringing cases and has not experienced massive staff turnover—most agencies are reasonably capable of investigating cases and designing remedies. As with any developing skill set, there may be weaknesses in analysis, and the process may not always be what is optimal under the circumstances. Weak analysis and process, measured against international best practice standards, may be attributable to insufficient experience applying them in actual practice, but may also result from a conscious decision by the agency or other political officials to deviate from these norms. These cases call for something other than training and capacity building.

Understanding international best practices and how to implement them are the stuff of capacity building; persuading enforcement agencies to follow them is a very different undertaking.

For competition authorities that have been operating for several years, therefore, more attention is given to helping with fine tuning statutes and regulations, analyzing complex issues, and applying sophisticated economic and other analytical tools.[30] The substantive content of the assistance program also covers a much broader array of issues and in much greater depth. For example, the FTC frequently sends attorneys and economists with relevant sectoral expertise to work with agencies in emerging economies that are

30 *See* Hughes, *supra* note 25.

dealing with newly liberalized sectors. It is also common for the assistance to shift to comments on, and assistance with, amending laws or regulations. Training that demonstrates through hands-on workshops how these amendments yield better results also strengthens the hand of those advocating the reforms.

The FTC's capacity building efforts over a period of approximately 10 years in several jurisdictions in Southeastern Europe and Southeast Asia are good examples of how content evolves to more technical economic and legal questions. The FTC's work has helped with the successful efforts by several ASEAN jurisdictions to create a small but capable core of enforcement officials with the tools to analyze and enforce their competition laws. Some staff in these agencies are capable of mentoring new hires and conducting their own assistance in jurisdictions in their region that are just beginning to implement competition laws and create competition institutions.

Several jurisdictions have recently realized the need for some major amendments to, or a substantial rewriting of, some parts of their competition laws and implementing regulations in order to bring them closer to international best practices. Many of them have successfully worked with the government to make these changes. The next steps in capacity building in these countries are easy enough to discern. The FTC's many years of experience in providing assistance in other countries has drawn a blueprint for the type of programs that will be needed.

3. Challenges for Future Technical Assistance

In the course of its work, the FTC has seen new competition authorities face major challenges. Three stand out. First, the public and business communities have little faith that competition law will be applied in accordance with the rule of law, free of corruption. Second, it is important to address actual and perceived deficiencies in investigation procedures, such as transparency and engagement with parties and protection of confidential information.[31] Third, competition authority staff and the judiciary have little, if any, cross-training in economics and law; this deficit must be addressed both at the university level and with on-the-job seminars.

The FTC and other technical assistance providers also face some challenging questions. Building an enforcement agency and staff with depth of experience is a lengthy undertaking. The FTC and many others institutions have been providing technical assistance for well over 10 years in many jurisdictions. What happens after a decade or more has passed, for example, in Indonesia, South Africa, Colombia, and Vietnam? Does the assistance just stop, or is there an "exit" or "graduation" strategy? Does capacity building and technical assistance eventually transition to a continuing-education program and become a way of promoting convergence and facilitating enforcement cooperation on cross-border transactions? Or does the relationship evolve toward cooperation between the US and foreign agencies in cases under common review, as has occurred with, for example, Mexico and Brazil?

---

31 *See generally* ICN, ICN Guidance on Investigative Process (2015), http://www.internationalcompetitionnetwork.org/uploads/library/doc1028.pdf.

VI. What is the Measure of Success?

A successful technical assistance program is a long-term endeavor. At the conference for which this article was prepared, Professor William Kovacic said that the appropriate time frame for grading an agency is 25 years. Success is often measured as the ratio between a recipient agency's steps forward and steps backwards. Many agencies that the FTC helped when they started one or two decades ago have evolved into capable and respected agencies with substantial achievements. For example, the FTC and DOJ provided assistance to Brazil's competition agencies when their modern competition law was coming on-stream. More recently, the FTC hosted several International Fellows from Brazil and has continued to provide assistance as needed to address particular topics. Brazil has developed a more efficient merger review system and has taken on high-profile cartel cases. The trajectory, however, was not one of smooth and continuous progress. In the early 2000s, Brazil was widely criticized for its inefficient merger review system. As the Brazilian competition agency matured, its capacity to influence Brazilian legislation to conform to international best practice and its ability to implement its authority soundly grew. Many other jurisdictions, such as Mexico, Colombia, South Africa, and countries across Central and Eastern Europe, show similar achievements.[32]

Such progress, however, can be fragile. For example, despite many years of technical assistance in the Ukraine in the 1990s, the FTC is restarting a technical assistance program there with an agency that is emerging from major setbacks. Commentators have also pointed to the difficult position in which the Hungarian competition authority, the GVH, finds itself: "The GVH has become an island in an increasingly incompatible environment in terms of . . . the concept of the liberal market economy as opposed to protectionism, paternalism, over-regulation and rent seeking."[33]

What ultimately matters is whether competition is contributing to an economic environment conducive to consumer welfare. A number of factors bear on this of which competition law enforcement is but one. Assessing the effect of competition law enforcement on economic growth is difficult in itself. The role that technical assistance has played—for example, how much has it helped the proponents of competition policies and competition law enforcement that, in turn, brought about measureable economic progress—may defy objective measurement.

The FTC's assistance is just one of the many factors that helped new agencies to improve performance. Other mature agencies and donors also provide assistance. The educational systems of these countries have begun to produce well-trained competition lawyers and economists. In many cases, political shifts resulted in greater political support for needed changes and resources. In addition, over time the new agencies learned from their own experiences, just as the FTC did over the past century. It is probably impossible to isolate the effect of technical assistance from other factors to allow for meaningful quantitative conclusions to be drawn.

---

32 To be sure, there have also been some failures, for example, because the agency failed to invest in staff, resulting in such rapid turnover that the impact of technical assistance evaporated, agency leadership and/or the government was insufficiently invested in the success of effective competition law enforcement, or mid- or top-level agency leaders restricted their staff's access to the advisors because they were uncomfortable with the advice being provided.

33 Csaba Kovacs & Andreas Reindl, *The Evolution of the Hungarian Competition Regime: Two Decades of Dynamic Change and Continuity*, *in* Building New Competition Law Regimes: Selected Essays 26, 73 (David Lewis ed., 2013).

Given the difficulty of quantitative assessment, the best measure of the success of technical assistance may be to look at the qualitative indicators of a successful agency[34] and to examine whether the assistance program has been able to reinforce them effectively. Questions to be asked in such an evaluation might include:

» Does the agency's work function within the context of an overall national strategy to promote competition and free markets?

» Are agency decisions to prosecute and adjudicate well-grounded in fact, law, and economics?

» Are agency procedures transparent and fair?

» Are sanctions and remedies well-tailored to address the harm at issue?

» Are agency resources effectively targeted towards the most important competition issues?

In the end, the best measure may be to ask the agency's stakeholders—practitioners, businesses, academics, government officials, and others who follow the evolution of competition policy—whether the agency's work is improving the well-being of consumers. The Federal Trade Commission will continue to ask these questions, and to strive to ensure that its technical assistance program, while fulfilling the convergence and other goals of the FTC, serves the needs of the recipient agencies and their consumers.

34 *See, e.g.*, William E. Kovacic, The Federal Trade Commission at 100: Into Our 2nd Century (2009), https://www.ftc.gov/system/files/documents/reports/federal-trade-commission-100-our-second-century/ftc100rpt.pdf; William E. Kovacic, *From Activity to Accomplishment: Competition Law and Performance Measurement*, 27 Antitrust 75 (2012); William E. Kovacic, *Rating the Competition Agencies: What Constitutes Good Performance?*, 16 Geo. Mason L. Rev. 903 (2009).

Editors' Bios

Harry First is the Charles L. Denison Professor of Law at the New York University School of Law and Co-Director of the School's Competition, Innovation, and Information Law Program. From 1999 to 2001 he served as Chief of the Antitrust Bureau of the Office of the Attorney General of the State of New York. Professor First is the co-author of the casebook *Free Enterprise and Economic Organization: Antitrust* (7th Edition, 2014), as well as a casebook on regulated industries. He was twice a Fulbright Research Fellow in Japan and taught antitrust as an adjunct professor at the University of Tokyo. Professor First's most recent scholarly work has focused on various aspects of antitrust enforcement and theory. These include: *The Microsoft Antitrust Cases: Competition Policy for the Twenty-first Century* (with Andrew I. Gavil) (MIT Press, forthcoming 2014); and "Your Money and Your Life: The Export of US Antitrust Remedies" in *Global Competition Law and Economics* (Stanford University Press, 2013). Professor First is a contributing editor of the *Antitrust Law Journal*, foreign antitrust editor of the *Antitrust Bulletin*, a member of the Executive Committee of the Antitrust Section of the New York State Bar Association, and a member of the Advisory Board and a Senior Fellow of the American Antitrust Institute.

Eleanor M. Fox is the Walter J. Derenberg Professor of Trade Regulation at the New York University School of Law. Before joining the School's faculty, Professor Fox was a partner at the New York law firm Simpson Thacher & Bartlett. She has served as a member of the International Competition Policy Advisory Committee to the Attorney General of the US Department of Justice (1997 to 2000) (President Clinton) and as a Commissioner on President Carter's National Commission for the Review of Antitrust Laws and Procedures (1978 to 1979). She has advised numerous younger antitrust jurisdictions, including South Africa, Egypt, Tanzania, Gambia, Indonesia, Russia, Poland, Hungary, and the Common Market for Eastern and Southern Africa. Professor Fox received an honorary doctorate degree from the University of Paris-Dauphine in 2009. She was awarded an inaugural Lifetime Achievement award in 2011 by the Global Competition Review for "substantial, lasting and transformational impact on competition policy." Her books include *The Design of Competition Law Institutions: Global Norms, Local Choices* (with Michael Trebilcock) (Oxford 2013), *US Antitrust Law in Comparative Context*, cases and materials (3rd Edition, West/Reuters 2012), and books on EU law and on developing countries and competition. Her recent papers include "Imagine: Pro-Poor(er) Competition Law" (OECD and UNCTAD, both 2013), and, with Deborah Healey, "When the State Harms Competition—The Role for Competition Law," forthcoming in the *Antitrust Law Journal*.

Nicolas Charbit, PhD, LLM, was admitted to the Paris Bar in 1994. He had been practicing from 1994 to 2005 in the field of competition law with strong emphasis on cartels and network industries. Nicolas wrote for French and international legal journals and taught these subjects at university and business schools. He has published several books and papers on EC and French competition law. He has completed a PhD thesis at Paris Sorbonne University on antitrust law and the public sector. He is the founding partner of the Institute of Competition Law and has been the Editor of Concurrences Review since 2004.

Elisa Ramundo graduated cum laude from the University of Bologna Law School (2002). Elisa holds a Master Degree in European Studies at European College of Parma (2004) and an LLM at the University of Chicago Law School (2010). Over the years, Elisa has gained professional experience in European, US, and International antitrust law. She worked at the US FTC (Washington, DC) as an international antitrust consultant, and in a tier-one Italian law firm as an associate in the competition practice (Rome/Milan). She also served as a legal intern at the European Commission (Brussels). Elisa is currently the Managing Editor of Concurrences Review and is based in New York City.

Contributors' Bios

Aditya Bhattacharjea is Professor and Head of the Department of Economics at the Delhi School of Economics, University of Delhi, India, where he teaches postgraduate courses in industrial organization and Indian economic development. He earlier taught for many years at St Stephen's College, Delhi, and has been a visiting associate professor at Duke University, USA. His research interests include trade policy under imperfect competition, labor market regulation, and competition (antitrust) law and policy. His articles have appeared in leading law and economics journals. Professor Bhattacharjea served as a member of the Expert Group on Trade and Competition Policy, Ministry of Commerce, Government of India, from 2002 to 2003. From 2005 to 2010, he was a resource person for the Competition Policy and Government Procurement sessions of the annual WTO Regional Trade Policy Courses for the Asia/Pacific region, which were conducted at Hong Kong University and then at the National University of Singapore. He served as a member of the Board of Directors of the Export-Import Bank of India from 2012 to 2015, and is currently a member of the Standing Committee on Industrial Statistics of the Ministry of Statistics and Programme Implementation. He holds an MPhil degree from the University of Cambridge and a PhD from Boston University.

George S. Cary is a partner based in the Washington, DC office of Cleary Gottlieb. Prior to joining Cleary Gottlieb in 1998, Mr. Cary served as Deputy Director of the US Federal Trade Commission's Bureau of Competition, where he oversaw a record number of merger transactions and was lead trial counsel in its successful challenge of the Staples/Office Depot merger, considered the most significant merger case of the decade. He has represented companies in many industry-transforming transactions, including most recently: Dow Chemical/DuPont, GlaxoSmithKline/Novartis, Medtronic/Covidien, Western Digital/SanDisk, Hertz/Dollar Thrifty, and Google/AdMob. He is currently defending Sabre Holdings, Sanofi U.S., and Keurig Green Mountain in closely watched monopolization cases and recently won a landmark preliminary injunction for Teladoc against the Texas Medical Board, enjoining a Board rule that would have ended telehealth in Texas. Chambers and Partners has ranked Mr. Cary in its top tier of global antitrust lawyers every year for the last decade; *Benchmark Litigation* named him "Antitrust Litigator of the Year" in 2016; *The National Law Journal* named him a "Trailblazer" in antitrust in 2015; *Law360* recognized him as an MVP in Competition in 2014; and *The Best Lawyers in America* named him Washington, DC's "Antitrust Lawyer of the Year" in 2016 and 2011 and "Antitrust Litigation Lawyer of the Year" in 2014.

Russell W. Damtoft is the Associate Director of the Federal Trade Commission's Office of International Affairs. He is responsible for relationships between the FTC and antitrust agencies in Canada, Latin America, and other countries, as well as helping to manage portions of the FTC's technical assistance program for developing competition and consumer protection agencies. He also manages the International Competition Network's Training on Demand Project and represents the FTC at meetings of the United Nations Conference on Trade and Development. Mr. Damtoft has been with the Federal Trade Commission since 1985. Before the Office of International Affairs was established, he performed similar duties in the Bureau of Competition. Prior to that, he served as Assistant Regional Director of the FTC's Chicago Regional Office, as an attorney and in other capacities in the Bureau of Consumer Protection, and as an Attorney-Advisor to a Commissioner. He has twice served as a long-term resident advisor to foreign competition and consumer protection authorities, once to Romania and once to the Baltic nations. He graduated from the University of Iowa College of Law in 1981 and from Grinnell College in 1976. He is a member of the American Bar Association, where he is on the editorial board of *Antitrust Source*.

Dennis M. Davis is a judge at the High Court of Cape Town, South Africa. He is also judge president of the Competition Appeal Court of Cape Town, a honorary professor of commercial law at the University of Cape Town, and a visiting professor at the Watson Institute for International Studies, among other institutions. During the negotiations for South Africa's new constitution, Judge Davis acted as a technical legal advisor both on electoral law to the Convention for a Democratic South Africa and on federalism to the Constitutional Assembly. His recent research has focused on competition and administrative law, constitutional law, human rights and litigation, and socio-economic rights. Judge Davis holds an MPhil from the University of Cambridge and a BCom and LLB from the University of Cape Town. He is the author and co-author of several books, including *Income Tax Cases and Materials* (1995), as well as numerous journal articles. Judge Davis is the former host of Future Imperfect and current host of Judge for Yourself, both of which are South African television programs that debate current political and socio-economic issues in the country.

Elaine Ewing is a partner based in the Washington, DC office of Cleary Gottlieb. Her practice focuses on all areas of antitrust law, including clearances of mergers and acquisitions from the US Federal Trade Commission (FTC) and Department of Justice (DOJ) and international competition authorities; civil antitrust litigation; criminal and civil antitrust investigations; and antitrust counseling. She joined the firm in 2007 and became a partner in 2016. Most recently, Ewing has represented companies in high-profile transactions including: Dow Chemical/DuPont, Air Liquide/Airgas, Coca-Cola Company/Monster Beverage Corporation, Medtronic/Covidien, Google/Motorola Mobility, Western Digital/Hitachi/HDD, and Hertz/Dollar Thrifty. She is currently defending Keurig Green Mountain in ongoing monopolization litigation brought by competitors and purported class action plaintiffs including successfully defeating a preliminary injunction seeking to block the launch of Keurig's 2.0 coffee brewer. In 2014, her co-authored article, "Divergence Then and Now: What Does the US/EU Experience Tell Us About Convergence With MOFCOM?," was selected as the winner of the Academic/Asia category for the Institute of Competition Law Antitrust Writing Awards.

Samir Gandhi heads the competition practice at AZB & Partners and deals with a broad range of competition law and policy issues, as well as international trade and World Trade Organization matters. Samir advises on all areas of competition law and policy and has previously served as counsel to the Competition Commission of India ("CCI") in major litigation, including in CCI v SAIL, the first substantive competition law case decided by the Indian Supreme Court. He advises clients, both as complainants and as defendants, in conduct cases before the CCI and the appellate and writ courts. Recent assignments include defending Daimler, Tata Motors, Google, and TAM Media Research in abuse of dominance cases; and Lafarge, JSW Steel and the Organization for Pharmaceutical Producers in India in cartel cases. Samir routinely advises companies on their competition compliance programs and is actively involved in competition policy issues as part of the activities of the International Competition Network. He has appeared before the Indian Parliamentary Standing Committee on Finance to comment on the proposed amendments to the Competition Act and in formulating competition policy for sovereign nations. Gandhi is a graduate of the National Law School of India University, Bangalore and the London School of Economics and Political Science, where he was a Commonwealth Scholar and Mahindra Trust Fellow. He was a visiting fellow at Columbia Law School and is admitted to practice in India.

J. Mark Gidley chairs the White & Case Global Antitrust/Competition practice. His practice focuses on mergers and acquisitions, cartel cases, class actions, and pharmaceutical antitrust cases. Gidley served as the Acting Assistant Attorney General for the US Department of Justice, Antitrust Division from 1992 to 1993 with responsibility for all of the Division's civil, criminal, and merger matters. Prior to that, he served as Deputy Assistant Attorney General for Regulated Industries in the Antitrust Division from 1991 to 1992, responsible for civil, criminal, and merger matters in the telecommunications, energy, computers, intellectual property, banking, and finance industries. From 1990 to 1991, Gidley served as Associate Deputy Attorney General under then Deputy Attorney William P. Barr, during the first Bush Administration. During his tenure at the Antitrust Division, he worked on a number of merger and acquisition investigations, including Bank of America's acquisition of Security Pacific National Bank and worked on the development of the seminal DOJ-FTC 1992 Horizontal Merger Guidelines. Gidley participated in Committee on Foreign Investment in the United States merger review deliberations, representing the Justice Department. He brought the successful lawsuit under Section 1 of the Sherman Act against the major US domestic air carriers for alleged price fixing and cartel behavior (the Airline Tariff Publishing Co.). Gidley also supervised the Division's investigation of price fixing in the US Treasury bond auction market, which resulted in a US$28 million asset forfeiture action against Salomon Brothers—at that time the largest antitrust penalty ever in the Division's history for cartel activity.

Kirti Gupta is a Director of Economic Strategy at Qualcomm Inc., where she serves as an in-house economist, specializing on Intellectual Property (IP) and competition policy and strategy. In this role, she is responsible for managing the substantive direction of the global IP policy and advocacy outreach efforts, and for conducting original research on issues related to IP and competition law and economics—published in both law and economics journals. She has been involved in various international antitrust and litigation cases. Kirti has also been responsible for developing economic models for determining Qualcomm's optimal IP strategy worldwide and on designing algorithms for IP portfolio valuation. Prior to her role as an economist, Kirti spent over a decade as a wireless systems engineering expert, working on research and development of third and fourth generation (3G and 4G) wireless cellular systems and has represented Qualcomm in various global technology standards bodies. She is a co-inventor of ten granted US patents and several pending patent applications in the field of wireless communications. Dr. Gupta holds a Master's degree in Electrical Engineering from Purdue University, and a PhD in Economics from the University of California, San Diego.

Timothy T. Hughes has been an attorney with the US Federal Trade Commission for 30 years. During the past 14 years he has served as Legal Counsel for International Technical Assistance. In that capacity, he has lived for extended periods in Indonesia, Romania and Vietnam providing training and counseling to the competition authorities of Southeast Europe and Southeast Asia, and has twice participated as a teacher-panelist at the OECD's annual Vienna training seminar for the competition authorities of Eastern Europe and the former Soviet Union. He has drafted training materials used by FTC attorneys in their technical assistance programs around the world, and has himself conducted short-term training missions throughout Southeast Europe, the Middle East, Latin America, and Southeast Asia. Prior to returning to the FTC in 2001, he practiced competition law in the private sector as a partner in the international law firm of Steel, Hector & Davis, headquartered in Miami, Florida, with offices in Brazil, the Dominican Republic, and Venezuela. While there he provided antitrust legal counsel to numerous multinational corporations doing business in Latin America, started the annual Latin American Competition & Trade Policy Roundtable, and served as the private sector representative to the Fair Competition Advisory Committee to the nations of the Caribbean Community and Common Market. He received his JD degree in 1976 from Northwestern University, Chicago, Illinois and completed his undergraduate studies in history and philosophy at Fordham University, New York.

Maxwell J. Hyman is an associate in the Washington, DC office of White & Case, where he specializes in complex trial and appellate litigation before federal courts. His practice concentrates on representing companies in antitrust cartel investigations. Prior to joining the Firm, Max served as a judicial clerk to The Honorable Stephanie D. Thacker of the US Court of Appeals for the Fourth Circuit.

Francis Wang'ombe Kariuki was appointed Director–General of the Competition Authority of Kenya on 9th January, 2013. His main interests are in competition regulation and also the economics of institutional development. In addition, he has been focusing on the impact of budget constraints on competition agencies' investigative process and human resource policy. He is also well known for his advocacy initiatives, nationally and internationally, geared towards entrenching competition in various sectors of the economy and boosting regional trade. Kariuki is a founding member and the current Chairman of the African Competition Forum—"A Network of African Competition Authorities which seeks to promote the adoption of Competition principles in the implementation of national and regional economic policies of African countries." He is a holder of a Master's of Science in Economic Regulation and Competition from City University- London; Bachelor in Economics & Business Studies from Kenyatta University; and various certificates in strategic leadership and corporate governance.

Carlos Mena-Labarthe was appointed Chief Prosecutor (*Autoridad Investigadora*) at the Federal Economic Competition Commission of Mexico in October 2014 for a four year term. He has worked for the Mexican competition authority since 2007. He was previously the Head of the Planning, Institutional Relations, and International Affairs Unit where he coordinated the efforts to create the first Strategic Plan and the first Annual Plan of the authority and represented it before Congress for the discussions of a new law in 2014. He was the Director of Cartels and Interstate Commerce from 2007 to 2008 and from 2008 to September 2013, he was the Director General of the Cartel Investigations Division. Mr. Mena has extensive experience in the fields of regulation and competition law. Prior to joining the Mexican competition authority, he worked for national and international law firms in their competition law practice. He was an International Fellow of the US Federal Trade Commission. He has also received training in investigations and the management of enforcement agencies at the European Commission (DG Comp), the Canadian Competition Bureau, and the Australian Competition and Consumer Commission. He has written for numerous publications and is the editor and co-author of five books on competition law, regulation, and public policy. Mr. Mena holds a Master's Degree in Business Law with honors from the Attorney Bar Association in Madrid, Spain; a Master's Degree in Regulation from the London School of Economics and Political Science with distinction for the best overall performance; and a Degree in Law with first-class honors from Instituto Tecnológico Autónomo de México.

Susan Ning joined King & Wood Mallesons in 1995. She is a senior partner and leads the International Trade and Antitrust & Competition Group. Since 2003 she has focused on two main areas: securing MOFCOM merger clearance for clients and advising on Anti-Monopoly Law compliance issues. During this time she has undertaken more than 150 antitrust merger control filings on behalf of blue-chip clients, which mostly consist of multinational corporations. Prior to the enactment of the AML in 2008, Ning took an active role in assisting and consulting with the Chinese Government on the drafting of the law. Since the enactment of the AML, she continues to be actively involved in drafting regulations and guidelines accompanying the AML. Through these consultations (and through her prior work with the Chinese Government on World Trade Organization issues), Ning built and maintained a close working relationship with the antitrust authorities in China.

Jonathan Orszag is a Senior Managing Director and member of the Executive Committee of Compass Lexecon, LLC, an economic consulting firm. As a consultant, Orszag has conducted economic and financial analysis on a wide range of complex issues in antitrust, regulatory, policy, and litigation matters for corporations and public-sector entities. These engagements have involved a wide array of mergers and other economic matters in various markets, such as the sports, media, telecommunications, financial services, and high-tech industries. He has testified before the United States Congress, US and international courts, the European Court of First Instance, and US and international regulatory authorities on competition and economic policy issues. In 2004, Orszag was named by the Global Competition Review as the youngest member of "the world's 40 brightest young antitrust lawyers and economists" in its "40 under 40" survey. In 2006, the Global Competition Review named Orszag as one of the world's "Best Young Competition Economists." Since 2007, Orszag has been named one of the foremost competition economists in The International Who's Who of Competition Economists. Prior to entering the private sector, Orszag served as the Assistant to the US Secretary of Commerce and Director of the Office of Policy and Strategic Planning. In this capacity, Orszag was the Secretary of Commerce's chief policy adviser and was responsible for coordinating the development and implementation of policy initiatives, from telecommunications issues to international trade issues. Previously, Orszag served as an economic policy advisor on President Clinton's National Economic Council. In 1999, the Corporation for Enterprise Development awarded Orszag its leadership award for "forging innovative public policies to expand economic opportunity in America."

Simon Roberts is Professor of Economics at the University of Johannesburg and Executive Director of the Centre for Competition, Regulation and Economic Development (CCRED). Roberts was Chief Economist and Manager of the Policy & Research Division at the Competition Commission of South Africa from November 2006 to December 2012. Prior to this appointment he was Associate Professor in Economics at the University of the Witwatersrand. At Wits he also directed the Corporate Strategy and Industrial Development research program, and previously held positions as Lecturer and Senior Lecturer. This followed positions as: Lecturer in Development Economics, University of East Anglia, UK; Senior Research Officer, Bank of Botswana; and, Lecturer in Economics, University College Cork, Ireland. He holds a PhD from University of London (Birkbeck College), MA from University of East Anglia, and BA (Hons) from Oxford University. He has been an adviser to competition authorities in a number of countries including Kenya.

Fiyanshu Sindhwani is a research scholar at the Department of Economics at the Delhi School of Economics, University of Delhi, India, where she is writing her PhD thesis under the guidance of Professor Aditya Bhattacharjea, with whom she has co-authored on "Competition Issues in the Indian Pharmaceutical Industry" for CUTS International. She has served as an Assistant Professor of Economics in Lakshmi Bai College, University of Delhi. She worked as a Consultant with Indian Council for Research on International Economic Relations for a project on pharmaceutical regulations in India. She was an intern at The Energy and Resource Institute, India at their Resources, Economic Regulation and Global Security Division. She holds a Masters Degree in Economics from the Jawahar Lal Nehru University, New Delhi, India.

Mariana Tavares de Araujo is a senior partner at Levy & Salomão Advogados, where she practices in the areas of Antitrust, Regulation & Infrastructure, and Product Liability. Prior to joining Levy & Salomão Advogados, Araujo worked with the Brazilian Government for nine years, four of which she served as head of the government agency in charge of antitrust enforcement and consumer protection policy. Araujo worked with international antitrust authorities throughout the world and served in leadership positions in key international competition organizations, such as chairing with the US Department of Justice the cartels sub-group of the International Competition Network ("ICN") (from 2004 to 2007). She also represented the Brazilian Government in meetings of the Organisation for Economic Co-operation and Development's Committee on Competition and of the United Nations Conference on Trade and Development. Araujo provides counseling in competition-related matters for the World Bank and served as a non-governmental advisor to the ICN. She is a member of the International Bar Association and of the American Bar Association's Section of Antitrust Law. She currently co-chairs the IBA Working Group on International

Cartels and is a member of the ABA International Cartel Task Force. She is also a Law Professor at the Graduate Program of Fundação Getúlio Vargas-RJ. Global Competition Review named her on its list of the "Top 100 Women in Antitrust" and Latin Lawyer included her among the "Inspiring Women in the Legal Profession." Who's Who Legal, Chambers Latin America, and Legal 500 listed her among the world's leading competition lawyers and she has been nominated by the members of the Latin American Corporate Counsel Association for inclusion in its list "LACCA Approved" (for 2013, 2014, and 2015).

Tara Tavernia is an associate based in the Washington, DC. office. Her practice focuses on antitrust and enforcement matters. Tavernia joined the firm in 2012. Her recent transactional highlights include Medtronic/Covidien, Platform Specialty Products/Alent, and 3M/Capital Safety Group, and she represented Keurig Green Mountain in successfully defeating a preliminary injunction seeking to block the launch of Keurig's 2.0 coffee brewer. She received a JD degree, with honors, in 2012 from the University of Chicago Law School and received her undergraduate degree, *magna cum laude* in English and with distinction in all subjects, from Cornell University in 2009.

Randolph Tritell is the Director of the Federal Trade Commission's Office of International Affairs. He is responsible for coordinating the FTC's international antitrust, consumer protection, and technical assistance policies and the FTC's involvement in cases that raise international issues. He represents the FTC in multilateral fora including the International Competition Network, in which he serves on the Steering Group, and the Organisation for Economic Co-operation and Development's Competition Committee. Tritell is also responsible for the FTC's negotiation and implementation of bilateral international cooperation agreements and competition and consumer protection provisions of US free trade agreements. Prior to joining the FTC in 1998, Tritell was a partner with the New York-based law firm of Weil, Gotshal & Manges LLP. Following six years in the firm's New York office, in 1992 he opened the firm's Brussels office where he practiced European Community and international competition law. Tritell began his career at the FTC serving as a staff attorney in the Bureau of Consumer Protection, Assistant to the Bureau of Consumer Protection Director, Timothy Muris, Attorney Advisor to Commissioner Terry Calvani, and Executive Assistant to the Chairman. Tritell obtained his law degree in 1977 from the University of Pennsylvania Law School, where he was an Editor of the *University of Pennsylvania Law Review*. He is a 1974 Phi Beta Kappa graduate of the State University of New York at Stony Brook. Tritell is active in the American Bar Association's Section of Antitrust Law, in which he co-chairs the International Task Force and serves on the Advisory Board of the Oxford Journal of Antitrust Enforcement and of the Fordham Corporate Law Institute. He is a frequent lecturer and author on international antitrust issues.

Concurrences Books

GLOBAL ANTITRUST ECONOMICS: CURRENT ISSUES IN ANTITRUST AND LAW & ECONOMICS

Douglas H. Ginsburg - Joshua D. Wright • 2016

CHOICE: A NEW STANDARD FOR COMPETITION LAW ANALYSIS?

Paul Nihoul • 2016

COMPETITION CASE LAW DIGEST: A SYNTHESIS OF EU AND NATIONAL LEADING CASES

Nicolas Charbit - Elisa Ramundo • December 2015

ANTITRUST IN EMERGING AND DEVELOPING COUNTRIES

Eleanor Fox - Harry First • October 2015

IAN S. FORRESTER QC LL.D. A SCOT WITHOUT BORDERS LIBER AMICORUM (VOL II)

Sir. David Edward, Jacquelyn MacLennon, Assimakis Komninos • 2015

IAN S. FORRESTER QC LL.D. A SCOT WITHOUT BORDERS LIBER AMICORUM (VOL I)

Sir. David Edward, Jacquelyn MacLennon, Assimakis Komninos • September 2015

WILLIAM E. KOVACIC: AN ANTITRUST TRIBUTE LIBER AMICORUM (VOL. II)

Nicolas Charbit - Elisa Ramundo • September 2014

COMPETITION LAW ON THE GLOBAL STAGE: DAVID GERBER'S GLOBAL COMPETITION LAW IN PERSPECTIVE

Nicolas Charbit - Elisa Ramundo • January 2014

WILLIAM E. KOVACIC: AN ANTITRUST TRIBUTE LIBER AMICORUM (VOL. I)

Nicolas Charbit - Elisa Ramundo • January 2013

All books are published in print and electronic format.

e-Competitions
Antitrust Case Laws e-Bulletin

e-Competitions Bulletin

CASE LAW DATABASE

e-Competitions is the only online resource that provides consistent coverage of antitrust cases from 55 jurisdictions, organized into a searchable database structure. e-Competitions concentrates on cases summaries taking into account that in the context of a continuing growing number of sources there is a need for factual information, i.e., case law.

- 12,000 case summaries
- 2,600 authors
- 55 countries covered
- 24,000 subscribers

SOPHISTICATED EDITORIAL AND IT ENRICHMENT

e-Competitions is structured as a database. The editors make a sophisticated technical and legal work on all articles by tagging these with key words, drafting abstracts and writing html code to increase Google ranking. There is a team of antitrust lawyers – PhD and judges clerks - and a team of IT experts. e-Competitions makes comparative law possible. Thanks to this expert editorial work, it is possible to search and compare cases.

PRESTIGIOUS BOARDS

e-Competitions draws upon highly distinguished editors, all leading experts in national or international antitrust. Advisory Board Members include: Sir Christopher Bellamy, Ioanis Lianos (UCL), Eleanor Fox (NYU), Damien Géradin (Tilburg University), Barry Hawk (Fordham University) Fred Jenny (OECD), Jacqueline Riffault-Silk (Cour de cassation), Wouter Wils (DG COMP), etc.

LEADING PARTNERS

- Association of European Competition Law Judges: The AECLJ is a forum for judges of national Courts specializing in antitrust case law. Members timely feed e-Competitions with just released cases.
- Academics partners: Antitrust research centres from leading universities write regularly in e-Competitions: University College London, King's College London, Queen Mary University, etc.
- Law firms: Global law firms and antitrust niche firms write detailed cases summaries specifically for e-Competitions: Allen & Overy, DLA Piper, Jones Day, Norton Rose Fulbright, Skadden Arps, White & Case, etc.

INSTITUTE of
Competition Law
Antitrust databases and resources

The Institute of Competition Law

The Institute of Competition Law is a publishing company, founded in 2004 by Dr. Nicolas Charbit, based in Paris and New-York. The Institute cultivates scholarship and discussion about antitrust issues though publications and conferences. Each publication and event is supervised by editorial boards and scientific or steering committees to ensure independence, objectivity, and academic rigor. Thanks to this management, the Institute has become one of the few think tanks in Europe to have significant influence on antitrust policies.

AIM

The Institute focuses government, business and academic attention on a broad range of subjects which concern competition laws, regulations and related economics.

BOARDS

To maintain its unique focus, the Institute relies upon highly distinguished editors, all leading experts in national or international antitrust: Bill Kovacic, Mario Monti, Eleanor Fox, Barry Hawk, Laurence Idot, Fred Jenny, etc.

AUTHORS

3,800 authors, from 55 jurisdictions.

PARTNERS

- Universities: University College London, King's College London, Queen Mary University, Paris Sorbonne Panthéon-Assas, etc.
- Law firms: Allen & Overy, Cleary Gottlieb Steen & Hamilton, DLA Piper, Hogan Lovells, Jones Day, Norton Rose Fulbright, Skadden Arps, White & Case, etc.

EVENTS

More than 250 events since 2004 in Brussels, London, New York, Paris, Singapour and Washington, DC.

ONLINE VERSION

Concurrences website provides all articles published since its inception.

PUBLICATIONS

The Institute publishes Concurrences Journal, a print and online quarterly peer-reviewed journal dedicated to EU and national competitions laws. e-Competitions is a bi-monthly antitrust news bulletin covering 55 countries. The e-Competitions database contains over 12,000 case summaries from 2,600 authors.

CPSIA information can be obtained
at www.ICGtesting.com
Printed in the USA
BVIC01n0814270317
479226BV00023B/137